Emerging Trends in IoT and Integration With Data Science, Cloud Computing, and Big Data Analytics

Pelin Yildirim Taser
Izmir Bakircay University, Turkey

A volume in the Advances in Web Technologies
and Engineering (AWTE) Book Series

Published in the United States of America by
    IGI Global
    Information Science Reference (an imprint of IGI Global)
    701 E. Chocolate Avenue
    Hershey PA, USA 17033
    Tel: 717-533-8845
    Fax: 717-533-8661
    E-mail: cust@igi-global.com
    Web site: http://www.igi-global.com

Library of Congress Cataloging-in-Publication Data

Names: Taser, Pelin Yildirim, 1990- editor.
Title: Emerging trends in IOT and integration with data science, cloud
    computing, and big data analytics / Pelin Yildirim Taser, editors.
Description: Hershey, PA : Information Science Reference, 2021. | Includes
    bibliographical references and index. | Summary: "This book contains
    research on emerging trends in the internet of things and integration
    with data science"-- Provided by publisher.
Identifiers: LCCN 2020013985 (print) | LCCN 2020013986 (ebook) | ISBN
    9781799841869 (h/c) | ISBN 9781799857167 (s/c) | ISBN 9781799841876
    (eISBN)
Subjects: LCSH: Internet of things--Industrial applications. | Big
    data--Industrial applications.
Classification: LCC TK5105.8857 .E444 2021 (print) | LCC TK5105.8857
    (ebook) | DDC 004.67/8--dc23
LC record available at https://lccn.loc.gov/2020013985
LC ebook record available at https://lccn.loc.gov/2020013986

This book is published in the IGI Global book series Advances in Web Technologies and Engineering (AWTE) (ISSN: 2328-2762; eISSN: 2328-2754)

British Cataloguing in Publication Data
A Cataloguing in Publication record for this book is available from the British Library.

All work contributed to this book is new, previously-unpublished material. The views expressed in this book are those of the authors, but not necessarily of the publisher.

For electronic access to this publication, please contact: eresources@igi-global.com.

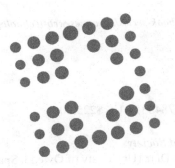

Advances in Web Technologies and Engineering (AWTE) Book Series

Ghazi I. Alkhatib
The Hashemite University, Jordan
David C. Rine
George Mason University, USA

ISSN:2328-2762
EISSN:2328-2754

MISSION

The **Advances in Web Technologies and Engineering (AWTE) Book Series** aims to provide a platform for research in the area of Information Technology (IT) concepts, tools, methodologies, and ethnography, in the contexts of global communication systems and Web engineered applications. Organizations are continuously overwhelmed by a variety of new information technologies, many are Web based. These new technologies are capitalizing on the widespread use of network and communication technologies for seamless integration of various issues in information and knowledge sharing within and among organizations. This emphasis on integrated approaches is unique to this book series and dictates cross platform and multidisciplinary strategy to research and practice.

The **Advances in Web Technologies and Engineering (AWTE) Book Series** seeks to create a stage where comprehensive publications are distributed for the objective of bettering and expanding the field of web systems, knowledge capture, and communication technologies. The series will provide researchers and practitioners with solutions for improving how technology is utilized for the purpose of a growing awareness of the importance of web applications and engineering.

COVERAGE

- Data analytics for business and government organizations
- Competitive/intelligent information systems
- Radio Frequency Identification (RFID) research and applications in Web engineered systems
- Information filtering and display adaptation techniques for wireless devices
- Knowledge structure, classification, and search algorithms or engines
- Integrated Heterogeneous and Homogeneous Workflows and Databases within and Across Organizations and with Suppliers and Customers
- Metrics-based performance measurement of IT-based and web-based organizations
- Web systems performance engineering studies
- Case studies validating Web-based IT solutions
- Data and knowledge capture and quality issues

IGI Global is currently accepting manuscripts for publication within this series. To submit a proposal for a volume in this series, please contact our Acquisition Editors at Acquisitions@igi-global.com or visit: http://www.igi-global.com/publish/.

Titles in this Series

For a list of additional titles in this series, please visit: http://www.igi-global.com/book-series/advances-web-technologies-engineering/37158

App and Website Accessibility Developments and Compliance Strategies
Yakup Akgül (Alanya Alaaddin Keykubat University, Turkey)
Engineering Science Reference • © 2022 • 322pp • H/C (ISBN: 9781799878483) • US $225.00

IoT Protocols and Applications for Improving Industry, Environment, and Society
Cristian González García (University of Oviedo, Spain) and Vicente García-Díaz (University of Oviedo, Spain)
Engineering Science Reference • © 2021 • 321pp • H/C (ISBN: 9781799864639) • US $245.00

Integration and Implementation of the Internet of Things Through Cloud Computing
Pradeep Tomar (Gautam Buddha University, India)
Engineering Science Reference • © 2021 • 357pp • H/C (ISBN: 9781799869818) • US $245.00

Design Innovation and Network Architecture for the Future Internet
Mohamed Boucadair (Orange S.A., France) and Christian Jacquenet (Orange S.A., France)
Engineering Science Reference • © 2021 • 478pp • H/C (ISBN: 9781799876465) • US $225.00

Challenges and Opportunities for the Convergence of IoT, Big Data, and Cloud Computing
Sathiyamoorthi Velayutham (Sona College of Technology, India)
Engineering Science Reference • © 2021 • 350pp • H/C (ISBN: 9781799831112) • US $215.00

Examining the Impact of Deep Learning and IoT on Multi-Industry Applications
Roshani Raut (Pimpri Chinchwad College of Engineering (PCCOE), Pune, India) and Albena Dimitrova Mihovska (CTIF Global Capsule (CGC), Denmark)
Engineering Science Reference • © 2021 • 304pp • H/C (ISBN: 9781799875116) • US $245.00

Result Page Generation for Web Searching Emerging Research and Opportunities
Mostafa Alli (Tsinghua University, China)
Engineering Science Reference • © 2021 • 126pp • H/C (ISBN: 9781799809616) • US $165.00

Building Smart and Secure Environments Through the Fusion of Virtual Reality, Augmented Reality, and the IoT
Nadesh RK (Vellore Institute of Technology, India) Shynu PG (Vellore Institute of Technology, India) and Chiranji Lal Chowdhary (School of Information Technology and Engineering, VIT University, Vellore, India)
Engineering Science Reference • © 2020 • 300pp • H/C (ISBN: 9781799831839) • US $245.00

701 East Chocolate Avenue, Hershey, PA 17033, USA
Tel: 717-533-8845 x100 • Fax: 717-533-8661
E-Mail: cust@igi-global.com • www.igi-global.com

Table of Contents

Chapter 14
Prototype Implementation of Innovative Braille Translator for the Visually Impaired With

    Soumen Santra, Techno International NewTown, India
    Arpan Deyasi, RCC Institute of Information Technology, India

Detailed Table of Contents

Chapter 1

Zuleyha Akusta Dagdeviren, International Computer Institute, Ege University, Turkey

Internet of things (IoT) has attracted researchers in recent years as it has a great potential to solve many emerging problems. An IoT platform is missioned to operate as a horizontal key element for serving various vertical IoT domains such as structure monitoring, smart agriculture, healthcare, miner safety monitoring, smart home, and healthcare. In this chapter, the authors propose a comprehensive analysis of IoT platforms to evaluate their capabilities. The selected metrics (features) to investigate the IoT platforms are "ability to serve different domains," "ability to handle different data formats," "ability to process unlimited size of data from various context," "ability to convert unstructured data to structured data," and "ability to produce complex reports." These metrics are chosen by considering the reporting capabilities of various IoT platforms, big data concepts, and domain-related issues. The authors provide a detailed comparison derived from the metric analysis to show the advantages and drawbacks of IoT platforms.

Chapter 2

Mobasshir Mahbub, Ahsanullah University of Science and Technology, Bangladesh

Many critical studies and research were carried out to improve the technologies of IoT. Nevertheless, several challenges need to be solved to determine the maximum value of IoT. These problems and concerns will be approached from specific IoT perspectives, such as applications, enabling technologies, issues, and so on. The key purpose of this work is to explore IoT technology in terms of technical and social aspects. The work discusses various challenges and major issues of IoT including detailed architecture and applications. The research further summarizes the recent literature of various areas of IoT and explains their importance. Moreover, the importance of integration of cloud in IoT infrastructure has been discussed. The research also mentioned and described various simulation tools through which the characteristics of the IoT environment can be analyzed empirically. This work lets the readers and the researchers grasp the IoT and its real-life applicability.

Arpit Kumar Sharma, Manipal University Jaipur, India
Arvind Dhaka, Manipal University Jaipur, India
Amita Nandal, Manipal University Jaipur, India
Akshat Sinha, Arya Institute of Engineering Technology and Management, Jaipur, India
Deepika Choudhary, Arya Institute of Engineering Technology and Management, Jaipur, India

The Android system operates on many smartphones in many locales. Websites and web tools have their own requirements in day-to-day life. To reach the maximum users, the app and website should handle all the resources such as text strings, functions, layouts, graphics, and any other static data that the app/website needs. It requires internationalization and localization of the website and app to support multiple languages. The basic idea of this chapter is to present an approach for localizing the Android application according to the location data that the app received from the device, but many users do not allow the "access location" feature so this approach will be a dead end in this case. The authors have proposed some other techniques to achieve this feature of localization and internationalization by implementing the "choose language" service so that the app can itself optimize its content and translate it into the user's native language.

Dragorad Milovanovic, University of Belgrade, Serbia
Vladan Pantovic, Union–Nikola Tesla University, Belgrade, Serbia

Multimedia-related things is a new class of connected objects that can be searched, discovered, and composited on the internet of media things (IoMT). A huge amount of data sets come from audio-visual sources or have a multimedia nature. However, multimedia data is currently not incorporated in the big data (BD) frameworks. The research projects, standardization initiatives, and industrial activities for integration are outlined in this chapter. MPEG IoMT interoperability and network-based media processing (NBMP) framework as an instance of the big media (BM) reference model are explored. Conceptual model of IoT and big data integration for analytics is proposed. Big data analytics is rapidly evolving both in terms of functionality and the underlying model. The authors pointed out that IoMT analytics is closely related to big data analytics, which facilitates the integration of multimedia objects in big media applications in large-scale systems. These two technologies are mutually dependent and should be researched and developed jointly.

Burak Karaduman, University of Antwerp and Flanders Make, Belgium
Bentley James Oakes, University of Antwerp and Flanders Make, Belgium
Raheleh Eslampanah, University of Antwerp and Flanders Make, Belgium
Joachim Denil, University of Antwerp and Flanders Make, Belgium
Hans Vangheluwe, University of Antwerp and Flanders Make, Belgium
Moharram Challenger, University of Antwerp and Flanders Make, Belgium

The Internet of Things and its technologies have evolved quickly in recent years. It became an umbrella term for various technologies, embedded devices, smart objects, and web services. Although it has gained maturity, there is still no clear or common definition of references for creating WSN-based IoT systems. In the awareness that creating an omniscient and ideal architecture that can suit all design requirements is not feasible, modular and scalable architecture that supports adding or subtracting components to fit a lot of requirements of various use cases should be provided as a starting point. This chapter discusses such an architecture and reference implementation. The architecture should cover multiple layers, including the cloud, the gateway, and the edges of the target system, which allows monitoring the environment, managing the data, programming the edge nodes and networking model to establish communication between horizontal and vertical embedded devices. In order to exemplify the proposed architecture and reference implementation, a smart irrigation case study is used.

Chapter 6

Zuleyha Akusta Dagdeviren, International Computer Institute, Ege University, Turkey
Vahid Akram, International Computer Institute, Ege University, Turkey

Internet of things (IoT) envisions a network of billions of devices having various hardware and software capabilities communicating through internet infrastructure to achieve common goals. Wireless sensor networks (WSNs) having hundreds or even thousands of sensor nodes are positioned at the communication layer of IoT. In this study, the authors work on the connectivity estimation approaches for IoT-enabled WSNs. They describe the main ideas and explain the operations of connectivity estimation algorithms in this chapter. They categorize the studied algorithms into two divisions as 1-connectivity estimation algorithms (special case for k=1) and k-connectivity estimation algorithms (the generalized version of the connectivity estimation problem). Within the scope of 1-connectivity estimation algorithms, they dissect the exact algorithms for bridge and cut vertex detection. They investigate various algorithmic ideas for k connectivity estimation approaches by illustrating their operations on sample networks. They also discuss possible future studies related to the connectivity estimation problem in IoT.

Chapter 7

Pelin Yildirim Taser, Izmir Bakircay University, Turkey
Vahid Khalilpour Akram, Ege University, Turkey

The GPS signals are not available inside the buildings; hence, indoor localization systems rely on indoor technologies such as Bluetooth, WiFi, and RFID. These signals are used for estimating the distance between a target and available reference points. By combining the estimated distances, the location of the target nodes is determined. The wide spreading of the internet and the exponential increase in small hardware diversity allow the creation of the internet of things (IoT)-based indoor localization systems. This chapter reviews the traditional and machine learning-based methods for IoT-based positioning systems. The traditional methods include various distance estimation and localization approaches; however, these approaches have some limitations. Because of the high prediction performance, machine learning algorithms are used for indoor localization problems in recent years. The chapter focuses on presenting an overview of the application of machine learning algorithms in indoor localization problems where the traditional methods remain incapable.

Explainable artificial intelligence (XAI) is a concept that has emerged and become popular in recent years. Even interpretation in machine learning models has been drawing attention. Human activity classification (HAC) systems still lack interpretable approaches. In this study, an approach, called eXplainable HAC (XHAC), was proposed in which the data exploration, model structure explanation, and prediction explanation of the ML classifiers for HAR were examined to improve the explainability of the HAR models' components such as sensor types and their locations. For this purpose, various internet of things (IoT) sensors were considered individually, including accelerometer, gyroscope, and magnetometer. The location of these sensors (i.e., ankle, arm, and chest) was also taken into account. The important features were explored. In addition, the effect of the window size on the classification performance was investigated. According to the obtained results, the proposed approach makes the HAC processes more explainable compared to the black-box ML techniques.

Animal activity recognition is an important task to monitor the behavior of animals to know their health condition and psychological state. To provide a solution for this need, this study is aimed to build an internet of things (IoT) system that predicts the activities of animals based on sensor data obtained from embedded devices attached to animals. This chapter especially considers the problem of prediction of goat activity using three types of sensors: accelerometer, gyroscope, and magnetometer. Five possible goat activities are of interest, including stationary, grazing, walking, trotting, and running. The utility of five ensemble learning methods was investigated, including random forest, extremely randomized trees, bagging trees, gradient boosting, and extreme gradient boosting. The results showed that all these methods achieved good performance (>94%) on the datasets. Therefore, this study can be successfully used by professionals such as farmers, vets, and animal behaviorists where animal tracking may be crucial.

Agriculture plays a major role in the socio-economic structure of India. A recent report claimed that population of India is increasing faster than its capability to produce rice, wheat, and vegetables. The challenges in the area of agriculture are farming, watering, weather forecasting, marketing, and transportation. These challenges are to be addressed towards proper solution. If the infrastructure and productivity of the food increases, then India can easily feed its population as well as improve the exports of wheat and rice around the world. Internet of things (IoT) is an emerging technical area of agriculture domain. The advantage of IoT is to implement a smart agriculture management system with the help of analyzing the weather conditions of the field in order to optimize the usage of water, energy, fertilizers so as to maximize the crop yield. The objective of this study is to explore the possible contributions of IoT in Indian agriculture towards the improvements in irrigation infrastructure, agricultural productivity, food security, and rural job opportunities.

Chapter 11

   Shailesh Pancham Khapre, Amity University, Noida, India
   Shraddha P. Satpathy, Amity University, Noida, India
   Chandramohan D., Madanapalle Institute of Technology and Science, India

The essence of blockchain is a decentralized distributed ledger system; the IoT is formed by accessing and interconnecting a large number of heterogeneous terminals and has a natural distributed feature. Therefore, the combination of the two IoT blockchains is widely optimistic. At the same time, due to the heterogeneity of IoT sensing terminals, limited computing storage, and data transmission capabilities, the IoT blockchain is facing greater challenges, among which cryptographic consensus technology has become a key issue. In this chapter, based on the summary of the current blockchain consensus algorithm, applicability to the IoT-blockchain has been analyzed, the application status of several major IoT-blockchain platforms and consensus mechanisms have been introduced, and also the IoT-blockchain research progress on optimization of consensus mechanism has been expounded. Looking forward to the optimization techniques of the IoT blockchain, potential research directions have been summarized.

Chapter 12

   Onur Ugurlu, Izmir Bakircay University, Turkey
   Nusin Akram, Ege University, Turkey
   Vahid Khalilpour Akram, Ege University, Turkey

The new generation of fast, small, and energy-efficient devices that can connect to the internet are already used for different purposes in healthcare, smart homes, smart cities, industrial automation, and entertainment. One of the main requirements in all kinds of cyber-physical systems is a reliable communication platform. In a wired or wireless network, losing some special nodes may disconnect the communication paths between other nodes. Generally, these nodes, which are called critical nodes, have many undesired effects on the network. The authors focus on three different problems. The first problem is finding the nodes whose removal minimizes the pairwise connectivity in the residual network. The second problem is finding the nodes whose removal maximizes the number of connected components. Finally, the third problem is finding the nodes whose removal minimizes the size of the largest connected component. All three problems are NP-Complete, and the authors provide a brief survey about the existing approximated algorithms for these problems.

Chapter 13

   Dmytro Zubov, University of Central Asia, Kyrgyzstan

Smart assistive devices for blind and visually impaired (B&VI) people are of high interest today since wearable IoT hardware became available for a wide range of users. In the first project, the Raspberry

Pi 3 B board measures a distance to the nearest obstacle via ultrasonic sensor HC-SR04 and recognizes human faces by Pi camera, OpenCV library, and Adam Geitgey module. Objects are found by Bluetooth devices of classes 1-3 and iBeacons. Intelligent eHealth agents cooperate with one another in a smart city mesh network via MQTT and BLE protocols. In the second project, B&VIs are supported to play golf. Golf flagsticks have sound marking devices with a buzzer, NodeMcu Lua ESP8266 ESP-12 WiFi board, and WiFi remote control. In the third project, an assistive device supports the orientation of B&VIs by measuring the distance to obstacles via Arduino Uno and HC-SR04. The distance is pronounced through headphones. In the fourth project, the soft-/hardware complex uses Raspberry Pi 3 B and Bytereal iBeacon fingerprinting to uniquely identify the B&VI location at industrial facilities.

Text-to-Braille conversion as well as speech-to-Braille conversion are not available in combined form so far for the visually impaired, and there is tremendous need of a device that can look after this special class of people. The present chapter deals with a novel model that is designed to help both types of impaired people, be it visual problem or related with hearing. The proposal is itself unique and is also supported by experimental results available within the laboratory condition. This device will help people to read from text with their Braille language and will also help to convert the same form to audio signal. Since text and audio are the two main interfaces for any person to communicate with the external world apart from functionalities of sensory organs, the work has relevance. With the help of DANET, the same data, in text or speech form, can be accessed in more than one digital device simultaneously.

Preface

Technological innovations and enormous advancements in computation, communications, and control have led to the development of various applications across all aspects of life, mainly autonomous communication between smart devices and cyberspace. Internet of Things (IoT) is a form of expanding network technology built on the foundation of the internet, is constantly being integrated into various applications within engineering and science. It presents a network of interconnected devices, objects, or living creatures and the capability to transmit data over the network without any human interaction. The IoT structure includes internet-enabled smart devices that collect, send, and act on data acquired from their environments through embedded systems such as processors, sensors, and communication hardware. Due to the enormous volume of data generated by a vast number of distributed sensors, collecting, integrating, storing, processing, and using this data has become a critical issue for IoT systems. To solve this issue, the cloud computing paradigm has been proposed for supporting big data technologies, e.g., big data storage and big data analytics. It enables data-driven services and tackles the complexities and resource demands for data storage, processing, and analytics. Furthermore, the large-scale data produced by the IoT devices require to be processed and converted into valuable knowledge by data science techniques in an efficient and low-cost way.

This book presents the theoretical frameworks, research findings, and state-of-the-art technologies on the combination of IoT with Data Science, Cloud Computing, and Big Data Analytics. The authors demonstrate the topics including IoT platforms, internet of media things, wireless sensor networks (WSN), wearable sensors, machine learning, artificial intelligence, and mobile computing. This book will serve as a good reference for data scientists, data analysts, IT specialists, academicians, professionals, researchers, and students working in the field of information and knowledge management in various disciplines, such as information and communication sciences, administrative management, education, sociology, and computer science. Moreover, the book provides insights and supports executives concerned with the management of expertise, knowledge, information, and organizational development in different types of work communities and environments. The book is thoroughly illustrated with examples and case studies to aid comprehension and includes a comprehensive bibliography of recent publications. I hope this book will shed light on developments in IoT technology, IoT-Based Data Science applications, and up-to-date IoT Cloud platforms.

ORGANIZATION OF THE BOOK

The well-structured book is organized into 14 chapters. The summary of each chapter is as follows.

Chapter Summaries

Chapter 1. A Comprehensive Evaluation of Internet-of-Things Platforms

Internet of Things (IoT) has attracted researchers in recent years as it has a great potential to solve many emerging problems. An IoT platform is missioned to operate as a horizontal key element for serving various vertical IoT domains such as structure monitoring, smart agriculture, healthcare, miner safety monitoring, smart home, and healthcare. In this chapter, the authors propose a comprehensive analysis of IoT platforms to evaluate their capabilities. The selected metrics (features) to investigate the IoT platforms are "ability to serve different domains," "ability to handle different data formats," "ability to process unlimited size of data from various context," "ability to convert unstructured data to structured data" and "ability to produce complex reports." These metrics are chosen by considering the reporting capabilities of various IoT platforms, big data concepts, and domain-related issues. The authors provide a detailed comparison derived from the metric analysis to show the advantages and drawbacks of IoT platforms.

Chapter 2. An Overview of IoT Infrastructure Architecture, Enabling Technologies, Issues, Integration of Cloud, and Simulation Tools

Many critical studies and research were carried out to improve the technologies of IoT. Nevertheless, several challenges need to be solved to determine the maximum value of IoT. These problems and concerns will be approached from specific IoT perspectives, such as applications, enabling technologies, issues, and so on. The key purpose of this work is to explore IoT technology in terms of technical and social aspects. The work discusses various challenges and major issues of IoT, including detailed architecture and applications. The research further summarizes the recent literature of various areas of IoT and explains their importance. Moreover, the importance of integration of cloud in IoT infrastructure has been discussed. The research also mentioned and described various simulation tools through which the characteristics of the IoT environment can be analyzed empirically. This work lets the readers and the researchers grasp the IoT and its real-life applicability.

Chapter 3. Location-Based Internationalization and Localization With Mobile Computing

The Android system operates on many smartphones in many locales. Websites and web tools have their own requirements in one day-to-day life. The application and website should handle all the resources such as text strings, functions, layouts, graphics, and any other static data that the application/website needs to reach the maximum users. It requires internationalization and localization of the website and application to support multiple languages. The basic idea of this chapter is to present an approach for localizing the Android application according to the location data that the application received from the device, but many users do not allow the "access location" feature, so this approach will be a halt in this case. Some other techniques have been proposed to achieve this feature of localization and internationalization by implementing the "choose language" service to optimize its content and translate it into the user's native language.

Chapter 4. Interoperability in Internet of Media Things and Integration Big Media: Conceptual Model and Frameworks

Multimedia-related Things is a new class of connected objects that can be searched, discovered, and composed on the Internet of Media Things (IoMT). A huge amount of data sets come from audio-visual sources or have a multimedia nature. However, multimedia data is currently not incorporated in the big data (BD) frameworks. The research projects, standardization initiatives, and industrial activities for integration are outlined in this chapter. MPEG IoMT interoperability and network-based media processing (NBMP) framework as an instance of the big media (BM) reference model are explored. Conceptual model of IoT and big data integration for analytics is proposed. Big data analytics is rapidly evolving both in terms of functionality and the underlying model. The authors pointed out that IoMT analytics is closely related to big data analytics, which facilitates the integration of multimedia objects in big media applications in large-scale systems. These two technologies are mutually dependent and should be researched and developed jointly.

Chapter 5. An Architecture and Reference Implementation for WSN-Based IoT Systems

The Internet of Things and its technologies have evolved quickly in recent years. It became an umbrella term for various technologies, embedded devices, smart objects, and web services. Although it has gained maturity, there is still no clear or common definition of references for creating WSN-based IoT systems. In the awareness that creating an omniscient and ideal architecture that can suit all design requirements is not feasible, modular and scalable architecture that supports adding or subtracting components to fit a lot of requirements of various use cases should be provided as a starting point. This chapter discusses such an architecture and reference implementation. The architecture should cover multiple layers, including the cloud, the gateway, and the edges of the target system, which allows monitoring the environment, managing the data, programming the edge nodes, and networking model to establish communication between horizontal and vertical embedded devices. In order to exemplify the proposed architecture and reference implementation, a smart irrigation case study is used.

Chapter 6. Connectivity Estimation Approaches for Internet of Things-Enabled Wireless Sensor Networks

Internet of Things (IoT) envisions a network of billions of devices having various hardware and software capabilities communicating through Internet infrastructure to achieve common goals. Wireless sensor networks (WSNs) having hundreds even thousands of sensor nodes, are positioned at communication layer of IoT. In this study, the authors work on the connectivity estimation approaches for IoT-enabled WSNs. They describe the main ideas and explain the operations of connectivity estimation algorithms in this chapter. They categorize the studied algorithms into two divisions as 1-connectivity estimation algorithms (special case for k=1) and k-connectivity estimation algorithms (the generalized version of the connectivity estimation problem). Within the scope of 1-connectivity estimation algorithms, they dissect the exact algorithms for bridge and cut vertex detection. They investigate various algorithmic ideas for k-connectivity estimation approaches by illustrating their operations on sample networks. They also discuss possible future studies related to the connectivity estimation problem in IoT.

Chapter 7. Machine Learning Techniques for IoT-Based Indoor Tracking and Localization

The GPS signals are not available inside the buildings; hence, indoor localization systems rely on indoor technologies such as Bluetooth, WiFi, and RFID. These signals are used for estimating the distance between a target and available reference points. By combining the estimated distances, the location of the target nodes is determined. The wide spreading of the Internet and the exponential increase in small hardware diversity allow the creation of the Internet of Things (IoT) based indoor localization systems. This chapter reviews the traditional and machine learning-based methods for IoT-based positioning systems. The traditional methods include various distance estimation and localization approaches; however, these approaches have some limitations. Because of the high prediction performance, machine learning algorithms are used for indoor localization problems in recent years. The chapter focuses on presenting an overview of the application of machine learning algorithms in indoor localization problems where the traditional methods remain incapable.

Chapter 8. XHAC: Explainable Human Activity Classification From Sensor Data

Explainable artificial intelligence (XAI) is a concept that has emerged and become popular in recent years. Even interpretation in machine learning models has been drawing attention, Human Activity Classification (HAC) systems still lack interpretable approaches. In this study, an approach, called eXplainable HAC (XHAC), was proposed, in which the data exploration, model structure explanation, and prediction explanation of the ML classifiers for HAR were examined to improve the explainability of the HAR models' components such as sensor types and their locations. For this purpose, various Internet of Things (IoT) sensors were considered individually, including accelerometer, gyroscope, and magnetometer. Besides, the location of these sensors (i.e., ankle, arm, and chest) was also taken into account. The important features were explored. In addition, the effect of the window size on the classification performance was investigated. According to the obtained results, the proposed approach makes the HAC processes more explainable compared to the black-box ML techniques.

Chapter 9. Animal Activity Recognition From Sensor Data Using Ensemble Learning

Animal activity recognition is an important task to monitor the behavior of animals to know their health condition and psychological state. To provide a solution for this need, this study is aimed to build an internet of things (IoT) system that predicts the activities of animals based on sensor data obtained from embedded devices attached to animals. This chapter especially considers the problem of prediction of goat activity using three types of sensors: accelerometer, gyroscope, and magnetometer. Five possible goat activities are of interest, including stationary, grazing, walking, trotting, and running. The utility of five ensemble learning methods was investigated, including Random Forest, Extremely Randomized Trees, Bagging Trees, Gradient Boosting, and Extreme Gradient Boosting. The results showed that all these methods achieved good performance (>94%) on the datasets. Therefore, this study can be successfully used by professionals such as farmers, vets, and animal behaviorists where animal tracking may be crucial.

Chapter 10. Essentials, Challenges, and Future Directions of Agricultural IoT: A Case Study in the Indian Perspective

Agriculture plays a major role in the socio-economic structure of India. A recent report claimed that the population of India is increasing faster than its capability to produce rice, wheat, and vegetables. The challenges in the area of agriculture are farming, watering, weather forecasting, marketing, and transportation. These challenges are to be addressed towards the proper solution. If the infrastructure and productivity of the food increases, then India can easily feed its population as well as improve the exports of wheat and rice around the world. Internet of Things (IoT) is an emerging technical area of the agriculture domain. The advantage of IoT is to implement a smart agriculture management system with the help of analyzing the weather conditions of the field to optimize the usage of water, energy, and fertilizers so as to maximize the crop yield. This study aims to explore the possible contributions of IoT in Indian agriculture towards the improvements in irrigation infrastructure, agricultural productivity, food security, and rural job opportunities.

Chapter 11. Optimization of Consensus Mechanism for IoT Blockchain: A Survey

The essence of blockchain is a decentralized distributed ledger system; the IoT is formed by accessing and interconnecting a large number of heterogeneous terminals and has a natural distributed feature. Therefore, the combination of the two IoT blockchains is widely optimistic. At the same time, due to the heterogeneity of IoT sensing terminals, limited computing storage, and data transmission capabilities, the IoT blockchain is facing more significant challenges, among which cryptographic consensus technology has become a vital issue. In this chapter, based on the summary of the current blockchain consensus algorithm, applicability to the IoT-blockchain has been analyzed, the application status of several major IoT-blockchain platforms and consensus mechanisms have been introduced, and also, the IoT-blockchain Research progress on optimization of consensus mechanism has been expounded. Looking forward to the optimization techniques of the IoT blockchain, potential research directions have been summarized.

Chapter 12. Critical Nodes Detection in IoT-Based Cyber-Physical Systems: Applications, Methods, and Challenges

The new generation of fast, small, and energy-efficient devices that can connect to the internet are already used for different purposes in healthcare, smart homes, smart cities, industrial automation, and entertainment. One of the main requirements in all kinds of cyber-physical systems is a reliable communication platform. In a wired or wireless network, losing some special nodes may disconnect the communication paths between other nodes. Generally, these nodes, which are called critical nodes, have many undesired effects on the network. This chapter focuses on different kinds of critical nodes, the existing methods for finding them, their effect on the cyber-physical systems, and the challenges for finding these nodes. More precisely, the chapter focuses on three different problems. The first problem is finding the nodes whose removal minimizes the pairwise connectivity in the residual network. The second problem is finding the nodes whose removal maximizes the number of connected components. Finally, the third problem is finding the nodes whose removal minimizes the size of the largest connected component. All three problems are NP-Complete and the authors provide a brief survey about the existing approximated algorithms for these problems.

Chapter 13. Mesh Network of eHealth Intelligent Agents for Visually Impaired and Blind People: A Review Study on Arduino and Raspberry Pi Wearable Devices

Smart assistive devices for blind and visually impaired (B&VI) people are of high interest today since wearable IoT hardware became available for a wide range of users. In the first project, the Raspberry Pi 3 B board measures a distance to the nearest obstacle via ultrasonic sensor HC-SR04 and recognizes human faces by Pi camera, OpenCV library, and Adam Geitgey module. Objects are found by Bluetooth devices of classes 1-3 and iBeacons. Intelligent eHealth agents cooperate with one another in a smart city mesh network via MQTT and BLE protocols. In the second project, B&VIs are supported to play golf. Golf flagsticks have sound marking devices with a buzzer, NodeMcu Lua ESP8266 ESP-12 WiFi board, and WiFi remote control. In the third project, an assistive device supports the orientation of B&VIs by measuring the distance to obstacles via Arduino Uno and HC-SR04. The distance is pronounced through headphones. In the fourth project, the soft-/hardware complex uses Raspberry Pi 3 B and Bytereal iBeacon fingerprinting to identify the B&VI location at industrial facilities uniquely.

Chapter 14. Prototype Implementation of Innovative Braille Translator for the Visually Impaired With Hearing Deficiency

'Text to Braille conversion' and 'Speech to Braille conversion' are not available in combined form so far for the visually impaired, and there is tremendous need of the device that can look after this special class of people. The present chapter deals with a novel model that is designed to help both types of impaired people, be it visual problem or related with hearing. The proposal is itself unique and is also supported by experimental results available within the laboratory condition. This device will help people to read from text with their Braille language and will also help to convert the same form audio signal. Since text and audio are the two main interfaces for any person to communicate with the external world apart from functionalities of sensory organs, the work has relevance. With the help of DANET, the same data, in text or speech form, can be accessed in more than one digital device simultaneously.

Acknowledgment

As the editor of this book, I would like to acknowledge the help of every individual, more specifically, to the authors and reviewers who took part in the review process. Without their kind support, this book would not have become a reality.

First, I would like to personally thank each author for their precious contributions. Sincere gratitude goes to the author/s of each chapter who worked very hard and contributed their valuable time and expertise to this book. Also, I wish to acknowledge the continuous and essential feedbacks of the reviewers regarding the improvement of quality, coherence, and content presentation of chapters. I highly appreciate both efforts of authors and reviewers for this book.

Second, I sincerely thank the IGI-Global production team and all personnel associated with this book for their outstanding support and excellent help at each stage of the book.

Finally, I would like to express my sincere gratitude to my family for supporting me spiritually throughout the preparation of this book and my life in general. I would not have been able to complete this book without their support and help.

Pelin Yildirim Taser
Izmir Bakircay University, Turkey

Chapter 1
A Comprehensive Evaluation of Internet–of–Things Platforms

Zuleyha Akusta Dagdeviren
International Computer Institute, Ege University, Turkey

ABSTRACT

Internet of things (IoT) has attracted researchers in recent years as it has a great potential to solve many emerging problems. An IoT platform is missioned to operate as a horizontal key element for serving various vertical IoT domains such as structure monitoring, smart agriculture, healthcare, miner safety monitoring, smart home, and healthcare. In this chapter, the authors propose a comprehensive analysis of IoT platforms to evaluate their capabilities. The selected metrics (features) to investigate the IoT platforms are "ability to serve different domains," "ability to handle different data formats," "ability to process unlimited size of data from various context," "ability to convert unstructured data to structured data," and "ability to produce complex reports." These metrics are chosen by considering the reporting capabilities of various IoT platforms, big data concepts, and domain-related issues. The authors provide a detailed comparison derived from the metric analysis to show the advantages and drawbacks of IoT platforms.

1. INTRODUCTION

Internet of Things (IoT), which was firstly remarked by Kevin Ashton to connect the radio frequency identification idea in a supply chain, has attracted researchers in recent years since it offers many capabilities in various areas (Rayes et al., 2019). Firstly, IoT aims to construct an ambient environment in which things are communicated through the Internet infrastructure, seamlessly. This will provide everyday objects around the people, that sense the events and communicate to accomplish missions without external commands. By achieving sensing, communication and analysis, IoT targets to take action to increase the quality of service experience and production. By utilizing IoT, vast amounts of structured and unstructured data, namely Big Data, is collected and analyzed from various resources such as healthcare systems, social media, factories and research institutes operating worldwide. In this manner, it is believed that IoT will be one of the important technological developments that ever seen

DOI: 10.4018/978-1-7998-4186-9.ch001

by the people since the existence of the world. IoT has already been a perfect storm driven by the factors such as convergence of operational technology and information technology, the astonishing introduction of Internet-based startups, mobile device explosion, analytics at the edge, cloud computing and virtualization, digital convergence and transformation, technological advancements in hardware/software technologies, enhanced user interfaces, fast rate of technological adoption, social network explosion, the rise of security requirements and the non-stop Moore's law.

Since IoT is envisioned to connect a tremendous amount of devices having different capabilities and running various applications through the Internet, one of the crucial missions for a successful IoT solution is to deploy an IoT services platform which manages plethora of devices and data sources (Terroso-Saenz et al., 2017) (Iyer et al., 2019) (Zamora-Izquierdo et al., 2019) (Xu et al., 2018) (Kuo et al., 2018) (Benammar et al., 2018) (Mahmud et al., 2018) (Dupont et al., 2018) (Rogojanu et al., 2018). A prosperous IoT platform functions as a horizontal solution for serving various vertical applications belonging to different business domains (Alonso et al., 2020) (Badii et al., 2020) (Foukalas, 2020) (Lee et al., 2020) (Sakthidasa Sankaran et al., 2020) (Sarmento et al., 2020) (Trilles et al., 2020) (Li et al., 2021) (Ramallo-Gonzalez et al., 2021) (Sagheer et al., 2021) (Yang et al., 2021). An IoT services platform is responsible to configure, deploy, secure, monitor and manage various devices (Motlagh et al., 2017) (Tsokov et al., 2017) (Shahzad et al., 2017) (Khazaei et al., 2017) (Ongenae et al., 2017) (Girau et al., 2017) (Abdelgawd et al., 2017) (Haghi et al., 2017) (Makinen et al., 2017) (Jamborsalamati et al., 2017) (Vergara et al., 2017). Besides that, it can handle software installation, debugging and starting/stopping. Moreover, an IoT services platform may provide advanced services such as closed-loop control, complex event handling and data analytics.

Figure 1. An IoT Architecture.

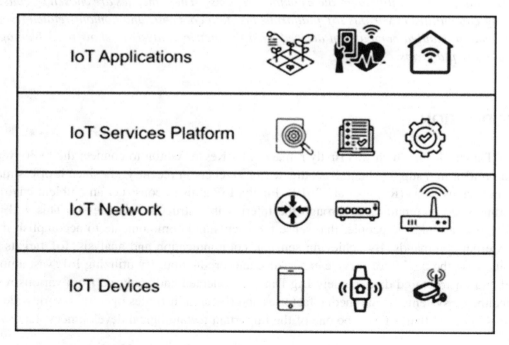

An example IoT architecture including IoT services platform is given in Figure 1 (Rayes ey al., 2019). At the top level, IoT applications such as healthcare, smart agriculture, miner safety monitoring, military surveillance, smart home, outer space exploration and structure monitoring are located. At the lowest level, physical IoT devices are located. These devices can be Teleosb, Iris, Aurdino and Raspberry Pi nodes. Core IoT devices for networking such as switches, access points, routers and gateways are placed in the layer one level above. Following that, IoT platforms are positioned at the third level.

In this chapter, we provide a comprehensive analysis of IoT platforms. Our metrics for this evaluation are "ability to serve different domains", "ability to handle different data formats", "ability to process unlimited size of data from various context", "ability to convert unstructured data to structured data" and "ability to produce complex reports". We provide a detailed analysis and review that shows the advantages and the drawbacks of the IoT platforms. In Section II (IoT Platforms), we survey the related IoT platforms. In Section III (Evaluation), we provide a detailed evaluation of the IoT platforms by considering the five metrics mentioned above. Finally, in Section V (Conclusion), we give the conclusions and discuss potential research issues for IoT platforms.

2. IOT PLATFORMS

In this section, we will investigate some selected IoT platforms operating on various application areas. Terroso-Saenz et al. provided a technique for device-to-device communication for indoor environment based on social IoT architecture (Terroso-Saenz, 2019). The quality of service evaluation and spectrum sensing was realized on Raspberry Pi devices. The system's stability was tested against illegitimate nodes which are transmitting misinformation. A multi-layer IoT platform based on cyber-physical systems layer linked with greenhouse operations, an edge computing plane and a cloud segment proposed by Zamora-Izquierdo et al. (Zamora-Izquierdo et al., 2019). The system was realized and tested in a greenhouse located in Spain.

Iyer et al. proposed a flying IoT platform designed to operate on insects (Iyer et al., 2019). This system has the advantage of using insects that provide efficient mobility. The platform is developed and deployed on bumblebees, and it can use backscatter communication, sensors, power source and self-localization. An IoT energy platform for providing a holistic solution for energy management was proposed in (Terroso-Saenz et al., 2019). The proposed platform is based on FIWARE and it includes various functions for tackling with data analytics and energy quality insurance. The IoT energy platform was tested with a real use case that has three buildings and hundreds of sensor devices. In (Xu et al., 2018), a cloud-based platform was proposed to increase the efficiency of lean prefabricated construction. As the building block of the IoT platform, cloud asset is adopted for the proposed IoT platform. Some Lego models are implemented to test the platform.

Kuo et al. proposed a IoT platform which is based on a wireless sensor network for heterogeneous application (Ku et al., 2018). The proposed IoT platform includes a database, multiple gateways, a web server and a connection between the sensor nodes to the database. The system is easy to integrate with open source projects. The wireless sensor network was selected to operate on IEEE 802.15.4e since this protocol provides multi-hop routing, energy-efficient operation, and collision-free communication. To increase the capacity of network and to decrease the energy consumption for battery-powered sensor networks, a burst communication feature and synchronization approach are given. The architecture of

Figure 2. The architecture of Kuo et al.'s IoT Platform.

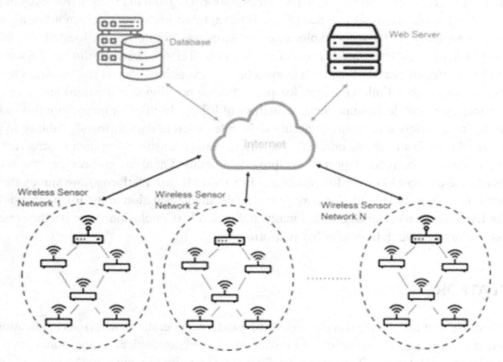

Figure 3. The architecture of NETIoT Platform.

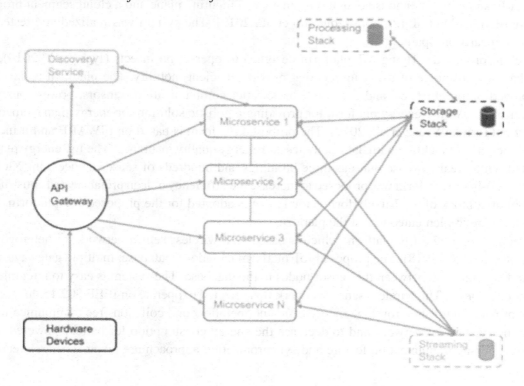

Kuo et al.'s IoT platform including wireless sensor networks, database and web server is depicted in Figure 2. The proposed system was tested by a campus implementation.

For monitoring air quality, a modular IoT platform is given in (Benammer et al., 2018). The system was designed to measure ambient temperature, relative humidity, Cl_2, O_3, NO_2, SO_2, CO and CO_2. The end users can access a web-server as a gateway to reach the collected air quality data. A restoration and backup mechanism of the sensed data against Internet faults was proposed. A modular system architecture was designed that provides integration of different standards and technologies. Mahmud et al. provided an IoT platform for monitoring structural health (Mahmud et al., 2018) that includes a Raspberry Pi, a wireless communication module (Wi-Fi is used) and analog to digital converter (MCP3008 is utilized). To gather data, piezoelectric sensors were used in the proposed system. MCP3008 provides the communication between Raspberry Pi and piezoelectric sensors. The needed computations to detect the status of structure are carried by Raspberry Pi.

An open IoT platform for solving some important real-life issues in African countries was proposed in (Dupont et al., 2018). To tackle with the problems, a full stack IoT framework was presented. The system was tested with real deployments in two different areas. A cloud hosted software was designed to deal with the economic, social and environmental requirements of the region. The water usage was targeted to reduce in the first test case. The important parameters such as pH and dissolved oxygen were monitored in the second test case. Additionally, to decrease the amount of wastes and to rise to recycle, a network of smart bins was implemented. Rogojanu et al. proposed the NETIoT (A Versatile IoT Platform Integrating Sensors and Applications) which is an IoT platform for the integration of applications and sensors to fulfill the needs of next generation IoT systems (Rogojanu et al., 2018). Supporting modular applications were targeted by the proposed platform. The microservices-based architecture of the platform aimed to provide high availability, to ensure scalability, to ease the deployment of applications. The architecture of the NETIoT platform with its components (services, gateway, stacks etc.) is depicted in Figure 3.

Figure 4. The architecture of Lysis Platform.

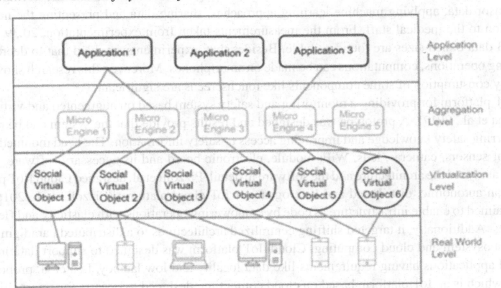

An unmanned aerial vehicle-based IoT Platform was proposed in (Motlagh et al., 2017) to operate in a crowd surveillance application based on face recognition. The researchers both studied the processing of video data locally on unmanned aerial vehicles and offloading the processing of data to a mobile edge computing node. In order to achieve this, a testbed was developed. The local binary pattern histogram method was utilized to recognize faces. Shahzad et al. tackled with the issues in industrial control systems and designed an IoT platform in this context (Shahzad et al., 2017). They modeled IoT supervisory control and data acquisition system, designed a security approach and presented a secure channel between the system and devices in the field by providing a cryptography-based technique.

Bonte el al. proposed the MASSIF (a modular and semantic platform for the development of flexible IoT services) given in (Bonte et al., 2017). MASSIF was designed as a data-driven platform for reasoning on IoT data. The platform allows high-level coordination of services and semantic annotation of collected data. The platform has been implemented and evaluated on two use cases: a media case and an eHomeCare case. An IoT platform named Lysis for supporting the deployment of applications by using socially connected objects was proposed in (Girau et al., 2017). The Lysis is a cloud-based IoT platform in which reusability allowing generation of templates of objects and services at various layers are regarded, the collected data can be controlled by the end users, the platform as a service model is applied and objects are configured as autonomous social agents by adopting the social IoT concept. The Lysis IoT platform's architecture is given in Figure 4. A use-case was presented by the researchers that show the features of Lysis and the implementation choices.

A smart campus IoT Platform's design, implementation and experimentation were given in (Haghi et al., 2017). The developed system is a generic platform which was built by students without IoT knowledge, in a short time (three months). The system is based on Microsoft Azure cloud services and commercial-off-the-shelf devices. The platform aims to enable the distribution of data related to academic activities and student-life. Vergara et al. proposed an IoT platform monitoring and supervising epilepsy data (Vergara et al., 2017). The researchers suggested to using a wearable sensor that is communicated with a smartphone which uses mobile cloud services and accesses cloud computing services. The target of the proposed platform is detecting the seizures, producing notifications and alarms, storing the collected sensor data, applying machine learning approaches, sharing data and presenting the necessary information to the medical staff. From the measurements taken from experimentation, 20.39 KB and 40.87 KB data bunch sizes are found suitable. Besides that, experiments revealed that to decrease the networking operations, computations can be made on smartphones. Moreover, this research showed that the energy consumption of some components like touchscreens are significant.

An IoT platform for providing a monitoring and safety system based on augmented and virtual reality (Alama et al., 2017). A prototype was designed and results provide that the system can be efficient in transferring safety knowledge and improving access to safety information. The head mounted system consists of sensors, cameras, leds, WiFi module, electronic board and its necessary software. The researchers analyzed the architecture and the software in detail. Pizzolli et al. designed Cloud4IoT platform which is an autonomic, distributed and heterogeneous IoT cloud platform (Pizzoli et al., 2016). This platform aimed to enable infrastructure as code by empowering operations with elasticity and flexibility of services. Additionally, it targeted shifting centralized architectures to a distributed paradigm to connect IoT ecosystem and cloud computing. Cloud4IoT platform was designed to support data intensive IoT-based applications having requirements like data locality and low latency. Lea et al. proposed the CityHub which is an IoT platform based on cloud computing, designed to operate for smart cities (Lea et al., 2014). Their approach is presented as a data hub via a platform as a service framework. The researchers implemented their testbed on two cases, one in Canada and one in the United Kingdom. They showed the advantages of the proposed IoT platform through these implementations and services designed for the hubs.

3. EVALUATION OF IOT PLATFORMS

In this section, we give our comprehensive comparison of IoT platforms. Our selected metrics (features) for the extensive evaluation of IoT platforms are "ability to serve different domains", "ability to handle different data formats", "ability to process unlimited size of data from various context", "ability to convert unstructured data to structured data" and "ability to produce complex reports". These metrics are chosen with regarding vertical domain (application) related issues, big data concepts and reporting capabilities of various IoT platforms.

Table 1 gives the comparison of IoT platforms where they are ordered historically. Totally, 42 IoT platforms are evaluated in this section. We use plus and minus signs to indicate that the platform has the corresponding feature or not. As an example, Park et al.'s IoT platform (given at the first row) is able to serve different domains (different application areas), is able to handle different data formats, is able to serve process unlimited size of data from various context but not able to convert unstructured data to structured data and not able to produce complex reports.

Results of our evaluation are given in Figure 5. We first investigate how many features are available in IoT Platforms in Figure 5.a. We find that 26% of IoT platforms have none of the features, 30% of them have only 1 feature, 22% of them have 2 features, 22% of them have 3 features and none of them has 4 and 5 features. These results show us that more than half of the IoT platforms only have at most 1 of our features, and none of them fulfills all abilities given in features. This further indicates us that our features are very selective to evaluate IoT platforms. Also, we obtain another important result that design and implementation of an IoT platform having at least 4 of our presented features are left an open research problem.

We study on how many IoT platforms have the first feature (ability to serve different domains), have the second feature (ability to handle different data formats), have the third feature (ability to process unlimited size of data from various context), have the fourth feature (ability to convert unstructured data to structured data) and have the fifth feature (ability to produce complex reports), respectively in Figures 5.b, 5.c, 5.d, 5.e and 5.f. As depicted in figures, the percentages of the IoT platforms having the first, second, third, fourth and fifth features are 33%, 33%, 26%, 7% and 24%, respectively. These results show us that for a specific feature, the probability of having that feature is at most 1/3 among investigated IoT platforms. Again, this finding is crucial to show that our selected features are selective for the evaluation. 67% of IoT platforms examined in this chapter serve for a single domain. Similarly, 67% of IoT platforms cannot handle different data formats. 74% of IoT platforms are not able to process an unlimited size of data from various context. More than 75% of the IoT platforms examined in this chapter do not produce complex reports. Another interesting result is that only 7% of the investigated IoT platforms can convert unstructured data to the structured data. Since big data is composed of huge amounts of structured and unstructured data, having the mentioned conversion capability will be a significant plus for an IoT platform.

Table 1. Comparison of IoT platforms

Platform/Feature	ability to serve different domains	ability to handle different data formats	ability to process unlimited size of data from various context	ability to convert unstructured data to structured data	ability to produce complex reports
Semantic Open IoT Service Platform Technology (Park et al., 2014)	+	+	+	-	-
A Health-IoT Platform Based on the Integration of Intelligent Packaging, Unobtrusive Bio-Sensor, and Intelligent Medicine Box (Yang et al., 2014).	-	-	-	-	-
CityHub: A cloud based IoT platform for Smart Cities (Lea et al., 2014).	+	+	-	-	+
Designing a Smart City Internet of Things Platform with Microservice Architecture (Krylovskiy et al., 2015).	+	+	+	-	-
SYNAISTHISI: An Enabling Platform for the Current Internet of Things Ecosystem (Pierris et al., 2015).	+	+	-	+	-
Do-it-Yourself Digital Agriculture Applications with Semantically Enhanced IoT Platform (Jayaraman et al., 2015).	-	-	-	-	-
A symbiotic resources sharing IoT platform (Silva et al., 2015).	+	-	-	-	-
Performance Characterization of the servIoTicy API: an IoT-as-a-Service Data Management Platform (Perez et al., 2015).	+	+	-	-	-
Design and Implementation of a Universal Smart Energy Management Gateway based on the Internet of Things Platform (Lee et al., 2016).	-	-	-	-	+
Adaptive Internet of Things and Web of Things convergence platform for Internet of reality services (Yu et al., 2016).	+	-	+	-	-
An Open Platform for Seamless Sensor Support in Healthcare for the Internet of Things (Miranda et al., 2016).	-	-	-	-	+
Cloud4IoT: a heterogeneous, distributed and autonomic cloud platform for the IoT (Pizzolli et al., 2016).	+	-	+	-	-
Rapid Interweaving of Smart Things with the meSchup IoT Platform (Kubitza et al., 2016).	+	-	-	-	-
The Sensorian IoT Platform (Mahmoud et al., 2016).	+	-	-	-	-
UAV Selection for a UAV-based Integrative IoT Platform (Motlagh et al., 2016). (UAV: Unmanned Aerial Vehicle)	-	-	-	-	-

Table 1. Continued

Platform/Feature	ability to serve different domains	ability to handle different data formats	ability to process unlimited size of data from various context	ability to convert unstructured data to structured data	ability to produce complex reports
Internet of Things Platform for Smart Farming: Experiences and Lessons Learnt (Jayaraman et al., 2016).	-	-	-		-
Reinventing Telecom Oss Toolkit as an IoT Platform (Zelenika et al., 2016).	+	-	-		
Enabling Synergy in IoT: Platform to Service and Beyond (Andersen et al., 2016).	+	+	+		
Architecture of an Interoperable IoT Platform Based on Microservices (Vresk et al., 2016).	+		+		
Design of open-source platform for introducing Internet of Things in university curricula (Dobrilovic et al., 2016).	-	+		-	-
A Cloud Platform for Big IoT Data Analytics by Combining Batch and Stream Processing Technologies (Dissanayake et al., 2017).	+	-		+	
Augmented and virtual reality based monitoring and safety system: A prototype IoT platform (Alama et al., 2017).	-	-	+	-	-
An IoT Platform for Epilepsy Monitoring and Supervising (Vergara et al., 2017).	-	-	-	-	+
Design and Implementation of a Cloud-based IoT Platform for Data Acquisition and Device Supply Management in Smart Buildings (Jamborsalamati et al., 2017).		-	-		+
ELIoT: Design of an Emulated IoT Platform (Makinen et al., 2017).	+	+	-		-
Fast-paced Development of a Smart Campus IoT Platform (Haghi et al., 2017).	-	+		-	-
Internet of Things (IoT) Platform for Structure Health Monitoring (Abdelgawad et al., 2017).	-	-	-		
Girau et al., Lysis: A Platform for IoT Distributed Applications Over Socially Connected Objects.	-	-	+	-	+

Continued on following page

Table 1. Continued

Platform/Feature	ability to serve different domains	ability to handle different data formats	ability to process unlimited size of data from various context	ability to convert unstructured data to structured data	ability to produce complex reports
The MASSIF platform: a modular and semantic platform for the development of flexible IoT services (Bonte et al., 2017).	+	+	+	-	-
SAVI-IoT: A Self-Managing Containerized IoT Platform (Khazaei et al., 2017).	+	-	-	-	+
Secure IoT Platform for Industrial Control Systems (Shahzad et al., 2017).	-	+	-	-	+
EcoLogic: IoT Platform for Control of Carbon Emissions (Tsokov et al., 2017).	-	-	-	-	-
UAV-Based IoT Platform: A Crowd Surveillance Use Case (Motlagh et al., 2017).	-	-	-	-	-
NETIoT: A Versatile IoT Platform Integrating Sensors and Applications (Rogojanu et al., 2018).	+	-	-	-	-
An Open IoT Platform to Promote Eco-Sustainable Innovation in Western Africa: Real Urban and Rural Testbeds (Dupont et al., 2018).	-	-	-	-	-
A Complete Internet of Things (IoT) Platform for Structural Health Monitoring (SHM) (Mahmud et al., 2018).	-	-	-	-	-
A Modular IoT Platform for Real-Time Indoor Air (Benammar et al., 2018).	-	-	-	-	-
Design of a Wireless Sensor Network-Based IoT Platform for Wide Area and Heterogeneous Applications (Kuo et al., 2018).	+	-	-	-	-
Cloud asset-enabled integrated IoT platform for lean prefabricated Construction (Xu et al., 2018).	-	+	-	+	+
Smart farming IoT platform based on edge and cloud computing (Zamora-Izquierdo et al., 2019).	-	+	+	-	-
Living IoT: A Flying Wireless Platform on Live Insects (Iyer et al., 2019).	-	-	-	-	-
An open IoT platform for the management and analysis of energy data (Terroso-Saenz et al., 2019).	-	+	+	-	+

Figure 5a. Percentages of IoT Platforms Having Feature Counts

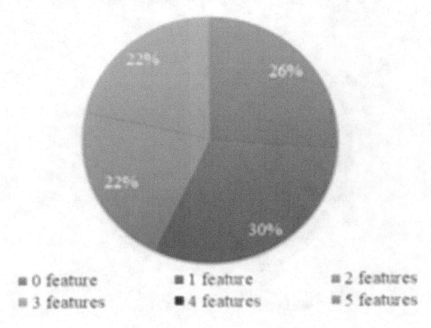

Figure 5b. Having First Feature

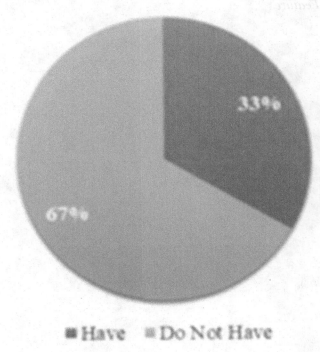

Figure 5c. Having Second Feature

Figure 5d. Having Third Feature

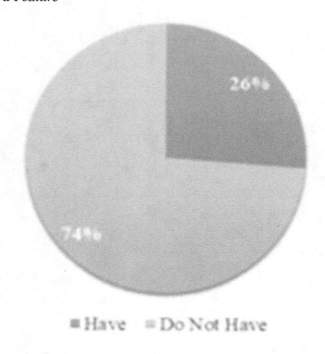

Figure 5e. Having Fourth Feature

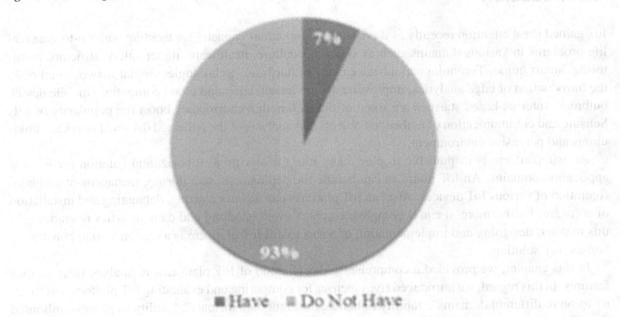

7%

93%

■ Have　■ Do Not Have

Figure 5f. Having Fifth Feature

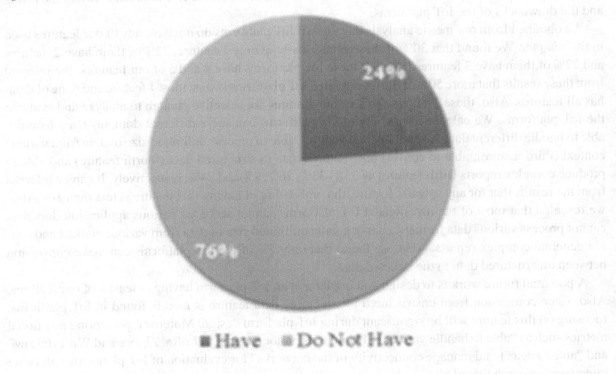

24%

76%

■ Have　■ Do Not Have

4. CONCLUSION

IoT gained great attention recently as it presents a tremendous capacity for tackling with up-to-date real life problems in various domains such as smart agriculture, healthcare, miner safety, structure monitoring, smart home. Technological advancements in hardware technologies, social network outbreak, the introduction of edge analytics, improvements in virtualization and cloud computing, mobile device outbreak, Internet-based startups are some of the factors that enormously boost the popularity of IoT. Sensing and communication of embedded objects and analysis of the collected data will provide a ubiquitous and pervasive environment.

An IoT platform is responsible to play a key role for serving as a horizontal solution for vertical application domains. An IoT platform can handle the deployment, monitoring, management and configuration of various IoT devices. Also, an IoT platform can achieve starting, debugging and installation of software. Furthermore, it can accomplish complex event handling and data analytics operations. In this manner, designing and implementation of a successful IoT platform is a crucial step to construct a holistic IoT solution.

In this chapter, we provided a comprehensive evaluation of IoT platforms to analyze their various features. In this regard, we introduced fives metrics for comparing and evaluating IoT platforms as "ability to serve different domains", "ability to handle different data formats", "ability to process unlimited size of data from various context", "ability to convert unstructured data to structured data" and "ability to produce complex reports". The reasons to select these features are to analyze big data-related issues, to investigate domain specific problems and to examine the reporting capabilities of these IoT platforms. We presented an extensive comparison extracted from analysis of these five features to reveal the favors and the drawbacks of the IoT platforms.

We obtained from our metric analysis that 26% of IoT platforms do not have any of our features used in this chapter. We found that 30% of these platforms have only 1 feature, 22% of them have 2 features and 22% of them have 3 features. None of these IoT platforms have 4 and 5 of our features. We inferred from these results that more 50% of the investigated IoT platforms own at most 1 feature and none of them has all features. Also, these findings show us our features are selective enough to analyze and evaluate the IoT platforms. We calculated how many IoT platforms can serve different domains (first feature), able to handle different data formats (second feature), able to process unlimited size of data from various context (third feature), able to convert unstructured data to structured data (fourth feature) and able to produce complex reports (fifth feature) as 33%, 33%, 26%, 7% and 24%, respectively. It can be inferred from the results that for any specific feature, the probability of having that feature is less than 1/3. Also, we revealed that most of the investigated IoT platforms cannot serve for various application domains, cannot process various data formats, cannot handle unlimited size of data from various context and cannot generate complex reports. Also, we found that only 7% of the IoT platforms can make conversion between unstructured data to the structed data.

A potential future work is to design and implement an IoT platform having at least 4 of our features. Also, since conversion from unstructured to structured data feature is merely found in IoT platforms, focusing on this feature will be significant during IoT platform design. Moreover, presenting additional metrics such as "able to handle various IoT link layer protocols such as LoRa, Zigbee and WiFi HaLow" and "able to detect and manage connectivity of the networks" for evaluation of IoT platforms will be an interesting research thread.

REFERENCES

Abdelgawad, A., & Yelamarthi, K. (2017). Internet of Things (IoT) Platform for Structure Health Monitoring. *Wireless Communications and Mobile Computing*, *2017*, 1–10. doi:10.1155/2017/6560797

Alam, M. F., Katsikas, S., Beltramello, O., & Hadjiefthymiades, S. (2017) Augmented and virtual reality based monitoring and safety system: A prototype IoT platform. *Journal of Network and Computer Applications, 89*, 109-119. doi:10.1016/j.jnca.2017.03.022

Alonso, R. S., Sittón-Candanedo, I., García, O., Prieto, J., & Rodríguez-González, S. (2020). An intelligent Edge-IoT platform for monitoring livestock and crops in a dairy farming scenario. *Ad Hoc Networks, 98*.

Andersen, M. P., Fierro, G., & Culler, D. E. (2016). Enabling Synergy in IoT: Platform to Service and Beyond. *2016 IEEE First International Conference on Internet-of-Things Design and Implementation (IoTDI)*, 1-12. 10.1109/IoTDI.2015.45

Badii, C., Bellini, P., Difino, A., & Nesi, P. (2020). Smart City IoT Platform Respecting GDPR Privacy and Security Aspects. *IEEE Access: Practical Innovations, Open Solutions, 8*, 23601–23623. doi:10.1109/ACCESS.2020.2968741

Benammar, M., Abdaoui, A., Ahmad, S. H. M., Touati, F., & Kadri, A. (2018). A Modular IoT Platform for Real-Time Indoor Air Quality Monitoring. *Sensors (Basel)*, *18*(2), 581. doi:10.339018020581 PMID:29443893

Bonte, P., Ongenae, F. D., & Backere, F. (2017). The MASSIF platform: A modular and semantic platform for the development of flexible IoT services. *Knowledge and Information Systems*, *51*(1), 89–126. doi:10.100710115-016-0969-1

Dissanayake, D. M. C., & Jayasena, K. P. N. (2017). A cloud platform for big IoT data analytics by combining batch and stream processing technologies. *2017 National Information Technology Conference (NITC)*, 40-45. 10.1109/NITC.2017.8285647

Dobrilovic, D., & Zeljko, S. (2016). Design of open-source platform for introducing Internet of Things in university curricula. *2016 IEEE 11th International Symposium on Applied Computational Intelligence and Informatics (SACI)*, 273-276. 10.1109/SACI.2016.7507384

Dupont, C., Vecchio, M., Pham, C., Diop, B., Dupont, C., Koffi, S., & Pathan, K. (2018). An Open IoT Platform to Promote Eco-Sustainable Innovation in Western Africa: Real Urban and Rural Testbeds. *Wireless Communications and Mobile Computing*, *2018*, 1–17. Advance online publication. doi:10.1155/2018/1028578

Foukalas, F. (2020). Cognitive IoT platform for fog computing industrial applications. *Computers & Electrical Engineering, 87*.

Girau, R., Martis, S., & Atzori, L. (2017, February). Lysis: A Platform for IoT Distributed Applications Over Socially Connected Objects. *IEEE Internet of Things Journal*, *4*(1), 40–51. doi:10.1109/JIOT.2016.2616022

Haghi, A., Burney, K., Kidd, F. S., Valiente, L. & Peng, Y. (2017). Fast-paced development of a smart campus IoT platform. *2017 Global Internet of Things Summit (GIoTS),* 1-6. . doi:10.1109/GIOTS.2017.8016214

Iyer, V., Nandakumar, R., Wang, A., Fuller, S. B., & Gollakota, S. (2019). Living IoT: A Flying Wireless Platform on Live Insects. In *The 25th Annual International Conference on Mobile Computing and Networking (MobiCom '19).* Association for Computing Machinery. 10.1145/3300061.3300136

Jamborsalamati, P., Fernandez, E., Hossain, M. J., & Rafi, F. H. M. (2017). Design and implementation of a cloud-based IoT platform for data acquisition and device supply management in smart buildings. *2017 Australasian Universities Power Engineering Conference (AUPEC),* 1-6. 10.1109/AUPEC.2017.8282504

Jayaraman, P. P., Palmer, D., Zaslavsky, A., & Georgakopoulos, D. (2015). Do-it-Yourself Digital Agriculture applications with semantically enhanced IoT platform. *2015 IEEE Tenth International Conference on Intelligent Sensors, Sensor Networks and Information Processing (ISSNIP),* 1-6. 10.1109/ISSNIP.2015.7106951

Jayaraman, P. P., Yavari, A., Georgakopoulos, D., Morshed, A., & Zaslavsky, A. (2016). Internet of Things Platform for Smart Farming: Experiences and Lessons Learnt. *Sensors (Basel),* 6(11), 1884. doi:10.339016111884 PMID:27834862

Khazaei, H., Bannazadeh, H., & Leon-Garcia, A. (2017). SAVI-IoT: A Self-Managing Containerized IoT Platform. *2017 IEEE 5th International Conference on Future Internet of Things and Cloud (FiCloud),* 227-234. 10.1109/FiCloud.2017.27

Krylovskiy, A., Jahn, M., & Patti, E. (2015). Designing a Smart City Internet of Things Platform with Microservice Architecture. *2015 3rd International Conference on Future Internet of Things and Cloud,* 25-30. 10.1109/FiCloud.2015.55

Kubitza, T., & Schmidt, A. (2016). Rapid interweaving of smart things with the meSchup IoT platform. In *Proceedings of the 2016 ACM International Joint Conference on Pervasive and Ubiquitous Computing: Adjunct (UbiComp '16).* Association for Computing Machinery.:10.1145/2968219.2971379

Kuo, Y., Li, C., Jhang J. & Lin, S. (2018). Design of a Wireless Sensor Network-Based IoT Platform for Wide Area and Heterogeneous Applications. *IEEE Sensors Journal, 18*(12), 5187-5197. . doi:10.1109/JSEN.2018.2832664

Lea, R., & Blackstock, M. (2014). City Hub: A Cloud-Based IoT Platform for Smart Cities. *2014 IEEE 6th International Conference on Cloud Computing Technology and Science,* 799-804. doi:10.1109/CloudCom.2014.65

Lee, C., & Lai, Y. H. (2016). Design and implementation of a universal smart energy management gateway based on the Internet of Things platform. *2016 IEEE International Conference on Consumer Electronics (ICCE),* 67-68. doi: 10.1109/ICCE.2016.7430524

Lee, D., Moon, H., Oh, S., & Park, D. (2020). mIoT: Metamorphic IoT Platform for On-Demand Hardware Replacement in Large-Scaled IoT Applications. *Sensors (Basel), 2020*(20), 3337. doi:10.339020123337 PMID:32545495

Li, X., Teng, L., Tang, H., Chen, J., Wang, H., Liu, Y., Fu, M. & Liang, J. (2021). ViPSN: A Vibration-Powered IoT Platform. *IEEE Internet of Things Journal, 8*(3), 1728-1739.. doi:10.1109/JIOT.2020.3016993

Mahmoud, Q. H. & Qendri, D. (2016). The Sensorian IoT platform. *2016 13th IEEE Annual Consumer Communications & Networking Conference (CCNC),* 286-287. . doi:10.1109/CCNC.2016.7444783

Mahmud, M. A., Bates, K., Wood, T., Abdelgawad, A., & Yelamarthi, K. (2018). A complete Internet of Things (IoT) platform for Structural Health Monitoring (SHM). *2018 IEEE 4th World Forum on Internet of Things (WF-IoT),* 275-279. 10.1109/WF-IoT.2018.8355094

Makinen, A., Jimenez, J., & Morabito, R. (2017). ELIoT: Design of an emulated IoT platform. *2017 IEEE 28th Annual International Symposium on Personal, Indoor, and Mobile Radio Communications (PIMRC),* 1-7. 10.1109/PIMRC.2017.8292769

Miranda, J., Cabral, J., Wagner, S. R., Fischer Pedersen, C., Ravelo, B., Memon, M., & Mathiesen, M. (2016). An Open Platform for Seamless Sensor Support in Healthcare for the Internet of Things. *Sensors (Basel), 16*(12), 2089. doi:10.339016122089 PMID:27941656

Motlagh, N. H., Bagaa, M., & Taleb, T. (2017, February). UAV-Based IoT Platform: A Crowd Surveillance Use Case. *IEEE Communications Magazine, 55*(2), 128–134. doi:10.1109/MCOM.2017.1600587CM

Park, D., Bang, H., Pyo, C. S., & Kang, S. (2014). Semantic open IoT service platform technology. *2014 IEEE World Forum on Internet of Things (WF-IoT),* 85-88. 10.1109/WF-IoT.2014.6803125

Pérez, J. L., & Carrera, D. (2015). Performance Characterization of the Servioticy API: An IoT-as-a-Service Data Management Platform. *IEEE First International Conference on Big Data Computing Service and Applications,* 62-71. 10.1109/BigDataService.2015.58

Pierris, G., Kothris, D., Spyrou, E., & Spyropoulos, C. (2015). SYNAISTHISI: an enabling platform for the current internet of things ecosystem. In *Proceedings of the 19th Panhellenic Conference on Informatics (PCI '15).* Association for Computing Machinery. DOI:10.1145/2801948.2802019

Pizzolli, D. (2016). Cloud4IoT: A Heterogeneous, Distributed and Autonomic Cloud Platform for the IoT. *2016 IEEE International Conference on Cloud Computing Technology and Science (CloudCom),* 476-479. 10.1109/CloudCom.2016.0082

Ramallo-Gonzalez, A. P., Gonzalez-Vidal, A., & Skarmeta, A. F. (2021). CIoTVID: Towards an Open IoT-Platform for Infective Pandemic Diseases such as COVID-19. *Sensors (Basel), 21*(2), 484. doi:10.339021020484 PMID:33445499

Rayes, A., & Samer, S. (2019). Internet of Things From Hype to Reality: The Road to Digitization. Springer Publishing Company.

Rogojanu, T., Ghita, M., Stanciu, V., Ciobanu, R. I., Marin, R. C., Pop, F., & Dobre, C. (2018). Netiot: A versatile iot platform integrating sensors and applications. *2018 Global Internet of Things Summit (GIoTS),* 1-6.

Sagheer, A., Mohammed, M., Riad, K., & Alhajhoj, M. (2021). A Cloud-Based IoT Platform for Precision Control of Soilless Greenhouse Cultivation. *Sensors (Basel), 21*(1), 223. doi:10.339021010223 PMID:33396448

Sakthidasan Sankaran, K., Vasudevan, N., & Verghese, A. (2020). ACIAR: Application-centric information-aware routing technique for IOT platform assisted by wireless sensor networks. *Journal of Ambient Intelligence and Humanized Computing, 11*(11), 4815–4825. doi:10.100712652-020-01748-y

Sarmento, R. M., Vasconcelos, F. F. X., Filho, P. P. R., & de Albuquerque, V. H. C. (2020). An IoT platform for the analysis of brain CT images based on Parzen analysis. *Future Generation Computer Systems, 105*, 135-147. doi:10.1016/j.future.2019.11.033

Shahzad, A., Kim, Y., & Elgamoudi, A. (2017). Secure IoT Platform for Industrial Control Systems. *2017 International Conference on Platform Technology and Service (PlatCon),* 1-6. doi:10.1109/PlatCon.2017.7883726

Silva, R., Silva, J. S., & Boavida, F. (2015). A symbiotic resources sharing IoT platform in the smart cities context. *2015 IEEE Tenth International Conference on Intelligent Sensors, Sensor Networks and Information Processing (ISSNIP),* 1-6. doi: 10.1109/ISSNIP.2015.7106922

Terroso-Saenz, F., González Vidal, A., Ramallo-González, A., & Skarmeta, A. (2017). An open IoT platform for the management and analysis of energy data. *Future Generation Computer Systems, 92,* 1066–1079. Advance online publication. doi:10.1016/j.future.2017.08.046

Trilles, S., González-Pérez, A., & Huerta, J. (2020). An IoT Platform Based on Microservices and Serverless Paradigms for Smart Farming Purposes. *Sensors (Basel), 20*(8), 2418. doi:10.339020082418 PMID:32344569

Tsokov, T., & Petrova-Antonova, D. (2017). EcoLogic: IoT Platform for Control of Carbon Emissions. Proc. ff ICSOFT, 178-185.

Vergara, P., Marín, E., Villar, J., González, V., & Sedano, J. (2017). An IoT Platform for Epilepsy Monitoring and Supervising. *Journal of Sensors, 2017,* 1–18. doi:10.1155/2017/6043069

Vresk, T., & Čavrak, I. (2016). Architecture of an interoperable IoT platform based on microservices. *2016 39th International Convention on Information and Communication Technology, Electronics and Microelectronics (MIPRO),* 1196-1201. 10.1109/MIPRO.2016.7522321

Xu, G., Li, M., Chen, C.-H., & Wei, Y. (2018). Cloud asset-enabled integrated IoT platform for lean prefabricated construction. *Automation in Construction, 93,* 123-134. doi:10.1016/j.autcon.2018.05.012

Yang, G., Xie, L., Mantysalo, M., Zhou, X., Pang, Z., Xu, L. D., Kao-Walter, S., Chen, Q., & Zheng, L.-R. (2014). A Health-IoT Platform Based on the Integration of Intelligent Packaging, Unobtrusive Bio-Sensor, and Intelligent Medicine Box. *IEEE Transactions on Industrial Informatics, 10*(4), 2180–2191. doi:10.1109/TII.2014.2307795

Yang, S., Xu, K., Cui, L., Ming, Z., Chen, Z. & Ming, Z. (2021). EBI-PAI: Toward an Efficient Edge-Based IoT Platform for Artificial Intelligence. *IEEE Internet of Things Journal, 8*(12), 9580-9593. . doi:10.1109/JIOT.2020.3019008

Yu, J., Bang, H. C., Lee, H., & Lee, Y. S. (2016). Adaptive Internet of Things and Web of Things convergence platform for Internet of reality services. *The Journal of Supercomputing, 72*(1), 84–102. doi:10.100711227-015-1489-6

Zamora-Izquierdo, M. A., Santa, J., Martínez, J. A., Martínez, V., & Skarmeta, A. F. (2019). Smart farming IoT platform based on edge and cloud computing. *Biosystems Engineering, 177*, 4-17. doi:10.1016/j.biosystemseng.2018.10.014

Zelenika, Z., & Pušnik, T. (2016). Reinventing telecom OSS toolkit as an IoT platform. *2016 International Symposium ELMAR,* 21-26. 10.1109/ELMAR.2016.7731746

Chapter 2
An Overview of IoT Infrastructure Architecture, Enabling Technologies, Issues, Integration of Cloud, and Simulation Tools

Mobasshir Mahbub

(iD) https://orcid.org/0000-0002-8272-7208

Ahsanullah University of Science and Technology, Bangladesh

ABSTRACT

Many critical studies and research were carried out to improve the technologies of IoT. Nevertheless, several challenges need to be solved to determine the maximum value of IoT. These problems and concerns will be approached from specific IoT perspectives, such as applications, enabling technologies, issues, and so on. The key purpose of this work is to explore IoT technology in terms of technical and social aspects. The work discusses various challenges and major issues of IoT including detailed architecture and applications. The research further summarizes the recent literature of various areas of IoT and explains their importance. Moreover, the importance of integration of cloud in IoT infrastructure has been discussed. The research also mentioned and described various simulation tools through which the characteristics of the IoT environment can be analyzed empirically. This work lets the readers and the researchers grasp the IoT and its real-life applicability.

INTRODUCTION

Internet of Things (IoT) is one of the emerging topics in recent times in terms of technical, social, and financial consequences. From the past decades, there is a significant development in the fields of wireless communication technology, information and communication systems, industrial designs, and electromechanical systems encouragements progress new technology named as the Internet of Things. The most

DOI: 10.4018/978-1-7998-4186-9.ch002

important intention of the IoT is to connect all or any devices to the internet or other connected devices (Sinche, 2020). IoT is the collection network of home appliances, physical devices, vehicular networks, and added devices fixed with sensors, electronics, and actuators along with network connectivity which make-possibility for mentioned objects to gather/accumulate and exchange information/data. IoT works as a massive network of organized things and people allocate those gathered resources in relation to the way they are utilized and also know regarding the surrounding atmosphere. Here each and everything typically identified with its corresponding computing system however it proficient to interoperate inside the existing internet infrastructure.

IoT is a paradigm where the real world is connected to the virtual world through the internet. IoT has wide scope in each trade of the world starting from engineering, medical, finance, food, energy, and agriculture. New devices, OS, architectures, platforms, security, and communication protocol are emerging in terms of IoT. As research is done in IoT, many new challenges are coming like massive connectivity, coverage, security, scalability. To achieve these goals that create problems a few years back now seems easy due to the interconnection of things. Both advancement and challenges are growing hand in hand. IoT adds a new taxonomy every day to its definition. It will take time to make IoT's boundary stable. IoT applications can be broadly categorized as consumer-based, industrial-based, and infrastructure-based applications. Some of the consumer-based applications are home automation, self-driven vehicles, smart wearable, automated healthcare, smart homes, etc. Major industrial application is smart manufacturing process and control system, smart retail and supply chain, internet industry, industrial automation etc. Infrastructure based applications are the smart city, habitat monitoring, smart environment, smart grid, etc. (Ngu, 2017).

IoT ecosystem is a system that brings together all the heterogeneous components of IoT in a managed way to build an efficient system. It is the integration of devices, operating system, controllers, gateways, middleware, and platform. All these elements are connected through communication protocol and interfaces like Zigbee, low power Wi-Fi, Message Queuing Telemetry Transport (MQTT), Low Power Personal Area Network for IPv6 (6LoWPAN), Near Field Communication (NFC), Bluetooth low energy (BLE), etc. IoT ecosystem connects a large number of physical devices in a single system. These connected devices have been increasing exponentially. In 2020 the count will increase to 50–100 billion according to various Information and Communication Technology (ICT) reports (Stoyanova, 2020). From the latest updates in the IoT field, there will be more than 30 billion things/devices continuously online and higher than 200 B. Chander and G. Kumaravelan billion things/devices infrequently online by the year 2020. In the early hours of 2000, Kevin Ashton one of the pioneer researchers of MIT institute AutoID Lab who made ground base work that comes out nowadays as the Internet of Things (IoT).

By the year 2022, up to 45 percent of all internet traffic will be projected by IoT. In addition to these predictions, the McKinsey Institute has stated that, over the last five years, the number of linked devices has risen 300 percent. IoT-based services can provide substantial economic development in the industry. It is estimated that the total annual economic impact of IoT will be $2.7 to $6.2 trillion by the year 2025.

This work will provide a study on pieces of literature that includes the core concepts of IoT such as IoT architecture, frameworks, enablers, issues, cloud-based IoT, etc. The increasing number of architecture proposed has yet to converge on a reference model. In the meantime, several initiatives such as IoT-A seek to develop specific architecture focused on the study of researchers and industry's needs. A three-layer design composed of the sensing, the network, and application layers are the primary architecture extracted from the set of proposals. However, several models that add further abstraction to the IoT architecture were proposed in the recent literature. The work will then provide a detailed overview of the layered structure of IoT such as three-layer, four-layer, IoT middleware architecture, including SOA-based architecture, etc. Further, it will describe the enabling technologies of IoT. Understanding the enabling technologies of IoT lets to achieve the necessary insight into the exact functionality of IoT. The enabling technologies are IoT devices, communications technologies, standards, protocols, etc. Understanding the objectives of IoT is not a straightforward task because of several issues to be addressed. Significant challenges involve accessibility, reliability, agility, efficiency, interoperability, scalability, privacy, and trust. Service providers, researchers, and designers should incorporate their programs effectively to adapt to these challenges. Such issues are elaborated broadly in this work. Cloud platforms enable third-party remote software and hardware resources to be used by individuals and businesses. Cloud infrastructure allows scientists and businesses to be able to centrally, efficiently, and cost-effectively access and manage a vast range of services. The IoT uses various embedded devices, such as sensors and actuators, which produce a large quantity of data, requiring complicated calculations to extract information. Consequently, cloud storage and computational services are the perfect options to process and store data for the IoT. This work moreover introduces a study on the integration of cloud technologies (including fog and edge computing) in IoT to serve the mentioned sophisticated purposes of IoT. Simulations are used to model system characteristics, where the simulation setting imitates and tests a particular situation until it is built or applied in real-life scenarios. The usage of simulation software to simulate the IoT environment is important because it allows the feasibility of an application to be measured effectively due to its precision and reliability. IoT is fully committed to providing community and citizens with new private and commercial benefits and enhancement. The work has mentioned the applications of IoT infrastructure in terms of smart cities, smart grid, smart transportation, smart agriculture, retail, industry, healthcare, etc. Finally, the work has proposed future research directions regarding IoT.

The chapter is structured as follows: Section 2 offers state-of-the-art information on major research that discusses various IoT problems and concerns. Section 3 discussed the architecture in detail. Section 4 focuses on enabling or supporting techs of IoT. The major challenges and issues of IoT are addressed in section 5. In section 6, the role and importance of integration of the cloud technologies in IoT are discussed. The discussions on IoT simulation tools are performed in section 7. The overview of the latest applications of IoT is given in section 8.

RELEVANT WORKS AND LITERATURE

The chapter differs from the existing literature as it gives an idea on IoT as a complete ecosystem in terms of architectures, requirements of IoT environments, core enabling technologies (computation, identification, sensing, communication, protocols and standards), integration of cloud technologies, simulation platforms. All these components work together to give an IoT application. A recent work (Sobin, 2020) covers IoT technologies and various applications of IoT. Various design aspects of OS and challenges are discussed in paper (Musaddiq, 2018). There is an overview on enabling technologies of IoT which also explains research issues on IoT (Čolaković, 2018). The paper (Kraijak, 2015) gives the literature review on IoT architectures, protocols, and applications. The survey on communication technologies and protocols is discussed in papers (Al-Masri, 2020; Lagkas, 2018; Al-Sarawi, 2017). An extensive study on the capabilities of IoT middleware (Razzaque, 2016) and components of platforms (Ojo, 2018) is explained in recent surveys. But there is no comprehensive literature on the complete IoT ecosystem which covers all IoT components and gives various applications as a complete IoT ecosystem.

ARCHITECTURES OF IOT

The architecture describes the main physical components, their practical alignment, and the concepts underlined. Various researchers have given different IoT architectures. IoT's first and foundational design is a three-layer design. This is composed primarily of three tiers, perception, network, and application layer. Sensor and actuation are the main components of the layer of perception. The network layer is in charge of information transmission and processing. The platform layer provides the consumer with certain functionality. There are two additional layers in five-layer architecture to allow the further abstraction of IoT architecture. The five distinctive layers are perception or sensing, processing, transport or network, middleware, and application.

Three-Tier Architecture

The architecture of IoT is typically divided into three fundamental layers (Gardašević, 2016): (i) application, (ii) network, and (iii) perception layer, which are described below.

(i) The perception or sensing layer is regarded as the down-most layer of the IoT design, also known as the sensor layer. The sensor layer deals with the usage of intelligent instruments (RFID, actuators, sensors, etc.) with specific gadgets and components. Its main purposes will consist of connecting things to the IoT network and measuring, collecting, and processing the information related to these things by deploying intelligent gadgets, transmitting processed data via layer interfaces to the top-level.

(ii) In IoT architecture, the network layer, also named as transmission layer, is considered as the middle layer. The network layer serves to receive the information provided by the perception layer and to establish the routes by which data and information can be passed through an integrated network to the IoT gadgets and appliances. The network layer is the most critical layer in IoT architecture as multiple gadgets (hub, routing, switching, cloud computing) and numerous networking technologies such as Bluetooth, Cellular networks (GSM, LTE), and Wi-Fi are embedded into the framework. The layer of the network should transmit data to and from different things or applications using interfaces and gateways between heterogeneous networks using different technologies and protocols of communication.

(iii) The top layer in IoT architecture is the application layer, also known as the business layer. The layer of application obtains data from the layer of the network and uses data for the services or operations required. The layer, for example, can supply the storage service for backup of data in a database or ensure the analysis to evaluate the information received to predict the future state of gadgets. Within this layer, there are many programs, each of which has specific specifications. Smart infrastructure, intelligent transport, smart towns, etc. are significant instances.

Five-Tier Architecture

The Penta-layer architecture is described in-depth as follows:

Objects Layer

Objects (gadgets) or sensing or perception layer is responsible for gathering and processing information via the sensors of an IoT ecosystem. This layer contains sensors and actuators to accomplish various functions such as position, temperature, weight, movement, vibration, distance, humidity, etc. The perceptual layer must be used to configure heterogeneous objects to standardized plug-and-play mechanisms. The selection layer scans and transmits data via protected channels to the Entity Abstraction layer. At this layer, the generations of massive data of an IoT infrastructure are initiated (Wang, 2020).

Object Abstraction Layer

Object abstraction layer transmits data generated by the perception layer via secure links to the service orchestration layer. Data may be transferred by different technologies, like RFID, UMTS, GSM, WLAN, Bluetooth, infra-red technology, ZigBee, etc. Additionally, this layer is responsible for other functions, like cloud computing and data management processes.

Service Orchestration Layer

Service orchestration or middleware layer pairs services dependent on address and name to the requestor. It enables IoT developers to deal with heterogeneous artifacts without considering a specified hardware platform. In addition, data obtained from this layer is analyzed, decisions are made and the services demanded are provided through networking protocols (Li, 2019).

Application Layer

The consumer's requested services are given through the application layer. For example, the application layer can provide the consumer with the data of temperature and air humidity measurements as per request. It is important for the IoT environment that this layer has the ability to provide well-furnished intelligent services to satisfy consumer requirements. The application layer includes many vertical services, for example, intelligent homes, intelligent buildings, smart transportation, industrial automation, and e-healthcare (Pérez, 2020).

Business Layer

This layer manages the total activities and services of IoT systems. Based on the data received from the application layer, the tasks of this layer are to develop a business model, graphs, flood charts, etc. IoT systems specific elements have also to be planned, analyzed, applied, assessed, tracked, and created. The layer of business orchestration enables the execution of decisions based on data analytics. Furthermore, the four layers are monitored and managed on this layer. This layer often contrasts each layer's performance with the projected production for better functionality and for the privacy of users.

SOA-Based Architecture

Architecture generally defines the technical roles and approaches need to be employed on a specific layer. To promote the mutual inter-operation between IoT environment and other networking services, SOA (Service Oriented Architecture) implements the most ambitious IoT design. SOA's success is evident in the widespread adoption of technologies, for example, cloud, web services, and more, in research and industry. In general, this design is divided into four layers (Chen, 2016).

Physical Layer

The object-oriented viewpoint defined in this layer contains many forms of physical entities that are interconnected. In essence, WSNs, RFIDs, and smart gadgets have found enormous applications and are key drivers of this IoT infrastructure. WSN, NFC, and RFID technologies are seen as leading-edge technologies that connect the physical and cyberspace together with gateways such as the servers, cloud, and mobile gadgets. The Unique/Universal/Ubiquitous Identifier (uID) (Ai, 2020) is an important element for overall visibility of items. It makes things easier to connect to each other and enables them to automatically sense and interchange information. For IoT services to be deployed in a large network, universal identities are essential.

Network Layer

The second layer reflects the network-oriented perspective by supporting the Web as one of the primary methods of connectivity for the interaction between IP artifacts. The key function is to ensure knowledge sharing and to ensure that knowledge not only comes from IoT apps but also from current IT systems is aggregated. Similar technologies typically exist in distributed networks. We may be combined in partnership to create internet infrastructure. IoT applications may be provided by the same system, local servers, or cloud/fog networks in terms of service requirements. The shortage of capacity, high latency, lossy network, hardware breakdown, and unnecessary data transmission, network assaults and several other reasons affect the IoT service providers' IoT services delivery. The restriction of resources is an important problem that leads to new protocols, for instance, 6LoWPAN and the Lossy Low-Power Routing Protocol, etc.

Service Layer

A third semantic method is supposed to push smooth connectivity between IoT and Internet providers at this second-highest stage. This is important to standardize the features offered by IoT. To meet consumer and other applications' demands, an IoT infrastructure is semi-defined by adopting SOA with a definition of specific client specifications and accessible via standard interfaces. Specifications mandating protocols and APIs that enable global interoperability are the key function of SoA. Different service providers having the same functionalities will be required to maintain quality of service (QoS), for example, response time, efficiency, error rate, and reputation will become the deciding element to differentiate between them. Physical and network levels at this stage do have a significant impact on QoS. For instance, resource constraints on the physical layer are responsible for delays in response time, and network architecture variations and modifications generally relate to connectivity and transmission loading capability.

Application Layer

This layer at the height of this design offers complete system-based support for end-users. Contrary to the traditional three-layer architecture, the framework layer is not regarded as a division of middleware, but rather orchestrates the middleware layer. It offers automated device interfacing by the delivery of heterogeneous networks and systems across protocols for standard user interfaces and app application structures. Intelligent infrastructure, smart transport, intelligent industry, smart care, etc. are all examples.

REQUIREMENTS OF IOT

An IoT framework consists of numerous blocks needed to promote the sensing, recognition, power, communication, and management for specific systems utilities (Minoli, 2017). The following are functional components:

Device: An IoT system consists of sensors, actuators, controls, and surveillance devices. Data communication with other linked devices may be performed through IoT devices, or data obtained by other devices can be processed locally or sent to the back-end data processing to remote repositories or cloud services, or operates on locally or through certain IoT network activities based on resources (e.g. power, computing capabilities, etc.). An IoT computer may consist of multiple wired and wireless connections to connect with other devices. These include (i) sensor input/output interfaces, (ii) communication interfaces, (iii) data and memory interfaces, and (iv) audio and video device interfaces. IoT systems will be diversified, e.g. smart sensors, autonomous gadgets, LED lighting, vehicles, and automotive robots. Almost all IoT devices produce data in a way that contributes to valuable knowledge when analyzed by data analytics programs, such as sensor data produced by a soil monitor in a greenhouse, when analyzed will help decide optimum watering plans locally or remotely. For example, the data can be collected by a sensor app.

Communication: The block of communication includes connectivity between gadgets and remote servers. IoT protocols typically operate in the data interface layer, network layer, transportation layer, and device layer.

Services: An IoT framework performs specific styles of functions including computer modeling facilities, application management, data representing, data processing, and object identification.

Management: The control or management framework offers different roles to handle an IoT device to look for fundamental IoT system management.

Security: The security functional framework provides the IoT device with authorization, approval, secrecy, and validity of the information and data protection functions.

Application: The application layer is the most relevant for consumers as it includes the modules required to manage and track many elements of the IoT network as an interface. Apps enable users to see and evaluate the present state of the program, and also to forecast potential prospects.

CORE COMPONENTS OF IOT INFRASTRUCTURE

Computation

Computational units such as microprocessors, microcontrollers, FPGAs, SOCs, and software platforms represent the "cerebrum" and the processing capacity of the IoT environment. Different IoT systems, including Arduino, Raspberry Pi, Intel Galileo, STM Development Boards, UDOO, Gadgeteer, FriendlyARM, Cubieboard, BeagleBone, Z1, Mulle, WiSense, and T-Mote Sky have been developed for the implementation of IoT applications. However, other IoT-functionalities are provided by various software frameworks. Operating systems are essential among these platforms because they run for the entire time a device is activated. Several real-time OS (RTOS) are well suited to developing RTOS-based IoT applications. Contiki RTOS, for example, has been widely used in IoT infrastructures. Contiki has an imitator called Cooja that simulates and emulates IoT and wireless network (WSN) networks for researchers and developers. LiteOS (Takahashi, 2009), TinyOS (Amjad, 2016), and Riot OS (Baccelli, 2018) also ensure light OS especially developed for IoT infrastructures.

Identification

To identify and align utilities with their application, an adequate identification approach is obvious for IoT. In the IoT, there are many authentication methods including electronic component codes (EPCs) and omnipresent codes (uCode) usable. Also, it is important to address the IoT objects to discern between the entity ID and its message. Object ID represents identifier and object address refers to its contact network address. Addressing IoT artifacts methods often contains IPv6 and IPv4. 6LoWPAN offers compression through the headers of IPv6, rendering it ideal for wireless low-power networks (Al-Kaseem, 2019). It is important to differentiate between entity identity and address as recognition approaches are not special worldwide and thus serve to recognize artifacts only. Moreover, network artifacts may use public and non-private IPs. The method of defining each target inside the network offers a simple identification.

Sensing and Sensors

The IoT-sensing method includes data collection and transfers to storage, database, or cloud from related gadgets inside the network. The data gathered are analyzed to take specific measures based on the services required. Smart switches, actuators, or portable sensing systems may be used with IoT sensors. Companies such as LikeWemo, Revolv, and SmartThings, for instance, offer intelligent hubs and mobile apps to track and control intelligent gadgets and appliances through smartphones. The following section provides a concise preview of these sensors:

Light sensor: It is an optical light detection system. The main role of these sensors is to provide light intensity, wavelength of light, light reflection, type (artificial, sunlight), and light intensity information. Many kinds of light sensors are available, such as UV sensors, photodiode, color sensors, IR sensors, etc. The light sensor is regarded as a rich data source at a very low cost because it consumes little energy.

Audio and microphone sensor: It offers details on specific sound forms with limited processing capability (noise, audio, speak).

Accelerometer sensor: It offers knowledge regarding the speed, acceleration, or propensity of mobile gadgets, which includes accelerometers, angular sensors, and mercury switches.

Location sensors: These types of sensors provide significant information on location, collocation, proximity, and position of gadgets, users, and surroundings. This kind of sensors can be used in many applications like GSM-locationing, GPS, and active signage systems.

Touch sensors: This type of sensors could be used by smart gadgets managed by users, because they can directly be implemented with specific conducting surfaces, such as skin conductivity or indirectly through temperature or light sensors. Such sensors tend to significantly reduce energy consumption, particularly for user-friendly devices.

Temperature sensors: The features of these sensors are easy to use and very inexpensive. This allows them to be applied in multiple application fields, including temperature estimation, smoke and flow gasses, body heat monitoring, rubber, and plastic development process applications, etc.

Pressure sensor: It is used for performing different types of measurements like fluid or gas pressure, altitude, and water level.

Medical Sensors: Enhancing the efficiency of biomedical systems and health infrastructures is one of the most demanding goals of our age, because of the need to provide quality healthcare for low-cost patients and to address the shortage of healthcare workers. The above-mentioned problems are solved by the use of IoT sensors, such as the blood glycoside, cardiac rates, blood pressure, respiratory rates, pulse rate, and temperature of the body of a patient, without human interference, through monitoring, and measuring. The purpose of medical applications is to remotely track the wellbeing of a patient and thus transfer sensed data to the doctors directly to determine properly.

Environmental and Chemical Sensors: These are used to detect physical, chemical, and biological environmental parameters such as pressure, humidity, temperature, air, and water pollution. The pressure and temperature parameter is measured by a barometer and thermometer, while air quality is monitored by sensors which detect the presence of gasses and other pollutants in the environment.

Communication Standards

Communications protocols constitute the backbone of IoT systems and allow network connectivity and connections to apps. Communication protocols enable network exchange of data by devices. The protocols define the formats for data exchange, data encoding, device address schemes, and packet routing from source to target. Other protocol functions include sequence control, control of flow, and the re-transmission of lost packets.

Near field communication (NFC): It allows wireless communication with a very short range (up to 10 cm). The technology stressed by NFC is RFID which uses the magnetic data region. There are two types of NFC communication: active and passive. In the active form, the power is controlled by both transmitted data transmission systems and passive technology, where one computer generates a magnetic field and another computer relies on data transmission modulation (Leikanger, 2017).

BLE: Bluetooth Low Energy (BLE) is an advanced Bluetooth technology that supports very small data packets while reducing the power usage of gadgets significantly respectively. BLE functions on a frequency of 2.4 GHz and utilizes hopping (frequency) mechanism. This mechanism utilizes the 2.4 GHz ISM band to counter the fading and interference. Now several mobile vendors continue to follow BLE, backed by leading operating systems such as Android, iOS, and Windows Phone.

IEEE 802.15.4 (WPAN): IEEE 802.15.4 is a Wireless Personal Area Network protocol designated for the physical and MAC layer (Choudhury, 2020). IEEE 802.15.4 seeks to focus on long-range wireless personal area networks (LRWPAN), providing efficient transmission rate, low cost, and energy-efficient connections to everyone in an operating area. The IEEE 802.15.4 protocol stack uses the OSI template to provide services, in which the transmission functions are separately implemented by each layer and lower layers can serve the upper layers. The IEEE 802.15.4 allows 868/915 MHz and 2.4 GHz bands and can reach a transfer rate of up to 20, 40, and 250 kbps for both bands respectively. IEEE 802.15.4 offers the foundation for a range of wireless technologies and standards like ZigBee, Wireless HART, and so forth.

IEEE 802.16 (WiMAX): IEEE 802.16 is a wideband wireless standard. The WiMAX (Worldwide Interoperability for Microwave Access) standard provides data rates up to 1.5 Mbps to 1 Gbps. The recent update (802.16 m) offers a data rate of 100 Mbps and 1 Gbps for fixed stations. The specifications of IEEE 802.16 can readily be found on the website of the working group (IEEE 802.16, 2014).

IEEE 802.11 (WLAN): The IEEE 802.11 collection contains the communication standards of Wireless Local Area Network (WLAN). For example, 802.11-a, functions in 5 GHz band, 802.11-b, and 802.11-g in the 2.4 GHz band, 802.11-n runs in both 2.4 and 5 GHz, and 802.11-ac in 5 GHz band. These standards provide 1 Mbps to 6.75 Gbps data rate. The communication range of WiFi can be between 20 meters (indoor) and 100 meters (outdoor).

Low-power Wireless Personal Area Network (6LowPAN) protocol: 6LoWPAN permits the Internet communication with intelligent users by utilizing the IPV6 standard, taking into consideration the complexity with wireless IoT networks and developing a very lightweight message header format. Also, the IPV6 protocol addressing barriers are broken down in terms of limited processing, low data rate, and limited power IoT objects, across the limited bandwidth of wireless networks.

ZigBee: ZigBee is a wireless communication technology designed to communicate on a short-term basis with low consumption (Li, 2019). Five layers of the ZigBee protocol are included: physical, MAC, transmission, application, and network layer. ZigBee networks have benefits such as low usage, low expense, low data speeds, low latency, stability, and protection. The ZigBee network will accept several topologies, such as the topologies of planets, trees, and mesh.

Z-Wave: This is a low-power MAC protocol dedicated to home automation and developed by Zensys18 (Qu, 2016). Z-Wave19 is suitable for small data packages up to 100kbps with a communication range of 30 meters (P2P) and operates with the 908 MHz band. It is not suitable for the streaming or transmission of critical time data due to the low data rate.

Cellular Communications: Any IoT service requiring long-distance operation can benefit from cellular technologies, such as GSM, UMTS, LTE or LTE-A and 5G NR, as it has the capabilities of transmitting large volumes of data packets, especially in 4G and 5G cellular technologies. On that basis, communication by cellular protocols for many applications is costly and extremely power-consuming.

NB-IoT - 3GPP (Third-generation Partnership Project) has introduced this technology. The combination of two cellular technologies namely LTE and GSM is the basis of NB-IoT. BPSK and QPSK are used for modulation by NB-IoT technology. Three types of operations exist in this technology-a standalone operation that only uses GSM, a guard band operation that uses a guard band, an in-band operation using the resource block of a carrier LTE. The quick modulation rate with small cost and high power consumption allows it more effective (Migabo, 2020).

Protocols and Services

Message Queue Telemetry Transport (MQTT): The Message Queue Telemetry Transportation (MQTT) is a communication protocol used to capture and transmit data on remote sensors to servers using publish and subscribe technology. MQTT is a lightweight and quick protocol that embraces low bandwidth and high latency networks. MQTT may be utilized on various platforms to connect IoT gadgets to the Internet, thus making MQTT an important message protocol in IoT between sensors, actuators, and servers (Kim, 2019).

Constrained Application Protocol: This protocol has been suggested by the IETF for the provision of flow management, efficient distribution, and easy congestion reduction for IoT applications to match resource-constrained and non-synchronized systems. It also supports the communication model based on publish-subscribe requests for multi-channel and unicast. CoAP runs through the User Datagram

Protocol (UDP) to manage resources reduce requirements for bandwidth and eliminate TCP's handshake overhead cost before transmission starts, because of its simplicity, small message size, and low code footprint. However, there are many deficiencies in this protocol as it increases latency and corruption of the supply of packets and transmits complex data (Park, 2020).

XMPP: The XMPP (Extensible Messaging and Presence Protocol), also known as Jabber, is an IETF standardized Protocol which is suitable to the IoT domain because it deals with issues of interoperability and security. However, bandwidth and processing power consumes it with no guarantee of QoS. This protocol is extremely scalable. XMPP offers a range of applications open source for servers, clients, and databases that enable various operating systems and provides an integrated interface that greatly eliminates expense and complexity (Dawei, 2018). This protocol essentially enables agnostic technology and protocol-independent data transport via wireless or wired internet-based networks. The XMPP supports a request-response model that allows bidirectional communication and also supports multi-directional communications utilizing the publishing and subscription model.

Hyper-Text Transfer Protocol: It was developed by Tim Berners-Lee in 1997 and supports the request-response representative state transfer (RESTful) feature, where clients submit HTTP request messages to the server. This web message has been built by Tim Berners-Lee. HTTP is dependent on TCP as the Transportation Layer Security or Secure Sockets Layer (TLS/SSL) protocol, which allows connection-orientated communication between the server and the client. However, IoT networking via the HTTP protocol leads to networking resources and a considerable overhead, because so many small packets have to be transferred (Park, 2018).

AMQP: The AMQP (Advanced Message Queuing Protocol) is an open-source protocol for communication through heterogeneous gadgets and networks across different applications. The protocol was developed initially for fast M2M communication. AMQP completely promotes practical interoperability between compliant clients and servers (brokers). AMQP is a multichannel, mediated, intermittent, secure, interactive, impartial, and powerful protocol (Uy, 2019).

DNS, mDNS & DNS-SD: Besides the transmission, communication, and messaging protocols, several other protocols or standards perform significant roles in the IoT ecosystem as well. E.g., Multicast DNS (mDNS) supports the name resolution processes in IoT gadgets. DNS Service Discovery (DNS-SD) may be used by customers in a specific network through mDNS for the discovery of requested services. This routing protocol is an independent protocol for lossy and low power networks, which can be used at resource-constricted nodes to establish routes through lossy and low power links. While they can be integrated into the IoT ecosystem, enhanced protocols are required to advance IoT development with additional security, credibility, and interoperability.

Data Distribution Service (DDS): DDS is focused on the publish-subscribe technique, inclusive of high-efficiency device-to-device communications. DDS is a data-centric protocol utilized mainly in the multicast network that offers a high QoS and lustiness and supported by the Object Management Group. It is suitable for IoT, device-to-device communication in real-time, utilizing the broker-free publish-subscribe technique. The level of scalability of DDS is much strong.

INTEGRATION OF CLOUD TECHNOLOGIES IN IOT

Cloud Computing

Cloud infrastructure is a modern technical paradigm for addressing the on-demand virtual capital network which is capable of configuring/managing assets such as networks, computers, and software which utilities. Cloud storage enables efficient and cost-optimized distributed usage and control of services. Cloud storage and computer resources allow IoT to manage this huge data and to store it and process it.

Thing-Worx, Google Cloud, OpenIoT, AWS, GENI, etc. are the major cloud servers for IoT infrastructure. Cloud storage handles large data that enables data collection and useful knowledge to be retrieved. However, it is a difficult task to implement IoT cloud computing. Several challenges are mentioned below:

- Synchronization and standardization of heterogeneous cloud services for the interoperability of real-time infrastructure.
- Maintaining equilibrium between IoT and cloud environments is a challenge in the case of IoT infrastructure.
- Due to the multi-domain security mechanisms involved in IoT layers, security is a major concern for IoT cloud.
- To maintain reliable infrastructure, cloud resources must be validated. In local infra resources, cloud computing is not necessary as there are limited data. If the cloud is triggered, the computing and operational costs should rise. To reduce internet data congestion, latency, and prices, raw data are needed to be stored on local nodes. This will further optimize the performances as well. Cloud is also used as a replacement for modern computational technologies such as Cloudlets and Fog Computing, which are intended to function as an alternative or a bridge to the cloud (De Donno, 2019).

Fog Computing

Fog might be elaborated as a "mobile" cloud. Another name of Fog Computing is Cloudlets. It is used for cloud processing and backup in a large-scale. This layer serves as a link between the layer of autonomous devices and the cloud storage layer. It empowers cloud storage infrastructure to be applied to edge gadgets. Similar to the web, Fog processing connectivity is strong for end-users and hence storage, time, quality, and efficiency are enhanced. It is regarded as a cloud of limited capacity. Fog computing reduces issues such as usability, trust, efficiency, etc. The Fog performs as a micro cloud in IoT. It offers limited capacity, for example, data storage, filtering, processing, and review to the edge of the network. Fog Computing capabilities include low latency, awareness of location, remote nodes, accessibility, the reaction in real-time, and cloud connectivity. In the case of IoT, the fog and cloud go hand in hand to achieve an optimal output (De Donno, 2019).

Edge Computing

The Edge Computing (EC), as the name suggests, involves computing at the edge of the network. EC aims to overcome restrictions related to the cloud-based model of computing. It operates as an interface for end-clients or products and the cloud and supports a vast range of IoT gadgets with processing and storage functions. The nearness of edge computers decreases the computing load of the central cloud data centers. The response to real-time and decreased latency will be enhanced (De Donno, 2019). The distributed nature of device mobility in heterogeneous networks is also an advantage of EC. Some of the supportive EC features are described below:

i) Geographically distributed, ii) Enhanced security by moving encrypted data to the core network, iii) Provides better response in real-time compared to the cloud model, iv) Improving virtualization scalability, v) Potential bottlenecks of communication are limited.

SIMULATION PLATFORMS FOR ANALYZING IOT INFRASTRUCTURE

Cooja simulator: The Cooja is a forum for simultaneous deployment in place of Contaki. It helps to determine exactly continuous applications which can be imported into physical nodes. Cooja assigns program engineers to their application to analyze; device logs on a different goal before activity (Chernyshev, 2018).

iFogSiM: iFogSim refers to simulation and modeling in the area of fog computation for the allocation of goals as well as resource control from coin to coin under various situations. iFogSim simulator primarily addresses the control of capital policies and their impacts on system congestion, running costs, electricity usage, and latency. This mainly focuses on the simulation of efficiency measurements for edge applications, networking links, and cloud data centers (Chernyshev, 2018).

Cloud2Sim: Cloud2Sim presents Cloud Simulation for distributed contemporary architecture. This may be expanded to cover many cases where server and VM workloads from several nodes are analyzed and returned to the data center broker. An adaptive procedure has been conducted and implemented to make resources available for simulation on an elastic scale (Chernyshev, 2018).

IoTSim: IoTSim has been developed to study IoT big data analysis and restore MapReduce. The efficiency of IoT-base appliances by both industry and market organizations can be generously assessed (Chernyshev, 2018).

MobIoTSim: MobIoTSim is a completely IoT emulator for android-based smartphones. It helps scientists to develop IoT gadgets without the need to buy real smart sensors for analyzing and express the IoT environments using multiple gadgets. The schemes built interconnect with gateway systems in the cloud including IBM Bluemix to handle virtual devices and provide essential sensor values with notification. MobIoTSim's main targets are to allow developers to monitor the performance of intelligent gadgets, hand-held IoT systems, etc. (Chernyshev, 2018).

Arduino Unit: Arduino unit is a device testing program that enables trivial library developers and researchers to quickly review their systems in the Arduino environment (Chernyshev, 2018).

IoTFIY: IoTFIY develops an IoT application without any dependence on hardware. The practical lab to build fixed models for system scaling and data generation is made available (Chernyshev, 2018).

APPLICATIONS OF IOT

Smart Cities: The systemic integration of IoT in urban smartness requires several applications: surveillance of car parks, surveillance of and identification of vibrations in buildings and bridges, measurements of sound frequency in vulnerable places, the intelligent control of streets lighting according to environmental conditions, the identification, and recycling of waste and garbage content levels.

Healthcare: The complete and accurate online preservation of patient statements, tracking, and identification to the success of the clinical operation, recognizing and authenticating patients to reduce adverse outcomes for particular patients are other benefits attributable to the participation of IoT in the medical care management. Automated data analysis and translation into various services and practices auditing clinics, devices that handle control to a specific stage, devices implanted in a patient's body with real-time shared feedback to patient safety issues, and patient behavior warnings. Smart sensor nodes are capable to track patient's blood flow, pulse rate, cholesterol, and glucose rates reliably.

Smart Home: It is popular because it improves the comfort of life all around the world. The intelligent devices like sensors and actuators together with wireless networks mature very quickly. This not only improves the quality of life but also improves home security. Automation and intelligence services are used with sensors that help automate daily activities. In the first place, the installation and operation of intelligent devices involve costs, but, in the long run, they help to conserve energy. Some examples include the switching off of light and electronic equipment regularization. Sensors collect ambient details such as temperature, humidity, light, moisture, gas, and smoke/fire. The intelligent home will track the safety of family members, from children to the elderly and emergency alarms.

Agriculture and Smart Farming: IoT in agriculture has recently been implemented and introduced. A vast variety of sensors are used to ensure that farmers are properly monitored with grown crops, soil water, nutrients, the amount with fertilizer they use, and the temperature of their stored commodity.

Retail and Logistics: IoT oriented retail system includes the monitoring of product and trace conditions, shopping centers' guides based on prearranged lists and processing payment processes in gyms and retail stores, automated product turning in the shelf, detection of product freshness such as time and data indications without particular attention to detail, location of objects, stockpiling of products and logistics.

Security and Emergency: Integration of IoT in emergency and security management includes perimeter access control to restrict the entry of people to safe regions, liquid detection in labs and explosive gas levels, detection of radiation levels at nuclear facilities, detection and alert messages about gas flows, chemical, coal mines, and the detection of disruptions in vehicles.

Smart Grid: The smart grid has been built through the combination of IoT and CPS to substitute conventional power grids to provide customers with safe and effective energy service. The smart gird implements centralized power plants to increase the usage of renewable energy capital, incorporates electric vehicles to boost the energy storage capacity and mitigate pollution of CO_2 as well as implements smart meters and bidirectional contact networks to accomplish consumer and service company experiences. The smart grid is able to achieve stability, performance, protection, and interactivity through these strategies.

Figure 1. Applications of IoT

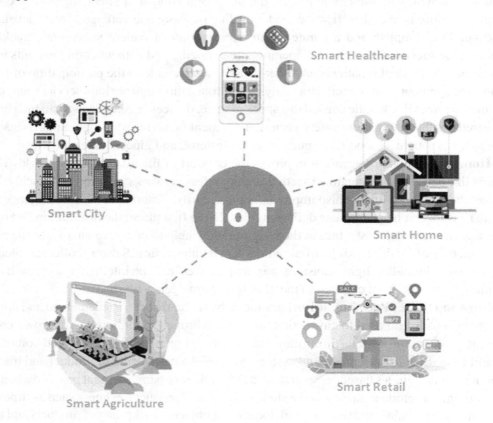

CHALLENGES AND ISSUES

IoT's a heterogeneous, highly complex network platform. This, on the other hand, makes various communication technologies more complex between different types of devices that show that the gross behavior of a network is fraudulent, delayed, and non-standardized. By promoting collaboration among different topics, for example, hardware and/or software products and managing them after approaching, identifying, or optimizing the interface or protocol stage, Bracciale et al. have indicated the management of connected objects. This is a significant research challenge.

Availability: It is a burden for consumers to reach hardware and applications at any time and everywhere. This is alluded to as IoT connectivity and interface tools or program performance. The performance of IoT systems in the design stage for optimum efficiency is being analyzed and explored.

Interoperability: The viability of sharing knowledge between various IoT devices and systems is interoperability. This knowledge sharing does not rely on the software and hardware deployed. The interoperability challenge arises because various technologies and solutions used to develop IoT have heterogeneous characteristics. The four stages of interoperability are scientific, semantic, syntactic, and organizational. To improve interoperability between various objects in a hetero space environment, IoT systems offer various functionalities.

Reliability: Reliability ensures that the machine works correctly according to its requirements. Trustworthiness is targeted at enhancing IoT service delivery performance. This has a similar connection to consistency as efficiency, we ensure knowledge and resources remain accessible over time. The usability of software in an emergency response becomes much more important and needs stricter. The core component of such networks is the transmission network that must be capable of failure tolerance to have a reliable delivery of knowledge. Software and hardware functionality across all IoT layers must be enforced.

Mobility: Mobility for IoT implementations is yet another challenge as the majority of services are intended for mobile users. It is an important premise of IoT to continuously connect users to your desired services while on the move. Mobile devices can be interrupted if these systems are moved from gateway to gateway. (Abbas, 2020) proposes a resource mobility scheme to encourage the continuity of service in two modes: cache and tunneling. In case of the temporary unavailability of resources, applications have access to IoT data. The vast number of intelligent devices in IoT systems needs powerful mobility control mechanisms as well.

Security and Privacy: Security is also a big concern in terms of complexity and a modular program. To maintain protection where heterogeneous interconnected systems and applications are involved, IoT apps gather tremendous data regarding individuals in daily life and can collectively produce extensively large amount of data so data safety and the secure flow of data is a major challenge in a wider environment. The lack of standards is a problem in IoT security. Data security is the IoT network profile control. Information transfers are a safe and privacy-free requirement. All communication tools need access that is clear and safe. To ensure the maturity of the method of access control in the program, initiative and standardization are required. Across all IoT modules, work is ongoing to develop protection and privacy.

Quality of Service (QoS): For IoT, QoS is another main element. QoS can be described as an evaluation measure for IoT devices, systems, and design functionality, output, and performance (Ahmad, 2020). Reliability, costs, energy consumption, safety, availability, and service time are the important and necessary QoS metrics for IoT applications. The requirements of the QoS standards must be met by a smarter IoT ecosystem. Also, QoS metrics must first be defined to ensure the reliability of all IoT services and devices. Moreover, users can also specify accordingly their needs and needs. There are several approaches available for QoS assessment but the quality factors and approaches have been combined, as mentioned by White et al. To solve this trade-off, high production versions will also be used.

CONCLUSION

In this chapter, an overview of IoT has been presented, including architectures, enabling technologies, and different issues, as well as the integration of cloud computing technologies and IoT to support diverse applications. Particularly, the relationship and difference between IoT and CPS have been clarified at the outset. Possible architectures for IoT have been discussed, including the traditional three-layer, five-layer architecture, and the SoA-based four-layer architecture. Enabling technologies have been detailed, respectively. To elaborate on the integration of fog and edge computing in IoT, the relationship between IoT and fog-edge computing has been discussed. Furthermore, different real-world applications of IoT are described which includes the smart cities, healthcare, smart home, smart agriculture, smart retail, etc. The chapter has included a description of IoT simulators as well through which an IoT infrastructure can be realized and observed virtually without the direct implementation. The work then elaborated on some research issues and challenges for further enhancement and development of the IoT environment. Finally, the chapter concluded with a conclusion describing the significant works performed in this work.

REFERENCES

Abbas, F., Liu, G., Fan, P., & Khan, Z. (2020). An Efficient Cluster Based Resource Management Scheme and its Performance Analysis for V2X Networks. *IEEE Access: Practical Innovations, Open Solutions*, 8, 87071–87082. doi:10.1109/ACCESS.2020.2992591

Ahmad, E., Alaslani, M., Dogar, F. R., & Shihada, B. (2020). Location-Aware, Context-Driven QoS for IoT Applications. *IEEE Systems Journal*, *14*(1), 232–243. doi:10.1109/JSYST.2019.2893913

Ai, Z., Liu, Y., Chang, L., Lin, F., & Song, F. (2020). A Smart Collaborative Authentication Framework for Multi-Dimensional Fine-Grained Control. *IEEE Access: Practical Innovations, Open Solutions*, 8, 8101–8113. doi:10.1109/ACCESS.2019.2962247

Al-Kaseem, B. R., Al-Dunainawi, Y., & Al-Raweshidy, H. S. (2019). End-to-End Delay Enhancement in 6LoWPAN Testbed Using Programmable Network Concepts. *IEEE Internet of Things Journal*, *6*(2), 3070–3086. doi:10.1109/JIOT.2018.2879111

Al-Masri, E., Kalyanam, K. R., Batts, J., Kim, J., Singh, S., Vo, T., & Yan, C. (2020). Investigating Messaging Protocols for the Internet of Things (IoT). *IEEE Access: Practical Innovations, Open Solutions*, 8, 94880–94911. doi:10.1109/ACCESS.2020.2993363

Al-Sarawi, S., Anbar, M., Alieyan, K., & Alzubaidi, M. (2017). Internet of Things (IoT) communication protocols: Review. *2017 8th International Conference on Information Technology (ICIT), Amman*, 685-690.

Amjad, M., Sharif, M., Afzal, M. K., & Kim, S. W. (2016). TinyOS-New Trends, Comparative Views, and Supported Sensing Applications: A Review. *IEEE Sensors Journal*, *16*(9), 2865–2889. doi:10.1109/JSEN.2016.2519924

Baccelli, E., Gundogan, C., Hahm, O., Kietzmann, P., Lenders, M. S., Petersen, H., Schleiser, K., Schmidt, T. C., & Wahlisch, M. (2018). RIOT: An Open Source Operating System for Low-End Embedded Devices in the IoT. *IEEE Internet of Things Journal*, *5*(6), 4428–4440. doi:10.1109/JIOT.2018.2815038

Bracciale, L., Loreti, P., Detti, A., Paolillo, R., & Melazzi, N. B. (2019). Lightweight Named Object: An ICN-Based Abstraction for IoT Device Programming and Management. *IEEE Internet of Things Journal*, *6*(3), 5029–5039. doi:10.1109/JIOT.2019.2894969

Chen, I., Guo, J., & Bao, F. (2016). Trust Management for SOA-Based IoT and Its Application to Service Composition. *IEEE Transactions on Services Computing*, *9*(3), 482–495. doi:10.1109/TSC.2014.2365797

Chernyshev, M., Baig, Z., Bello, O., & Zeadally, S. (2018). Internet of Things (IoT): Research, Simulators, and Testbeds. *IEEE Internet of Things Journal*, *5*(3), 1637–1647. doi:10.1109/JIOT.2017.2786639

Choudhury, N., Matam, R., Mukherjee, M., & Lloret, J. (2020). A Performance-to-Cost Analysis of IEEE 802.15.4 MAC with 802.15.4e MAC Modes. *IEEE Access: Practical Innovations, Open Solutions*, 8, 41936–41950. doi:10.1109/ACCESS.2020.2976654

Čolaković, A., & Hadžialić, M. (2018). Internet of Things (IoT): A review of enabling technologies, challenges, and open research issues. *Computer Networks*, *144*, 17–39. doi:10.1016/j.comnet.2018.07.017

Dawei, X., & Liqiu, J. (2018). Design of Real-Time Communication Social Software Based on XMPP. *2018 IEEE International Conference of Safety Produce Informatization (IICSPI)*, 829-833. 10.1109/IICSPI.2018.8690410

De Donno, M., Tange, K., & Dragoni, N. (2019). Foundations and Evolution of Modern Computing Paradigms: Cloud, IoT, Edge, and Fog. *IEEE Access: Practical Innovations, Open Solutions*, *7*, 150936–150948. doi:10.1109/ACCESS.2019.2947652

Gardašević, G., Veletić, M., Maletić, N., Vasiljević, D., Radusinović, I., Tomović, S., & Radonjić, M. (2016). The IoT Architectural Framework, Design Issues and Application Domains. *Wireless Personal Communications*, *92*(1), 127–148. doi:10.100711277-016-3842-3

Kim, G., Kang, S., Park, J., & Chung, K. (2019). An MQTT-Based Context-Aware Autonomous System in oneM2M Architecture. *IEEE Internet of Things Journal*, *6*(5), 8519–8528. doi:10.1109/JIOT.2019.2919971

Kraijak, S., & Tuwanut, P. (2015). A survey on IoT architectures, protocols, applications, security, privacy, real-world implementation and future trends. *11th International Conference on Wireless Communications, Networking and Mobile Computing (WiCOM 2015)*, 1-6. 10.1049/cp.2015.0714

Lagkas, T. D. (2018). Network Protocols, Schemes, and Mechanisms for Internet of Things (IoT): Features, Open Challenges, and Trends. *Wireless Communications and Mobile Computing*, *2018*, 1–23.

Leikanger, T., Schuss, C., & Häkkinen, J. (2017). Near field communication as sensor to cloud service interface. 2017 IEEE Sensors, 1-3.

Li, J., Liu, Y., Xie, J., Li, M., Sun, M., Liu, Z., & Jiang, S. (2019). A Remote Monitoring and Diagnosis Method Based on Four-Layer IoT Frame Perception. *IEEE Access: Practical Innovations, Open Solutions*, *7*, 144324–144338. doi:10.1109/ACCESS.2019.2945076

Li, P., Yan, Y., Yang, P., Li, X., & Lin, Q. (2019). Coexist WiFi for ZigBee Networks With Fine-Grained Frequency Approach. *IEEE Access: Practical Innovations, Open Solutions*, *7*, 135363–135376. doi:10.1109/ACCESS.2019.2941963

Migabo, E. M., Djouani, K. D., & Kurien, A. M. (2020). The Narrowband Internet of Things (NB-IoT) Resources Management Performance State of Art, Challenges, and Opportunities. *IEEE Access: Practical Innovations, Open Solutions*, *8*, 97658–97675. doi:10.1109/ACCESS.2020.2995938

Minoli, D., Sohraby, K., & Occhiogrosso, B. (2017). IoT Considerations, Requirements, and Architectures for Smart Buildings—Energy Optimization and Next-Generation Building Management Systems. *IEEE Internet of Things Journal*, *4*(1), 269–283. doi:10.1109/JIOT.2017.2647881

Musaddiq, A., Zikria, Y. B., Hahm, O., Yu, H., Bashir, A. K., & Kim, S. W. (2018). A Survey on Resource Management in IoT Operating Systems. *IEEE Access: Practical Innovations, Open Solutions*, *6*, 8459–8482. doi:10.1109/ACCESS.2018.2808324

Ngu, A. H., Gutierrez, M., Metsis, V., Nepal, S., & Sheng, Q. Z. (2017). IoT Middleware: A Survey on Issues and Enabling Technologies. *IEEE Internet of Things Journal*, *4*(1), 1–20.

Ojo, M. O., Giordano, S., Procissi, G., & Seitanidis, I. N. (2018). A Review of Low-End, Middle-End, and High-End Iot Devices. *IEEE Access: Practical Innovations, Open Solutions*, 6, 70528–70554. doi:10.1109/ACCESS.2018.2879615

Park, C. (2020). Security Architecture for Secure Multicast CoAP Applications. *IEEE Internet of Things Journal*, 7(4), 3441–3452. doi:10.1109/JIOT.2020.2970175

Park, S., Kim, M., & Lee, S. (2018). Anomaly Detection for HTTP Using Convolutional Autoencoders. *IEEE Access: Practical Innovations, Open Solutions*, 6, 70884–70901. doi:10.1109/ACCESS.2018.2881003

Pérez, S., Hernández-Ramos, J. L., Raza, S., & Skarmeta, A. (2020). Application Layer Key Establishment for End-to-End Security in IoT. *IEEE Internet of Things Journal*, 7(3), 2117–2128. doi:10.1109/JIOT.2019.2959428

Qu, L., Zhang, R., Shin, H., Kim, J., & Kim, H. (2016). Performance enhancement of ground radiation antenna for Z-wave applications using tunable metal loads. *Electronics Letters*, 52(22), 1827–1828. doi:10.1049/el.2016.1682

Razzaque, M. A., Milojevic-Jevric, M., Palade, A., & Clarke, S. (2016). Middleware for Internet of Things: A Survey. *IEEE Internet of Things Journal*, 3(1), 70–95. doi:10.1109/JIOT.2015.2498900

Sinche, S., Raposo, D., Armando, N., Rodrigues, A., Boavida, F., Pereira, V., & Silva, J. S. (2020). A Survey of IoT Management Protocols and Frameworks. *IEEE Communications Surveys and Tutorials*, 22(2), 1168–1190. doi:10.1109/COMST.2019.2943087

Sobin, C. C. (2020). A Survey on Architecture, Protocols and Challenges in IoT. *Wireless Personal Communications*, 116(3), 1383–1429. doi:10.100711277-020-07108-5

Stoyanova, M., Nikoloudakis, Y., Panagiotakis, S., Pallis, E., & Markakis, E. K. (2020). A Survey on the Internet of Things (IoT) Forensics: Challenges, Approaches, and Open Issues. *IEEE Communications Surveys and Tutorials*, 22(2), 1191–1221. doi:10.1109/COMST.2019.2962586

Takahashi, M., Hussain, B., & Tang, B. (2009). Demo abstract: Design and implementation of a web service for liteos-based sensor networks. *2009 International Conference on Information Processing in Sensor Networks*, 407-408.

Uy, N. Q., & Nam, V. H. (2019). A comparison of AMQP and MQTT protocols for Internet of Things. *2019 6th NAFOSTED Conference on Information and Computer Science (NICS)*, 292-297.

Wang, Y., Jin, J., Li, Y., & Choi, C. (2020). A Reliable Physical Layer Authentication Algorithm for Massive IoT Systems. *IEEE Access: Practical Innovations, Open Solutions*, 8, 80684–80690. doi:10.1109/ACCESS.2020.2989395

Chapter 3
Location–Based Internationalization and Localization With Mobile Computing

Arpit Kumar Sharma
Manipal University Jaipur, India

Arvind Dhaka
Manipal University Jaipur, India

Amita Nandal
Manipal University Jaipur, India

Akshat Sinha
Arya Institute of Engineering Technology and Management, Jaipur, India

Deepika Choudhary
Arya Institute of Engineering Technology and Management, Jaipur, India

ABSTRACT

The Android system operates on many smartphones in many locales. Websites and web tools have their own requirements in day-to-day life. To reach the maximum users, the app and website should handle all the resources such as text strings, functions, layouts, graphics, and any other static data that the app/website needs. It requires internationalization and localization of the website and app to support multiple languages. The basic idea of this chapter is to present an approach for localizing the Android application according to the location data that the app received from the device, but many users do not allow the "access location" feature so this approach will be a dead end in this case. The authors have proposed some other techniques to achieve this feature of localization and internationalization by implementing the "choose language" service so that the app can itself optimize its content and translate it into the user's native language.

DOI: 10.4018/978-1-7998-4186-9.ch003

1. INTRODUCTION

Mobile applications and web tools play an integral part in our everyday life. The mobile application development has rapidly increased in the past few years (Awwad, 2017). In order to compete in global markets, the development companies need to deploy world-ready products. If an app is going to be released or a web site is going to be hosted in various countries or regions, it should support the native language and the languages of the target market. This can be done by internationalization and localization of the application and web site/web tool (Awwad & Slany, 2016). There are many contents and information on the internet which is really helpful but due to language many people cannot access it and the information doesn't help them at all. So, the feature of "choose language" in localization and internationalization would be fruitful. The interaction between user and software or the web content will be improved by localization and internationalization. The cultural graphical content can also help users to understand the content because user finds the application or the web content more familiar if the user interface is related to their culture or region. This will also increase the user experience. Fig.1 illustrates 'Hello' in different languages at different location.

Figure 1. 'Hello' in different languages at different location (Ma, 2018)

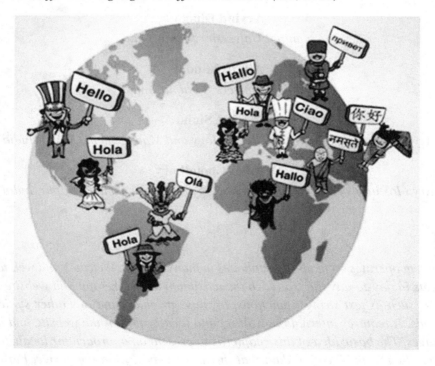

The steps involved in internationalization and localization are very crucial in deploying the apps and websites to various countries of the world. Users feel more comfortable if the content talks to them in their native language and shows their cultural values. Every region has its own native language, customs and tradition as India is a land of tradition and customs so, does the other countries are. The revenue and downloads will increase if this feature is implemented but due to privacy many of the users refuse to accept the location services (Luhana et al., 2018). But if the application or website asks for the language change then the user will not get offended regarding their privacy.

The location based service (LBS) has become very common these days as if a person wants to use online food delivery application or online Cab services then he/she must enable their location to access their pickup point but, if a normal application asks for the location service then maximum user refuse to accept it. The location based service is very helpful for android devices to find the best services based on their surroundings. Location based services also helps to find the lost device and present a richer user experience (Ferreira et al., 2017).

In this paper the LBS is used to localize and internationalize the android application and websites from the original language to other languages according to the location information that the app receives from the mobile device (Ma, 2018).

According to data collected by Google and Admob in March 2014, many users have stopped using the application due to lack of localization in selected countries which varies between 34% - 48% including the countries (United States, China, Japan, United Kingdom, and South Korea)(Xia et al., 2013). This shows that the localization and internationalization is really needed to improve the user experience (Xu & Xu, 2017). Figure 2 illustrates the distribution of available apps in leading app stores.The data shows the changes in app download with localized and globalized services.

Figure 2. Available apps in leading app stores (Xu & Xu, 2017)

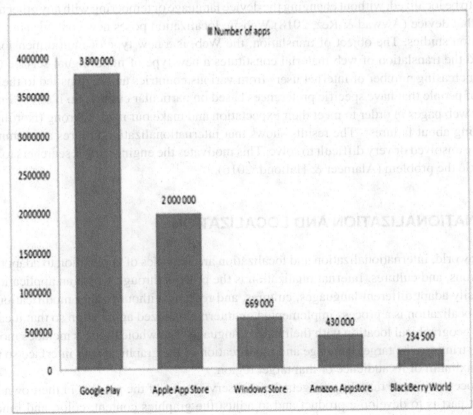

41

2. LITERATURE REVIEW

According to literature review Cristian LAKO says in his research paper "Subsequent to the process of globalization, within the GILT processes, is internationalization (I18n)". Schäler defines the term as "the process of designing (or modifying) software so as to enable users to work in the language of their choice (even if the software is not localized) and to isolate the linguistically and culturally dependent parts of an application in preparation for localization" (IEEE Draft, 2019). Gesus Cardenosa suggested that "Internationalization of software as a previous step for localization is usually taken into account during early phases of the life-cycle of software development" (Gama & Lopes, 2017). Benjamin's says "Research related with internationalization and localization is new and is more and more solicited by language businesses, software developers, translation agencies, international multilingual organizations, universities, language planning policy makers and standardization institutes" (Zhang & Hu, 2014). Ricky pointed out and suggested that "Online marketplaces like eBay and Amazon make it easy to buy products from businesses or individuals on the other side of the planet" . Even products sold in traditional brick-and-mortar stores like target often make stops in several different countries before reaching their final destinations. Consumer electronics, for example, are commonly sourced from raw materials in India, made in China, then sold in America (Liu et al., 2015). according to author, many stores already imposed this technique worldwide, based on the longitudinal study of images on the homepages. Chinese online store websites had diverge increasingly from U.S sites over time (Zhang & Herring, 2012). Using location sensor, locale switching feature is enriched with location information which allows the android application to be localized, without changing the device language or tempering with any other application present on that device (Awwad & Rez, 2018).Website localization poses new challenges to translators and translation studies. The object of translation, the Web, is a new type of multidimensional source material and the translation of web material constitutes a new type of multilingual service (Sandirini, 2014). An increasing number of internet users from various countries and regions led to the formation of a group of people that have specific preferences based on particular culture. So it's very important to localize our web pages in order to meet their expectation and make our market strong (Nordin & Singh, 2016). Talking about failures:- The results shows that internationalization failures are common in the web. And are unsolved or very difficult to solve, This motivates the engineering researchers to do further ways to tackle the problem (Alameer & Halfond, 2016).

3. INTERNATIONALIZATION AND LOCALIZATION

In computer world, internationalization and localization are activities of application to adapt the locales of other regions, and cultures. Internationalization is the process through which an application or software can easily adapt different languages, cultures, and regions without further modification (Teng et al., 2017). Localization is a process implemented on internationalized application so that it can be used in a specific geographical location with their native language. The whole process includes modification of language strings to the target language and modification of the graphical user interface so that it can influence maximum of its audience of that target region.

These processes ensure that the user gets the best services out of the product in their own language. The difficult part is to develop a product and to adjust the graphics content, color, and functions according to the regions and this should be performed by those who are actually familiar with that locale.

The localization and internationalization make sure that the user's expectations are fulfilled in terms of features, language, culture, content and user experience (Wang et al., 2013). The process of localization and internationalization include several steps as shown in figure 3.

Some of the major aspects to be considered while internationalization of the software, website and application are:-

- Time and dates formats
- Measurement and calendar formats
- Contents(name and title formats)
- User interface
- Language character and etc.

Some of the major aspects to be considered while localizing the software, website and applications are:-

- Spelling and language translation
- Cultural values and images
- Visuals (logos and icons) etc.

According to software without frontiers, the design aspects to consider when internationalizing a product are "data encoding, data documentation, software construction, hardware device support, user interaction"; while the key design areas to consider when making a fully internationalized product from scratch are "user interaction, algorithm design and data formats, software services, documentation".

Translation is the most typical and time consuming component of localization and internationalization, which involves.

- For film, video and audio, translation of spoken words and music lyrics are often dubbed or shown using subtitles.
- Text translation for printed materials, digital media (possibly include error message and documentation).

The image below shows the flow of process in the making of fully functional localized and internationalized product.

At first the sample app or web-tool is created with a rough blue-print, and when the web-tool and app is created then several steps are used to make a globalized service which can talk with you in your native language (Schiller & Voisard, 2004).

The images and text translation takes maximum time to reach to its final stage, but when it's done we have our fully functional localized and globalized product wither application or a webtool.

There are more aspects to be concerned while creating a global product which we want to capture the market and do the required business (Garybadze & Reger, 1997). Fig.4 illustrates the process of internationalization.

The android device can provide the location of the user by invoking the activate location service by using the below ——code (Huang et al., 2019)-

Figure 3. Localization and internationalization process (Wang et al., 2013)

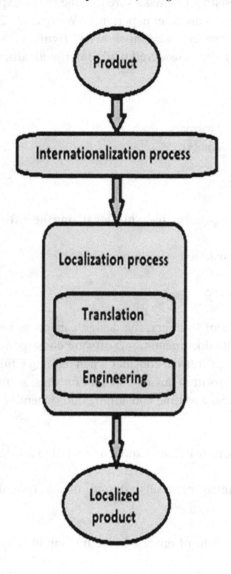

```
locationManager = (LocationManager)getSystemService(Context.LOCATION_SERVICE);
String provider = locationManager.getBestProvider(new Criteria(), true); Loca-
tion locations = locationManager.getLastKnownLocation(provider); List<String>
providerList = locationManager.getAllProviders(); double longitude = loca-
tions.getLongitude();
```

The above code can translate the street location to latitude and longitude coordinates with the help of Android Geocoder. This will show a prompt asking the users to enable the location services or GPS so that the app can address the actual coordinates.

Figure 4. Internationalization (Garybadze & Reger, 1997).

A.Location Provider

Location is something which tells the longitude and latitude of someone based on the location's component. Location provider is an abstraction for several technologies that are used to find the location of the devices. Based on the technology present in the device the location varies as every technology has its own power consumption factor, accuracy and various capabilities (Mvon, 2004).

B.GPS Location Provider

There are 27 satellites known as "Global navigation satellite system" in the space, each revolves around the earth every 12 hours regularly broadcasting the changing position data. 24 satellites are active and 3 satellites are backup. Every mobile device is equiped with global positioning system (GPS) sensors which can track the location of that device along with the latitute and longitude. The mobile phone can determine the location by using 3 of these satellites atleast by performing data computation (Mvon, 2004). The GPS location provider uses global navigation satellite system and time to find the exact location of the device (Hau & Aparicio, 2008). Fig.5 shows Magellan GPS Tracker.

Figure 5. Magellan GPS Tracker (Hau & Aparicio, 2008)

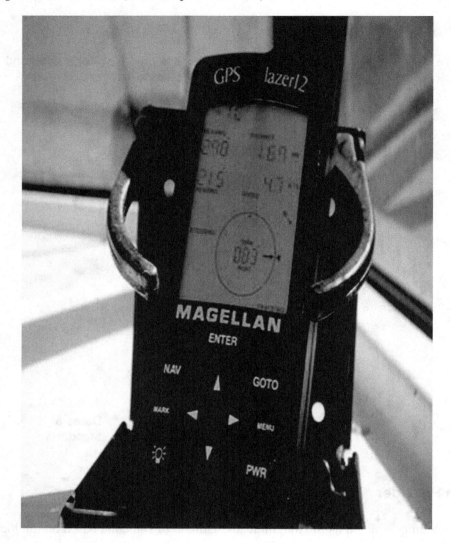

C.Cell-Tower Location Provider

Anther efficient way to track someone's location is by cell-tower location provider (Ohagan, 2009). When a mobile device is switched on it gets connected to the tower near by and is in regular contact with a cell-tower enclosing it. So, if we know the identity of the cell-tower we can track the device name and location and other requried details (Cristian, 2015).

D.Wi-Fi Network Location Provider

The least efficient way of tracking location of a device is the method known as Wi-Fi network location provider(Cardenosa et al., 2006). The current signal strength and access points examines the service provider against the database to understand the location (Lionbridge, 2019).

E. Location Based Services

Figure 6. Location Based Services (Guo et al., 2008)

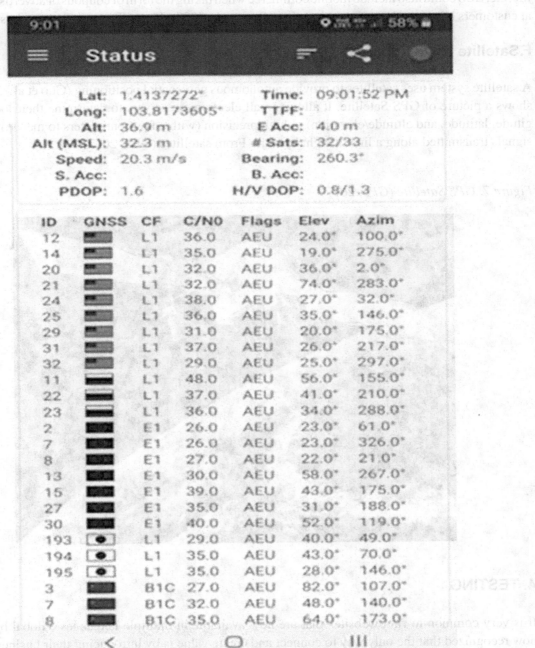

A location-based services (LBS) is a general term denoting software services that utilize geographic data and information to provide services or information to users (Floros & Charlampidou, 2019).

LBS is used in a variety of context, such as health, indoor object search, entertainment, work, personal life, etc. LBS could also include mobile commerce when taking the form of coupons or advertising directed at customers based on their current location (Guo et al., 2008). Fig.6 illustrates location based services.

F.Satellite Navigation

A satellite system uses satellites to provide autonomous geo-spatial positioning (Guo et al., 2011). Fig.7 shows a picture of GPS Satellite. It allows small electronic receivers to determine their location (longitude, latitude, and altitude/elevation) to high precision (with a few centimeters to meters) Using time signals transmitted along a line of sight by radio From satellites (GPS, 2017).

Figure 7. GPS Satellite (GPS, 2017)

4. TESTING

It is very common to find websites that are now available in multiple languages. Global brands have now recognized that the only way to connect and create value is by introducing their business to locals in the language that is truly local.

This process of adapting a product to a different language, region and locale are called localization. A localized product creates more business opportunities and caters for growth and expansion. Fig. 8 shows Localization Testing and Fig. 09 shows Globalization Testing.

Figure 8. Localization Testing (GPS, 2017)

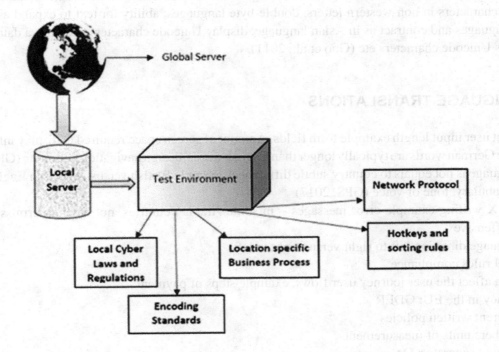

Figure 9. Globalization Testing (GPS, 2017)

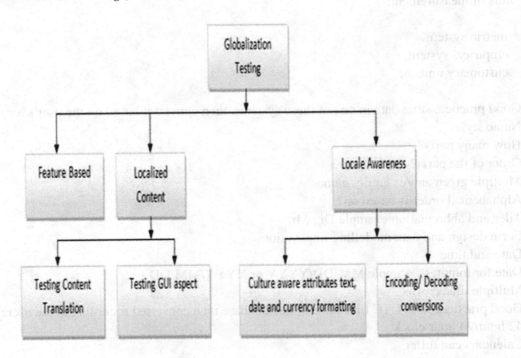

An internationalized product/application design is the one that can accommodate localized content such as characters in non-western letters, double-byte languages, ability for text to expand as in European languages and contract as in Asian language, display Unicode characters and have a database that supports Unicode characters etc (Guo et al., 2011).

5. LANGUAGE TRANSLATIONS

Different user input length example form fields. Amount of screen space required to display information example German words are typically longer than English words, design navigation button etc (GPS, 2017).

Language is not equals to country subtle differences example British versus American English spelling, vocabulary, tone of voice (GPS, 2017)

You X writing example error messages – in some Arabic countries, not having permissions may sound offensive

Language direction left to right versus right to left

Legal rules compliance

It can affect the user journey user flows, example steps of payment

Privacy in the EU: GDER

Different written policies

Numbers units of measurement

Decimal separator: Or,

Thousand separator: __or,

Form validation!

Required input formats

Units of measurement:

1. metric system
2. empirical system
3. customary units

Good practice: store data in one of these systems, then convert it based on the user's location

Name styles

How many parts?

Order of the parts?

Multiple given and/or family names

Alphabetical order is based on?

Tiles and abbreviation example Dr., Mr.

Form design and data modelling implications

Date and time

Date for minutes, example MM/DD/YYYY or YYYY/MM/DD

Multiple times owns

Good practice: store UTC time zone in the database then converted according to the users times and 42 hour/24 hour clock

Calendars can differ

Currency

Decimal and thousand separator

Negative value: place of the minus (-) sign

Currency symbol

Exchange rate

Some questions

Does the app handles multiple currencies?

Is conversion needed?

If yes: where will it get the exchange rates from?

Contact information

Phone number: different length and format

Address: different parts

Visuals

Colour: different meaning

Imagery-offensive?

Symbols, icons, metaphor-meaning the first

Using flags (country versus region)

Lot of additional cultural characteristics example cultural dimensions-GEERT Hofstede's E-D model

6. PROPOSED WORK

We had conducted a survey in Arya Institute of Engineering Technology and Management, Jaipur in which we found that 90% of the users doesn't want any application or website to use their location except the food delivering apps and cab services. Due to their privacy concern they want an application to be isolated which does not use their mic, camera and location indeed. So, the method of invoking the location acceptance service will be a halt in many cases an we cannot achieve the localization and internationalization. Instead of asking for the location we can give them an option to change their language preference according to their choice and based on the native language preference the graphic visuals will be adjusted.

- *Example 1:*

```
//16th of June 1998
var date = new Date(1998, 6, 16);
// 16/6/1998"
console.log(new Intl.DateTimeFormat(it-IT').format(date));
// "6/16/1998"
console.log(new Intl.DateTimeFormat('en-US').formate(date));
// "16/06/1998"
console.log(new Inti.DateTimeFormat('en-GB').formate(date));
```

As we all know our search results and history are used againts us for marketing and advertisement so, the fear of privacy leakage is a major concern for the users which is the drawback of Location Based Service method (GPS, 2018). We have found that if we provide a fill up space for country and region then we can also get the coordinates of the users and then the localization and internationalization will be based on the approx location not exact but that won't affect much because the culture and tradition is of a state and city not an individual.

JavaScript can be used to localize and internationalize the website or a web tool and hybrid applications too.

In example1 if we want to internationalize the date format for the locale such as IT, US and GB we can implement the resource bundles as set of resource files which are sharing a common base name with an additional language specification.

In example 1, we employ *"DateTimeFormat"* constructor for creating the new date formatter by using the given locale ("it-IT", "en-US", "en-GB") and invoke the *"format"* method to format the date format accordingly. Similarly we can implement such functions to other major aspects of the localization and localization too.

A. PROPOSED ALGORITHM

- **Step 1. Managing Application Framework**

The application framework will be the major criteria for the internationalization and localization and it should contain following content:-
Resources files:The resource file for the specified language will contain the respective resources.

- **Step 2. The Planning of the text in Different Languages**

The translated language may take more space or less space depending on the language used, apparently which will cause more congestion or even indecipherable when translated.

- **Step 3 Unicode/UTF-8 (Global Expansion)**

The reinsertion of strings will take place when we perform internationalization, in this case the use of UTF-8 is the best option unless you are using Asian language, as Asian language uses UTF-16.

- **Step 4 Deal with your Strings**

Before the actual translation process we must focus on the strings, and the best approach could be:
Concatenation should be avoided: developers uses concatenation of two strings to save space but words varies as we go for other languages which results in translation error.
Hard-coded strings should be avoided: The replacement of strings with regular expression using pseudo localization which is often performed by a separate branch of localization testing.

7. APPLICATION NEEDED ENHANCEMENT

There is current outbreak of Coronavirus (Covid-19) disease.

Coronaviruses (CoV) are a large family of viruses that cause illness ranging from the common cold to more severe diseases such as Middle East Respiratory Syndrome (MERS-CoV) and Severe Acute Respiratory Syndrome (SARS-CoV). A novel coronavirus (nCoV) is a new strain that has not been previously identified in humans.

In this pandemic situation Indian government launched an application that can help people from every corner of India. *Aarogya Setu* is an Indian open-source CoVID-19 "Contact tracing, Syndromic mapping and Self-assessment" digital service, primarily a mobile app, developed by the National Informatics Centre under the Ministry of Electronics and Information Technology (Aarogyasetu, 2020). Fig. 10 shows Aarogya Setu app Advertisement.

This application is available in 12 different languages. Once the app is downloaded, it asks the user to pick a language and displays a list wherein one can pick English, Assamese, Gujarati, Hindi, Punjabi, Marathi, Bangla, Telugu, Tamil, Kannada, Malayalam or Odia – a total of 12 languages.This are the mostly spoken languages in India which cover 90% of population (Aarogyasetu, 2020). Fig.11 shows Aarogya Setu app language changing option snapshot.

This app ask location only for tracing virus infection by smartphone's GPS and Bluetooth features. So we can see that we can provide language choosing option to user so that need not to give location access for changing language and can secure there privacy.

Every country is fighting against covid-19 so does India we are facing lock down in India and during these days app is being launched by the government of India which is arogya setu app the setu app ask you questions regarding your health the questions includes some of the basic things like are you having headache? Do you have a runny nose? Etc and on the basis of your answers the aarogyasri to app will judge whether you have the symptom of covid-19 or not this application also include internationalisation and localisation based on your selection of language is given inside the app the application will pop up a form in the beginning when you login which will ask you about the language preference it could be Hindi English Marathi Gujarati anything but our concept is to provide you a form in which you will provide your state your belonging so that the application can perform is algorithm and find out your approximate longitude and latitude which will be further used to identify your location and your native languages and eventually you application will be translated according to your native language and your culture.

This could be a major change which we can bring to any application out in the market we can bring revolution in a digital market the applications which are already running on this algorithm which type of form in which you will have to select your language preference could be changed into a form which can ask you about your residence so that your native language could be identified and your app could show you images which belong to your culture and tradition so that would be more familiar.

Figure 10. Aarogya Setu app Advertisement (Aarogyasetu, 2020)

Figure 11. Aarogya Setu app language changing option snapshot(Aarogyasetu, 2020).

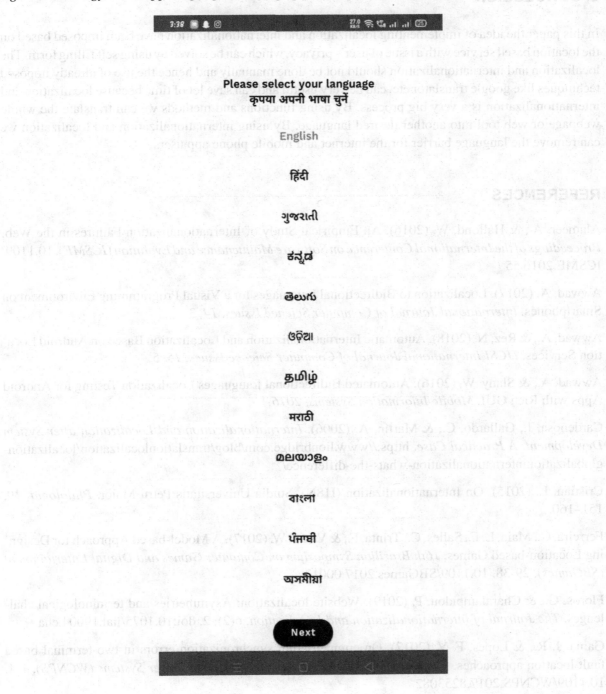

8. CONCLUSION

In this paper the idea of implementing localization and internationalization have been imposed based on the location based service with a issue of user's privacy, which can be solved by using self filling form. The localization and internationalization should not be done manually and hence the use of already imposed techniques like google translator etc. can be very useful and can save lot of time because localization and internationalization is a very big process. By using functions and methods we can translate the whole webpage or web tool into another desired language. By using internationalization and localization we can remove the language barrier for the internet and mobile phone app users.

REFERENCES

Alameer, A., & Halfond, W. (2016). An Empirical Study of Internationalization Failures in the Web. *Proceedings of the International Conference on Software Maintenance and Evolution (ICSME).* 10.1109/ICSME.2016.55

Awwad, A. (2017). Localization to Bidirectional Languages for a Visual Programming Environment on Smartphones. *International Journal of Computer Science Issues, 14*, 3.

Awwad, A., & Rez, N. (2018). Automatic Internationalization and Localization Based on Android Location Services. *IJCSI International Journal of Computer Science Issues, 15*, 5.

Awwad, A., & Slany, W. (2016). Automated Bidirectional Languages Localization Testing for Android Apps with Rich GUI. *Mobile Information Systems, 2016.*

Cardeñosa, J., Gallardo, C., & Martín, A. (2006). *Internationalization and Localization after System Development: A Practical Case.* https://www.lionbridge.com/blog/translationlocalization/localization-globalizationinternationalization-whats-the-difference/

Cristian, L. (2015). On Internationalization (I18N). Studia Universitatis Petru Maior. *Philologia, 19*, 151–160.

Ferreira, C., Maia, L. F., Salles, C., Trinta, F., & Viana, W. (2017). A Model-based Approach for Designing Location-based Games. *16th Brazilian Symposium on Computer Games and Digital Entertainment (SBGames)*, 29-38. 10.1109/SBGames.2017.00012

Floros, G., & Charalampidou, P. (2019). Website localization: Asymmetries and terminological challenges. *The Journal of Internationalization and Localization, 6*(2), 2. doi:10.1075/jial.19004.cha

Gama, J. R., & Lopes, F. V. (2017). On compensating synchronization errors in two-terminal based fault location approaches. *Workshop on Communication Networks and Power Systems (WCNPS)*, 1-4. 10.1109/WCNPS.2017.8253082

Gerybadze, A., & Reger, G. (1997). Internationalization of R&D and global management of technological competencies within transnational corporations. Innovation in Technology Management. The Key to Global Leadership. PICMET '97, 979-982. doi:10.1109/PICMET.1997.653755

GPS. (2017). GPS: Global Positioning System (or Navstar Global Positioning System). In *Wide Area Augmentation System (WAAS) Performance Standard, Section B.3, Abbreviations and Acronyms*. Wayback Machine.

Guo, A., Satake, S., & Imai, M. (2008). Home-Explorer: Ontology-based Physical Artifact Search and Hidden Object Detection System. *Mobile Information Systems, 4*(2), 2. doi:10.1155/2008/463787

Guo, B., Fujimura, R., Zhang, R., & Imai, M. (2011). Design-in-Play: Improving the Variability of Indoor Pervasive Games. *Multimedia Tools and Applications, 59*(1), 259–277. doi:10.100711042-010-0711-z

Hau, E., & Aparício, M. (2008). Software internationalization and localization in web based ERP. *Proceedings of the 26th annual ACM international conference on Design of communication*, 175-180. 10.1145/1456536.1456570

Huang, X., Chen, H., Wang, L., & Zeng, S. (2019). How Does Leader Narcissism Influence Firm Internationalization? *IEEE Transactions on Engineering Management*, 1–14. doi:10.1109/TEM.2019.2900169

IEEE Draft Recommended. (2019). *Practice for Common Framework of Location Services (LS) for Healthcare*. IEEE P1847/D1.

Liu, W., Li, W., Yin, X., Yu, Q., & Jiang, H. (2015). Single terminal traveling wave fault location based on fault location algorithm integrating MMG with correlation function. *IEEE 5th International Conference on Electronics Information and Emergency Communication*, 289-292. 10.1109/ICEIEC.2015.7284541

Luhana, K. K., Schindler, C., & Slany, W. (2018). Streamlining mobile app deployment with Jenkins and Fastlane in the case of Catrobat's pocket code. *IEEE International Conference on Innovative Research and Development (ICIRD)*, 1-6. 10.1109/ICIRD.2018.8376296

Ma, M. (2018). Enhancing Privacy Using Location Semantics in Location Based Services. *IEEE 3rd International Conference on Big Data Analysis (ICBDA)*, 368-373. 10.1109/ICBDA.2018.8367709

Mvon, Z. (2004). International R&D by Chinese companies. *IEEE International Engineering Management Conference, 1*, 6-10.

Nordin, H., & Singh, D. (2016). The Internationalization of E-Learning Websites. *Methodology*.

O'Hagan, M. (2009). The evaluation of pragmatic and functionalist aspects in localization: Towards a holistic approach to Quality Assurance. *The Journal of Internationalisation and Localisation, 1*, 60–93. doi:10.1075/jial.1.03jim

Sandrini, P. (2014). *Website Localization and Translation*. Project: Website Translation.

Schiller, J., & Voisard, A. (2004). Location based services. Elsevier.

Teng, J., Zhan, X., Xie, L., Zeng, X., Liu, Y., & Huang, L. (2017). A novel location method for distribution hybrid lines. *IEEE Conference on Energy Internet and Energy System Integration (EI2)*, 1-5. 10.1109/EI2.2017.8245425

Wang, X., Zhang, L., Xie, T., Mei, H., & Sun, J. (2013). Locating Need-to-Externalize Constant Strings for Software Internationalization with Generalized String-Taint Analysis. *IEEE Transactions on Software Engineering, 39*(4), 516-536.

Xia, X., Lo, D., Zhu, F., Wang, X., & Zhou, B. (2013). Software Internationalization and Localization: An Industrial Experience. *18th International Conference on Engineering of Complex Computer Systems*, 222-231. 10.1109/ICECCS.2013.40

Xu, C., & Xu, C. (2017). Predicting Personal Transitional Location Based on Modified-SVM. *2017 International Conference on Computational Science and Computational Intelligence (CSCI)*, 340-344. 10.1109/CSCI.2017.57

Zhang, G., & Herring, C. (2012). Globalization or localization? *Proceedings Cultural Attitudes Towards Technology and Communication*, 430-445.

Zhang, J., & Hu, C. (2014). The research and application on the optimal location model of project. *The 26th Chinese Control and Decision Conference (2014 CCDC)*, 2208-2210. 10.1109/CCDC.2014.6852535

Chapter 4
Interoperability in Internet of Media Things and Integration Big Media:
Conceptual Model and Frameworks

Dragorad Milovanovic
University of Belgrade, Serbia

Vladan Pantovic
Union–Nikola Tesla University, Belgrade, Serbia

ABSTRACT

Multimedia-related things is a new class of connected objects that can be searched, discovered, and composited on the internet of media things (IoMT). A huge amount of data sets come from audio-visual sources or have a multimedia nature. However, multimedia data is currently not incorporated in the big data (BD) frameworks. The research projects, standardization initiatives, and industrial activities for integration are outlined in this chapter. MPEG IoMT interoperability and network-based media processing (NBMP) framework as an instance of the big media (BM) reference model are explored. Conceptual model of IoT and big data integration for analytics is proposed. Big data analytics is rapidly evolving both in terms of functionality and the underlying model. The authors pointed out that IoMT analytics is closely related to big data analytics, which facilitates the integration of multimedia objects in big media applications in large-scale systems. These two technologies are mutually dependent and should be researched and developed jointly.

INTRODUCTION

Internet of things (IoT) and big data (BD) are used in a variety of applications. The key value of IoT technology is the innovative processing of collected data, which is increasingly becoming multimedia. The Internet of multimedia things (IoMT) currently drives a large number of research and development

DOI: 10.4018/978-1-7998-4186-9.ch004

efforts related to multimedia communication and big media (BM) (Nauman, 2020). It is very important to jointly analyze the latest trends. Advanced applications that connect IoT and BD analytics have been in focus. IoT is a usable technology and at the same time a significant driver of innovation (Vermesan, 2013; Stankovic, 2014). It is obvious that the Internet of multimedia objects and big data are evolving step-by-step and transforming many areas of everyday life. We would like to point out that these technological achievements are mutually dependent and joint development is necessary in the future (Seng, 2018).

The rapid development of IoT embeds a large number of sensors in a number of devices from personal to industrial machines that are connected to a reliable Internet. Embedded sensors collect a variety of data, including process, transportation, medical, personal, and mobile equipment. This is crucial for the adoption of IoT applications in multimedia big data development. BM have different characteristics compared to typical BD as a result of different heterogeneities, data types (video, audio, images, interactive 3D models) and unstructured features.

IoT can be seen as a global infrastructure that enables advanced services by interconnecting (physical and virtual) facilities based on interoperable computing and communication technologies (ICT) that are in development (Al-Fukaha, 2015). The basic IoT concept is to connect the vast majority of systems with a common infrastructure. Within the large IoT field, applications and services of IoMT enable the delivery, interpretation, representation and analysis of multimedia content are a special challenge. IoMT is a particular type of objects with all multimedia characteristics, which by definition may sense or act in the physical/virtual environment. Applications and services are designed and implemented based on cloud technology, content streaming and caching, big data for multimedia analytics. New challenges in real-time multimedia communication within the IoMT system are the following: acquisition of multimedia data from objects, communication protocols and standards, analysis of multimedia content and event detection, security and privacy, multimedia processing and storage, distributed/centralized perceptual multimedia compression, scalable encoding of data sources with low delay, scalable management of big data in IoT systems.

The variety of research work associated with IoT convergence are reviewed in (Milovanovic, 2017) and are mainly focused on standardization activities, frameworks, and emerging applications. Interoperability is considered as the most important enabler in integration of IoMT ecosystems, so it is comprehensive survey on IoT interoperability is given in (Wu, 2020) from different perspectives.

The chapter is organized as follows. The fundamental concepts of multimedia-centric IoT and big data are presented in the first part. The conceptual model of IoMT and big media is outlined in the second section. Next, MPEG IoMT standardization process and reference architecture for big data applied to media are presented. The IoT and big data integration for analytics is proposed in the fourth part. It should be noted that there is a close relation between multimedia IoT analytics with big data analytics, which facilitates the integration on multimedia objects in big media applications in large scale systems. These two technologies are mutually dependent and should be developed together.

CONCEPTUAL MODEL FOR BIG MEDIA

In the continuous development of multimedia technology, IoT is becoming one of the main sources of big data. The multimedia data thus collected are heterogeneous and unstructured. Data collection for an IoT application includes data acquisition, compression and formatting. Data acquisition is carried out in several areas such as Internet of multimedia things and Industrial IoT (IIoT) (see Figure 1). Designing a new method for data acquisition requires consideration of the following factors: heterogeneous sources, unstructured data, multimode, dynamic evolution, user requirements, spatial/temporal information, semantics, and distributed data (Meddeb, 2016; Gazis, 2016).

Figure 1. Integration of Big Data and multimedia into IoT domains

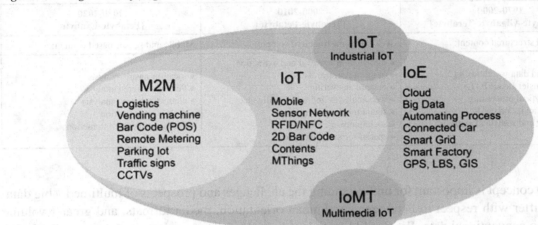

A significant feature of IoT devices is the noticeable limitations in terms of processing, storage and communication capabilities. Careful design of algorithms at all levels of design is necessary. For example, the IoMT camera partially analyzes the recorded video in order to retrieve only significant (and compressed) information from the environment. Another feature of IoMT system is belonging to larger systems that can contain many similar or different IoT objects. Some systems can be large-scale (urban video surveillance systems) or small-scale (bio-signal recording systems), so that a significant variety of services and applications is enabled (ISO/IEC, 2015; Kafle, 2016; ITU-T, 2012).

Multimedia contains various videos, audio content, speech, online video streaming, documents, graphics, geospatial data, 3D virtual models, etc. Multimedia big data is unstructured data, which is more complex to analyze compared to typical big data. The main challenge of BM acquisition is to increase the quantity and quality of multimedia data as a consequence of the fact that application users easily and instantaneously perceive unstructured data. Additionally, it is generally assumed that large-scale BM data is collected from a source containing incomplete data that is uncertain, and that communication errors are inevitable.

The term big data has multiple meanings and is used to represent a range of related concepts. The evolution of meaning has been influenced by the interaction of the following aspects: data processing features, datasets analysis, performance of data management systems, new engineering techniques, and analysis for distributed data processing. In the development of data processing systems, the need for efficient analysis has caused changes in existing technologies. For example, the transition to a relational model occurred when methods for reliably handling changes to structured data led to the use of relational databases (RDBMS) (see Table 1). However, the relational model is not able to efficiently process of large and unstructured data sets. It is not just that the amount of data that is being processed now is higher than in the previous period, but the amounts are steadily increasing from decade to decade. Many of the conceptual foundations of BD have been around for years, but in the last 25 years there has been an explosion of scaling technologies and their maturation and application to data systems.

Table 1. The evolution of BD processing systems according to the data size of order

1970-2000 [Megabyte–Gigabyte-Terabyte]	2000-2010 [Terabyte-Petabyte]	2010-2020 [Petabyte-Exabyte]
DBMS-based structured content:	Web-based unstructured content:	Mobile and sensor-based content:
• RDBMS and data warehousing • Extract Transfer Load (ETL) • online analytical processing • dashboards and scorecards • data mining and statistical analysis	• information retrieval and extraction • opinion mining • custom answering • web analytics and web intelligence • social media analytics • social network analysis • spatial-temporal analysis	• location-aware analysis • Person-centered analysis • context-relevant analysis • mobile visualization • human-computer interaction

The BD concept is important for understanding the challenges and prospects of multimedia big data. BM data differ with respect to heterogeneity, human orientation, media formats, and greater volume compared to conventional data. We would like to highlight the following characteristics (see Table 2):

- BMs include a huge number of data types compared to traditional BDs.
- BM data have a higher processing complexity to process because they include several kinds of audio-video recordings such as interactive videos, stereoscopic 3D videos, 3D interactive models.
- BM modeling and representation is complex because data are retrieved from different (heterogeneous) sources such as ubiquitous mobile devices, devices with built-in sensors, IoT, Internet, virtual worlds and social media.
- BM content and context analysis is complex because vary over time and in 3D space.
- BM data needs to be processed instantly and continuously to avoid speed limitation of network transport. For real-time computing, it is necessary to archive BM data in order to enable the transport of a huge amount of data.

Table 2. Characteristics of BM data

Characteristics	Typical datasets	Big data	Multimedia
Volume	less	medium	big
Data size	definite	uncertain	uncertain
Inferring video	not at all	no	yes
Representation of data	structured data	structured data	unstructured data
Real-time	not at all	yes	yes
Human-centric	not at all	no	yes
Response	no	no	yes
Data source	centralized	heterogeneous distributed	heterogeneous distributed
Complexity	low	medium	high:

Challenges related to the processing, storage, communication and analysis of BM data determine the direction of research in the field. Traditional data processing and analysis is no longer able to process BD sets due to the large amount and increased complexity. The huge volume of data sets is structured but also unstructured. Unstructured data can take the form of image files, audio-visual files, web pages, and various types of multimedia content, for example. Compared to traditional text-based databases, BM data presents further intricacies with respect to fundamental operations, such as storage of huge data sets, processing, transmitting, and analyzing data. Some of the challenges of multimedia data are given as follows:

- **Real time and quality of experience requirements.** BM services are in real time. Online streaming and concurrently data processing for analysis are required, so requirements of quality of experience (QoE) are complex.
- **Unstructured and multimodal data.** Since multimodal data are collected from heterogeneous sources, representation and storage of BM data are challenging, as well as difficult to model. The transformation of unstructured BM data into structured data is complex due to data are being collected from diverse sources.
- **Perception and understanding complexity.** Multimedia data is not easy to interpret by a computer because there is a semantic gap at a high/low - level. In addition, multimedia data varies over time and in 3D space.
- **Scalability and efficiency.** BM systems require huge computation, so it is necessary to improve the resources of communication, computing and storage.

The role of multimedia communication is key to big data development. BM data are massive in size, compression is necessary to continue processing, transport and storage. The techniques used for compressing BM data are more challenging in contrast to conventional data sets and techniques. The limitations in storage, processing and computing capacities, has made efficient compression based on digital signal processing (DSP) necessary. At the same time, there is a correlation between the available communication technologies (Internet, IP, 5G, WiFi) and the amount of data available for analysis. Over the past two decades, communication bandwidth has witnessed an exponential rise. These technologies have also become more accessible via the web and smartphones. We are now at the beginning of a new generation of applications and a much larger set of data sources and consumer analysis results, based on social networks, fifth generation (5G) wireless networks, software-defined networks (SDNs) and network function virtualization (NFV). Network and service operations, customer service, security, and augmented reality (AR) are the main applications that drive the communications industry. All these applications have been driven by successively larger and more accessible multimedia data sources.

In the telecommunications sector, a conceptual model of the BD ecosystem is presented in Supplement 40 ITU-T Recommendations Y.3600 (ITU-T, 2016). The recommendation describes the conceptual BD ecosystem and related technical areas, as well as the activities of standards development organizations (SDOs). The reference architecture provides guidelines for the development of system architecture, solutions and applications, including its decomposition and design patterns. A high level of abstraction that can be applied to several use cases and instances of the system, is presented. The concept of reference architecture encompasses different perspectives of selected actors, as well as the ones associated with function, information, communication, integration, asset, usage, implementation, process, and the system. The reference architecture is usable as a general guideline that abstracts specific needs and technologies in different applications and use cases. The roles and sub-roles of the BD ecosystem are shown in Figure 2. The roles of the Data Provider (DP) consist of the sub-roles of the data provider (DS) and the data intermediary broker (DB). The service provider (SP) can act as an extension of the existing data analytics platform for big data. A customer of a big data service (DC) is an end-user or system that uses the results or services of a service provider.

Figure 2. Conceptual model of Big Data ecosystem (ITU-T, 2016)
Source: ITU-T, 2016

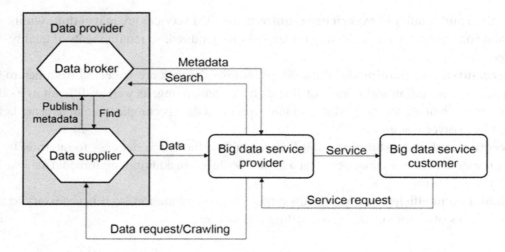

The focus of the MPEG working group (ISO/IEC SC29/WG11) is on the analysis of missing standards and on the development of a conceptual model for functions related to BM data. The technical committee JTC1 has established a BD working group (ISO/IEC, 2014) to develop core standards, including reference architecture and vocabulary standards, as well as to liaise with all relevant SDOs that may propose BD-related activities. On the other hand, the MPEG Exploration Part 21 (Big Media) is focused on developing a conceptual model for multimedia functionalities in the context of big data (MPEG N16565, 2016). Also, in 2016, MPEG identified the need to enable interoperability among IoMT and published the FDIS 23093 standard in March 2019.

INTEROPERABILITY FRAMEWORK FOR MULTIMEDIA THINGS

The connection between IoMT and BM can be observed at the level of advanced signal processing collected from devices in large-scale systems. Currently, MPEG working group standardizes IoMT which simplifies the integration of multimedia objects into BM applications (MPEG Exploration, 2020). The connection is generic and does not apply to only one component.

The MPEG working group recognizes the requirement for interoperability of multimedia Internet things. MThing is defined as an object capable of sensing, acquiring, actuating, or processing digital media or metadata. The standard describes communication commands, protocols and the format of aggregated and synchronized data that allow the application of complex media systems on a large scale that allow the exchange of data interoperable between media objects and media wearables (MPEG Exploration, 2016). In the first phase of standardization, MPEG issued a public call for proposals (CfP) and considered the received solution (MPEG, 2016a) together with the collected use cases (MPEG, 2016b) and requirements (MPEG, 2016c). The CfP document requires data representation (XML schema, API) for MThing object interfaces, media wearables, and multimedia systems. The published ISO/IEC 23093 standard specifies the architecture and program application interfaces APIs, as well as the compressed data format that MThings exchanges. The standard has been published in four parts: (1) Architecture, (2) Discovery and communication API, (3) Media data formats and API, (4) Reference software and conformance (March 2019 FDIS approval).

However, there is still a lack of a standard framework that enables large-scale communication, storage, analysis, interpretation and retrieval of BM data emerging from IoMT devices. It is essential that standards provide the basis for new multimedia content services. Standards enable the realization of interoperable IoMT applications on a large-scale. The MPEG working group Exploration Part 21 (Big Media) is focused on the analysis of the lack of standards and on the formulation of a theoretical model for multimedia functionalities in the BD context (MPEG, 2016d).

IOMT INTEROPERABILITY

A number of international consortia have been formed, such as the Internet Industrial Consortium (IIC), the Alliance for Internet of Things Innovation (AIOTI), the Internet of Things Architecture (IoTA), the WSO2 reference architecture for the IoT, the M2M and OIC, with the aim of providing IoMT interoperability. Consortia are guided by specific requirements and focus on specific challenges.

The MPEG working group recognizes the need for interoperability of IoMT systems and focuses on multimedia content processing. The expert group was set up by ISO/IEC to originally specifies the audio-video compression and transmission standards (MPEG, 2016e). The ISO/IEC 23093 standard specifies an IoMT set of interfaces, protocols, and associated media representations that enable advanced services and applications based on human-device interaction, in a physical and virtual environment. The IoMT architecture, generic with respect to the target application, specifies three types of interfaces among and between the various entities in any application associated with MThings objects:

- MThings API enables the discovery, connection and efficient exchange of data in the network. It also supports transaction tokens to access significant MThings functionality, resources and data.
- Information related to multimedia objects includes discovery data, system designer setup information, raw and processed sensor data, and actuation information. The ISO/IEC 23093 standard specifies data formats for input/output from multimedia sensors, actuators, storages, analyzers, as well as reference software and conformance bit streams for data formats.
- Multimedia analyzers processes data in a cascade with the aim of extracting semantic information. The standard does not specify how the detection and analysis process is carried out, but rather only the interface of multimedia objects.

The global IoMT architecture from Part 1 of the standard is presented in Figure 3, which illustrates a set of interfaces, protocols and corresponding information representations that are associated with media:

- **Interface 1** user commands (setup information) between a system manager and an MThing.
- **Interface 1'** user commands (setup information) relayed between one an MThing to another, probably in a changed form (subset of Interface 1).
- **Interface 2** captured data (raw/processed data, compressed/semantic extraction) and actuation information.
- **Interface 2'** transformation for individual data exchange channels (for transmission).
- **Interface 3** discovery MThing characteristics.

Figure 3. MPEG IoMT architecture

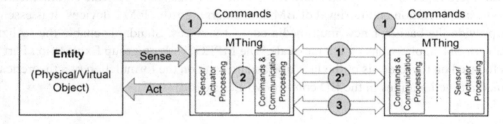

The MPEG IoMT standard covers three aspects covered in individual sections:

- **Discovery and communication API.** Information related to multimedia objects contains features and discovery data, system setup information, raw and processed sensor data and actuator information. The ISO/IEC 23093 standard specifies data formats for input/output of multimedia sensors, actuators, storages, analyzers, etc. Multimedia analyzers generate data from multimedia sensors and cascading processing is possible to extract semantic information. The standard specifies software APIs for detecting and communicating between MThings in the network and other APIs to support transactions between MThings, which are implemented to discover other multimedia objects in the network, connect/disconnect MThings, transaction payments using media tokens.
- **Media data formats and API.** Normative programming APIs are listed in Part 2 of the standard. Part 3 contains tools for describing data exchanged between multimedia objects (e.g. multimedia sensors, actuators, analyzers, storages) for their program APIs.
- **Reference software and conformance.** Part 4 of the standard specifies the conformance and reference software implementing the normative clauses in Part 3. This part also provides means for conformance testing (bit-streams).

Applications and services of IoMT can be designed and developed using a large number of available technologies such as information-centric networking, multimedia analytics, cloud technologies, BD for multimedia content, content streaming and caching. However, there are still additional requirements for orchestration and synchronization of all components, as well as advanced analytics.

BM REFERENCE ARCHITECTURE

The MPEG working group standardizes IoMT with a focus on multimedia objects and thus simplifies the integration of such objects into BM applications. The group's activities include the specification of the acquisition, processing/analysis and visualization of multimedia data acquired by or used to control IoT entities. Working group IoMT communicates with BM group in conceptual model development.

The vast amount of data comes from audio-visual sources or is multimedia in nature. However, audio-visual data are not currently covered by the BD standardization paradigm. The goal of the MPEG working group is to standardize specific audio-visual data and make them exploitable and usable for different applications. MPEG has initiated an analysis of the BM standard requirements. The set of use cases was completed and analyzed against existing MPEG standards (MPEG, 2016f).

The MPEG working group cooperates with JTC1 WG9, work program was launched in 2015 and then moved to SC42 / WG2 in May 2018, which defines the big data reference architecture (BDRA) (IS/IEC 20547-3, 2019) (see Figure 4a). Within this framework, existing MPEG standards have been identified that are related to different parts/aspects of the reference architecture. Additionally, MPEG analyzes the NIST Big Data reference architecture (NBDIF NBD-RA) (see Figure 4b) (Ünal, 2019).

Figure 4a. BD reference architecture: ISO/IEC BDRA functional components

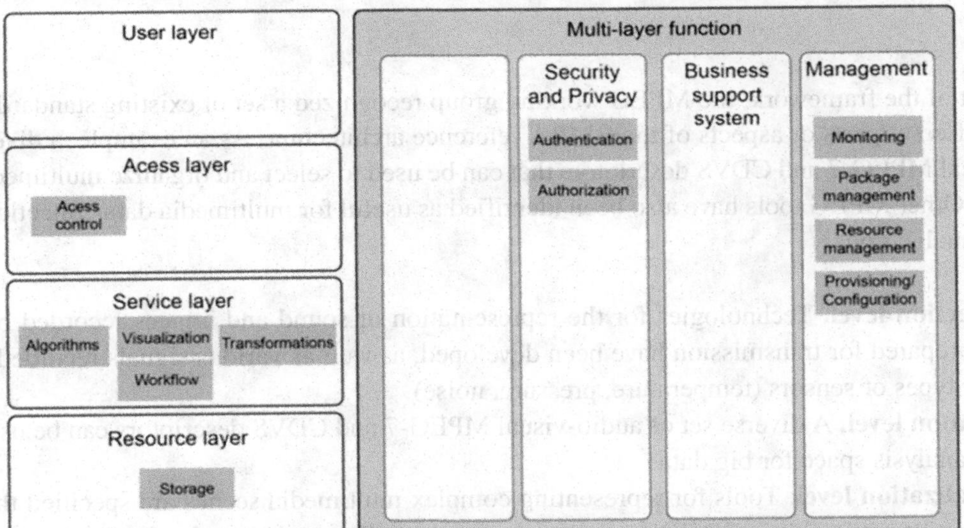

Figure 4b. NIST conceptual model.

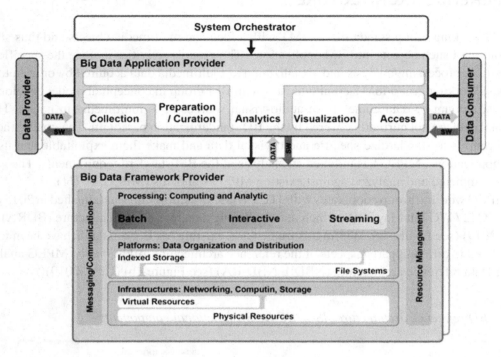

As part of the framework, the MPEG working group recognized a set of existing standards that can address different parts or aspects of the BMRA reference architecture. As an example, a diverse set of audio-visual MPEG-7 and CDVS descriptors that can be used to select and organize multimedia data ia specified. Other MPEG tools have also been identified as useful for multimedia data collection, analytics and visualization:

- **Collection level.** Technologies for the representation of sound and images recorded by sensors and prepared for transmission have been developed, as well as various signals recorded by many other types of sensors (temperature, pressure, noise).
- **Curation level.** A diverse set of audio-visual MPEG-7 and CDVS descriptors can be used to prepare analysis space for big data.
- **Visualization level.** Tools for representing complex multimedia scenes are specified that enable interactive navigation in 2D/3D complex environments. The tools can also be used to visualize the results of big data analytics.
- **System orchestration level.** The MPEG-M specification set allows software APIs to access MPEG components. It is possible to use them in the context of big data because there are no restrictions on where the data is located or how it is transmitted. In general, APIs provide access in load/save modes.
- **Analytics side.** The MPEG working group has not standardized the analytics tool, but multimedia content description technology can be used to prepare the space for analysis using descriptors.

The aim of the BM activities in the MPEG working group is to specify the necessary standards for multimedia databases in order to make them exploitable and usable for different applications. In the use case of the IoMT in smart cities, embedded devices are becoming smarter and more connected to the Internet. In most cases, complex processing cannot be performed directly on the device, so intelligent data collection and device synchronization is necessary:

- collecting data from a large number of IoMTs, such as surveillance cameras, tracking devices, sensors
- correlating the data on a BD platform that is capable of extracting useful information
- BD platform for providing useful information (video traffic analysis, free parking spaces via image or sensor processing, chemical/audio pollution for traffic redirection and balancing)
- providing means to protect the platform and provide privacy where necessary.

We present the focus of the MPEG working group on the study of the development of new standards and a conceptual model for functions related to BM data. Future standardization activities include the specification of software APIs between the basic components of the functional architecture of application providers for BD. It is possible to standardize APIs between the analytical component and acquisition, preparation, visualization, and access, as well as between these components and system orchestration. Further development of the reference BD architecture will enable the working group to align with the conceptual model for BM-related functions.

NBMP Framework

The framework allows users to describe multimedia operations that will be performed online. The MPEG working group is exploring how network media processing (NBMP) can become an instance of the BMRA reference model (ISO/IEC, 2019). The standard specifies framework for content and service providers to describe, deploy, and control multimedia processing. Framework contains an abstraction layer that can be deployed on existing commercial cloud platforms and integrated with 5G core and mobile edge computing (MEC) (Botta, 2016). Processing flow manager (NBMP PFM) enables the composition of multiple tasks to process incoming multimedia and metadata from sources and to produce multimedia streams and metadata that are ready for distribution.

Multimedia processing is constantly evolving and is focused on increasingly complex tasks and services. Applications are diverse and limited only by the complexity of the algorithm and the processing power of the target devices. On the other hand, the 3GPP consortium that standardizes mobile network architectures is powered by newer cloud technologies (SDN, NFV, MEC) that enable intensive computing applications (Battisti, 2021). Network operators seek to use the services of cloud service operators and provide the basic infrastructure for required services to end users. In turn, content/service providers use the services of network operators and cloud service operators to set up hardware and platforms, so they can focus only on the functionality of the services they provide.

The MPEG-I (ISO/IEC 23090 Coded representation of immersive media, Part 8) network processing method has been developed with a focus on fragmentation and a unique way of processing multimedia on a cloud platform and on any IP network. It enables multimedia service providers and network/cloud service providers to work together to provide their customers with customized services available anywhere. given With the current surge in demand for digital media delivery in 5G networks, efficient multimedia network processing, requires solutions with limited processing units in networks, as well as challenges in new network settings (MPEG, 2018). Service providers and end users can execute online multimedia processing operations with NBMP. NBMP defines the framework: interfaces for multimedia processing functions in networks/cloud, additional information for multimedia processing, format for standardization, chaining and composition of multimedia processing functions in the network. NBMP also provides a software API for multimedia processing. The MPEG-I Part 8 specification reached the FDIS phase of the standardization process in January 2020.

Figure 5. NBMP Reference architecture for network media processing

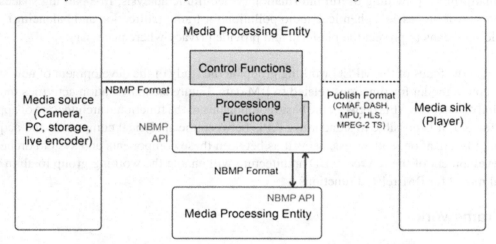

To allow the configuration of functions and effective communication of multimedia data, the NBMP framework specifies the interfaces of multimedia processing functions in networks as well as cloud environments. Interfaces also enable a better compromise of resource allocation (bandwidth, compute, storage) in these environments by having additional information that is useful for multimedia processing. NBMP provides a software API for media processing and describes the formats for connecting and constituting of media processing function. Multimedia processing tasks on input data and associated metadata are performed by the processing unit. Control functions specified by the NBMP are used to compose and configure transport methods for communication between media sources and multimedia processing entities (see Figure 5).

INTEGRATION OF IoT AND BIG DATA BY ANALYTICS

Integration of IoT and BD enables understanding of context and situation, real-time actions, performance optimization and proactive/predictive knowledge. Analysis technologies are advancing in all areas with implications in everyday life. From sensor technology to the convergence of information and communication technologies (ICT), a multitude of domains and users are generating more and more data. However, challenges must be overcome in order for data to be used optimally. It is necessary to pay attention to the growing volume of data, their diverse structure, real-time processing, security and privacy policies (Kumar, 2020).

BM data includes a group of huge and complex data sets. The advent of IoT devices significantly affects the life cycle of BM data: acquisition, processing, storage, sharing and visualization of data. The following characteristics can describe multimedia data (see Table 3):

- Volume represents the huge amount of data produced by the IoT, portals, and the Internet. With the advent of technological advancements and internet technologies, each device generates large amounts of multimedia data. It is very challenging to process BM data in the phase of acquisition, storage, analysis, pre-processing, sharing and visualization.
- Velocity indicates the speed of data generation, how fast the data arrives. To operate at the speed imposed by BM data, effective management tools and techniques are needed.
- Variety refers to the diversity of data. It is very complex to process unstructured data as it does not have a fixed format. To process unstructured data in a short time interval, the clustering method is employed. It is more challenging to analyze, preprocess, and extract valuable data, from unstructured BM data.
- Veracity means data uncertainty, noise and data deviation. It is very challenging to maintain the accuracy of the data which renders it equally difficult to compute the reliability of the data.
- Value is the most crucial component, which means using and finding valuable information in a large amount of heterogeneous data. For data analysis, filtering, sorting and selecting the data is necessary.
- Visualization involves the use of available tools that are limited by available working memory, functionality, extensibility, and response time. New methods of data representation such as data clustering, parallel coordinates, circular network diagrams, sunbursts are required for BM data.
- Vulnerability refers to security issues related to BM data.
- Validity indicates the accuracy of the data for the intended use.
- Variability represents the number of discrepancies in the data, in addition to the rate of loading BM into the database.
- Volatility refers to the validity period for data storage before it becomes useless for any analysis.

Table 3. Five V's of multimedia Big Data

Volume	Veracity	Velocity	Value	Variety
• yottabyte of data • mobile devices • social media	• multimedia quality • multimedia uncertainty • accuracy • security	• real-time • efficiency • speed of data • stream/batch	• usage/retrieval valuable data • filter/sort/select • statistical events • correlation	• diversity of data • structure/unstructured • image/audio/video/text • sensors, social media

The features that drive interoperability towards greater efficiency are the characteristics of the data set and the diversity of data from several domains:

- It is not possible to efficiently process BD datasets for a particular problem domain at a given time, using current/existing/traditional technologies and techniques to extract the new value.
- In order to achieve the scalability necessary for efficient processing of large data sets, the BD paradigm distributes the data systems through horizontally linked independent resources.
- BD models are based on logical data models (relational and non-relational) and processing/computational models (batch, streaming, transactional) for data storage and manipulation on horizontally scaled resources.
- BD analytics is evolving rapidly in terms of both functionality and models. Analytical functions support the integration of parallel-derived results from one or more data sources. Advanced analytics is a faster insight through various techniques, such as long tail analyzes, micro-segmentations and others, which are not feasible if there are limitations of smaller volumes, slower velocities, narrower varieties, and undetermined veracities.

Convergence of Technologies

The true value of IoT lies in its innovative processing of gathered data, which is why it converges on BD analytics in the design and implementation of advanced applications. BD are essentially dynamic, heterogeneous, and unstructured data. They require more sophisticated, more specific analytics that would make them meaningful. The rise of cloud computing and BD analytics allows for the wider application and use of sophisticated IoT analytics applications (Sharma, 2020).

IoT generates unprecedented amounts of data and this affects the entire BD ecosystem. Technologies are obviously evolving step-by-step. Also, IoT analytics and BD analytics are closely related. In fact, IoT data is essentially big data (Martino, 2017):

- data sources generate in most cases very large amounts of data, which usually exceeds the storage and processing capabilities of conventional database systems
- data streams have very high input data ingestion rates, they are generated continuously, with high frequency and periodically in very short time intervals
- due to the great variety of IoT devices, data sources are very heterogeneous both in terms of semantics and data formats
- data is a classic example of data with noise, which is characterized by uncertainty.

All these facts are the reason that, systems, tools and techniques for development of BD applications (databases, data storages, streaming middleware and engines, data mining techniques and development tools) represent a good starting point for IoT analytics. Analytical applications are very often applied within edge and/or cloud computing infrastructures, so the benefits of IoT analytics are in capacity, performance and scalability (Botta, 2016; Battisti, 2021). Edge computing decentralizes data processing at the very edge of the network, while transporting only selected IoT data from edge devices to the cloud. However, IoT data and analytics applications in most cases face their own challenges, which are not always common for high-volume applications and high-speed transactions. The main challenges facing the development and application of IoT analytics applications include: heterogeneity of IoT data flows, different data quality, nature of real-time IoT datasets, dependence of IoT flows on time and location, sensitivity to privacy and security and data bias.

BD Analytics

It is in fact possible to perform analytics on small data sets without BD processing. However, the impact of affordable tools for distributed computing and parallel processing of large data sets has strongly influenced the field of analytics. Additionally, the flexibility of cloud computing and the accessibility of open source tools for distributed computing have together given a new dimension to performing analytics. In the period preceding big data, supercomputers and huge large databases were not available to most data scientists. Technological constraints gave scientists no choice but to make compromises when performing analyzes and have on several occasions determined the selection of a statistical model. With the revolution of cloud computing as well as the release of open source tools to configure and operate distributed computing environments, the spectrum of techniques and analytics tools available to scientists has also evolved (Pouianfar, 2018). Some examples of big data analytics changes are as follows:

- processing of ever increasing sample sizes and thus modifying the sampling error of statistical results
- scaling out instead of scaling up is enabled to reduce the cost of storing large data sets with BD technology
- in-memory analytics and faster delivery of results
- streaming or real-time analytics and application of real-time statistical learning models
- advanced visualization techniques to improve understanding
- cloud-based analytics has also given individuals huge capacities of computing power in a short time period
- creation of a tool for structuring unstructured data for analysis
- transition from operational to analytical focus with databases specifically designed for analytics
- analysis of increasingly unstructured (non-relational) data
- focus of data science analysis has shifted from causal to correlation
- creation of data lakes, where the data model is not predefined prior to creation or analysis
- execution speed of computer-intensive machine learning (ML) algorithms that have become practical for analysis has increased
- ML algorithms have been improved by increasing data sets for training and testing, leading to more accurate predictive models
- enabling deep learning techniques
- behavioral data analyzes were initiated by BD tools providing computational capacity for analyzing data sets such as Web traffic or location data.

Conventional analysis has focused on the development of causal models, on the basis of which predictions can be made. Causal models are based on analyzing the factors that lead to change in the physical world. The introduction of BD analysis, however, has caused practical changes in model development. The large data made it possible to shift the focus from cause-effect to correlation. It is increasingly common to know that when variables are correlated it leads to better decisions. Big data analytics has enabled a transition whereby the focus is more on understanding. With the evolution of BD technologies, identifying correlations instead of causal models is still being considered as more important. Data virtualization (federation) is one of the basic building blocks of integration, which consists of redirecting from analysis to data, as opposed to transporting data from a storage location to a data warehouse for analysis. BD analytics and constant changes in technology due to advances in big data processing have indicated a lack of related standards. Big data analytics has produced the interest of organizations participating in the process of de jure standards, industrial consortia and open source organizations (see Figure 6) (NIST, 2019a; NIST, 2019b):

- **Fair data** [https://www.rd-alliance.org/groups/go-fair-ig] is based on concepts that enable the search ability, accessibility, interoperability, and reusability of data sets.
- **Open Data** [https://ieeesa.io/bdgmm] uses machine-readable and standard data infrastructures to enable data mashup between heterogeneous data sets from diversified domain repositories.
- **AI/ML Data** [https://www.iso.org/committee/6794475.html] allows high quality data sets to be produced, used and/or trained using algorithms such as traditional statistical methods, machine learning (ml) and deep learning (dl). The is made possible by data preparation processes such as data cleansing, labeling and evaluation,
- **Big Data Analytics** [https://bigdatawg.nist.gov] applies good practices of software development (dev) and it operations (ops) for packaging analytical algorithms/tools with clear input and output parameters as analytics payload services/libraries. The tools are now reusable, deployable, and operational across multi-cores cpu/gpus computing platforms.
- **Big Data Architecture** [https://bigdatawg.nist.gov] enables vendor-neutral, technological and infrastructural agnostic architecture, and consists of functional components connected by interoperable interfaces (services). The task is to enable systems engineers, data scientists, software developers, data architects, and decision makers to apply bd analytics packages for reuse in an interoperable big data ecosystem.

Figure 6. NIST Big Data analytics and beyond roadmap

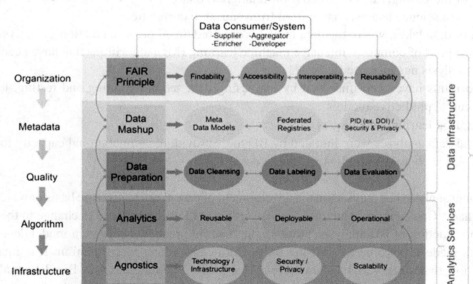

BM Analytics

BM exploited innovative technologies to address the demands of digital multimedia. Specifically, novel techniques are being explored to reclaim and remove values from diverse, unstructured, or semi-structured and dynamic sources. Mass internet services and mobile technologies have enabled era of multimedia big data (BM). Extensive research is conducted in the field of multimedia, focusing on various aspects of analytics, such as acquisition, storage, indexing, mining and retrieval. However, there is a lack of BM analytics research, which includes challenges and opportunities, and promising research directions (see Table 4) (Hu, 2014).

Table 4. BM analytics modules and challenges

Multimedia data extraction	Multimedia database	Multimedia data sharing	Multimedia data mining
Data types: videos, audio, text, IoT devices	Data storage: MMDBMS, NoSQL, GraphDB, Key-value store Data management: data indexing, spatio-temporal analysis, network analytics	Sharing system: Cloud, online file sharing system, wireless sharing	Data processing: data cleaning, data transformation, data reduction Machine learning: supervised, unsupervised
Challenges: volume, real-time, unstructured, uncertainty	Challenges: store, manage, extract/retrieve, unstructured data, heterogeneous data sets	Challenges: more storage, bandwidth limit, maximum file size, data types, app supports, human efforts	Challenges: multimodality representation, complexity, noise, semi-structured data efficiency, real-time, accuracy

The BD system can be decomposed into four sequential modules: data generation, collection, storage and analytics. These four modules form the BD value chain. The last and most important phase of the value chain is data analysis aimed at extracting useful data, proposing conclusions and/or supporting decision-making. BM analytics research covers a wide range of topics, including multimedia summarization, annotation, indexing and retrieval, recommendation, and event detection (see Table 5) (Seng, 2018).

Table 5. BM analytics modules and challenges

Analysis domain	Sources	Characteristics	Approaches
Structured data analytics	transaction records	structured records (less volume and real-time)	data mining, statistical analysis
Text	logs, email, documents, text web pages, comments	unstructured, rich textual, context, semantic, language dependent	document presentation, NLP, information extraction, topic model, summarization, categorization, clustering, question answering, opinion mining
Multimedia analytics	multimedia documents, surveillance, eHealth	image, audio, video massive, redundancy semantic gap	summarization, annotation, indexing and retrieval, recommendation, event detection
Mobile analytics	mobile apps, sensors	location based, person specific, fragmented info	monitoring, location-based mining

The huge amount of data and applications leads to the emergence of mobile data (MD) analytics. However, analytics faces challenges posed by inherent data characteristics, such as mobile awareness, activity sensitivity, noisiness, and redundancy richness. With the rapid growth of mobile computing, more and more mobile terminals (such as mobile phones, sensors) and applications are being applied globally. New architectures, platforms and solutions are emerging and integrating new enabling technologies such as artificial intelligence (AI), secure distributed general ledger (DLT) technology or advanced 5G communication networks, to meet new user demands for service quality (Bojkovic, 2020). Interactive platforms enable real-time control, event-driven contextual services, with more intelligence on the edge. To support trust and security, information flows are stay close to users, decisions are made at the point of interest, where data is both collected and processed locally. It is necessary that edge computing applications and mobile autonomous systems use AI technologies (Battisti, 2021).

CONCLUDING REMARKS

Recently, many applications and services have been directly or indirectly linked to IoT and BD. Technologies are mutual dependent and should be developed jointly. In fact, IoT data is essentially big data, and analytics are closely related. The convergence of IoT and BD is notable in the creation and deployment interoperable applications, instead of simple sensor data processing applications. Challenges related to the representation and modeling, processing, storage, transmission and analysis of BM data determine the direction of research in the field, such as real-time requirements and quality of experience, unstructured and multimodal data, perception and understanding of complexity, as well as scalability and efficiency.

The BM involves a group of huge and complex data sets. Integrated multimedia signal sensors are becoming a significant source of IoT data, leading to the IoMT. With the spread of cloud services and mobile technologies, the growth of multimedia content is causing a huge amount of BM data. IoMT enables integration and collaboration between heterogeneous multimedia devices with different sensing, computing and communicating capabilities and resources. Multimedia sensors generate continuous, massive data streams of complex structure and temporal significance. Compressing BM data brings with it more challenges compared to traditional data sets and BD techniques. There is high heterogeneity in the multimedia communication protocols and data formats used by the devices, adding an additional level of complexity in data acquisition, processing and data consumption. It is necessary to develop new techniques, standards and frameworks that will deal with these new challenges.

The BD concept is essential for understanding the challenges and opportunities of BM data. We further summarized such challenges to identify current research directions. Very little research provides an overview of the possibilities of directing research towards multimedia BD analysis. Moreover, the standard framework of BM data derived from massively multimedia-oriented IoMT systems is missing. We presented the MPEG working group in standardizing IoMT interoperability and network-based media processing frameworks (NBMP) as an example of a BDRA reference architecture that facilitates the integration of multimedia objects in media applications into large scale systems. Finally, we identified open issues and future directions of IoT research and BD integration for analytics.

In future solutions, the importance of multimedia data will succeed and continue to grow. Sophisticated and specific analytics are required to make it meaningful. Further joint development of IoMT and BM ecosystem is needed for efficient big data analytics. We look forward to subsequently analyze the feasibility of combining IoMT with emerging technologies such as advanced 5G communication networks and artificial intelligence (AI).

REFERENCES

Al-Fuqaha, A., Guizani, M., Mohammadi, M., Aledhari, M., & Ayyash, M. (2015). Internet of Things: A survey on enabling technologies, protocols, and applications. *IEEE Communications Surveys and Tutorials*, 4(17), 2347–2376. doi:10.1109/COMST.2015.2444095

Battisti, A. L., & Wen, M.-S. (2021). Enabling Internet of Media Things with edge-based virtual multimedia sensors. *IEEE Access: Practical Innovations, Open Solutions*, 9, 59255–59269. doi:10.1109/ACCESS.2021.3073240

Bojkovic, Z., Milovanovic, D., & Fowdur, T. P. (Eds.). (2020). *5G Multimedia Communication: Technology, multiservices, and deployment*. CRC Press. doi:10.1201/9781003096450

Botta, A., Donato, W., Persico, V., & Pescape, A. (2016). Integration of cloud computing and Internet of Things: A survey. *Future Generation Computer Systems*, 56, 684–700. doi:10.1016/j.future.2015.09.021

Gazis, V. (2016). A survey of standards for Machine to Machine (M2M) and the Internet of Things. *IEEE Communications Surveys and Tutorials*, 19(1), 482–511. doi:10.1109/COMST.2016.2592948

Hu, H., Wen, Y., Chua, T.-S., & Li, X. (2014). Toward scalable systems for Big Data analytics: A technology tutorial. *IEEE Access: Practical Innovations, Open Solutions*, 2, 652–687. doi:10.1109/ACCESS.2014.2332453

ISO/IEC JTC1/SC42/WG2 IS 20547-3 (2019) *Big data Reference architecture.*

ISO/IEC JTC1/WG10 (2015) *Internet of Things*. Retrieved from http://isotc.iso.org/livelink/livelink/open/jtc1wg10 ISO/IEC JTC1/WG9

ISO/IEC JTC1/WG9 (2014) *Big data Preliminary report.*

ITU-Telecommunication Standardization Sector. (2012). *ITU-T Y.4000/Y.2060 Overview of the Internet of things*. Retrieved from https://www.itu.int/en/ITU-T/gsi/iot/

ITU-Telecommunication Standardization Sector. (2016). *ITU-T Series Y Supplement 40, Big data standardization roadmap*. Retrieved from https://www.itu.int/en/ITU-T/techwatch/Pages/big-data-standards.aspx

Kafle, V. P., Fukushima, Y., & Hara, H. (2016). Internet of Things Standardization in ITU and prospective networking technologies. *IEEE Communications Magazine*, 54(9), 43–49. doi:10.1109/MCOM.2016.7565271

Kumar, D., Kumar, P., & Ashok, A. (2020). Introduction to multimedia big data computing for IoT. In S. Tanwar, S. Tyagi, & N. Kumar (Eds.), *Multimedia big data computing for IoT applications* (pp. 3–36). Springer.

Martino, B., Cretella, G., & Esposito, A. (2017). Big Data, IoT and semantics. In Handbook of Big Data technologies. Springer.

Meddeb, A. (2016). Internet of Things standards: Who stands out from the crowd? *IEEE Communications Magazine - Communications Standards Supplement, 7*(54), 40–47.

Milovanovic, D., Pantovic, V., & Gardasevic, G. (2017). Converging technologies for the IoT: Standardization activities and frameworks. In P. Kocovic, R. Behringer, M. Ramachandran, & R. Mihajlovic (Eds.), *Emerging trends and applications of the Internet of Things* (pp. 71–103). IGI Global. doi:10.4018/978-1-5225-2437-3.ch003

MPEG (2016a) N16535 *Call for Proposals on Internet of Media Things and Wearables*

MPEG (2016b) N16533 *Use cases for Internet of Media Things and Wearables*

MPEG (2016c) N16534 *Requirements for Internet of Media Things and Wearables*

MPEG (2016d) N16565 Liaison Statement from SC29/WG11 to JTC1/WG9

MPEG (2016e) W16316 *Strategic Standardization Roadmap*

MPEG (2016f) N16540 *Vision, objectives, and plan for Big Media*

MPEG (2018) N17503 *Call For Proposals on NBMP*

MPEG Exploration. (2016). *Internet of Media Things and Wearables.* Retrieved from https://mpeg.chiariglione.org/standards/exploration/internet-media-things-and-wearables

MPEG Exploration. (2020). *Big Media.* Retrieved from https://mpeg.chiariglione.org/standards/exploration/big-media

Nauman, A., Qadri, Y. A., Amjad, M., Zikria, Z. B., Afzal, M. K., & Kim, S. W. (2020). Multimedia Internet of Things: A comprehensive survey. *IEEE Access: Practical Innovations, Open Solutions, 8*, 8202–8250. doi:10.1109/ACCESS.2020.2964280

NIST Big Data Public (2019a) NBD-PWG SP 1500-7 *Big Data interoperability framework: Standards roadmap*

NIST Big Data Public (2019b) NBD-PWG *Big Data analytics and beyond roadmap*

Pouyanfar, S., Yang, Y., Chen, S.-C., Shyu, M.-L., & Iyengar, S. S. (2018). Multimedia Big Data Analytics: A Survey. *ACM Computing Surveys, 51*(1), 10–34. doi:10.1145/3150226

Seng, K. P., & Ang, L. M. (2018). A Big data layered architecture and functional units for the Multimedia Internet of Things. *IEEE Transaction on Multi-Scale Computing Systems, 4*(4), 500–512. doi:10.1109/TMSCS.2018.2886843

Sharma, R., Agarwal, P., & Mahapatra, R. P. (2020). Evolution in Big Data analytics on Internet of Things: Applications and future plan. In S. Tanwar, S. Tyagi, & N. Kumar (Eds.), *Multimedia Big Data computing for IoT applications* (pp. 453–477). Springer. doi:10.1007/978-981-13-8759-3_18

Stankovic, J. A. (2014). Research directions for the Internet of Things. *IEEE Internet of Things Journal, 1*(1), 3–9. doi:10.1109/JIOT.2014.2312291

Ünal, P. (2019). Reference architectures and standards for the Internet of Things and Big Data in Smart Manufacturing. *Proc. International Conference on Future Internet of Things and Cloud*, 243-250. 10.1109/FiCloud.2019.00041

Vermesan, O., Friess, P., Guillemin, P., Giaffreda, R., Grindwoll, H., Eisenhauer, M., Serrano, M., Moessner, K., Spirito, M., Blystad, L.-C., & Tragos, E. Z. (2013). Internet of Things beyond the Hype: Research, innovation and deployment. In O. Vermesan & P. Friess (Eds.), *Internet of Things: Converging technologies for smart environments and integrated ecosystems* (pp. 15–118). River Publishers.

Wu, Y., Wu, Y., Guerrero, J. M., Vasquez, J. C., Palacios-Garcia, E. J., & Li, J. (2020). Convergence and interoperability for the Energy Internet: From ubiquitous connection to distributed automation. *IEEE Industrial Electronics Magazine, 14*(4), 91–105. doi:10.1109/MIE.2020.3020786

Chapter 5
An Architecture and Reference Implementation for WSN-Based IoT Systems

Burak Karaduman

iD https://orcid.org/0000-0002-7262-992X

University of Antwerp and Flanders Make, Belgium

Joachim Denil

iD https://orcid.org/0000-0002-4926-6737

University of Antwerp and Flanders Make, Belgium

Bentley James Oakes

University of Antwerp and Flanders Make, Belgium

Hans Vangheluwe

University of Antwerp and Flanders Make, Belgium

Raheleh Eslampanah

iD https://orcid.org/0000-0001-8188-7464

University of Antwerp and Flanders Make, Belgium

Moharram Challenger

University of Antwerp and Flanders Make, Belgium

ABSTRACT

The Internet of Things and its technologies have evolved quickly in recent years. It became an umbrella term for various technologies, embedded devices, smart objects, and web services. Although it has gained maturity, there is still no clear or common definition of references for creating WSN-based IoT systems. In the awareness that creating an omniscient and ideal architecture that can suit all design requirements is not feasible, modular and scalable architecture that supports adding or subtracting components to fit a lot of requirements of various use cases should be provided as a starting point. This chapter discusses such an architecture and reference implementation. The architecture should cover multiple layers, including the cloud, the gateway, and the edges of the target system, which allows monitoring the environment, managing the data, programming the edge nodes and networking model to establish communication between horizontal and vertical embedded devices. In order to exemplify the proposed architecture and reference implementation, a smart irrigation case study is used.

DOI: 10.4018/978-1-7998-4186-9.ch005

1. INTRODUCTION

The Internet of Things (IoT) is a paradigm that aims to connect physical objects, intelligent devices, vehicles, machines, buildings and/or sensors to the Internet using communication protocols, wired/wireless hardware and embedded software (Karimpour, et al., 2019). The background technology of IoT includes radio-frequency identification (RFID), near-field communication (NFC), Wireless Sensor Networks (WSN), and other wired or wireless communication. Generally, IoT is based on establishing a bridge between the digital and the physical world by sensors and actuators. According to a study (Sharma et al., 2019), over 70 billion devices will be connected to the Internet by 2025, and the world will become more digitized through smart, distributed and power-efficient nodes.

In order to increase the network coverage of an area, these IoT devices can create ad-hoc networks with their neighbor nodes, termed a Wireless Sensor Network (WSN). The WSN paradigm is well-suited for distributed data acquisition using low-power antennas and embedded devices for various applications (Arslan, et al., 2017). Generally, wireless sensor networks use routing protocols to send a packet from a source node to the sink node. If a gateway transmits this data from a sink node and sends it to a computer or log manager system, that WSN system can be considered part of an IoT ecosystem. Inside the IoT ecosystem, various platforms can be included, such as IoT nodes, WSN nodes, Long Range Wide Area Network (LoRaWAN) and Bluetooth Low Energy (BLE) devices. The common basis of these systems is embedded computing systems designed to perform tasks such as measuring environmental changes and converting them into a human-readable format or digital data. These systems can perform the tasks in an event-based or real-time manner. Additionally, the embedded systems may have an operating system to manage the system resources and have an antenna to establish wireless communication. Therefore, hardware and an accompanying protocol are required to create a network between embedded systems to wirelessly collect data in a wide area.

1.1 Motivation

IoT systems should be designed considering both environmental and user-oriented requirements. They are inherently connection-based systems, and as expected, there will be billions of these devices where scalability becomes an essential feature in the future. Moreover, these devices may not have any user interface or maybe abstracted from human intervention. Therefore, they need a log and event management system that handles changes in the environment by remotely controlling IoT devices. However, the design constraints of the system should be aligned considering the conditions of the environment. In particular, the lifetime of the IoT node is essential when these nodes are deployed in vast rural areas. It may not be possible to find a power source to provide continuous energy to these nodes. Therefore, the dependency on the power source should be reduced to increase nodes' lifetime. The necessity of creating a network without requiring a direct Internet connection has emerged.

For these reasons, IEEE 802.15.4-based WSN nodes are suitable since they are designed for low-power and long life-time dependent applications. When this low-power antenna technology is merged with energy-efficient micro-controllers (Chéour et al., 2020), it can create a mesh network without requiring a direct Internet connection and any power source. WSN nodes create their dynamic network, and new nodes can be easily added/removed. The network can organize itself if the topology changes. The WSN can be opened to the Internet. When the sink is connected to the gateway, data can reach to Internet level via a gateway. Internet level may also have IoT nodes. Suitable communication protocols should be selected considering user requirements and environmental conditions. In addition, variants of operating systems and devices may create indecision for practitioners. For these reasons, we provide a reference architecture of physical components, operating systems, embedded hardware and software covering IoT layers while integrating IoT and WSN systems. The WSN empowers the communication of IoT devices in a wide area (using IEEE 802.15.4) where direct Internet connection (IEEE 802.11) is not available. In this study, we present our architecture integrating the WSN paradigm into the IoT eco-system. The architecture acts as a reference for how a WSN-based IoT system design could be defined.

1.2 Case Study: Smart Irrigation System

In order to assess our architecture's benefits and evaluate the proposed architecture, a case study of a smart irrigation system is analyzed, designed, and implemented. The irrigation system includes both WSN and Wi-Fi modules to detect the soil's moisture level in an area such as large fields, vineyards, and gardens.

The distributed nodes continuously sample the moisture level of a field, while each IoT node controls a solenoid valve to irrigate a part of a field. The distributed data is collected by the sink node and delivered to the Log Manager system. Log Manager logs the data and monitors the state changes in target fields while comparing the desired moisture level with collected moisture values. When the system detects any moisture drop in the field, the log manager requests the corresponding IoT node to irrigate that part by controlling the solenoid valve. This case study demonstrates how the WSN paradigm can enhance an IoT system addressing irrigation. It shows the distribution of WSN nodes across large fields with many IoT components attached to water pipes to control specific zones of those fields. In addition, the irrigation case study also contains a complex, layered IoT system starting from sensor sampling, routing protocol creation, gateway implementation, to log/event management.

The primary motivation for this architecture is that series of case studies are established based on the provided reference architecture. Provided architecture is applied (Asici et al., 2019; Marah et al,. 2020; Karaduman et al,. 2018a; Karaduman et al,. 2020a; Karaduman et al,. 2020b) where fire detection, lighting automation and emergency control systems are implemented using reference operating systems and hardware.

1.3 Contributions

This study contributes a reference architecture and implementation for WSN-based IoT systems. The WSN paradigm is integrated into the IoT ecosystem such that IoT systems can benefit from the advantages of the settled WSN technologies. In this way, IoT systems are empowered with low-power, low-cost and well-established WSN technology as well as providing distributed topology to increase the coverage for IoT. Moreover, our architecture also eases the problems of resource-constrained environments where the energy source is limited or not continuous.

With the integration of the WSN, we also provide a self-sustainable network where the nodes can act as a subsystem as centralized and decentralized operation modes. We present an architecture that can be scale-able via dynamic network behaviour where new WSN nodes can be added or removed easily. Considering the environmental conditions of operation area the coverage may be extended, so WSN should also adopt these physical extensions by adding new nodes to their network. We show how IoT and WSN systems can be implemented by showing the implementation details and engineering methodologies starting from edge nodes to the cloud log manager. In the fog level, we present how a gateway can be created to read incoming data and transfer them to the Internet level. Lastly, we provide a comprehensive case study to show the applicability of our architecture. Specifically, this study provides assistance in resolving hardware selection confusion while also eliminating the operating system selection problem.

When two paradigms must be merged to solve a complex problem, then architectural requirements can be complex. Because of the variety of the firmware and hardware, the research and development phase can be delayed until a suitable architecture, development environment, and development boards are found. Then, developers start to seek references that will take them to the next step in the software life-cycle.

In this chapter, we have addressed these architectural challenges and included these requirements. The architectural requirements are the gateway and log manager of our architecture. In this way, developers are not only going to know about only operating systems and supported devices. They are also going to have an idea of how and why these requirements are filled and what are the alternatives. Using this reference architecture, an implementer can have a starting point for how to design and implement a WSN empowered IoT system.

This chapter is organized as follows: Section 2 provides an overview of the proposed architecture. The reference implementation is demonstrated in Section 3. Section 4 describes the implementation workflow for a case study. The chapter is concluded in Section 5, along with a discussion of possible future work.

2. PROPOSED ARCHITECTURE

The proposed architecture is discussed in this section. It includes high-level design, including required components to create a WSN-based IoT system.

2.1 High-Level Design of the System

The architecture proposed in this study covers a high-level design of a WSN based IoT system. As illustrated in Figure 1, the high-level design includes the different groups of components such as WSN nodes, IoT devices, a gateway and cloud level log manager. WSN nodes can cover a large area using low-power motes, while IoT devices provide computation power and control for resource and response demanding tasks by directly accessing the Internet. These tasks can be related to M2M communication or human interaction. Specifically, IoT nodes may listen to a port for incoming requests to actuate a physical and electronic component like a servo motor to control a door lock mechanism. Cloud level log management systems can be implemented from scratch or pre-ready technologies such as ThingSpeak (Maureira et al., 2011), Google Cloud (Korobeinikova et al., 2020), Azure IoT (Klein, 2017) and AWS IoT (Kurniawan, 2018) are also preferable. Alternatively, graphical-based programmable solutions like Node-RED are also a choice to customize the cloud level. Specifically, these cloud technologies should be convenient for data-visualisation, logical comparison, rule definition and storing data.

Figure 1. The general view of the proposed architecture.

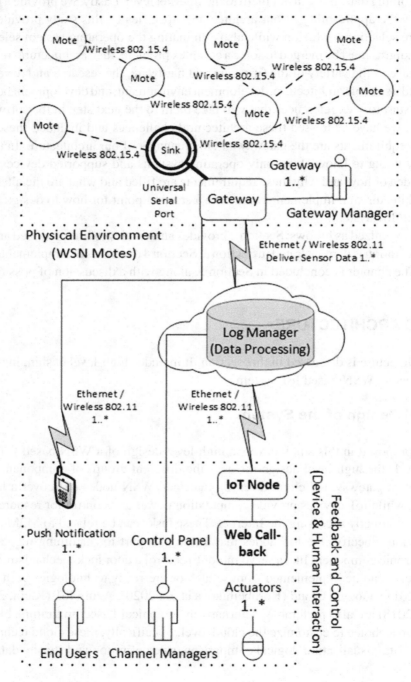

WSN-based Sensors

WSN is a suitable technology while there is no possibility to establish a direct Internet connection in the environment (Akyildiz et al., 2002). Using the multi-hopping feature of WSNs, they can have their coverage widened. These devices can create their network using IP-based protocols. They are also adaptable for low-power transmission (Toscano and Bello, 2012). Moreover, most of the WSN devices' microprocessors are designed considering low power consumption. They can yield the processor to switch to ultra-low-power when there is not an ongoing process. In this way, they provide additional energy-saving by going into the deep-sleep mode to minimize power consumption.

As the WSN nodes use the IEEE 802.15.4 protocol, the collected data from the environment is delivered to the sink node using a routing algorithm between source nodes. WSN nodes can convey their sensor data node-to-hand to reach the sink node. The sink node starts the routing algorithm as the root device to establish a network tree. This node acquires the environment information. That information is forwarded by distributed source nodes. In WSNs, intermediate nodes between the source node and the sink node cooperate with each other by forwarding each other's packets to achieve distributed data collection. This enables multi-hopping where a node cannot reach the sink node directly. In this way, wide areas can be covered, and data can be sampled and distributed.

Finally, all data received by the sink node must be stored, processed and probably forwarded to the Internet. This is done by a computer playing the role of a gateway and sending the data using its direct Internet connection. The gateway reads the data from the sink node using a Universal Serial Port (USB). Therefore, the data can be sent to a cloud or a Log Manager system, which is discussed in the following subsections.

IoT-based Nodes

Wi-Fi-based IoT nodes are useful when there is direct Internet connectivity. They can communicate using IEEE 802.11 protocol and can be utilized with socket programming techniques. Low-end devices such as ESP32/8266, MSP430, Particle Photon can be preferred for low-power and long-term tasks, while high-end single board computers such as RaspberryPi, Jetson Nano and BeagleBoard devices are suitable for real-time and high-computation demanding tasks.

Compared with WSN Motes, IoT-based nodes might consume more power. To ease this problem, some operations such as enabling deep-sleep mode, constraining computation by switching ultra-low power operation and implementing energy harvesting solutions can be preferred.

As illustrated in Figure 1, Web-based sensors can be used in connection with Wi-Fi connectivity modules. Also, in addition to using physical sensors, these devices can request data from a web resource such as a weather forecast website by sending a simple web request or using an API since they are directly connected to the Internet. As a result, if Internet connectivity is available in the area, the user should prefer to use Wi-Fi connectivity modules while using WSN motes to create a distributed network through a wide area.

Feedback and Control

In the proposed architecture, the feedback and control section includes the user system notifications, e.g., mobile notifications for the user. These notifications also provide two-way confirmation as they send a fail or success message to the sender when a notification or actuation is realised. Generally, these control messages are sent from the cloud to the edge level as feedback messages are created by edge devices and delivered to the cloud level. Specifically, if an event is triggered, like a rise in moisture level inside a farm, then the log manager in cloud level can send an action request to an actuator to open the irrigation valve to raise the soil's moisture. Then the farmer confirms whether irrigation is completed as planned and presses the Irrigation is completed button to notify the log manager. The log manager receives this feedback manager and marks that area as irrigated. Thus, human-machine interaction can be achieved using two-way confirmation through feedback and control messages.

Gateway

WSN devices benefit from gateways to reach cloud services. A gateway has an application that acts as an intermediate component. At some point, distributed data should be delivered to the cloud level by connecting the sink node of the WSN to itself and being connected to an access point wireless or cable. In this way, the gateway creates interoperability between the WSN and IoT.

Log Manager

The number of IoT devices like smart houses to intelligent transport systems and production systems to public services is increasing day by day. This technological advancement necessitates the storing, visualisation and management of the information generated by these devices. Moreover, change in the context of data can trigger various events to take necessary actions. Therefore, a log manager has to store this data, visualise it for the system administrator and take actions according to these changes.

In the scope of this study, the record management system is called the Log Manager, which can transfer the data coming from the devices located in different locations quickly and produce the desired events reports. To support the system's heterogeneity, the cloud-based log manager proposed in this architecture accepts the requests and sensor data via standard web-based requests, and the feedback can be a form of web-based callback, mobile notification, SMS, or email. These features can be extended depending on the requirements.

Log manager should operate independently from any platform or device. Therefore, the sensor data is received as a key-value with the key as a predefined tag in the log manager. So, each sensor has a tag in the log manager, and the sensor sends its data using this tag to the log manager. Unlike the available log managers such as Think Speak, the proposed log manager has no limitation to submit data at specific periods. Also, the log manager proposed in this architecture is much easier to use and configure compared to the available fully-fledged log manager such as AWS. Finally, it can also analyze the data based on the user's queries and report the results in the user's predefined forms such as charts and graphs.

2.2 Lifecycle of WSN-based IoT Systems

In addition to reference architectures, the lifecycle of WSN-based IoT systems guides developers to implement their systems, starting from bare-metal programming to fully functioning systems. It begins with System Analysis, System Design, System Modelling and Simulation, Implementation and ends with System Test. SysML diagrams (Holt and Perry, 2008) might be preferred to describe different phases of the development life-cycle of these systems, see Figure 2.

System Analysis: In this phase, the functional and non-functional requirements of the system are defined. Moreover, Use Case Diagrams are provided to describe user-system interactions. Specifically, use case specifications elaborate on the events and specifications of the system.

System Design: In order to model the system components, Block Definition Diagrams (BDD) are preferred to describe the types of hardware components, hardware connections of components, and hierarchies of software. A detailed design can be realized by providing Internal Block Diagrams (IBD). The BDD and IBD can provide the required structural modeling of the system. State machine diagrams and Activity diagrams are useful to model the system behaviour. These diagrams can be developed using the use case scenarios provided in the analysis phase.

In addition to this diagram, the other behavioural diagrams of SysML can be used, such as sequence diagrams, depending on the needs of the system under development (SUD). Early verification of system design can be made using Petri-Net models. This can help to check the important system properties, such as reach-ability, live-ness, traffic/load, and so on, to check whether the development of the system under design is feasible and efficient (Karaduman et al,. 2020a).

Figure 2. Lifecycle of WSN-based IoT Systems.

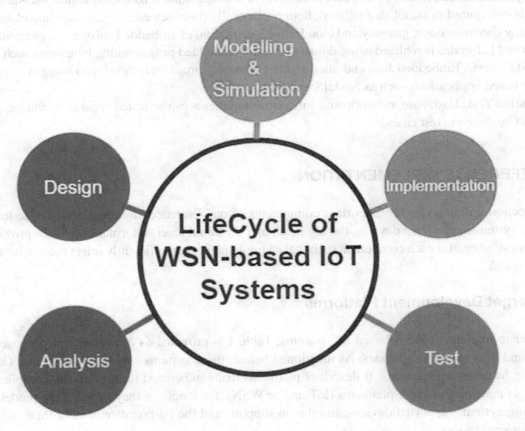

System Modeling and Simulation: WSN-based IoT systems are composed of various hardware, network and software components, a bottom-up approach can be a valuable way to develop the system. In order to realize the system modeling and simulation, these steps can be applied:

First, the system modeling can start with the physical model of the system where the hardware has interaction with mechanical or physical components. For example, a Cyber-physical system (CPS) with a servo motor component used for lifting weight can be modelled by physical rules to be used later in the implementation phase. Second, the development of a setup model for the configuration of sensors and actuators with micro-controllers or development boards. This can be realized in different hardware modeling environments depending on the level of modeling, such as Proteus. Third, the WSN program and topology can be simulated in application-specific or general-purpose WSN or network simulators. Then, the software can be modelled using UML diagrams such as Class Diagram, Object diagram and Interaction Diagram to model the structural and behavioural aspects of the system software. These diagrams are useful to model software components and the hierarchy of the WSN-based IoT systems. Domain-specific modelling languages are preferable technologies to generate code for target systems. In case of using DSMLs in the development of WSN-based IoT systems, they can automatically synthesize code artefacts for the target system.

Implementation: In this phase, hardware setup is realized using sensors and actuators. Networking setup is configured to establish a network both horizontally (between edges, gateways and clouds) and vertically (between edge, gateway and cloud). Implementation of embedded software to program WSN Motes and IoT nodes is realized using domain-specific embedded programming languages such as Embedded C, nesC, Embedded Java and microPython. Gateway program is developed using web based or socket-based applications such as NodeJS and Perl.

System Test: Hardware, network, and software components can be tested separately and integration test can be done via test cases.

3. REFERENCE IMPLEMENTATION

This section will describe the important components of our reference implementation: edge level operating systems, edge level devices, the fog level, and the cloud level. Information will be provided on different solutions for each component such that an implementer can efficiently select the one best suited for their task.

3.1 Target Development Platforms

In order to implement WSN-based IoT systems, Table 1 is provided as a summary of proposed platforms and their supported devices. As mentioned before, these systems consist of WSN, IoT, Gateway and Log Manager components. It describes platforms that can be used to develop these applications, the target paradigm of these platforms (IoT and/or WSN), the language they support, the model of the operating system, supported devices, simulation support, and the on-board sensors of their supported development devices.

Overall, the WSN part can be implemented using either TinyOS or ContikiOS. These operating systems are one of the most preferred technologies to create distributed and ad-hoc wireless sensor networks. They use common hardware devices so developed software can be deployed using the same hardware technology. In this way, the developer does not have to deal with emerged heterogeneity because of hardware complexity. Both operating systems have simulation support.

Target devices have onboard sensors to help developers by abstracting away from hardware connections. They have an event-driven operating system model which works using event definitions such as network event when a message packet is received or generation of timer event when the duration of a timer is expired.

On the WSN side, Contiki operating system is programmed using C language while TinyOS applications are developed using nesC language, a dialect of C. On the IoT side, RIOT and Arduino IDE are some of the commonly preferable development environments. They are suitable for real-time applications. To eliminate hardware heterogeneity, we also present common supported hardware for RIOT and Arduino IDE. Both firmware applications can be developed using C/C++. However, they do not have specific simulation support currently.

Gateway programs can be implemented using general-purpose programming languages. To this end, serial port communication and socket programming libraries are required. According to project requirements, API's can also be added. For example, PushBullet API can be added into a Java program that runs in a RaspberryPi. Then, according to incoming data, notifications can be sent to the user via this API.

A log management system is required at the cloud level to visualize data, handle data-based events, and store data. This cloud level software can be a custom log manager implemented using a server side programming language, such as NodeJS. Alternatively, Node-RED, ThingSpeak, Google Cloud, Azure IoT and AWS IoT can also be preferred. From our point of view, Node-RED comes forward among them as a free tool to visualize data, customize/define events and establish network operations.

The operating system is important for the requirements of the tasks. Generally, it depends on the environmental conditions. Since environmental changes occur based on events and periods between events, a real-time model cannot be preferred where these events occur rarely. Moreover, when hardware capabilities and environmental changes are considered, it is not convenient to use battery-powered devices using a real-time operating system since real-time operation consumes battery. On the other hand, an event-driven operating system processes tasks when there is an event. Then, once that event is completed, it stops the CPU and goes to sleep mode to save energy.

Table 1. Summary table of proposed architecture's components.

Platform	IoT	WSN	Language	OS Model	Supported Devices	Simulation Support	On Board Sensors
RIOT	X	X	C	Real-time	ESP32, ESP8266, ARM	-	Specific Verion
Arduino IDE	X		C/C++	Real-time	ESP32, ESP8266, ARM	-	Specific Verion
ContikiOS		X	C	Event-driven	TmoteSky, IRIS, Z1	CooJA	Yes
TinyOS		X	nesC	Event-driven	TmoteSky, IRIS, Z1	ToSSiM	Yes
Gateway	X	X	Java, Python	Real-time	RaspberryPi	Not Required	Not Required
Log Manager	X	X	NodeJS, Perl	Real-time & Event-driven	PC, RaspberryPi	Not Required	Not Required

As proposed in section 2, WSN creates distributed and multi-hop topology of the architecture using event-based models. At the same time, the IoT side provides single-hop topology to support real-time activities. In case of multiple arbitrary or parallel requests sent to an IoT device, a real-time operating system should collect and handle these requests.

3.2 Edge Level Operating Systems

As mentioned, WSN and IoT have received immense attention in the research community that leads to the emergence of various operating systems and development environments. Because of the variety of operating systems and embedded technologies, development boards are also gaining popularity, creating extra decision challenges for the developers. This subsection discusses edge-level operating systems, and in Section 3.3, supported and practised devices are given.

WSN and IoT are highly dynamic networks, and their embedded devices are mostly battery powered. Those nodes may become deactive quickly because of frequent antenna usage. Moreover, these devices are equipped with constrained resources such as memory and computation power. In many cases, it is impossible to replace the sensor device after deployment. Therefore the first objective may be to optimize the sensor devices lifetime.

These challenges of WSN and IoT bring additional solutions like creating a specialized OS. According to the needs, various operating systems are designed for these devices. Therefore, operating systems for WSN and IoT have been studied to provide a reference. These features are considered: Architecture, Programming Approach, Programming Architecture, Programming Model, Threading, Scheduling, Real-time, and Memory Management.

RIOT OS

Table 2. Features of RIOT

Architecture	Microkernel
Programming Approach	Thread-base
Programming Architecture	Event/Threads
Programming Model	Multithreaded
Threading	POSIX-like API
Scheduling	Tickless, Priority-based
Real-time	Yes
Memory Management	Dynamic/Static/File System/Device Driver Protection

Table 2 describes the features of the RIOT operating system. RIOT is an open-source microkernel-based operating system designed to match the requirements of IoT and WSN devices. RIOT requires a very low memory footprint and high energy efficiency while has real-time capabilities, support for a wide range of hardware, and communication stacks for wireless and wired networks. It provides an abstract API that eliminates embedded level configurations and enables ANSI C and C++ application programming, including multi-threading, IPC, system timers and mutexes. It uses a tickless scheduler (Baccelli et al., 2013) to reduce power consumption. The system enters sleep mode by switching to idle thread whenever there are no pending tasks, and it remains in sleep mode until an interrupt wakes it up. RIOT has a modular Internet stack which is more flexible than a layered stack as modules can be separately maintained. Its communication protocols 6LoWPAN and RPL are provided with support to TCP, UDP and IPv6 protocols.

Arduino IDE

Arduino is an open-source embedded programming platform for creating IoT applications using various development boards. Recently, Arduino IDE and its libraries created a legacy to program different development boards using wrappers that consist of Arduino-like programming. By adapting its functions and libraries, it enlarged the scope of its supported boards. Arduino programming language is similar to C++, with some additional predefined functions and constants. Minimal Arduino code consists of two functions which are setup and loop. Function setup is called once when the program starts after power-up or board reset. It is usually used to initialize variables, libraries, or I/O pins. It uses freeRTOS for threading, and it has platform-independent libraries to create a network and establish a connection. It has various communication protocol libraries such as TCP, UDP, CoAP, MQTT etc., including communication stacks such as lwIP and uIP. Table 3 shows the features of the Arduino development environment.

Table 3. Features of Arduino.

Architecture	Microkernel
Programming Approach	Setup/Loop functions, FreeRTOS
Programming Architecture	Task and Function Creation
Programming Model	Functional and/or Multithreaded
Threading	POSIX-like API
Scheduling	Tickless, Priority-based, Round-Robin
Real-time	Yes
Memory Management	Memory Coalescence

ContikiOS

Contiki (Dunkels et al., 2004) is an operating system that implements the Protothreads threading (Dunkels et al., 2006) model that supports both event-driven and multi-threading. Protothreads provide lightweight and stack-less multi-threading to save ROM and RAM requirements. Multiple threads share a common stack. There is no explicit mechanism in Contiki to switch to deep sleep mode. The applications in execution are self-responsible to save battery power by observing event-queue size. When there are no events scheduled on the queue, the processor can go to sleep mode until an interrupt caused by an event wakes it up.

ContikiOS supports dynamic memory allocation, but there is not a Memory Protection Unit (MPU). For establishing network and M2M communication, ContikiOS has microIP (uIP) (Dunkels, 2003) and Rime stacks (Dunkels et al., 2007). Rime stack contains a set of custom lightweight protocols and application layer functions, while uIP stack is also a lightweight stack that supports IPv6. Specifically, uIP stack is developed for low-power and wireless memory-constrained sensor devices. Table 4 summarizes the features of the Contiki operating system.

Table 4. Features of ContikiOS.

Architecture	Modular
Programming Approach	Thread-based
Programming Architecture	Event/Threads
Programming Model	Events and Protothreads
Threading	Protothreads, Multi-Threads (Alternatively)
Scheduling	Earliest Deadline First
Real-time	Partially with Protothreads, but no guarantee
Memory Management	No Support.

TinyOS

Table 5. Features of TinyOS.

Architecture	Monolithic
Programming Approach	Component-based
Programming Architecture	Commands/Events/Tasks
Programming Model	Event-Driven
Threading	TOS Threads
Scheduling	Non-preemptive, Earliest Deadline First
Real-time	No Support.
Memory Management	Memory Recovery, Pointer and Array Error Tracking

TinyOS (Levis et al., 2005) is a component-based operating system where components stick together to form statically linked programs. Specifically, these components are software modules and wrappers around hardware. It has non-preemptive tasks management and preemptive events mechanisms. Tasks cannot preempt each other, but events can preempt tasks and other events. Events represent hardware interrupts. TinyOS has cooperative TOS threads. In other words, the user is responsible for yielding the CPU explicitly when it is not in use. Task scheduler executes as a high priority thread and schedules threads using FIFO preemptive scheduling model. TinyOS is written in nesC, a dialect of C (Gay et al., 2003). nesC is a component-based and event-driven programming language to develop WSN-based applications. TinyOS has a low-power Internet Stack that consists of TCP, UDP, ICMPv6 and IPv6, including support for 6LoWPAN, RPL and CoAP. Features of TinyOS are shown in Table 5.

3.3 Edge Level Devices

In this section, edge level components that are used with respect to the proposed architecture are mentioned. Although both WSN and IoT sides have various Edge level nodes, we have investigated two pieces of hardware that are commonly preferred and low-cost. Moreover, we also test these devices considering power consumption, support level (partial or full), and availability on the market. We concluded that TmoteSky motes are suitable for implementing the WSN side while ESP32's can be preferred to develop IoT applications.

Tmote-Sky Mote

Figure 3. Tmotesky Mote.

TmoteSky is a low power wireless sensor device. It offers a high data rate sensor network for applications requiring ultra-low power. It also provides high reliability and ease of development. It has multiple integrated peripherals including a 12-bit ADC, 12-bit DAC, Timer, and UART bus protocols. It has an antenna chip that is IEEE 802.115.4 compliant and sensors for measurements such as humidity, temperature, and light. Figure 3 displays the TmoteSky motes used to implement the smart fire detection and the smart lighting system in our previous work (Karaduman et al., 2018a; Karaduman et al., 2018b; Karaduman et al., 2020b).

ESP32-WROOM-32

ESP32-WROOM-32 is a 32-bit, low-cost and dual-core microcontroller, seen in Figure 4. It has integrated Wi-Fi and Bluetooth modules that target a wide variety of applications ranging from low-power sensor networks to the most demanding tasks. It supports 802.11 b/g/n Wi-Fi connectivity with speeds up to 150 Mbps. It has 520 KB of SRAM, 448 KB of ROM and 16 KB of RTC SRAM. In addition, it is equipped with 34 Programmable GPIOs. 18 GPIO's can operate as 12-bit ADC and two of them can work as 8-bit DAC.

Figure 4. ESP32 Node.

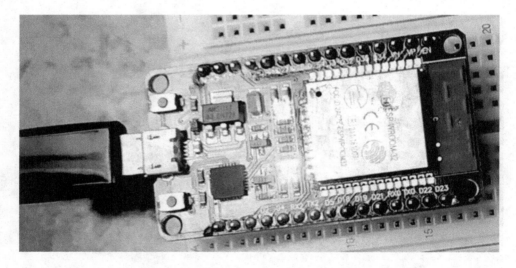

3.4 Fog Level System

The Fog layer resides on top of the edge layer and forms the network backbone between Edge and Cloud. In the Fog layer, we have placed a gateway to creating a bridge between the cloud and edge layers. The gateway plays an intermediate role in the architecture. Its basic function is moving data between Edge nodes and Cloud devices. Since they are more advanced high-end computational devices, they are usually powered by stable power sources and can also perform data processing.

WSN devices can be connected to the Internet using a single gateway. As mentioned, each source node samples environmental data and sends it to the sink node. Then, the sink node aggregates distributed data and delivers it to the gateway. The sink node is connected to the gateway physically via USB and the gateway is connected to the Internet using either Wi-Fi or Ethernet cable. Therefore, gateway devices have to have embedded features such as USB, Wi-Fi, Ethernet port, and advanced operating systems like Linux. We refer to RaspberryPi 3. It uses the Raspbian operating system, including the aforementioned hardware components.

Gateway

A gateway is a bridge that connects between the Internet network and the wireless sensor network. To this end, it should have enough capabilities to combine two different networks. Customization of the gateway depends on the system requirements, e.g., network protocols and data parsing, and hardware features of the components such as port types and power requirements. Moreover, hardware selection for the gateway is important because it should handle requests that come from nearly 50-60 WSN nodes and deliver them to the cloud level without any significant delay. The operating system of the gateway level should be able to run applications that are written for high-level and object-oriented languages such as Java, Python and C/C++. Therefore, data operations can also be applied at the fog level.

Fog Device: RaspberryPi 3

The RaspberryPi 3 seen in Figure 5 is the successor of the RaspberryPi. It has a BCM2837 microprocessor with a 1.2 GHz 32/64-bit quad-core processor. In addition, the Broadcom BCM43438 microchip has been added that provides the RPi 3 with a Wi-Fi 802.11n 2.4 GHz and a Bluetooth 4.1 Low Energy (BLE) connection. It has a camera interface, Ethernet port and four USB ports. It can be booted from USB or microSD. It uses Rasbpian operating system. It is a special Linux/Debian distribution. It has 40-pin GPIO pins which can be used for PWM, digital or analogue input/output. It has an HDMI port that can be connected to a monitor to be visually controlled by an operator.

Raspbian operating system lets a RaspberryPi be programmed using Python, Java, and C/C++. It can also run web-based applications and it is possible to create a web server. Compared to the edge level devices, RaspberryPi has better capabilities but higher power consumption since it requires 5V and 1A to operate. Therefore these kinds of devices have to be supplied by a limitless power source instead of battery-powered approaches.

Figure 5. RaspberryPi 3 with the TmoteSky sink mote (Kamgueu et al., 2017).

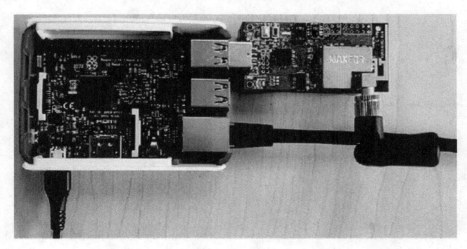

In the proposed architecture, we used RaspberryPi 3 to create a gateway between the edge and cloud. We used a USB port to attach the sink node. The USB of the RaspberryPi 3 also feeds the sink node, which means the sink node is plugged into a limitless power source. Then, a serial port reader application is written using Java to receive aggregated data from the sink node. We programmed the gateway in the manner that once it receives data, it immediately sends it to the cloud with the information of source nodes' IP and measurement value. Figure 5 represents a RaspberryPi 3 (left side) gateway with TmoteSky (right side) mote connected as a sink node. To connect those two hardware USB port is preferred. Tmotesky is roled as the sink node and deliveres incoming information to the gateway.

Cloud Level: Log Manager

Generally, IoT Systems require cloud level logging systems. In order to visualize the collected data, the Log Manager system should reflect this information graphically. This feature enables the user to track the changes in the environment and to analyse the system statistically. Figure 6 represents environmental data that are collected from a sensor. This figure shows 17 samples taken from moisture sensor. Values represent decimal value ranging between 0-255. Sampling time starts from 8:16 am (morning) and continues until 3:46 pm (afternoon). The figures can be interpreted that the moisture level did not change considerably for 7 hours, maybe due to a rainy or cloudy day.

Since WSN systems are written in an event-based application manner, these events should be handled by a log manager and turned into action by IoT nodes. A notification is sent to the log manager by an IoT node (e.g. irrigation valve is opened). Then the log manager should send a callback to the IoT node automatically to close the valve. The same behavior can also be applied for e-mailing aggregated data or sending notifications to users' mobile phones. Figure 7 illustrates a Node-RED diagram that visualizes moisture level and provides an interface to set threshold. In the Node-RED model shown in this figure, the threshold can be set by the user. It is set to decimal value of 47. Periodically, system receives sensor values. Model elements describe capabilities of Node-RED. Logic flow is established using model elements that are colored differently.

Figure 6. Measured sensor values are represented by a graph.

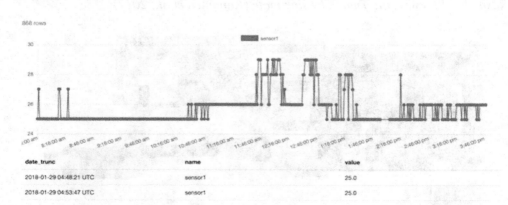

Moreover, Node-RED can also be connected to a database to log moisture data. It can send GET and SET requests to nodes for collecting moisture data or updating threshold values. Further, different sensor types can also be used, such as temperature, pressure and humidity. It has a future to create user-defined functions. In this way, users can customize functionalities of the Node-RED, and users can also add JSON elements to parse JSON coded information.

Figure 7. Node-RED diagram logs and visualizes data and sends requests when a certain threshold is exceeded.

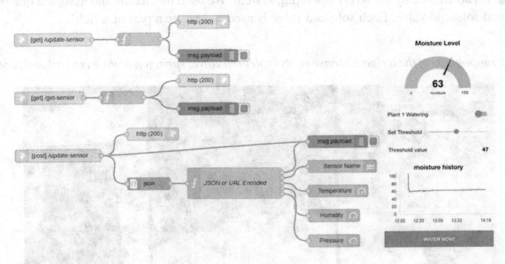

4. IMPLEMENTATION WORKFLOW FOR A CASE STUDY

This section will present the workflow for the implementation of our architecture for the irrigation case study.

4.1 Case Study Implementation

The irrigation case study is implemented based on the reference architecture and components. It is represented by Figure 8. The system is firstly tested in a wide garden then adapted to a large area. Since farm fields are large areas where it is hard to establish an Internet connection or is not possible due to green farming, lack of power source and lack of infrastructure. Therefore, distributed WSN motes should create a network between each other using IEEE 802.15.4 technology. Moreover, they should be battery-powered and have a deep-sleep operation. Therefore, proposed operating systems can automatically switch to a deep-sleep mode where there is no pending task or event.

We distributed TmoteSky motes to these fields and measured the moisture level of the soil. Because it is not an area that receives sunlight for a long time in a day, it was not possible to use solar batteries. Therefore, we used standard 2xAA batteries for each WSN mote. When a sensor node has detected dryness, it sends its IP address and measurement data to the neighbour node through the sink node. The gateway reads this data from the sink node via a USB port and has delivered it to the cloud. Lastly, the cloud level logs this data, including date and time, then sends a request to an ESP32 IoT node (IEEE 802.11) that controls a solenoid valve. We selected the TmoteSky node since it has built-in solutions such as in-board sensors, battery packs, and it is a well-supported device by Contiki operating system and its simulation CooJa. Moreover, we selected ESP32 since it has well-designed analogue I/O pins and a high-frequency CPU. Therefore, it can easily control a solenoid valve that draws many currents and requires a fast and smooth operation to arrange its water consumption. We selected the RIOT operating system because we wanted to use a real-time operating system that controls more than one solenoid valve attached to one ESP32 mote. Moreover, the software complexity which is derived from hardware connections is abstracted by the RIOT operating system. We used its threads and assigned one thread to each I/O and solenoid valve. Each solenoid valve is used to irrigate a part of a field.

Figure 8. Components of the irrigation case study (solenoid valve, springer, mobile control and prototype).

As a gateway, we preferred a RaspberryPi since we can feed four sink nodes using its USB ports and even read incoming data from these USB ports and transmit them to the cloud simultaneously. As a log management system, we preferred to use Node-RED because it has a graphical and user-friendly interface/data visualization.

4.2 Workflow

Figure 9 illustrates the workflow of the irrigation case study. The columns list the different components within the architecture, while the steps within the workflow specify how we implemented each component. Broadly, there are four phases to our workflow. Requirements are about gathering the requirements and deciding on the specification of each component. Then, implementation is about implementing and configuring the component software. Testing concerns the unit and integration testing of each component, and then finally, deployment deploys the components to the field.

Figure 9. Workflow of the irrigation case study using proposed architecture.

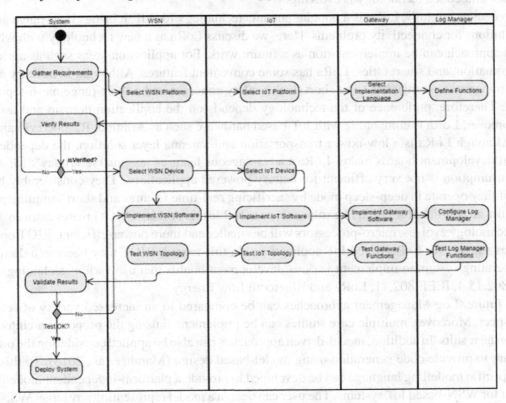

5. CONCLUSION AND FUTURE WORK

In this chapter, an architecture and reference implementation are proposed to eliminate unpredictable technical challenges that system designers will encounter in the development of WSN-based IoT systems. Moreover, this chapter discusses a gateway and log manager, which are architectural requirements for creating WSN-based IoT systems. Considering the device and operating system variety, we shared our experience to provide a reference architecture and implementation. In this way, designers can use the provided information to eliminate the decision problem and immediately begin developing their systems. An irrigation system is given as a case study. There is sufficient complexity since it has many components interacting with each other to control the moisture level of farm fields. Operating systems handle these components' power consumption while aggregated data is delivered to the Log manager via a gateway.

This architecture and reference implementation are helpful for designers who want to benefit from distributed data aggregation using WSN motes while empowering the system IoT nodes to control actuator components. WSN motes can be distributed along with the large fields and IoT nodes can actuate electronic components to influence the environment.

However, because of device constraints on the WSN side, they are not suitable for real-time applications. Moreover, there is no simulator for IoT side OS and platforms to simulate the WSN-based IoT and application software. However, the RIOT operating system follows a hybrid model to support WSN and IoT devices. In this way, it may be possible to create distributed topology using power-efficient IoT nodes since embedded technology is evolving.

As a recent technology, LoRa is a popular antenna technology for IoT, it brings long-range and low-power solutions for connectivity problems. Here, we discuss LoRa as a new technology with which the proposed approach can be implementation as a future work. For application areas such as agriculture, home automation, and smart cities, LoRa has some convenient features. Although, in military applications the transmission range has to be short due to safety concerns and a short-range mesh-topology is preferred. Therefore, preference of the technology depends on the application domain and task to be done. Moreover, LoRa is compatible with IoT-based hardware such as Arduino, RaspberryPi and STM boards. Although LoRa is a low-power transportation and antenna layer solution, the dependency on traditional development boards makes LoRa's advantageous features less visible. Today's IoT boards' power consumption is not very efficient for battery-powered applications. They considerably become efficient if they operate in deep-sleep mode by sacrificing real-time features and short sampling periods. They require an additional solution like solar energy to tackle this problem, yet it creates extra cost. However, as technology evolves, micro-processors will be smaller and more power-efficient. RIOT operating system has support for LoRa-based IoT applications. In this regard, RIOT may become a dominating hybrid operating system to implement various development boards that use various technologies such as IEEE 802.15.4, IEEE 802.11, LoRa and Bluetooth Low Energy.

In the future, Log Management approaches can be compared to an increased variety of selections in this respect. Moreover, multiple case studies can be implemented using the proposed architecture to generalize the results. In addition, model-driven approaches can also be applied considering the proposed architecture to provide code generation using model-based design (Marah, et al., 2018). To this end, a domain-specific modelling language can be developed to provide a platform-independent modelling environment for WSN-based IoT systems. The user can design a model representing any target WSN-based IoT system and select a specific platform to transform the platform-independent model to a platform-specific model. The user can add platform-specific elements to the model and automatically generate codes for TinyOS, Arduino, Contiki, RIOT OS and/or Java platforms. In addition, an agent-oriented paradigm can be applied for programming WSN-based IoT systems (Tezel, et al., 2016). As software agents provide a higher-level of abstraction to develop software, they can be used to ease the control of distributed WSN topology, as agents are collaborative software entities. Agents can be deployed at any level of the provided architecture to solve complex problems.

REFERENCES

Akyildiz, I. F., Su, W., Sankarasubramaniam, Y., & Cayirci, E. (2002). Wireless sensor networks: A survey. *Computer Networks*, *38*(4), 393–422. doi:10.1016/S1389-1286(01)00302-4

Arslan, S., Challenger, M., & Dagdeviren, O. (2017). Wireless sensor network based fire detection system for libraries. In *2017 International Conference on Computer Science and Engineering (UBMK 2017)*, (pp. 271-276). IEEE 10.1109/UBMK.2017.8093388

Asici, T. Z., Karaduman, B., Eslampanah, R., Challenger, M., Denil, J., & Vangheluwe, H. (2019). Applying model driven engineering techniques to the development of contiki-based IoT systems. In *2019 IEEE/ACM 1st International Workshop on Software Engineering Research & Practices for the Internet of Things (SERP4IoT)* (pp. 25-32). IEEE. 10.1109/SERP4IoT.2019.00012

Baccelli, E., Hahm, O., Günes, M., Wählisch, M., & Schmidt, T. C. (2013). RIOT OS: Towards an OS for the Internet of Things. In 2013 IEEE conference on computer communications workshops (INFOCOM WKSHPS) (pp. 79-80). IEEE.

Chéour, R., Khriji, S., & Kanoun, O. (2020). Microcontrollers for IoT: Optimizations, Computing Paradigms, and Future Directions. In *2020 IEEE 6th World Forum on Internet of Things (WF-IoT)* (pp. 1-7). IEEE.

Dunkels, A. (2003, May). Full TCP/IP for 8-bit architectures. In *Proceedings of the 1st international conference on Mobile systems, applications and services* (pp. 85-98). Academic Press.

Dunkels, A. (2007). Rime-a lightweight layered communication stack for sensor networks. In *Proceedings of the European Conference on Wireless Sensor Networks (EWSN), Poster/Demo session, Delft, The Netherlands* (Vol. 44). Academic Press.

Dunkels, A., Gronvall, B., & Voigt, T. (2004). Contiki-a lightweight and flexible operating system for tiny networked sensors. In *29th annual IEEE international conference on local computer networks* (pp. 455-462). IEEE. 10.1109/LCN.2004.38

Dunkels, A., Schmidt, O., Voigt, T., & Ali, M. (2006). Protothreads: Simplifying event-driven programming of memory-constrained embedded systems. In *Proceedings of the 4th international conference on Embedded networked sensor systems* (pp. 29-42). 10.1145/1182807.1182811

Gay, D., Levis, P., Von Behren, R., Welsh, M., Brewer, E., & Culler, D. (2003). The nesC language: A holistic approach to networked embedded systems. *ACM SIGPLAN Notices*, *38*(5), 1–11. doi:10.1145/780822.781133

Holt, J., & Perry, S. (2008). *SysML for systems engineering* (Vol. 7). IET. doi:10.1049/PBPC007E

Kamgueu, P. O., Nataf, E., & Djotio, T. (2017). Architecture for an efficient integration of wireless sensor networks to the Internet through Internet of Things gateways. *International Journal of Distributed Sensor Networks*, *13*(11), 1550147717744735. doi:10.1177/1550147717744735

Karaduman, B., Aşıcı, T., Challenger, M., & Eslampanah, R. (2018). A cloud and Contiki based fire detection system using multi-hop wireless sensor networks. In *Proceedings of the Fourth International Conference on Engineering & MIS 2018* (pp. 1-5). 10.1145/3234698.3234764

Karaduman, B., Challenger, M., & Eslampanah, R. (2018). ContikiOS based library fire detection system. In *2018 5th International Conference on Electrical and Electronic Engineering (ICEEE)* (pp. 247-251). IEEE. 10.1109/ICEEE2.2018.8391340

Karaduman, B., Challenger, M., Eslampanah, R., Denil, J., & Vangheluwe, H. (2020). Analyzing WSN-based IoT Systems using MDE Techniques and Petri-net Models. Academic Press.

Karaduman, B., Challenger, M., Eslampanah, R., Denil, J., & Vangheluwe, H. (2020). Platform-specific Modeling for RIOT based IoT Systems. In *Proceedings of the IEEE/ACM 42nd International Conference on Software Engineering Workshops* (pp. 639-646). 10.1145/3387940.3392194

Karimpour, N., Karaduman, B., Ural, A., Challenger, M., & Dagdeviren, O. (2019). IoT based Hand Hygiene Compliance Monitoring. In *2019 International Symposium on Networks, Computers and Communications (ISNCC)*, (pp. 1-6). IEEE.

Klein, S. (2017). *IoT Solutions in Microsoft's Azure IoT Suite*. Apress. doi:10.1007/978-1-4842-2143-3

Korobeinikova, T. I., Volkova, N. P., Kozhushko, S. P., Holub, D. O., Zinukova, N. V., Kozhushkina, T. L., & Vakarchuk, S. B. (2020). Google cloud services as a way to enhance learning and teaching at university. *Proceedings of the 7th Workshop on Cloud Technologies in Education (CTE 2019)*.

Kurniawan, A. (2018). *Learning AWS IoT: Effectively manage connected devices on the AWS cloud using services such as AWS Greengrass, AWS button, predictive analytics and machine learning*. Packt Publishing Ltd.

Levis, P., Madden, S., Polastre, J., Szewczyk, R., Whitehouse, K., Woo, A., & Culler, D. (2005). TinyOS: An operating system for sensor networks. In *Ambient intelligence* (pp. 115–148). Springer. doi:10.1007/3-540-27139-2_7

Marah, H. M., Challenger, M., & Kardas, G. (2020). RE4TinyOS: A Reverse Engineering Methodology for the MDE of TinyOS Applications. In *2020 15th Conference on Computer Science and Information Systems (FedCSIS)* (pp. 741-750). IEEE. 10.15439/2020F133

Marah, H. M., Eslampanah, R., & Challenger, M. (2018). DSML4TinyOS: Code Generation for Wireless Devices. *2nd International Workshop on Model-Driven Engineering for the Internet-of-Things (MDE4IoT), 21st International Conference on Model Driven Engineering Languages and Systems (MODELS2018)*.

Maureira, M. A. G., Oldenhof, D., & Teernstra, L. (2011). ThingSpeak–an API and Web Service for the Internet of Things. *World Wide Web (Bussum)*.

Sharma, N., Shamkuwar, M., & Singh, I. (2019). The history, present and future with IoT. In *Internet of Things and Big Data Analytics for Smart Generation* (pp. 27–51). Springer. doi:10.1007/978-3-030-04203-5_3

Tezel, B. T., Challenger, M., & Kardas, G. (2016). A metamodel for Jason BDI agents. In *5th Symposium on Languages, Applications and Technologies (SLATE'16)*. Schloss Dagstuhl-Leibniz-Zentrum fuer Informatik.

Toscano, E., & Bello, L. L. (2012). Comparative assessments of IEEE 802.15. 4/ZigBee and 6LoWPAN for low-power industrial WSNs in realistic scenarios. In *2012 9th IEEE International Workshop on Factory Communication Systems* (pp. 115-124). IEEE.

Chapter 6
Connectivity Estimation Approaches for Internet of Things–Enabled Wireless Sensor Networks

Zuleyha Akusta Dagdeviren
International Computer Institute, Ege University, Turkey

Vahid Akram
International Computer Institute, Ege University, Turkey

ABSTRACT

Internet of things (IoT) envisions a network of billions of devices having various hardware and software capabilities communicating through internet infrastructure to achieve common goals. Wireless sensor networks (WSNs) having hundreds or even thousands of sensor nodes are positioned at the communication layer of IoT. In this study, the authors work on the connectivity estimation approaches for IoT-enabled WSNs. They describe the main ideas and explain the operations of connectivity estimation algorithms in this chapter. They categorize the studied algorithms into two divisions as 1-connectivity estimation algorithms (special case for k=1) and k-connectivity estimation algorithms (the generalized version of the connectivity estimation problem). Within the scope of 1-connectivity estimation algorithms, they dissect the exact algorithms for bridge and cut vertex detection. They investigate various algorithmic ideas for k connectivity estimation approaches by illustrating their operations on sample networks. They also discuss possible future studies related to the connectivity estimation problem in IoT.

1. INTRODUCTION

Internet of Things (IoT) will include billions of computational devices communicating through Internet infrastructure (Xu, 2014) (Giri, 2017) (Lee, 2017) (Rehman, 2017) (Balaji, 2019) (Yugha, 2020). A robust network for IoT must deal with the malfunctions without losing its connectivity. Robust networks are one

DOI: 10.4018/978-1-7998-4186-9.ch006

of the important requirements in Internet of Things (IoT) because they provide a reliable infrastructure for communication of other devices. The nodes (vertices) in IoT systems are usually connected to each other over wireless channels and communicate by message passing. Hence failures in relay nodes can destroy the data transmission paths among nodes and waste many active resources. So, the underlying communication infrastructure of a reliable IoT should be able to tolerate the failures and keep the connectivity of active nodes.

Wireless sensor networks (WSNs) compose of motes which have the abilities of sensing from the environment and transmission of the collected data in a wireless manner (Akyildiz, 2002) (Arampatzis, 2005) (Paradis, 2007) (Alemdar, 2010) (Rawat, 2014) (Jino Ramson, 2017). WSNs are crucial technologies for IoT and positioned at the communication layer. WSNs can be used in various practical scenarios such as smart cities, healthcare, military surveillance, target tracking and habitat monitoring. Generally, WSNs include at least one special node called the sink in which the data is collected. An example WSN modeled with a graph is given in Figure 1. In this network model, there are 14 sensor nodes, and the ID of each node is written inside it. The vertex set $V=\{0, 1, 2, 3, 4, 5, 6, 7, 8, 9, 10, 11, 12, 13\}$. Transmission ranges are depicted as dashed circles. Possible communication channels (edges) between nodes are drawn with solid lines. The edge set $E=\{(0,4), (0,12), (1,10), (2,5), (2,9), (2,13), (3,7), (3,8), (5,11), (5,12), (5,13), (6,8), (6,11), (6,12), (7,10), (8,13), (9,10), (11,12), (11,13)\}$.

Figure 1. Network Model

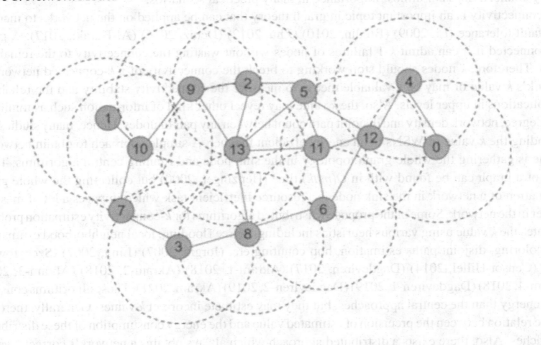

A WSN is connected if at least one communication path between every pair of nodes is present. Since WSNs are designed to operate in a distributed manner, maintaining network connectivity is of utmost importance to achieve common application goals by transmitting messages between nodes. If a vertex's removal partitions the communication network into disjoint segments, we call this vertex as cut vertex (articulation point). Identifying cut vertices are very important for wireless networks to expose their connectivity properties and vulnerable parts. In Figure 1, nodes 10 and 12 are cut vertices as removal of them partitions the network into 2 disjoint segments. If we remove node 10 from the network, the first connected component will include only node 1 and the second connected component will consist of other remaining nodes. Similarly, if we remove node 12 from the graph in Figure 1, the first segment will include nodes 0 and 4, and the other segment will consist of other remaining nodes. A bridge is an edge whose removal partitions the communication network into disjoint segments. In Figure 1, the edge (1,10) is a bridge which connects node 1 to the rest of network. Detections of bridges and cut vertices are crucial operations to investigate the link robustness of a WSN (Dagdeviren, 2013) (Akram, 2013) (Dagdeviren, 2014) (Dagdeviren 2016).

Connectivity is an essential requirement for many WSN applications belonging to various domains. For example, in a target tracking application utilized for military surveillance, the trajectory of the target can be monitored in a real time manner, if the sensor nodes are connected to the sink node. The monitoring nodes should send their sensed data in a timely manner to provide latest trajectory data of the target. If the connectivity of a network is corrupted, then ensuring data transfer from the sensor nodes is not possible. WSNs designed to operate in harsh environment such as mines, volcanic areas and rainforests may face with node faults. A failed node may completely stop the execution or it may transmit unwanted signals to the network. In order to reach a correct global decision, the nodes should execute consensus protocols where the network connectivity is an indispensable requirement. Hence, estimation and maintaining connectivity is of utmost importance in many practical scenarios.

k-connectivity is an important topic in graph theory that can be applied on the networks to increase their fault tolerance (Li, 2009) (Bredin, 2010) (Zhu, 2012) (Deniz, 2016) (Al-Karaki, 2017). A graph is k-connected if it can admit k-1 failures of nodes without wasting the connectivity to the remaining nodes. Therefore, k nodes should stop working to break the connectivity of a k-connected network. A network's k value of may be a valuable metric to measure the connectivity stability and the reliability of applications in upper levels. Also, the k value may reveal other kind of information such as minimum node degree, network density and disjoint path count between any pair of nodes. Hence, many studies aim for finding the k value of WSNs in an energy efficient manner. A simple approach to obtain network's k value is gathering the whole graph topology in the sink node and running central algorithms. The k value of a graph can be found with in $O(mnk)$ time (Henzinger, 2000) but collecting the whole graph information of a network in the sink node is a resource inefficient task which imposes a lot of message transfer in the network. Some of the proposed distributed algorithms for k-connectivity estimation problem estimates the k value using various heuristics including degree flooding, local neighborhood estimation, edge coloring, disjoint paths estimation, hop counting etc. (Jorgic, 2007) (Ling, 2007) (Szczytowski, 2012) (Censor-Hillel, 2014) (Dagdeviren, 2017) (Akram-1, 2018) (Akram-2, 2018) (Akram-3, 2018) (Akram-4, 2018) (Dagdeviren-1, 2019) (Dagdeviren-2, 2019) (Akram, 2021). These algorithms consume lower energy than the central approaches, but they may estimate incorrect k values. Generally, there is a reverse relation between the precision of estimated value and the energy consumption of these distributed approaches. Also, there exists a distributed approach which always obtains a network's correct k value, having less energy consumption compared to the central approach. However, the energy consumption of this exact algorithm is higher than the other distributed approaches.

In this chapter, we focus on the connectivity estimation problem for IoT enabled WSNs. We review the approaches for connectivity estimation, describe their main ideas and explain their operation by illustrating on example networks. We divide the connectivity estimation problem into 2 categories as the connectivity estimation algorithms for $k=1$ and the connectivity estimation algorithms for general k values. We examine the bridge and cut vertex detection algorithms for $k=1$ special case. We also study on the open research problems for connectivity estimation. The rest of the chapter is given as following. In Section II, we dissect important approaches to achieve connectivity (1-connectivity) estimation. In Section III, we will study on the k-connectivity estimation algorithms in detail. In the last section, Section IV, we will draw conclusions and provide open research problems in this area.

2. ALGORITHMS FOR CONNECTIVITY (1-CONNECTIVITY) ESTIMATION

In this section, we will cover cut vertex and bridge detection algorithms as they reside in 1-connected WSNs. A three-stage algorithm is proposed by Pritchard for bridge detection in WSNs (Pritchard, 2006). This algorithm constructs a distributed breadth-first search (BFS) tree in the first stage. After that, Pritchard's algorithm finds preorder labels and subtree sizes. Finally, bridges are identified in the last stage. The I-PRITCHARD algorithm (Improved Pritchard) has 2 phases and aims to find bridges of a WSN (Dagdeviren, 2013). The algorithm targets to reduce the energy consumption by decreasing the number of transmitted messages. This algorithm merges the first and second stages of the Pritchard's algorithm (Pritchard, 2006). The nodes find their subtree sizes (desc) during the backward process in the first stage to accomplish the convergecast process. A new field which includes the subtree size, is added to the messages in backward process. Second stage is not executed after the backward stage is terminated, thus the messages needed for the flooding operation is saved. Also, Preorder and Announcement messages are transmitted as unicast to prevent the energy consumption occurred by the sending of header fields of the separate messages.

An example operation is given in Figure 1. The first stage of the algorithm is executed in Figure 1.a. IDs, desc values and preorder labels are shown for each node. The result of the second stage of the I-PRITCHARD algorithm is shown in Figure 1.b. For each node, low value and high value are given. The edges (0,1), (0,3), (1,2) and (6,9) are identified as bridges. The dashed edges given in both networks in Figure 1 are cross edges of the BFS tree.

Similar to the I-PRITCHARD algorithm, ENBRIDGE (Energy-Efficient Bridge Detection) algorithm aims to identify bridges for a WSN (Dagdeviren, 2013). ENBRIDGE consists of two stages where an extended BFS algorithm is applied in the first stage. This stage is also divided into two steps as forward and backward. An extended BFS algorithm is executed in the forward step. The states of edges of the nodes are multicasted (sent to their neighbors as a radio packet) in the backward stage. An edge's state can be BRIDGE, CHILD and CROSS. Since the edge states are multicasted, each node learns the 2-hop information. Each node uses this information and finds the state of the edge which connects it to its parent by executing ENBRIDGE Classify algorithm. This algorithm has 5 rules where rules are ordered according to their computational complexities. After ENBRIDGE Classify is executed, nodes inform their parent whether they can classify their parent link by filling a 1-bit field at the backward process. This field will be 1, if a node and its descendants can classify the link, otherwise it will be equal to 0 during the convergecast process. In this manner, the sink node can identify if at least one edge is not classified. If any node informs "unclassified" to its parent, the parent does not need to run ENBRIDGE Classify which will lead to save processing power. The sink terminates the algorithm if it finds that all edges are classified. In the other case, the second stage of the algorithm is started since there are unclassified edges in the network. In this phase, an improved depth-first search (DFS) algorithm is applied where nodes use multicast communication to transmit *SEARCH* messages instead of unicast communication.

Figure 2. a) Stage 1 of I-PRITCHARD Algorithm b) Stage 2 of I-PRITCHARD Algorithm

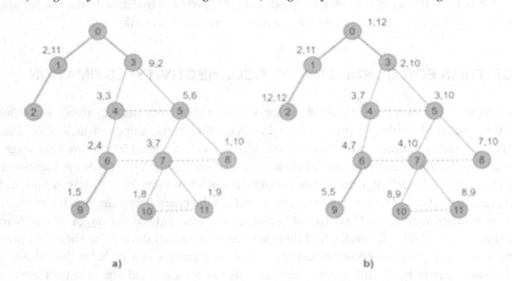

Figure 3 shows the example operations for the algorithms. In the first network given in Figure 3.a, ENBRIDGE Classify can obtain the states of all edges so the second stage of the algorithm is not run. In this example, the states of (1,2) and (3,4) edges can be identified as bridge by Rule 1 (R1) of the ENBRIDGE Classify Algorithm. The states of (4,5), (5,6), (7,8), (9,10), (9,11) and (9,12) are found as nonbridge by executing Rule 2 (R2). The edge (8,9) is a bridge found from Rule 3 (R3). Rule 4 (R4) can identify the state of edges (0,7) and (0,6) as nonbridge. The edge (8,9) is classified as nonbridge from Rule 5 of the ENBRIDGE Classify algorithm. The second example network is depicted in Figure 3.b where some edges cannot be classified by the ENBRIDGE Classify algorithm, so second stage is executed by the nodes. The edges (1,2), (2,3), (3,4), (4,5) and (5,6) are classified as nonbridge by the ENBRIDGE Classify algorithm. However, the states of the edges (2,3) and (3,4) cannot be identified by the algorithm, so the improved DFS based stage is executed to find their states (shown with DFS in Figure 3.b).

Milic proposed a bridge detection approach that is based on BFS tree and has two stages (Milic, 2007). Milic's algorithm's first stage (forward stage) is very similar to the those of BFS tree construction process. In the backward stage, the nodes find cross edges list where these lists are transmitted to their parents. Since then, the size of the messages is depended on the cross edge count. The execution of the algorithm is terminated as the BFS tree construction ends.

E-MILIC (Extended Milic) algorithm targets to decrease the transmitted message size of the Milic algorithm by providing additional rules (Akram, 2013). In the first rule, when node *i* finds a cross edge (*i,j*), only *j*'s ID is sent to the parent of node *i* instead of sending the information of (*i,j*) which includes 2 node IDs. In this manner, the transmitted byte count needed for this information is reduced to its half.

In the second rule, the node executes a *k*-cycle detection approach after the cross edge information is collected.

Figure 3. a) Stage 1 of ENBRIDGE Algorithm b) Stage 2 of ENBRIDGE Algorithm

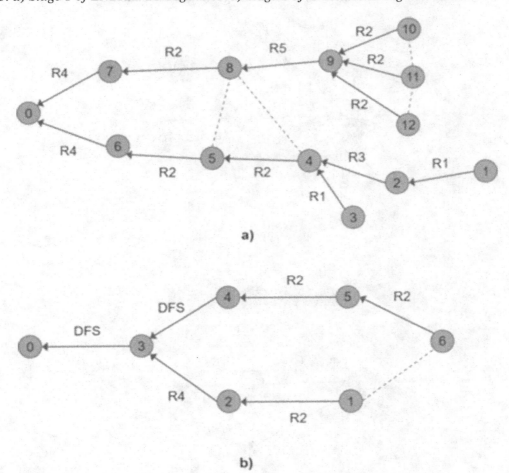

Example operations of the Milic's algorithm and E-MILIC algorithm are given in Figure 4. In the first step, node 1 sends the list of cross edges to its parent node 6 as (1,4), (1,5) in Figure 4.a (The edges are written by concatenation of two endpoints in the figure). At the same time nodes 4 and 5 transmit their cross edge lists to their parents (node 2). After these processes are executed, 7 cross edge information is transmitted. Node 2 matches (4,5) from both lists sent by nodes 4 and 5. Since, the cross edge list of node 7 is empty, the edge (3,7) is identified as a bridge. Totally, information for 15 edges (30 vertex information) is sent in Milic's algorithm. When we use E-MILIC algorithm to detect bridges, nodes 1, 4 and 5 apply Rule 1 and send only one vertex information. Nodes 4 and 5 do not send the information of edge (4,5) by detecting a three-cycle. Similar, operations are applied for other nodes for decreasing the total transmitted bytes. Finally, by executing E-MILIC algorithm on Figure 4.b, only 13 vertex information is needed for the transmission between nodes. Since, generally, communication is the dominant criteria for the energy consumption in battery powered WSNs, more than 50% decrease in the total energy consumption is achieved for this example (with regarding to the transmission of cross edges information).

Figure 4. a) Milic Algorithm's Execution b) E-MILIC Algorithm's Execution

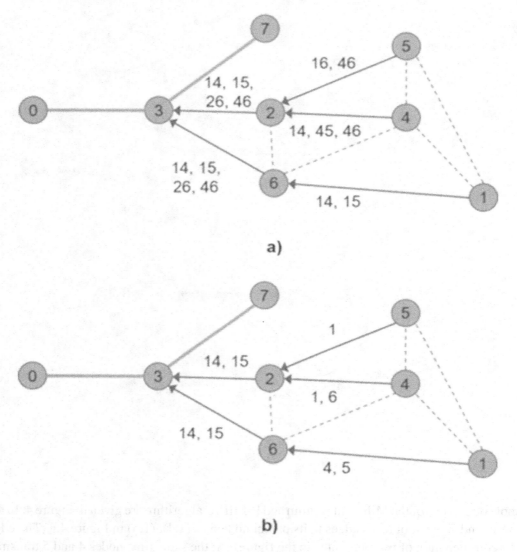

Similar to the E-MILIC, ABIDE (Ancestral knowledge for bridge detection) algorithm targets to find bridges. When the cross edge count is not low, E-MILIC algorithm can transmit large packets which may lead to drain of batteries of the sensor nodes. ABIDE algorithm runs with a distributed BFS algorithm. It consists of backward and forward stages. In the first stage, a spanning tree is constructed. In the latter stage, backward messages are convergecasted on the tree formed in the previous state. The sink node initiates the first stage by multicasting a forward message to its immediate neighbors. When a node gathers a forward message, it sets itself as visited, assigns the ID of sender as the ID of its parent and multicasts a forward message to its neighbors. Each node adds its parent ID to the list of ancestors in the forward message. In this manner, the paths between the sink node to any other node are constructed. Leaf nodes start the backward stage which will be terminated at the sink node.

Figure 5. a) Stage 1 of ABIDE Algorithm b) Stage 2 of ABIDE Algorithm

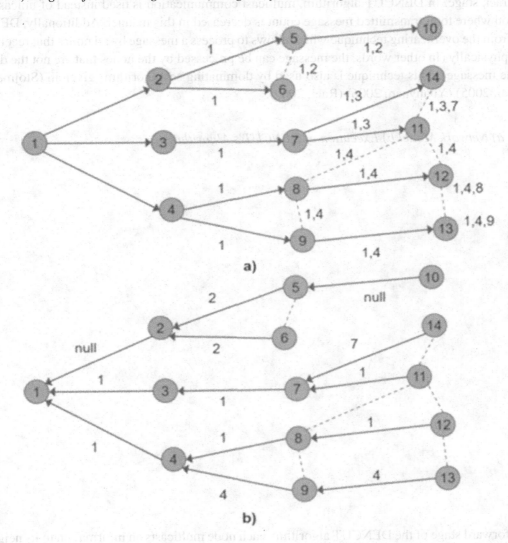

An example operation for the ABIDE algorithm is depicted in Figure 5 where there are 15 nodes in the network. Node 1 is the sink which initiates the execution of the approach. Arcs show the transmission of forward and backward messages. Dashed edges are non-tree edges that do not belong to the BFS tree. In Figure 5.a, the forward step is illustrated. In Figure 5.b, the backward step of the ABIDE algorithm is depicted. In Figure 5.a, ancestor lists of the forward messages are given. The identifiers of the cycles are given in Figure 5.b.

DENCUT (Distributed Energy-Efficient Cut Vertex Detection) algorithm aims to find cut vertices in a WSN by applying a distributed DFS algorithm (Dagdeviren, 2014). DENCUT algorithm is initiated by the sink and it is executed in a fully distributed manner. It consists of forward and backward stages similar to the aforementioned algorithms. In the forward stage, each node discovers its neighbors and adds undiscovered neighbors to its list of children. After discovering all neighbors, each node executes the backtrack stage. In DENCUT algorithm, multicast communication is used instead of unicast communication where total transmitted message count is decreased in this manner. Additionally, DENCUT benefits from the overhearing technique which allows to process a message by all nodes that receives the message physically (In other words, the message can be processed by the nodes that are not the destination of the message). This technique is also used by dominating set algorithms given in (Stojmenovic, 2002) (Dai, 2005) (Yuanyuan, 2006) (Raei, 2009).

Figure 6. a) Network Model b) Execution of DENCUT's Algorithm

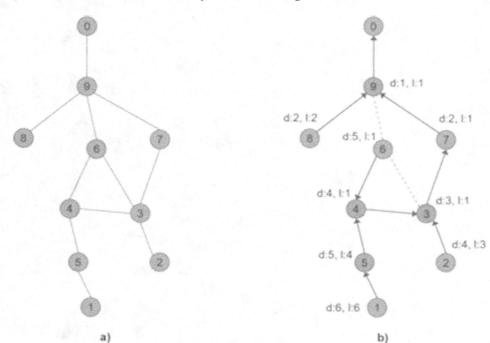

In the forward stage of the DENCUT algorithm, each node multicasts an information to its neighbors when it is discovered. In the backward stage, this operation is repeated. Also, the algorithm is suddenly finished, when a discovery information is overheard by a leaf node (a node whose degree equals to 1). At the beginning of the algorithm, the nodes store a set of its neighbors' states. Since the algorithm is DFS based, the nodes use depth and low variables. Additionally, each node stores variables for its parent IDs, root state (a boolean variable that equals to true if it is root, otherwise it is false), cut vertex state (whether it is cut vertex or not) and the algorithmic state (the state variable used during the execution of the DENCUT algorithm). A neighbor state of a node can either in BACK_CHILD, CHILD, BACK_NODE, UNVISITED and PARENT states. Initially, all neighbors of nodes are in UNVISITED state.

The parent of a node will be in PARENT state. Similarly, the children of a node are set to CHILD state. If a node gathers a BACKTRACK from its child, it assigns the state of this child to BACK_CHILD. If a BACKTRACK message is overheard by a node from one of its children that is not in CHILD or PARENT states, it sets this child's state to BACK_NODE state.

BACKTRACK, DISCOVER, FINISH and START messages are used in the DENCUT algorithm. START message is utilized to initiate the approach by the sink. Each node initializes its variables after this message is received. DISCOVER messages are sent by a node which has found an undiscovered neighbor as operated in the distributed DFS algorithm. FINISH message is sent from a leaf node when it receives a DISCOVER message. BACKTRACK message is transmitted by a node which does not have any CHILD neighbor.

An example operation for the DENCUT is given in Figure 6. The initial network showing the nodes and communication links are given in Figure 6.a. There are 10 nodes in the network and node 0 is the root of the DFS tree which will start the neighbor discovery process (the sink node that is not depicted in the figure, sends a START message to node 0 to trigger the execution of the DENCUT algorithm). The final status of the network after executing the DENCUT algorithm is depicted in Figure 6.b. The arcs show the parents of the nodes. Depth and low values of each node are written with d and l letters, respectively in the figure. Cut vertices are filled in blue. Nodes 3, 4, 5 and 9 are identified as cut vertices in this example after processing the DENCUT algorithm. The edges (0,9), (8,9), (7,9), (4,6), (3,4), (3,7), (4,5), (1,5) and (2,3) are classified as DFS tree edges. Other edges, (6,9), (3,6) are non-tree edges.

3. ALGORITHMS FOR *k*-CONNECTIVITY ESTIMATION

The stability estimation of connections (SECO) algorithm in (Akram-1, 2018) tries to find the maximum possible node-disjoint DFS trees in a WSN. Since the nodes in the detected depth-first trees are disjoint, each detected DFS tree will be a disjoint path between all nodes in the network. The number of detected DFS trees can be considered as an estimation of k value of the given WSN. The SECO uses two kinds of messages named Forward and Backward messages to find disjoint DFS trees in the network. In the SECO, the sink node starts the distributed DFS operation by selecting a neighbor node, say node z, and broadcasting a Forward $(1,0,z)$ where 1 is the number of current DFS, 0 is the hop value and z is the ID of the target node. The hop value is used to determine how many nodes are already added to the DFS. After gathering a Forward message each node accumulates the sender in a local set named R to avoid sending the same Forward to that node because it already participates in the DFS tree. Node z, as the target of Forward message, increases the node count of the tree, selects a neighbor say node w, and multicasts Forward$(1,1,w)$. This process continues until the target receiver of Forward message has no unvisited neighbors. The node u cannot continue the Forward sending process if it's all neighbor's already broadcasted Forward message. In this situation, node u transmits a Backward to its parent nodes (the node who has sent Forward to node u). The Backward messages include the visited node count in the DFS tree. In this manner, the parent nodes are able to know the count of visited nodes in their subtrees and can pass the sum of these values to their parent. So, the parent nodes can determine how many nodes have already been added to the tree and how many nodes remain unvisited.

After receiving a Backward message, the node returns Backward to its parent if it has no unvisited neighbor. Otherwise, the node sends Forward to its unvisited neighbor. This operation goes on till all vertices are added to the DFS tree and the base station (the sink) node receives backward from its all neighbors. After receiving the Backward from all neighbor nodes, if the count of covered vertices in the backward messages is same with the count of available nodes in the network then the established DFS tree has already passed over all nodes and we have found disjoint paths. In this case, the base station increases the DFS tree number and broadcasts a new Forward (2,0,z) message where z has not sent Backward (is not a direct child of sink) in the previous tour. In the second tour, each receiver of Forward, say node u, ignores its children in the previous phase and tries to send Forward messages to the nodes who have not sent Backward to u in the previous phase. In this way, the second established DFS tree will use disjoint edges from the previous DFS tree. The algorithm continues in this way until the last established DFS tree does not cover all the nodes. In this case, the total count for visited vertices in the returned Backward messages to the sink node will not equal to the network's node count. In this way, the sink node gets notified that the last DFS tree establishment is unsuccessful and terminates the algorithm. The number of established DFS trees will be considered as an estimation of the k value of the network. Figure 7 shows a 2-connected network and two possible DFS trees in this network. The directions of arrow are from child nodes to the parent node. In this sample, the number of detected paths is equal to the k value of the network however the algorithm may find less than k DFS tree in the network.

Figure 7. Establishing two disjoint DFS tree in a sample network

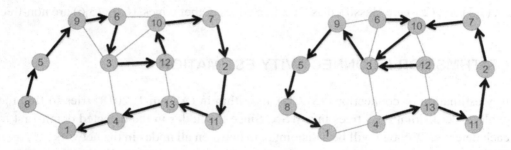

The SECO algorithm may construct at most k DFS trees. For establishing a DFS tree, a node may send at most Δ1 Forward and 1 Backward message (where Δ is the maximum node degree). Both Forward and Backward messages carry $O(\log_2 n)$ bit data. Therefore, the bit complexity of SECO algorithm is $O(n\Delta k \log_2 n)$. A DFS tree can be established in $O(n)$ time unit therefore the time complexity of SECO algorithm is $O(nk)$. The space complexity is $O(\Delta)$ since a node keeps the set of its children in the previous phases to escape transmitting Forward to them in next phases. The maximum count for children in each node is limited by Δ. The proposed algorithm in (Akram-2,2018) obtains a lower and upper limit for the k value and takes their average as an estimation for the general k value. In any graph, the minimum node degree δ is an upper limit for the k value since deleting δ nodes disconnects at least one node.

In the proposed local neighborhood information for k-connectivity estimation (NIKE) the nodes send their degree as upper limit of the k value to the sink. For the lower bound each node constructs its 2-hop subgraph and obtains its k value. In any k-connected network, the k value of the 2-hop subgraph of at least one node will be less than or at most equal to the k value of the general graph. So, if all nodes obtain the k of their subgraphs, at least one of the detected values will be less than the k value of the general graph. In NIKE, the sink initiates the approach by multicasting a Start that is remulticasted by the other nodes. Based on the number of received Start messages the nodes obtain their degrees. Also, each node transmits its neighbor list to its neighbors that lets the node to form their 2-hop subgraphs. After finding the *k* value of subgraph, the nodes send their degree as upper bound and their local *k* as lower bound for *k* to the sink node over multi hop connections. The intermediate nodes combine the gathered data from the other nodes by selecting the highest value of the received lower bounds and the smallest value of the received upper bound. In this way, the number of sent messages in the network will be bounded by the number of nodes because each node sends exactly one message containing the lower and upper bounds. However, broadcasting the entire neighbors list increase the bit complexity of the algorithm to $O(n\Delta k \log_2 n)$. The time complexity of the NIKE algorithm is $O(n)$ because a Start message is flooded to the network in $O(n)$ time and the estimations are returned in the reverse direction in $O(n)$ time.

Figure 8a. A sample 2-connected network and its BFS tree rooted by node 1.

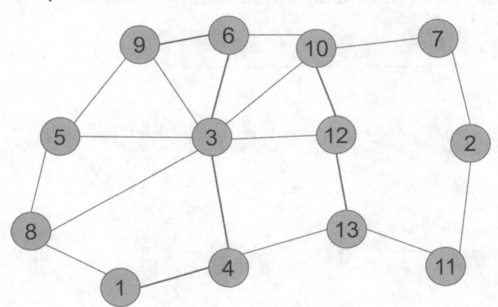

The proposed algorithm in (Akram-3,2018) establishes a BFS tree and estimates the *k* value based on the node count in each level of BFS and the minimum degree of nodes. Like the NIKE algorithm, BFS estimates an upper limit for the *k* value based on the degree and node count in the narrowest level in the tree. In each BFS tree, removing all nodes from any layer of the tree disconnects all paths between the adjacent level. Finding the layer with the minimum node count and removing the nodes from that level causes to a disjoint graph. Therefore, the number of nodes in the narrowest layer can be utilized as an estimation of the upper limit of the *k* value in the general graph. Also, the minimum node degree is another upper bound for the *k*. So, the BFS algorithm finds both the minimum degree and the node count in the narrowest level and takes their minimum value.

The sink node initiates the BFSK algorithm by multicasting a Forward message that is rebroadcasted by the other nodes to construct a BFS tree. In the backward phase, all nodes send their degree and the level number in the tree to their parent. The parent nodes combine the received data from their children by taking the minimum of nodes degree and node count in the next level. This data is returned to the sink and the sink takes the minimum of smallest degree and the smallest node count in a level as the *k* value. Figure 8.a depicts a 2-connected graph and Figure 8.b shows the BFS tree of this network rooted by node 1. The BFSK algorithm finds the *k* value of this graph by taking the minimum of node degrees (which is 3) and the number of nodes in the narrowest level (level 1) which is 2. Therefore, the algorithm finds the correct *k*=2.

Figure 8b.

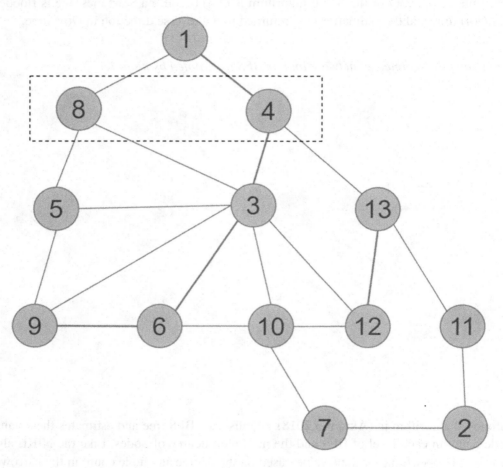

The bit complexity of establishing a BFS tree, which is dominant task in the BFSK algorithm, is $O(mn \log_2 n)$. Therefore, the bit complexity of the BFSK algorithm is $O(mn \log_2 n)$. The time complexity of the BFSK algorithm is $O(D^2)$ because the nodes in each level send their estimations to sink from the last level up to first level.

The proposed algorithm in (Dagdeviren, 2017), uses disjoint paths to estimate the *k* value of the network. The path coloring based *k*-connectivity detection algorithm (PACK) obtains the *k* by detecting the number of disjoint paths between the sink and the other remaining nodes. PACK has two general phases which are the Detection and Notification phases. In the Detection phase, each node finds the disjoint path count between itself and the sink node. In the Notification phase, the minimum number of detected path count is determined and is transmitted to the sink. The minimum number of detected path count is regarded as an estimation of the k value.

PACK uses an edge coloring schema to detect the disjoint paths between the sink and the other remaining nodes. Initially, the sink node assigns a separate color to each neighbor. The neighbors multicast the received colors to their neighbors. Each node that gathers a color from an uncolored edge, marks the edge with that color and increases its disjoint path count by 1. The nodes ignore upcoming redundant colors or incoming colors from colored edges. Since the nodes accept only one color from each edge, the number of accepted colors by each node will be a lower bound for the disjoint path count among that node and the sink. Videlicet, if node u accepts 3 colors from their neighbors, then it has at least 3 disjoint paths to the sink node. After finishing the detection phase, the nodes transmit their accepted color count to the sink and the sink chooses the smallest received value as an estimation to the k value. Using the coloring schema, some nodes may miss their existing paths to the sink. Therefore, the found k value can be smaller than the actual k value of the network. However, PACK never overestimates the k because the proposed coloring method guarantees that the nodes cannot overestimate the disjoint path count to the sink node.

In the Detection Phase each node may receive at most Δ colors where Δ is the maximum node degree. If all nodes accept all incoming messages and rebroadcast them then the total number of broadcasted messages in the Detection phase will be $O(\Delta n)$. Each color message carries $O(\log_2 n)$ bits. Therefore, the bit complexity of the algorithm in the Detection phase is $O(\Delta n \log_2 n)$. In the Notification phase, the nodes transmit their accepted color count to the sink which leads to $O(n)$ messages in total. Considering that each message carries the color count and the ID of node, the bit complexity of algorithm in Notification phase is $O(n \log_2 n)$. Hence, the overall bit complexity of the PACK is $O(\Delta n \log_2 n)$. In the PACK algorithm the color messages are broadcasted to the entire network at the same time that causes to $O(D)$ time but accepting all colors and returning the accepted color count to the sink may take $O(n)$ time unit. Therefore, the time complexity of PACK algorithm is $O(n)$.

The proposed algorithm in (Akram-4,2018), detects the exact value of the given WSN by sending more messages. The distributed exact k-connectivity detection algorithm (DECK) obtains the k value of a given network in 3 stages. In the first stage, the sink node begins the approach by multicasting a Hello message. Each node that gathers a Hello for the first time multicasts the message to its neighbors. In this manner, the nodes learn their 1-hop neighbor lists. Then, the nodes multicast their detected 1-hop neighbor lists to their neighbors which allows them to form their 2-hop subgraphs. Using this 2-hop local subgraph, each node predicts a k value by finding the k value of its subgraph. These estimated values generally will be less than the global k. In the second stage, a distributed linked list is constructed among the nodes which report the smallest k values. In the third stage, the sink finds the number of disjoint paths between itself and the nodes that report minimum local k values. In this way, the correctness of the estimated values is validated. If the disjoint path count between the sink and a node is equal to the estimated value by that node then the estimated value is correct, and the algorithm terminates by reporting the exact value. Otherwise, if the detected path count is bigger than the second smallest estimated value, the sink finds the count of disjoint paths to the nodes that have reported the second smallest k value. This process continues until the exact value is detected. The bit and time complexity of DECK is $O(n^2 k \log_2 n)$ and $O(n^2 k)$ respectively, which is considerably higher than other k-connectivity detection approaches. However, DECK can find the exact k value of the network while all other algorithms provide an estimation for it.

The proposed *k*-connectivity estimation using independent paths (KEIP) completely relies on the number of disjoint paths between the nodes (Dagdeviren-1,2019). In this method, a special case of disjoint paths, named independent paths, are defined which may have common nodes. Two paths are called independent if we can extract disjoint paths from them. In other words, independent paths are paths with possible common nodes that can generate disjoint paths. The proposed relations in the KEIP algorithm allow the node to differentiate the independent paths. In the KEIP algorithm, the sink node multicasts a path message to allows the other nodes to find the existing paths to the sink node. Each node that gathers a path message attaches its ID to the end of the path and multicasts the path to their neighbors. If the received new paths are completely disjoint from the previously accepted paths or if node *u* can generate disjoint paths from the incoming paths by attaching the nodes in right and left-hand sides of the paths, it accepts the path and rebroadcasts it to the neighbor nodes. In this way, all nodes will accept some of the received path messages and estimate their disjoint paths to the sink node. Finally, all nodes send their accepted path count to the sink and the sink node chooses the smallest value as the *k* of the general network.

By using the concept of the independent paths, the KEIP algorithm may find more close estimation to the *k* value of the graph. However, since all nodes attach their ID to the path messages, the size of multicasted messages can reach to $O(n \log_2 n)$ bits. In the worst case, all nodes may accept and multicast the incoming message from their neighbors which may lead to $O(n\Delta)$ paths. Therefore, the worst-case bit complexity of the algorithm will be $O(n^2 \Delta \log_2 n)$ which is higher than the other estimation approaches. The time complexity of the KEIP algorithm is $O(n)$ because all path messages are broadcasted simultaneously by the nodes.

4. CONCLUSION

Internet of Things (IoT) is a network of vast quantity of nodes that are equipped with different software and hardware abilities communicating through Internet infrastructure for accomplishing common objectives. Faults on nodes may break down the communication paths and may consume network wide resources. So, monitoring and controlling the connectivity of IoT infrastructures are very important. WSNs are essential IoT technologies that reside at the communication layer of IoT. Maintaining the connectivity of a WSN is of utmost importance to provide data transfer for IoT applications.

In this chapter, we studied on the connectivity estimation algorithms for IoT enabled WSNs. Firstly, we worked on the 1-connectivity estimation problem by dissecting cut vertex and bridge detection algorithms. Within this scope, we investigated Pritchard, I-PRITCHARD, ENBRIDGE, Milic and E-MILIC algorithms in terms of bridge identification with sample applications in detail. Additionally, we studied on DENCUT algorithm for cut vertex detection problem in 1-connected networks. Following to the 1-connectivity estimation, we worked on *k*-connectivity estimation problem in WSNs. Estimating the *k* value of a network is very important for finding important network parameters such as minimum node degree and disjoint path count between nodes. We described various *k*-connectivity estimation algorithms such as SECO, NIKE, PACK, DECK and KEIP with their main ideas and sample operations in various networks.

Integration of the connectivity estimation algorithms with other graph theoretic structure such as matching, independent set and vertex cover is an interesting future research subject. This integration will decrease the total resource consumption of connectivity estimation and graph theoretic structure construction. Design and implementation of self-stabilizing connectivity estimation algorithms is appealing for fault-tolerant WSNs in which node and edge leaves/joins are present. In this manner, the connectivity value of the network will be converged by the algorithm in a finite amount of time. Determining the lower bounds for time, message, bit and computational complexities of fully distributed and asynchronous k-connectivity estimation algorithms is also a very important future research thread. These complexity bounds will guide the algorithm designers theoretically. Finally, implementing connectivity estimation algorithms on different testbeds will be beneficial for researchers to measure their practical performance for various IoT applications.

REFERENCES

Akram, V. K., & Dagdeviren, O. (2013). Breadth-first search-based single-phase algorithms for bridge detection in wireless sensor networks. *Sensors (Basel)*, *13*(7), 8786–8813. doi:10.3390130708786 PMID:23845930

Akram, V. K., Arapoglu, O., & Dagdeviren, O. (2018). A Depth-First Search based Connectivity Estimation Approach for Fault Tolerant Wireless Sensor Networks. *2018 International Conference on Artificial Intelligence and Data Processing (IDAP)*, 1-6. 10.1109/IDAP.2018.8620883

Akram, V. K., & Dagdeviren, O. (2018). k-Connectivity Estimation from Local Neighborhood Information in Wireless Ad Hoc and Sensor Networks. *2018 IEEE International Black Sea Conference on Communications and Networking (BlackSeaCom)*, 1-5. 10.1109/BlackSeaCom.2018.8433701

Akram, V. K., Asci, M., & Dagdeviren, O. (2018). Design and Analysis of a Breadth First Search based Connectivity Robustness Estimation Approach in Wireless Sensor Networks. *2018 6th International Conference on Control Engineering & Information Technology (CEIT)*, 1-6. 10.1109/CEIT.2018.8751850

Akram, V. K., & Dagdeviren, O. (2018). DECK: A distributed, asynchronous and exact k-connectivity detection algorithm for wireless sensor networks. *Computer Communications*, *116*, 9–20. doi:10.1016/j.comcom.2017.11.005

Akram, V. K., Dagdeviren, O., & Tavli, B. (2021). Distributed k-connectivity restoration for fault tolerant wireless sensor and actuator networks: Algorithm design and experimental evaluations. *IEEE Transactions on Reliability*, *70*(3), 1112–1125. doi:10.1109/TR.2020.2970268

Akyildiz, I. F., Su, W., Sankarasubramaniam, Y., & Cayirci, E. (2002). Wireless sensor networks: a survey. *Computer Networks, 38*(4), 393-422.

Al-Karaki, J. N., & Gawanmeh, A. (2017). The optimal deployment, coverage and connectivity problems in wireless sensor networks: Revisited. *IEEE Access: Practical Innovations, Open Solutions*, *5*, 18051–18065. doi:10.1109/ACCESS.2017.2740382

Alemdar, H., & Ersoy, C. (2010). Wireless sensor networks for healthcare: A survey. *Computer Networks, 54*(15), 2688-2710.

Arampatzis, T., Lygeros, J., & Manesis, S. (2005). A Survey of Applications of Wireless Sensors and Wireless Sensor Networks. *Proceedings of the 2005 IEEE International Symposium on, Mediterrean Conference on Control and Automation Intelligent Control*, 719-724. 10.1109/.2005.1467103

Balaji, S., Nathani, K., & Santhakumar, R. (2019). IoT Technology, Applications and Challenges: A Contemporary Survey. *Wireless Personal Communications*, *108*(1), 363–388. doi:10.100711277-019-06407-w

Bredin, J. L., Demaine, E. D., Hajiaghayi, M. T., & Rus, D. (2010). Deploying sensor networks with guaranteed fault tolerance. *IEEE/ACM Transactions on Networking*, *18*(1), 216–228. doi:10.1109/TNET.2009.2024941

Censor-Hillel, K., Ghaffari, M., & Kuhn, F. (2014). Distributed connectivity decomposition. *Proc. ACM Symp. Principl. Distrib. Comput. (PODC)*, 56–165.

Dagdeviren, O., & Akram, V. K. (2013). Energy-efficient bridge detection algorithms for wireless sensor networks. *International Journal of Distributed Sensor Networks*, *9*(4), 867903. doi:10.1155/2013/867903

Dagdeviren, O., & Akram, V. K. (2014). An energy-efficient distributed cut vertex detection algorithm for wireless sensor networks. *The Computer Journal*, *57*(12), 1852–1869. doi:10.1093/comjnl/bxt128

Dagdeviren, O., Akram, V. K., Tavli, B., Yildiz, H. U., & Atilgan, C. (2016). Distributed detection of critical nodes in wireless sensor networks using connected dominating set. *IEEE SENSORS*, *1-3*, 2016. doi:10.1109/ICSENS.2016.7808815

Dagdeviren, O., & Akram, V. K. (2017). PACK: Path coloring based k-connectivity detection algorithm for wireless sensor networks. *Ad Hoc Networks*, *64*, 41-52.

Dagdeviren, O., & Akram, V. K. (2019). KEIP: A distributed k-connectivity estimation algorithm based on independent paths for wireless sensor networks. *Wireless Networks*, *25*(8), 4479–4491. doi:10.100711276-018-1739-7

Dagdeviren, O., Akram, V. K., & Farzan, A. (2019). A Distributed Evolutionary algorithm for detecting minimum vertex cuts for wireless ad hoc and sensor networks. *Journal of Network and Computer Applications*, *127*, 70-81. doi:10.1016/j.jnca.2018.10.009

Dai, F., & Wu, J. (2005) On Constructing k-connected k-dominating Set in Wireless Networks. In *Proc. 19th Int. Parallel and Distributed Processing Symposium (IPDPS)*. IEEE. 10.1109/IPDPS.2005.302

Deniz, F., Bagci, H., Korpeoglu, I., & Yazici, A. (2016). An adaptive, energy-aware and distributed fault-tolerant topology-control algorithm for heterogeneous wireless sensor networks. *Ad Hoc Networks*, *44*, 104–117. doi:10.1016/j.adhoc.2016.02.018

Giri, A., Dutta, S., Neogy, S., Dahal, K., & Pervez, Z. (2017). Internet of things (IoT): a survey on architecture, enabling technologies, applications and challenges. In *Proceedings of the 1st International Conference on Internet of Things and Machine Learning (IML '17)*. Association for Computing Machinery. 10.1145/3109761.3109768

Henzinger, M. R., Rao, S., & Gabow, H. N. (2000). Computing vertex connectivity: New bounds from old techniques. *Journal of Algorithms*, *34*(2), 222–250. doi:10.1006/jagm.1999.1055

Jorgic, M., Goel, N., Kalaichevan, K., Nayak, A., & Stojmenovic, I. (2007). Localized detection of k-connectivity in wireless ad hoc, actuator and sensor networks. *Proceedings of 16th International Conference on Computer Communications and Networks, ICCCN 2007*, 33-38. 10.1109/ICCCN.2007.4317793

Jino Ramson, S. R., & Moni, D. J. (2017). Applications of wireless sensor networks - A survey. *International Conference on Innovations in Electrical, Electronics, Instrumentation and Media Technology (ICEEIMT)*, 325-329. 10.1109/ICIEEIMT.2017.8116858

Lee, S. K., Bae, M., & Kim, H. (2017). Future of IoT Networks: A Survey. *Applied Sciences (Basel, Switzerland)*, 7(10), 1072. doi:10.3390/app7101072

Li, J., Andrew, L. L., Foh, C. H., Zukerman, M., & Chen, H.-H. (2009). Connectivity, coverage and placement in wireless sensor networks. *Sensors (Basel)*, 9(10), 7664–7693. doi:10.339091007664 PMID:22408474

Ling, Q., & Tian, Z. (2007). Minimum node degree and *k*-connectivity of a wireless multihop network in bounded area. *IEEE Global Telecommunications Conference. GLOBECOM'07*, 1296-1301. 10.1109/GLOCOM.2007.249

Milic, B., & Malek, M. (2007). Adaptation of the breadth first search algorithm for cut-edge detection in wireless multihop networks. *Proceedings of the 10th ACM Symposium on Modeling, Analysis, and Simulation of Wireless and Mobile Systems (MSWiM '07)*, 377–386.

Paradis, L., & Han, Q. (2007). A Survey of Fault Management in Wireless Sensor Networks. *Journal of Network and Systems Management*, 15(2), 171–190. doi:10.100710922-007-9062-0

Pritchard, D. (2006). An optimal distributed bridge-finding algorithm. *Proceedings of the 25th Annual ACM SIGACT-SIGOPS Symposium on Principles of Distributed Computing (PODC '06)*.

Raei, H., Tabibzadeh, M., Ahmadipoor, B., & Saei, S. (2009). A Self-Stabilizing Distributed Algorithm for Minimum Connected Dominating Sets in Wireless Sensor Networks with Different Transmission Ranges. *Proc. 11th Int. Conf. on Advanced Communication Technology, ICACT'09*, 1, 526–530.

Rawat, P., Singh, K. D., Chaouchi, H., & Bonnin, J. M. (2014). Wireless sensor networks: A survey on recent developments and potential synergies. *The Journal of Supercomputing*, 68(1), 1–48. doi:10.100711227-013-1021-9

Rehman, H. U., Asif, M., & Ahmad, M. (2017). Future applications and research challenges of IOT. *2017 International Conference on Information and Communication Technologies (ICICT)*, 68-74. 10.1109/ICICT.2017.8320166

Szczytowski, P., Khelil, A., & Suri, N. (2012). DKM: Distributed k-connectivity maintenance in wireless sensor networks. *Proc. Annual Conf. Wireless On-Demand Netw. Syst. Serv. (WONS)*, 83–90.

Stojmenovic, I., Seddigh, M., & Zunic, J. (2002). Dominating sets and neighbor elimination-based broadcasting algorithms in wireless networks. *IEEE Transactions on Parallel and Distributed Systems*, 13(1), 14–25. doi:10.1109/71.980024

Xu, L. D., He, W., & Li, S. (2014). Internet of Things in Industries: A Survey. IEEE Transactions on Industrial Informatics, 10(4), 2233-2243. doi:10.1109/TII.2014.2300753

Yuanyuan, Z., Jia, X., & Yanxiang, H. (2006). Energy Efficient Distributed Connected Dominating Sets Construction in Wireless Sensor Networks. *Proc. 2006 Int. Conf. on Wireless Communications and Mobile Computing, IWCMC'06*, 797–802. 10.1145/1143549.1143709

Yugha, R., & Chithra, S. (2020). A survey on technologies and security protocols: Reference for future generation IoT. *Journal of Network and Computer Applications*, 169.

Zhu, C., Zheng, C., Shu, L., & Han, G. (2012). A survey on coverage and connectivity issues in wireless sensor networks. *Journal of Network and Computer Applications*, 35(2), 619–632.

Chapter 7
Machine Learning Techniques for IoT-Based Indoor Tracking and Localization

Pelin Yildirim Taser

https://orcid.org/0000-0002-5767-2700

Izmir Bakircay University, Turkey

Vahid Khalilpour Akram

Ege University, Turkey

ABSTRACT

The GPS signals are not available inside the buildings; hence, indoor localization systems rely on indoor technologies such as Bluetooth, WiFi, and RFID. These signals are used for estimating the distance between a target and available reference points. By combining the estimated distances, the location of the target nodes is determined. The wide spreading of the internet and the exponential increase in small hardware diversity allow the creation of the internet of things (IoT)-based indoor localization systems. This chapter reviews the traditional and machine learning-based methods for IoT-based positioning systems. The traditional methods include various distance estimation and localization approaches; however, these approaches have some limitations. Because of the high prediction performance, machine learning algorithms are used for indoor localization problems in recent years. The chapter focuses on presenting an overview of the application of machine learning algorithms in indoor localization problems where the traditional methods remain incapable.

INTRODUCTION

The popularity of the Internet, smartphones, and different kinds of wireless devices has enabled the provision of new services such as indoor localization and tracking systems. Indoor localization is the process of detecting the real-time location of wireless devices in an indoor environment with a bounded error rate. Indoor localization and tracking of mobile objects have extensive and increasing applications in dif-

DOI: 10.4018/978-1-7998-4186-9.ch007

ferent fields such as healthcare, advertisements, marketing, monitoring, security, building management, surveillance, and warehousing (Karimpour, 2019)(Khelifi, 2019). For example, in a hospital, tracking the assets, patients, and medical staff can increase the service quality and lead to efficient resource planning. As another example, the indoor localization of customers in a big shopping center can help send more efficient advertisements and analyze customers' behavior and shopping interests. Finally, the indoor localization of assets in a big warehouse can help to find the assets or free spaces faster and simpler.

The GPS signals are not available inside the buildings; hence the indoor tracking and localization systems try to use other signals such as Bluetooth Low Energy (BLE), WiFi, RFID, Wireless Sensor Networks (WSN), and Ultra-Wide Band signals (UWB). Receiving the signals from different sources allows the localization systems to merge the information and estimate the location of target assets. Recent advances in wireless communication modules, low energy BLE modules, sensors, memory chips, and processors have emerged a new generation of small and powerful devices that can store and run programs, measure the signal's strength and communicate over radio channels. The wide spreading of the Internet and the exponential increase in the diversity of small hardware allow us to create a network of devices that communicate over the Internet and form an Internet of Things (IoT). The IoT-based tracking systems allow the real-time positioning and monitoring of different assets. The precision of available localization systems generally depends on the underlying hardware and localization method. This chapter reviews the traditional and machine learning-based methods for IoT-based positioning systems and discusses their challenges and limitations.

An ideal indoor localization system should determine the exact location of the desired number of mobile targets inside a large building with minimal energy consumption, small mobile devices, and low cost. The main properties of an ideal indoor localization system are as follow:

1. **Accuracy:** Accuracy is the most important property of an indoor localization system. An ideal localization system detects the exact and real-time coordinates of the mobile targets using the available anchor points. Developing accurate indoor localization systems is a hard challenge because wireless signals are affected by different obstacles in the environment, which leads to incorrect distance estimation. Different methods are available to increase the accuracy of indoor localization systems; however each approach has some limitations and disadvantages. For example, increasing the number of anchor points may help increase the accuracy but also increase the cost and energy consumption of the system.

2. **Cost:** Generally, a localization system consists of many anchors and mobile nodes that communicate over radio channels. The anchor nodes are distributed in the environment in predefined (known) locations, and the mobile nodes are attached to the mobile target assets. The recent advances in hardware and IoT devices have led to the production of small, low-cost, and energy-efficient devices useful in indoor localization systems.

3. **Energy Efficiency:** Generally, indoor localization systems are expected to work for a long time. In some approaches, the nodes are battery-powered, and the batteries should be replaced periodically. Different approaches have different battery-replacing periods. In some approaches, the nodes can work with a battery for many years, while in some other approaches, the batteries should be recharged every day. Therefore, energy efficiency is an important factor of a localization system that directly affects the quality of provided services.

4. **Size:** To track and locate the mobile assets in the environment, a device should be attached to the assets. Such a device should be able to send or receive the radio signals and may have some pro-

cessing and memory units. Generally, attaching extra hardware to the assets affects the usability of the system. In some cases, attaching an extra tracking device to mobile assets is simply impossible. For example, it is hard to attach a device to the medical staff or patients to track them in a hospital. In these cases, the localization system should track their smartphones or use other approaches such as image or video processing. By wide-spreading of mobile phones, most of the recently developed localization systems track the mobile phones to locate the people in the environment.

5. **Scalability:** An ideal localization system should be able to locate and track any number of mobile targets in the entire environment. However, due to various reasons such as cost, energy consumption, communication bound, channel capacity, packets interferences, and harsh environments, tracking many assets in the entire environment can be complicated. For example, sometimes placing anchors in desired places in a building is impossible, which creates a blind spot in the system. As another example, locating a large number of mobile assets in a bounded area inside a building increases packet interference and affects the system's accuracy.

In the remaining parts of this chapter, we will examine the recent technologies and methods that are used in the localization systems.

Existing Studies and Technologies for IoT-Based Localization

Recent advances in the production of small IoT devices have led to the generation of efficient low cost, low energy, and multipurpose hardware such as Arduino, RasperiPy, Node MCU, and different wireless modules such as Bluetooth, WiFi, and Ultra Wide Band (UWB). These modules can be used as building blocks of localization systems. This section provides a brief survey about the available technologies for localization systems. Most of the available indoor localization systems are developed based on the Received Signal Strength Indicator (RSSI). The Received Signal Strength (RSS) is the power strength of the received radio signal on the receiver side. The RSS value is usually measured in decibel-milli-watts (dBm) or milli-Watts (mW) and can be used as a metric to estimate the distance between the sender and receiver of the signal. Generally, the power strength of the signals is decreased while the signals are propagated in the environment. So, the receivers in the shorter distances of the sender get higher RSS values than the receivers in remote distances. In Figure 1, for example, if node S broadcasts a signal periodically, the expected received signal strength in node R1 will be higher than the received signal strength in R2.

Theoretically, the exact distance can be estimated from the received RSS value using the signal propagation model and the received signal power at a reference point. However, various factors can affect the signal strength and the correctness of the calculated distance. The RSSI value is a relative measurement of the signal strength in which the manufacture of the device defines its units. For example, the RSSI range of the produced WiFi module by the Atheros company is between 0 and 60, while the RSSI range in Cisco WiFi modules varies between 0 and 100. In the simple path-loss propagation model, the distance between sender and receiver can be calculated using the following relation:

$$RSSI = -10n \log_2 d + d_0 \tag{1}$$

Where d is the distance, n is the path loss factor and d_0 is the RSSI value at an initial distance to the sender. The path loss factor may differ between 2 in outdoor up to 4 in indoor environments. The path loss factor may differ between 2 in outdoor up to 4 in indoor environments. Relying on pure RSSI values generally leads to poor localization accuracy, especially if some obstacles, such as walls or big objects, change the signal strength between the sender and receiver. The obstacles usually affect the signal strength and reduce the accuracy of the estimated distance; hence some of the approaches need a line of sight (no obstacle) between sender and receiver. Usually, different filters, averaging mechanisms, and algorithms are used to increase the precision of the RSSI-based methods, which will be discussed in the following sections. The remaining part of this section discusses the available wireless technologies that can be used in localization systems.

Figure 1. The propagation of signal decreases its power strength

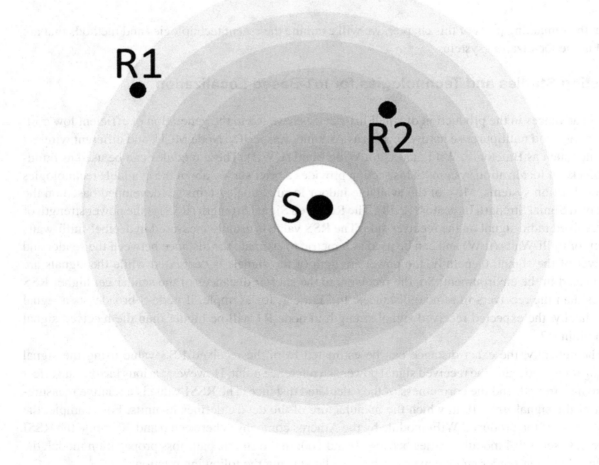

Radio Frequency Identification Device

Radio Frequency Identification Device (RFID) is primarily invented for storing and transferring electromagnetic data (Holm, 2009). An RFID system has at least one reader that can communicate with RFID tags. An RFID tag can hold a small amount of data that is readable by the RFID reader. Generally, there are Active and Passive RFID types. The Active RFID systems work in the Ultra High Frequency (UHF) and microwave frequency range. The tags are equipped by a power source (usually a small battery) in the active RFID systems and periodically transmit their ID and optional data. The readers can read the broadcasted data by the active tags from a far distance. Hence, Active RFID tags can be used for localization because they have a reasonable range and can be easily attached to the target assets. However, the active RFID technology may have a few meters error rate in the estimated distance, which is unacceptable in most applications. Passive RFID tags work without a battery and have a limited communication range (usually less than 5 m). The passive tags are smaller, lighter, and cheaper than the active tags and can work in the low, high, UHF, and microwave frequency range. The passive tags don't need the battery, but the limited range of passive tags considerably restricts their application in localization systems. Figure 2 shows a 2.4GHz-NRF24l01 active RFID module, some passive tags, and an RFID reader device.

Figure 2. (a) 2.4GHz-NRF24l01 Active RFID module, (b) Passive RFID tags, (c) Long range RFID reader

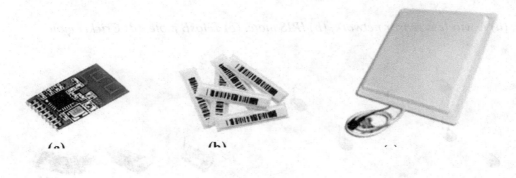

(a) (b) (c)

WiFi

WiFi is wireless networking technology based on the IEEE 802.11 standard, which is commonly used in local area networks to provide wireless internet connection for different devices. WiFi-based wireless networks usually have special hardware called access points that bridge between wireless devices and the underlying local area network. The indoor Access Points can work in 2.4 and 5 GHz frequencies and usually have a communication range between 20 up to 150 m. Almost all available smartphones, computers, and many other portable devices support WiFi, and WiFi signals are available in many buildings. Hence many researchers have focused on WiFi-based indoor localization systems (Ali, 2019)(Zafari, 2019). The propagated radio signals from the available WiFi access points in a building can be used as reference signals in localization systems. A simple localization system with reasonable accuracy can be built by comparing the RSSI of access points and setting the location of the target node near the access point with the highest RSSI. Efficient algorithms have been proposed in the literature that improves WiFi-based localization systems' accuracy to less than 1 m.

Wireless Sensor Network

Wireless sensor networks are generally used for sensing different quantities from the environment in different applications such as monitoring, automation, healthcare, and target tracking. Each node has at least a wireless communication module, a processor, and some memory for local processing in a wireless sensor network. The nodes communicate with remote nodes over multi-hop radio messages, and the sensed data usually are sent to a base station (sink node). The base station connects to a processing center and transfers the gathered data to a high-level application (Figure 3.a). Several standards, such as IEEE 802.15.4, Thread, and ZigBee, have been developed for wireless communication in wireless sensor networks. Most of these standards work at 2.4 GHz frequency with up to 250kbit/s data rate. The wireless sensor nodes, also called mote, are equipped with different sensors and devices to measure environmental conditions. For example, Figures 3.b, 3.c and 3.d show the IRIS, TelosB, and Cricket motes, respectively, manufactured by the MEMSİC company. The IRIS mote has an extension socket for attaching different sensors. The TelosB mote has built-in temperature, light, and humidity sensors. The Cricket motes have an ultrasound module to measure the distance between motes and obstacles.

Figure 3. (a) A wireless sensor network, (b) IRIS mote, (c) TelosB mote, (d) Cricket mote

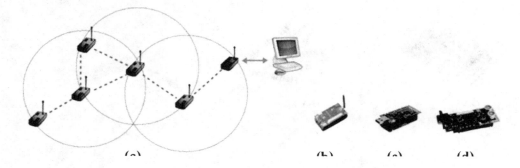

Almost all motes types in wireless sensor networks can measure the RSSI of the received signals. The received signal power can be used to estimate the distance between motes and locate the mobile nodes in the network area. However, in most applications (for example, in shopping centers or hospitals), attaching a sensor mote to the mobile entities (customers or patients) is impossible, which restricts the usage of wireless sensor networks in indoor localization.

Bluetooth

Bluetooth, which is also known as IEEE 802.15.1 standard, is a wireless technology for transferring data between devices using short-wavelength UHF radio waves from 2.400 to 2.485 GHz. Bluetooth includes the physical and MAC layers protocols and is currently used in a wide variety of electronic devices. The initial versions of Bluetooth standards suffer from high energy consumption; however, the recent version, known as Bluetooth Low Energy (BLE), consumes lower energy than the older versions, provides up to 24Mbps data rate, and has up to 100-meter coverage range (Zafari, 2019). Just like the other radio frequency-based technologies, the strength of Bluetooth signals goes down when the signal passes a long distance. Hence, the RSSI of Bluetooth signals is used in various localization solutions. Relying on pure RSSI limits its accuracy of localization; hence different methods and algorithms have been proposed to improve the accuracy of BLE-based systems. Apple has developed a BLE base localization solution known as iBeacons two BLE-based protocol in 2013 (Newman, 2014). Google rolled out an open-source solution called Eddystone in 2015 (Amadeo, 2015).

Figure 4. An iBeacon device

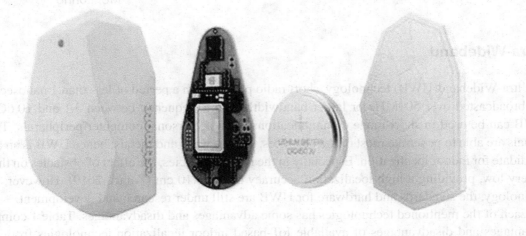

In the iBeacons and Eddystone solutions, a special BLE device periodically broadcasts BLE signals (beacons). Figure 4 shows an iBeacons beacon device. Each beacon message has a Universally Unique Identifier (UUID) field with 16 bytes length and an optional two bytes data. Any BLE device in the environment, can receive these beacon messages and estimates its distance to the beacon source using RSSI. The UUID and RSSI of the received beacon signals are sent to a server or a cloud by the mobile device. The application running in the server combines the received information and estimates the location of the mobile device. Different approaches can be used for combining the received information. In the simplest way, the server can calculate the weighted average of the iBeacon locations where the weight of each iBeacon is its RSSI. If the data transfer rate between a mobile device and the server is less than the period of beacon signals, the mobile device sends the average of received signals in the last period. For example, if the mobile device receives iBeacon signals every 50 ms and sends data to the server every 100 ms, the average of the last two RSSI will be sent to the server in each message. Figure 5 shows the general architecture of these approaches. The iBeacons and Eddystone solutions are currently used in different industrial and business applications.

Figure 5. General architecture of a BLE based system

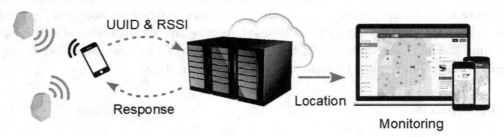

Ultra-Wideband

In Ultra-Wideband(UWB) technology, short radio pulses, with a period of less than 1 nanosecond (ns), are broadcasted over 500MHz or larger bandwidth with a frequency between 3.1 and 10.6GHz. The UWB can be used in short-range communications, such as personal computer peripherals. The UWB signals are able to penetrate most of the obstacles, such as walls and metals; hence UWB is an attractive candidate for indoor localization. Especially in the low frequencies, the effect of obstacles on the signals is very low, providing a high localization accuracy of up to 10 cm (Zafari, 2019). However, as a new technology, the standards and hardware for UWB are still under research and development.

Each of the mentioned technologies has some advantages and disadvantages. Table 1 compares the advantages and disadvantages of available IoT-based indoor localization technologies from different perspectives.

Table 1. Caption should be sentence case with no ending punctuation if only one sentence

Technology	Accuracy	Scalability	Power Consumption	Maximum Rang	Cost	Advantages	Disadvantages
RFID	1-5 m	Medium	Low	5 m	Low	Medium accuracy and low power consumption	Expensive readers. Short range
WiFi	1-10 m	High	Moderate	150 m	Low	Medium accuracy and no need for infrastructure in most cases	Very sensitive for noises
WSN	1-10 m	Medium	Moderate	150 m	Medium	Medium accuracy	Very sensitive for noises
Bluetooth	1-5 m	High	Low	100m	Low	Acceptable accuracy, low cost and low power consumption	Sensitive for noises
Ultra-Wideband	1-10 cm	Low	Moderate	10-20m	High	High accuracy	High cost, low range and low scalability

Traditional Methods

To increase the accuracy of the localization systems, many RSSI-based methods have been proposed by researchers. These methods use different properties of radio signals, and each one has some advantages and disadvantages. This section presents some of the most important traditional methods for indoor localization systems.

Fingerprinting

The idea behind the fingerprinting method is to build a map of the RSSI values for all possible locations of the target environment (Yiu, 2017). To create such a map, the indoor target area should be divided into regular cells, and the RSS of available signals should be recorded for each cell. After creating the radio map, the localization problem can be considered an optimization problem. The input is an RSS value of a mobile node with an unknown location, and the output is its estimated location using the previously recorded radio map. The location of the target node is calculated by a reverse mapping function that accepts the reported RSS by the mobile node and compares this value with the recorded values in the maps. Different methods have been proposed for calculating the location of a node using the RSSI and radio map. For example, in the Probabilistic methods, a likelihood value is calculated for each possible position in the area, and the location with the highest likelihood value is selected as the estimated location. Artificial Neural Networks, Support Vector Machine, and k-Nearest Neighbors are some of the other techniques that have been proposed for estimating the location from the given RSSI and a radio map. The fingerprinting method uses a grid-based model of the target area and can be applied to all types of radio signals such as BLE or WiFi. However, due to the underlying gird based model, the fingerprinting method provides discrete location estimation. Increasing the number of sample points on the map can help increase the accuracy, but if we take too many samples, the difference between recorded RSSI values in different locations will be small, leading to incorrect location estimations. Also, any environmental change, such as moving the obstacles or changing the location or transmission power of the signal sources, will dramatically affect the entire locating system because sampled signals on the radio map will not be valid after any environmental change. Figure 6 shows the general schema of the fingerprinting method.

Figure 6. General schema of fingerprinting method

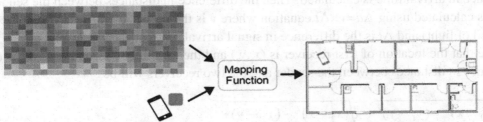

Angle of Arrival (AoA)

The angle of Arrival (AoA) based methods need a set of special antennas to estimate the angle of received signals (Rong, 2006). The receiver should be equipped with an array of antennas capable of calculating the angle of the received signal. After calculating the angle of the received signal by each antenna, the location of the signal source can be calculated using the detected angle, the time difference of signal arrival by different antennas, and the distance between antennas. The AoA can estimate the correct location of target nodes for the short distances or in the application that provides a line of sight between the sender and receiver. However, this method needs special hardware and precise calibration and synchronization between the receivers, which are not feasible in most applications. Also, it is hard to provide a line of sight between the sender and receiver in most indoor applications.

Time of Arrival

In the Time of Arrival (ToA) or Time of Flight (ToF) method, the receiver calculates the signal propagation time to estimate the distance to the sender (Aditya, 2018). Considering the $d=v{\times}t$ relation between distance (d, speed (v and time (t, if the receiver calculates the propagation time of the signal, it can find the distance to the sender because the propagation speed of radio signals is almost equal to the speed of light. The main drawback of the ToA method is the hardness of calculating the propagation time of the signals. To find the signal's propagation time, the sender can put the sent time of the signal in the message, and the receiver can calculate the difference between sent and received time. However, the sender and receiver clocks should be strictly synchronized because a very small difference between the clocks leads to incorrect estimation. Synchronizing the sender and receiver clocks is a hard task and is not feasible in most applications. Also, the possible obstacles between the sender and receiver can affect the signal propagation path and increase the propagation time. Therefore, besides clock synchronization, ToA needs a line of sight between sender and receiver, which is not feasible in most applications.

Time Difference of Arrival

he Time Difference of Arrival (TDoA) is similar to ToA, which uses the time difference of arrived signal instead of the signal sent time (McClelland, 2017). In the TDoA method, the sender does not attach any timestamp to the message, and the receivers record only the receiving time. This method needs to at least two receivers with strictly synchronized clocks. After receiving the signal at two receiver nodes, the difference in arrival time is calculated. Then the difference in distances between the sender and the receivers is calculated using $\Delta d=v{\times}\Delta t$ equation where v is the propagation speed (usually considered as the speed of light) and Δt is the difference in signal arrival times at each receiver.

Assume that the location of first receiver is (x_1,y_1) and the location of second receiver is (x_1,y_1). So the difference in distances between the sender and the two receivers will be

$$\Delta d = \sqrt{(x_1 - x)^2 - (y_1 - y)^2} - \sqrt{(x_2 - x)^2 - (y_2 - y)^2}$$

where (x,y) is the unknown location of signal's sender. By replacing Δd in the previous equation we get

$$\sqrt{(x_1 - x)^2 - (y_1 - y)^2} - \sqrt{(x_2 - x)^2 - (y_2 - y)^2} = v \times \Delta t .$$

In this equation, except the (x,y) we have the value of all variables. This equation can be converted to the hyperbola form and solved using nonlinear regression. Similar to the ToA, the TDoA needs strict synchronization between receiver nodes which is a hard task. The estimation accuracy in TDoA depends on the existence of obstacles, the line of sight between sender and receivers, and the precision of the synchronized clocks.

Trilateration

In the trilateration method, the location of the target node is determined by finding the distance to 3 reference points (Shchekotov, 2014). The target node receives the broadcasted signals from 3 reference senders with known locations and estimates the distance to that point using RSSI values. The intersection of the estimated distance determines the location of the target node. Figure 7 illustrates the location estimation in the trilateration method. In this figure, nodes A, B, and C are reference points with known locations. By receiving the broadcasted signal from these reference points, the target node estimates its distance to each point and selects the intersection of estimated distances as its location.

Figure 7. Calculating the target location using the Trilateration method

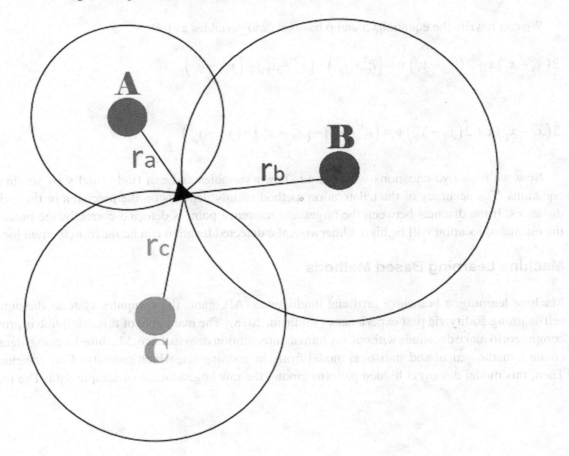

Assuming that the location of the target node is (x,y) we can find the intersection of estimated distances using the circle equation as follow:

$$\left(x_A - x\right)^2 - \left(y_A - y\right)^2 = r_a^2 \tag{2}$$

$$\left(x_B - x\right)^2 - \left(y_B - y\right)^2 = r_b^2 \tag{3}$$

$$\left(x_C - x\right)^2 - \left(y_C - y\right)^2 = r_c^2 \tag{4}$$

By removing both sides of equations 2 and 3 from equation 4 we will have:

$$\left(x_A - x\right)^2 - \left(x_C - x\right)^2 + \left(y_A - y\right)^2 - \left(y_C - y\right)^2 = r_A^2 - r_C^2 \tag{5}$$

$$\left(x_B - x\right)^2 - \left(x_C - x\right)^2 + \left(y_B - y\right)^2 - \left(y_C - y\right)^2 = r_B^2 - r_C^2 \tag{6}$$

We can rewrite the equations 5 and 6 base on (x,y) variables as follow:

$$2\left(x_3 - x_1\right)x + 2\left(y_3 - y_1\right)y = \left(r_1^2 - r_3^2\right) - \left(x_1^2 - x_3^2\right) - \left(y_1^2 - y_3^2\right) \tag{7}$$

$$2\left(x_3 - x_2\right)x + 2\left(y_3 - y_2\right)y = \left(r_2^2 - r_3^2\right) - \left(x_2^2 - x_3^2\right) - \left(y_2^2 - y_3^2\right) \tag{8}$$

Now we have two equations with two unknown variables and can find x and y by solving these equations. The accuracy of the trilateration method mainly depends on the precision of the estimated distances. If the distance between the target and reference point is detected correctly, the precision of the estimated location will be high. Otherwise, the detected location can be far from the real location.

Machine Learning Based Methods

Machine learning, a branch of artificial intelligence (AI), gains the computer systems the automatic self-learning ability via past experiences (Yildirim, 2018). The main goal of this discipline is providing computers to make decisions without any human intervention or assistance. Machine learning algorithms create a mathematical and statistical model from the training set, which consists of observation data. Then, this model discovers hidden patterns among the raw huge amount of sample data. The machine learning tasks are categorized into two main types: supervised learning and unsupervised learning, as shown in Figure 8.

Figure 8. Types of machine learning

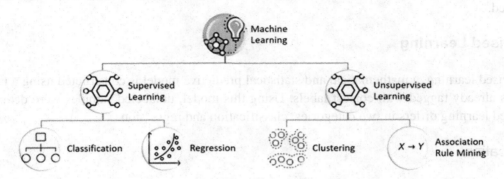

Because most of the traditional approaches have limited precision for target localization, the machine learning algorithms have started to be implemented in indoor localization problems in recent years by providing high prediction performance. The following figure demonstrates the general architecture of the indoor localization estimation system using machine learning algorithms.

Figure 9. The general architecture of a machine learning based indoor localization system

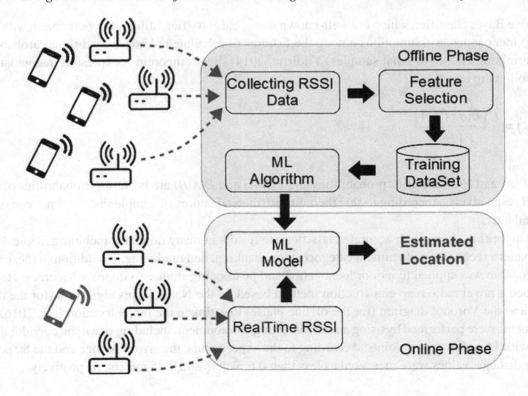

As shown in figure 9, in the offline phase, location data obtained from the access points are collected. Then, the irrelevant attributes of the records that affect estimating the sample's location are determined and eliminated in the feature selection step. Afterward, the selected ML algorithm was trained using the training data set constructed after the feature selection step. In the online phase, a new real-time RSSI data was given to the ML model as an input to estimate its location, and the estimated location value is determined.

Supervised Learning

In supervised learning, a mathematical and statistical predictive model is constructed using a raw data set that is already tagged with correct labels. Using this model, unlabeled samples were determined. Supervised learning differs in two categories: classification and regression.

Classification

The most known and commonly used supervised learning method is classification. This method categorizes new unlabeled samples into predefined classes. The classification algorithms try to discover relationships between features of samples in the training dataset $D = (R_1, R_2, ..., R_n)$ which has n records R including m attributes $R = (a_1, a_2, ..., a_m)$ and predict unknown target output (a_m) based on a given input. The mainly utilized classification algorithms in the literature are Naive Bayes, Support Vector Machines, K-Nearest Neighbor, Artificial Neural Networks, and Decision Tree (C4.5).

Naive Bayes

The Naive Bayes classifier, which is a well-known statistical classifier, utilizes Bayes theorem with naive (strong) independence assumptions among the features to calculate unknown conditional probabilities for determining classes of input samples (Yildirim, 2014). Bayes theorem is expressed mathematically as the following equation:

$$P(A|B) = \frac{P(B|A)P(A)}{P(B)} \qquad (9)$$

where $P(A)$ and $P(B)$ are prior probabilities and $P(B|A)$ and $P(A|B)$ are posterior probabilities of event A and B respectively. According to this theorem, attributes/features of sample instances are considered independently.

The algorithm shows high accurate classification results in many domains, including medical diagnosis, pattern recognition, document categorization, banking, and marketing. In addition to these areas, this algorithm was applied to indoor localization and positioning studies to improve accuracy. He et al. developed a novel radio map construction method based on the Naive Bayes algorithm (for the online phase) and the Voronoi diagram (for the offline phase) to estimate the target location (He, 2016). The experiments were performed by using an indoor testing environment, including one main corridor and 13 rooms with 15 active access points. According to the experiments, the error distance and the 80 percent of error distance values were measured as less than 0.6 meters and 0.25 meters, respectively.

The main problem of the Naive Bayes classifier is zero probability which occurs when the training set does not include a sample's category value. Several indoor localization studies proposed a solution to this problem (Haq, 2017)(Bozkurt, 2015). In another study, a novel weighting classification method called improved Multinomial Naive Bayes was proposed to increase the accuracy of the localization system using Wi-Fi fingerprinting by resolving zero probability issues of the traditional Naive Bayes algorithm (Haq, 2017). The experimental results obtained from the application of the novel technique on the data collected by the Wi-Fi analyzer and HTC One from three Wi-Fi access points indicated that the proposed method requires fewer computations and eliminates the zero probability problem. Zhang et el al. (Zhang, 2014)) also developed an Improved Naive Bayes Simple learning algorithm, namely INBS, based on the data characteristics used to solve the zero probability problem. The proposed method was compared with the traditional k-NN and Naive Bayes algorithms in terms of accuracy. The obtained results from the experiments revealed that the INBS produced more accurate estimation results than the traditional methods.

k-Nearest Neighbor (k-NN)

k-Nearest Neighbor is a non-parametric lazy learning classifier that predicts the sample's class label as a majority vote of its *k* neighbors that have certain class labels. When determining the *k* nearest neighbors of a sample data point, the algorithm uses specific distance metrics such as Euclidean, Manhattan, Minkowski, and so on. The commonly used distance metrics in the *k*-NN algorithm and their formulas are listed in Table 2.

Table 2. Commonly used distance metrics in k-NN algorithm

Distance Metric	Attribute Type	Formula (k: dimension number, x: data point in training set, y: data point in new sample, p: norm order)	
Euclidean	Continuous	$\sqrt{\sum_{i=1}^{k}\left(x_i - y_i\right)^2}$	
Manhattan	Continuous	$\sum_{i=1}^{k}\left|x_i - y_i\right|$	
Minkowski	Continuous	$\left(\sum_{i=1}^{k}\left(\left|x_i - y_i\right|\right)^q\right)^{1/q}$	
Hamming	Categorical	$\sum_{i=1}^{k}\left|x_i - y_i\right|$	$x = y \circledR D = 0$ $x^1 y \circledR D = 1$

In this approach, the *k* value is a user-defined constant. The optimal *k* value is generally specified empirically. As a well-established and practicable classification algorithm, the k-NN algorithm has been widely used to overcome estimation problems in indoor tracking and localization studies (Bozkurt, 2015)

(Xie, 2016)(Peng, 2016). Bozkurt et al. (Bozkurt, 2015) compared several well-known machine learning algorithms (k-NN, Sequential minimal optimization (SMO), Decision Tree (C4.5), Naive Bayes, Bayesian Network, and ensemble methods such as AdaBoost and Bagging) for the estimation of fingerprinting based indoor positions in terms of positioning accuracy and computation time. UJI IndoorLoc indoor positioning dataset, which is stored in the UCI Machine Learning Repository, was selected for the experiments of this study. As a result of the experiments, k-NN algorithms were determined as the most appropriate classifier for the indoor positioning systems. Furthermore, in another study (Xie, 2016), an improved Spearman-distance-based k-NN method was developed for the indoor localization problem based on the fingerprint of RSSI. The experimental results from this study demonstrated that the proposed method shows more successful results than the traditional technique. Peng et al. (Peng, 2016) proposed an Iterative Weighted KNN (IW-KNN) solution for the indoor localization problem based on RSSI of the Bluetooth Low Energy (BLE) environment. Thus, while the accuracy of the position estimation increased, the mean error decreased by 1.5 to 2.7 meters.

Support Vector Machine (SVM)

Support vector machine (SVM), which is based on statistical learning theory, the concept of decision planes and structural risk minimization is proposed for classification and regression problems. The SVM algorithm sets each record in the dataset as a point in n-dimensional space, where n is the number of attributes in the dataset. Then, a hyperplane is constructed to separate the two different classes. Selecting the maximum margin for the hyperplane is very important for avoiding overfitting and misclassification problems.

In some of the indoor localization studies, the SVM-based classifiers were used (Chriki, 2017) (Farjow, 2011). Chriki et al. (Chriki, 2017) suggested applying a multi-class SVM model for the indoor localization problem in wireless sensor networks. The proposed approach was applied to two different real-world datasets, including a hospital and a laboratory building, and compared with the ANN in terms of response time and correctly classified data rate. According to the experimental results, the proposed method offers over 80% accuracy in affordable response time. Researchers of another study (Farjow, 2011) utilized the SVM model for the estimation of the node positions of the IEEE802.15.4/ZigBee-based sensor networks. The introduced method provided higher prediction performance with minimal setup time in the experiments of the study.

Artificial Neural Network (ANN)

Artificial Neural Network (ANN) is a supervised learning technique inspired by the biological neural structure of the brain, which determines the target attribute value of the new sample depending on input data. The ANN model includes interconnected multiple layers of nodes in a weighted directed graph.

In one of the indoor localization studies, Fang and Lin (Fang, 2008) introduced a novel discriminant-adaptive neural network (DANN) model for the indoor localization process in a real-world IEEE 802.11 WLAN environment. In this approach, multiple discriminant analysis was used for the extraction of useful discriminative information in the fingerprint data. The proposed approach was compared with the weighted k-NN, maximum likelihood (ML), and MLP algorithms in terms of accuracy rate, and the results indicated that this proposed method outperforms the existing techniques. Dai et al. (Dai, 2015) suggested a multi-layer neural network (MLNN) solution for RSS-based indoor localization problems.

This model consists of three sections such as transforming section, denoising section, and locating section. In the experiments, the proposed model was compared with maximum likelihood estimation (MLE), generalized regression neural network (GRNN), and fingerprinting methods, and it provided higher estimation accuracy than the others.

Decision Tree

A decision tree is one of the most popular classification techniques that generate a tree consisting of a conjunction of rules to classify unknown target attribute values of the new sample (Yildirim, 2018). Internal nodes, branches, and leaf nodes which are the components of the tree, represent attributes, attribute values, and class labels, respectively. There are several decision tree algorithms in the literature, including C4.5, C5, ID3, CART, and CHAID.

The decision tree algorithms have also been applied to indoor localization systems to increase the position estimation accuracy. For example, Yim (Yim, 2008) proposed a novel decision tree-based indoor location fingerprinting technique that creates a decision tree in the offline phase using a training set. With this decision tree, the user's location in the online phase is estimated. Compared with the existing methods (probabilistic method, k-NN, and ANN), the proposed tree-based approach is more efficient than others, especially in response time in the online phase.

In the positioning literature, there are several studies that combine different classification algorithms with improving the accuracy of the position estimations. For example, Zhao et al. (Zhao, 2016) proposed a novel estimation method that combines the universal Kriging (UK) interpolation method (to reduce the number of training points), weighted k-NN, and Naive Bayes classifiers (to merge candidates) for WiFi fingerprinting based indoor positioning systems. In the experiments, the average positioning error that the proposed hybrid approach provided was measured as 1.265 meters.

Unsupervised Learning

The unsupervised learning technique trains the system using unlabeled observation data, which has not any prior information about the output value. There are two main techniques in this approach: clustering and association rule mining.

Clustering

Clustering is an unsupervised learning technique that groups a set of objects into clusters based on similarity (Yıldırım, 2018). To identify the resemblance of objects depending on their features, similarity measures are used. The most popular and commonly applied similarity measures in the clustering task are Manhattan, Euclidean, and Minkowski for numerical valued objects and Jaccard's distance for categorical valued objects. The clustering task of ML has been proven useful in many areas, ranging from image processing to pattern recognition and from information retrieval to segmentation. The most popular and applied clustering algorithms in the literature are K-Means, K-Means++, Fuzzy C-Means, DB-SCAN, and Self Organizing Maps (SOM).

K-Means

K-Means is a popular, efficient, simple computable clustering algorithm which divides the given n observations $X = \{x_1, x_2, ..., x_n\}$ into predefined k clusters $C = \{c_1, c_2, ..., c_k\}$ by considering the centroids of each cluster. First, k initial centroids are randomly chosen for each cluster and then each object in the data set is assigned to a cluster that has the nearest centroid to the object. In each iteration, centroids are updated, and the clustering process is repeated until no non-clustered object remains.

In the indoor localization literature, the K-Means algorithm has widespread usage in estimating positions, especially for reducing computational complexity (Saadi, 2016). Razavi et al. (Razavi, 2015) proposed a novel K-Means-based method used to estimate the floor by favor of fingerprint clustering of WiFi and other positioning sensor outputs. This approach's main goal is to cluster the whole fingerprinting data to reduce the data size via the K-Means algorithm. The experimental results presented that the proposed clustering method improves the computational time complexity of the floor estimation algorithm. Similarly, Bai and Wu (Bai, 2013) used the K-Means algorithm to cluster the fingerprint data at the anchors in the indoor localization system. Therefore, the response time of the online phase was significantly decreased.

Fuzzy C-Means

Fuzzy C-Means, also known as Soft K-Means, is very similar to the K-Means clustering algorithm, but objects in the data set can be assigned to more than one cluster. The Fuzzy C-Means algorithm is as widely used as the K-Means algorithm in indoor localization systems. For example, Suroso et al. (Suroso, 2011-Dec) clustered feature vectors of the fingerprint data set into the classes of the different amounts of RSSI values using the Fuzzy C-Means algorithm. In another study, the same researchers proposed the Fuzzy C-Means clustering algorithm again but for radio frequency (RF) fingerprint technique-based localization system (Suroso, 2011-Nov). In (Zhou, 2014), Zhou and Van developed a novel fingerprint algorithm based on Fuzzy C-means clustering to reduce the computing time of the location estimation in the underground parking area.

Besides the K-Means and Fuzzy C-Means, several positioning studies implement K-Means++ (Kanmaz, 2019), K-Medoids (Naga, 2019), which are the different improved versions of K-Means and Competitive Agglomeration (CA) (Jiang, 2015) algorithms.

Hybrid Approaches (Merging Classification and Clustering Algorithms)

There are many studies that implement hybrid approaches that combine classification and clustering algorithms with improving accuracy and efficiency for estimating indoor positions. Gutierrez et al. (Gutierrez, 2014) developed a hybrid approach that merges Naive Bayes classifier and K-Means clustering algorithms to estimate mobile devices' location depending on the measured Wi-Fi signal strength and building floor plan. First, the dataset is clustered as a predefined cluster number via K-Means, and then, using the Naive Bayes algorithm, the location of mobile devices is predicted. Similarly, Berz et al. (Berz, 2015) combined SVM classifier and K-Means clustering algorithms to estimate RSSI fingerprinting based locations and Sun et al. (Sun, 2009) merged Fuzzy C-Means clustering algorithm and k-NN classifier to improve the accuracy of the indoor location system in WLAN.

CONCLUSION

Indoor tracking and localization systems are widely used in many applications such as target tracking, monitoring, advertising, and healthcare. In the lack of GPS signals, the indoor localization systems try to use other signal types such as BLE, WiFi, RFID, and UWB. The widespread of the internet and recent advances in wireless communication modules, sensors, memory chips, and processors have simplified indoor localization systems. These systems measure the received signal strength in the target nodes and estimate the distance between target nodes and the signal sources. The estimated distances are merged using some algorithms, and the real-time location of the target node is determined. In the literature, various traditional and machine learning-based methods have been proposed to estimate target nodes' location from RSSI values. While the traditional methods, such as ToA, TDoA, Trilateration, and Fingerprinting mainly rely on mathematical modeling and calculation, the ML-based approaches focus on using different learning-based methods such as classification and clustering algorithms. In this chapter, the traditional and ML-based methods for IoT-based positioning systems were discussed.

Generally, most of the traditional approaches have limited precision for target localization. However, ML methods provide more promising results in indoor localization systems. The ML algorithms are generally classified into two categories: supervised learning algorithms and unsupervised learning algorithms. Supervised learning focuses on predicting outputs of unlabeled samples using labeled data. The most known and commonly used method in supervised learning is classification. The mainly used classification algorithms in the indoor localization systems are Naive Bayes, Support Vector Machines, K-Nearest Neighbor, Artificial Neural Networks (Multilayer Perceptron), and Decision Tree (C4.5). In unsupervised learning, the system is trained by using unlabeled data to find hidden patterns from it. It consists of two main techniques: clustering and association rule mining. In the indoor localization literature, K-Means and Fuzzy C-Means clustering algorithms have widespread usage in estimating positions. This chapter shows that the classification studies are more common in indoor localization than the studies that implement the clustering technique. To the best of our knowledge, no association rule mining studies have been carried out in this area yet. The chapter also concluded with accuracy and feasibility analysis of the traditional and machine learning approaches.

REFERENCES

Aditya, S., Molisch, A. F., & Behairy, H. M. (2018). A survey on the impact of multipath on wideband time-of-arrival based localization. *Proceedings of the IEEE, 106*(7), 1183–1203. doi:10.1109/JPROC.2018.2819638

Ali, M. U., Hur, S., & Park, Y. (2019). Wi-Fi-based effortless indoor positioning system using IoT sensors. *Sensors (Basel), 19*(7), 1496. doi:10.339019071496 PMID:30934799

Amadeo, R. (2015). *Meet Google's "Eddystone"-a flexible open source iBeacon fighter*. Ars Technica.

Bai, S., & Wu, T. (2013). *Analysis of K-Means algorithm on fingerprint based indoor localization system*. Paper presented at the meeting of the 5th IEEE International Symposium on Microwave, Antenna, Propagation and EMC Technologies for Wireless Communications. 10.1109/MAPE.2013.6689952

Berz, E. L., Tesch, D. A., & Hessel, F. P. (2015). *RFID indoor localization based on support vector regression and k-means.* Paper presented at the meeting of the 2015 IEEE 24th International Symposium on Industrial Electronics (ISIE), Rio de Janeiro, Brazil. 10.1109/ISIE.2015.7281681

Bozkurt, S., Elibol, G., Gunal, S., & Yayan, U. (2015, September). *A comparative study on machine learning algorithms for indoor positioning.* Paper presented at the meeting of the 2015 International Symposium on Innovations in Intelligent SysTems and Applications (INISTA), Madrid, Spain. 10.1109/INISTA.2015.7276725

Chriki, A., Toutai, H., & Snoussi, H. (2017). *SVM-Based Indoor Localization in Wireless Sensor Networks.* Paper presented at the meeting of the 13th International Wireless Communications and Mobile Computing Conference (IWCMC), Valencia, Spain. 10.1109/IWCMC.2017.7986446

Dai, H., Ying, W., & Xu, J. (2015). Multi-layer neural network for received signal strength-based indoor localisation. *IET Communications*, *10*(6), 717–723. doi:10.1049/iet-com.2015.0469

Fang, S.-H., & Lin, T.-N. (2008). Indoor Location System Based on Discriminant-Adaptive Neural Network in IEEE 802.11 Environments. *IEEE Transactions on Neural Networks*, *19*(11), 1973–1978. doi:10.1109/TNN.2008.2005494 PMID:19000967

Farjow, W., Chehri, A., Hussein, M., & Fernando, X. (2011). *Support Vector Machines for indoor sensor localization.* Paper presented at the meeting of the 2011 IEEE Wireless Communications and Networking Conference, Cancun, Mexico. 10.1109/WCNC.2011.5779231

Gutierrez, N., Belmonte, C., Hanvey, J., Espejo, R., & Dong, Z. (2014, April). Indoor localization for mobile devices. In *Proceedings of the 11th IEEE International Conference on Networking, Sensing and Control* (pp. 173-178). IEEE. 10.1109/ICNSC.2014.6819620

Haq, M. A. U., Kamboh, H. M. A., Akram, U., Sohail, A., & Hifsa, I. (2017). Indoor Localization Using Improved Multinomial Naïve Bayes Technique. In *Proceedings of the Third International Afro-European Conference for Industrial Advancement — AECIA 2016* (vol. 565, pp. 321-329). Springer.

He, C., Guo, S., Wu, Y., & Yang, Y. (2016). A novel radio map construction method to reduce collection effort for indoor localization. *Measurement*, *94*, 423–431. doi:10.1016/j.measurement.2016.08.021

Holm, S. (2009, April). Hybrid ultrasound-RFID indoor positioning: Combining the best of both worlds. In *2009 IEEE International Conference on RFID* (pp. 155-162). IEEE.

Jiang, Q., Li, K., Zhou, M., & Tian, Z. (2015). Indoor Location in WLAN Based on Competitive Agglomeration Algorithm. *International Journal of Innovative Science, Engineering & Technology*, *2*(1).

Kanmaz, M., & Aydın, M. A. (2019). Comparison of dv-hop based indoor positioning methods in wireless sensor networks and new approach with k-means++ clustering method. *Journal of the Faculty of Engineering and Architecture of Gazi University*, *34*(2), 975–986.

Karimpour, N., Karaduman, B., Ural, A., Challengerl, M., & Dagdeviren, O. (2019, June). IoT based Hand Hygiene Compliance Monitoring. In *2019 International Symposium on Networks, Computers and Communications (ISNCC)* (pp. 1-6). IEEE.

Khelifi, F., Bradai, A., Benslimane, A., Rawat, P., & Atri, M. (2019). A survey of localization systems in internet of things. *Mobile Networks and Applications, 24*(3), 761–785. doi:10.100711036-018-1090-3

McClelland, K., Flinner, E. H., Abler, E. R., & Edu, G. (2017, September). Time Difference of Arrival Localization Testbed: Development, Calibration, and Automation. In *Proceedings of the GNU Radio Conference* (*Vol. 2*, No. 1, pp. 8-8). Academic Press.

Naga, R. A., Elias, R., & Nahas, A. E. (2019). Indoor Localization Using Cluster Analysis. In Artificial Intelligence and Soft Computing. ICAISC 2019. Lecture Notes in Computer Science (vol. 11509, pp. 3-13). Springer.

Newman, N. (2014). Apple iBeacon technology briefing. *Journal of Direct, Data and Digital Marketing Practice, 15*(3), 222–225. doi:10.1057/dddmp.2014.7

Peng, Y., Fan, W., Dong, X., & Zhang, X. (2016). *An Iterative Weighted KNN (IW-KNN) based Indoor Localization Method in Bluetooth Low Energy (BLE) Environment.* Paper presented at the meeting of the 2016 Intl IEEE Conferences on Ubiquitous Intelligence & Computing, Advanced and Trusted Computing, Scalable Computing and Communications, Cloud and Big Data Computing, Internet of People, and Smart World Congress, Toulouse, France.

Razavi, A., Valkama, M., & Lohan, E.-S. (2015). *K-Means Fingerprint Clustering for Low-Complexity Floor Estimation in Indoor Mobile Localization.* Paper presented at the meeting of the 2015 IEEE Globecom Workshops (GC Wkshps), San Diego, CA. 10.1109/GLOCOMW.2015.7414026

Rong, P., & Sichitiu, M. L. (2006, September). Angle of arrival localization for wireless sensor networks. In *2006 3rd annual IEEE communications society on sensor and ad hoc communications and networks* (Vol. 1, pp. 374-382). IEEE.

Saadi, M., Ahmad, T., Zhao, Y., & Wuttisttikulkij, L. (2016). *An LED based Indoor Localization System using k-means Clustering.* Paper presented at the meeting of the 2016 15th IEEE International Conference on Machine Learning and Applications. 10.1109/ICMLA.2016.0048

Shchekotov, M. (2014, October). Indoor localization method based on Wi-Fi trilateration technique. In *Proceeding of the 16th conference of fruct association* (pp. 177-179). Academic Press.

Sun, Y., Xu, Y., Ma, L., & Deng, Z. (2009, December). KNN-FCM hybrid algorithm for indoor location in WLAN. In *2009 2nd International Conference on Power Electronics and Intelligent Transportation System (PEITS)* (Vol. 2, pp. 251-254). IEEE.

Suroso, D. J., Cherntanomwong, P., Sooraksa, P., & Takada, J. I. (2011, December). Fingerprint-based technique for indoor localization in wireless sensor networks using Fuzzy C-Means clustering algorithm. In *2011 International Symposium on Intelligent Signal Processing and Communications Systems (ISPACS)* (pp. 1-5). IEEE. 10.1109/ISPACS.2011.6146167

Suroso, D. J., Cherntanomwong, P., Sooraksa, P., & Takada, J. I. (2011, November). Location fingerprint technique using Fuzzy C-Means clustering algorithm for indoor localization. In *TENCON 2011-2011 IEEE Region 10 Conference* (pp. 88–92). IEEE. doi:10.1109/TENCON.2011.6129069

Xie, Y., Wang, Y., Arumugam, N., & Lina, W. (2016). An Improved K-Nearest-Neighbor Indoor Localization Method Based on Spearman Distance. *IEEE Signal Processing Letters, 23*(3), 351–355. doi:10.1109/LSP.2016.2519607

Yildirim, P., & Birant, D. (2014, June). Naive Bayes classifier for continuous variables using novel method (NBC4D) and distributions. In *2014 IEEE International Symposium on Innovations in Intelligent Systems and Applications (INISTA) Proceedings* (pp. 110-115). IEEE.

Yıldırım, P., & Birant, D. (2018). Bulut bilişimde veri madenciliği tekniklerinin uygulanması: Bir literatür taraması. *Pamukkale Üniversitesi Mühendislik Bilimleri Dergisi, 24*(2), 336–343.

Yildirim, P., Birant, D., & Alpyildiz, T. (2018). Data mining and machine learning in textile industry. *Wiley Interdisciplinary Reviews. Data Mining and Knowledge Discovery, 8*(1), e1228. doi:10.1002/widm.1228

Yim, J. (2008). Introducing a decision tree-based indoor positioning technique. *Expert Systems with Applications, 34*(2), 1296–1302. doi:10.1016/j.eswa.2006.12.028

Yiu, S., Dashti, M., Claussen, H., & Perez-Cruz, F. (2017). Wireless RSSI fingerprinting localization. *Signal Processing, 131*, 235–244. doi:10.1016/j.sigpro.2016.07.005

Zafari, F., Gkelias, A., & Leung, K. K. (2019). A survey of indoor localization systems and technologies. *IEEE Communications Surveys and Tutorials, 21*(3), 2568–2599. doi:10.1109/COMST.2019.2911558

Zhang, W., Wang, L., Zhenquan, Q., Zheng, X., Sun, L., Jin, N., & Lei, S. (2014). *INBS: An Improved Naive Bayes Simple Learning Approach for Accurate Indoor Localization.* Paper presented at the meeting of the 2014 IEEE International Conference on Communications (ICC), Sydney, Australia. 10.1109/ICC.2014.6883310

Zhao, H., Huang, B., & Jia, B. (2016). *Applying Kriging Interpolation for WiFi Fingerprinting based Indoor Positioning Systems.* Paper presented at the meeting of the 2016 IEEE Wireless Communications and Networking Conference, Doha, Qatar. 10.1109/WCNC.2016.7565018

Zhou, H., & Van, N. N. (2014, January). Indoor fingerprint localization based on fuzzy c-means clustering. In *2014 Sixth International Conference on Measuring Technology and Mechatronics Automation* (pp. 337-340). IEEE. 10.1109/ICMTMA.2014.83

ADDITIONAL READING

AlHajri, M. I., Ali, N. T., & Shubair, R. M. (2018). Classification of indoor environments for IoT applications: A machine learning approach. *IEEE Antennas and Wireless Propagation Letters, 17*(12), 2164–2168. doi:10.1109/LAWP.2018.2869548

AlHajri, M. I., Ali, N. T., & Shubair, R. M. (2019). Indoor localization for IoT using adaptive feature selection: A cascaded machine learning approach. *IEEE Antennas and Wireless Propagation Letters, 18*(11), 2306–2310. doi:10.1109/LAWP.2019.2915047

Lashkari, B., Rezazadeh, J., Farahbakhsh, R., & Sandrasegaran, K. (2018). Crowdsourcing and sensing for indoor localization in IoT: A review. *IEEE Sensors Journal, 19*(7), 2408–2434. doi:10.1109/JSEN.2018.2880180

Löffler, C., Riechel, S., Fischer, J., & Mutschler, C. (2018, September). Evaluation criteria for inside-out indoor positioning systems based on machine learning. In *2018 International Conference on Indoor Positioning and Indoor Navigation (IPIN)* (pp. 1-8). IEEE. 10.1109/IPIN.2018.8533862

Ramnath, S., Javali, A., Narang, B., Mishra, P., & Routray, S. K. (2017, May). IoT based localization and tracking. In *2017 International Conference on IoT and Application (ICIOT)* (pp. 1-4). IEEE.

Sadowski, S., & Spachos, P. (2018). Rssi-based indoor localization with the internet of things. *IEEE Access: Practical Innovations, Open Solutions, 6*, 30149–30161. doi:10.1109/ACCESS.2018.2843325

Zafari, F., Gkelias, A., & Leung, K. K. (2019). A survey of indoor localization systems and technologies. *IEEE Communications Surveys and Tutorials, 21*(3), 2568–2599. doi:10.1109/COMST.2019.2911558

KEY TERMS AND DEFINITIONS

Classification: The most known and commonly used supervised learning method is classification. This method categorizes new unlabeled samples into predefined classes.

Clustering: Clustering is an unsupervised learning technique that groups a set of objects into clusters based on similarity.

Indoor Localization: Indoor localization is the process of detecting the real-time location of wireless devices in an indoor environment with a bounded error rate.

Internet of Things: The Internet of Things (IoT) is a system of interconnected, internet-connected devices that are capable of collecting and transmitting data via a wireless network.

Machine Learning: Machine learning, a branch of artificial intelligence (AI), gains the computer systems the automatic self-learning ability via past experiences.

Supervised Learning: In supervised learning, a mathematical and statistical predictive model is constructed using a raw data set that is already tagged with correct labels.

Unsupervised Learning: The unsupervised learning technique trains the system using unlabeled observation data, which has not any prior information about the output value.

Chapter 8
XHAC:
Explainable Human Activity Classification From Sensor Data

Duygu Bagci Das
Dokuz Eylul University, Turkey

Derya Birant
iD https://orcid.org/0000-0003-3138-0432
Dokuz Eylul University, Turkey

ABSTRACT

Explainable artificial intelligence (XAI) is a concept that has emerged and become popular in recent years. Even interpretation in machine learning models has been drawing attention. Human activity classification (HAC) systems still lack interpretable approaches. In this study, an approach, called eXplainable HAC (XHAC), was proposed in which the data exploration, model structure explanation, and prediction explanation of the ML classifiers for HAR were examined to improve the explainability of the HAR models' components such as sensor types and their locations. For this purpose, various internet of things (IoT) sensors were considered individually, including accelerometer, gyroscope, and magnetometer. The location of these sensors (i.e., ankle, arm, and chest) was also taken into account. The important features were explored. In addition, the effect of the window size on the classification performance was investigated. According to the obtained results, the proposed approach makes the HAC processes more explainable compared to the black-box ML techniques.

INTRODUCTION

Nowadays, millions of people and billions of objects use the Internet of Things (IoT) technologies. Besides, it is expected that these statistics will be exponentially increased in the future. IoT systems consist of hardware, software, data, and service components. Although the potential of their technology and the variety of their usage fields, the boundary of IoT components remains undetermined. In addition, it is challenging to process and analyze the heterogeneous data, which are produced by IoT.

DOI: 10.4018/978-1-7998-4186-9.ch008

IoT systems interact with the physical environment through sensors, storing long-term data, and making data analyses to improve efficiency. Machine learning (ML) algorithms have been used in IoT systems for many purposes such as optimization, estimation, pattern recognition, data classification, outlier data detection, fault detection (Walter, 2019; Li et al., 2018; Dziubany et al., 2019; Zantalis et al., 2019). Besides, the search for optimal and explainable machine learning models has been undertaken in many different fields (Shanthamallu et al., 2017; Shafique et al. 2018). Especially the explainability is essential for multiple hardware/software components and systems that include heterogeneous sensor data.

Explainable Artificial Intelligence (XAI) has become a significant area of interest due to trust issues in the machine learning model's decision (Dosilovic et al., 2018; Rudin, 2019). XAI presents more explainable machine learning models without affecting their performance. Besides, it provides extra information, which can be understood by humans and therefore improves their trust in the models (Barredo-Arrieta et al., 2020). It improves the transparency of ML models by providing a human-understandable justification to the decisions.

Human activity classification (HAC) is the process of automatically and correctly categorizing the actions performed by the user by analyzing video or IoT sensor data. It is useful for understanding the behavioral patterns present in an environment, such as walking, standing, running, and eating. One of the main problems in the current HAC systems is providing results without interpretability. Although there are several studies covering HAC and XAI, it is still needed to investigate the XAI concept on the HAC in a more comprehensive way. Our study focuses on the topic in many respects, including data exploration, prediction explanation, and model interpretation. The proposed approach provides many properties such as interpretability, explainability, transparency, effectiveness, verifiability, scrutability, understandability, explainability, trust, and technical robustness.

The main aim of this study is to provide a basic, interpretable, and robust approach to HAC problems. For this purpose, an approach, called explainable human activity classification (XHAC), is proposed. In this study, the data exploration, prediction explanation, and model explanation of the four machine learning models have been employed to perform HAR with XAI using the MHEALTH dataset, including Decision Trees (DT), Partial Decision Tree (PART), Naive Bayes (NB), and K-Nearest Neighbors (KNN). It is aimed to improve the explainability of the HAC models' components such as sensor types and sensor locations. For this purpose, each sensor (accelerometer, gyroscope, and magnetometer) data has been considered individually. Besides, the locations of these sensors (ankle, arm, and chest) have also been examined. In accordance with the aims of this study, the following research questions were considered.

R1: Do raw signals give sufficient information about the related human activity?

R2: Is feature extraction necessary for human activity recognition? Which features provides the most meaningful information?

R3: In preprocessing phase, what is the importance of the window size in the performance of the human activity classification

R4: Which activities can be easily or hardly classified?

R5: Does the transparent machine learning models give accurate result in the explainable human activity classification? What is the effect of the sensor location on the model performance?

R6: How sensor type affected the human activity classification performance?

R7: No matter which sensor and machine learning model is considered, what is the best sensor location for human activity classification?

R8: Considering the sensor location and type of each participant, are there any changes in the algorithm performance?

BACKGROUND

XAI has been employed in various fields (Daglarli, 2021, Farrugia et al., 2021, Anguita-Ruiz et al., 2020) such as neuroscience (Fellous et al., 2019), engineering (Chen & Lee, 2020), medicine (Hossain et al., 2020), and computer vision (Meske & Bunde, 2020). Although it has been considered in various domains, the studies lack in certain cases when it is applied for human activity recognition problems.

Human Activity Recognition (HAR) systems have been considered in two main parts called ASHAR (Ambient Sensor-Based Human Activity Recognition) and WSHAR (Wearable Sensor-Based Human Activity Recognition). ASHAR comprises cameras, GPS systems, and ambient sensors. On the other hand, WSHAR includes data of several sensors such as accelerometer, gyroscope, magnetometer, biosensors that are placed on body parts (arm, chest, foot, and head) via various devices (smartphone, smartwatches, googles, shoes, belts). The data, which obtained from those sensors are used for many purposes in various fields such as medicine, security, and rehabilitation (Wang et al., 2019). In this perspective, HAR is a popular field of usage for IoT technology due to its characteristics.

Even explainability is critical in terms of evaluating ML models and further analysis, only a few systems in HAR literature are capable of generating interpretable results. Some of the main focus of those studies can be briefly summarized as follows. Khodabandehloo et al. (2021) proposed an explainable and flexible artificial intelligence system to capture the early symptoms of cognitive diseases in smart homes. They validated their approach using a dataset, which includes data of people who have MCI and dementia. They also allowed clinicians to examine the anomalies with predictions' explanations. They concluded that the explanation of the proposed system is useful for not only task performance but also for increasing trust. Slijepcevic et al. (2020) presented an XAI method, namely Layer-wise Relevance Propagation (LRP), for gait analysis. They evaluate the explanations considering the statistical analysis of the corresponding data with Statistical Parametric Mapping and a clinical expert's qualitative evaluation. They used a dataset including gait patterns of patients having different lower-body gait disorders and healthy people. They concluded that LRP gives good statistical properties, which are in line with the clinical gait patterns. Souza et al. (2020) examined hybrid intelligent models for human fall detection systems. They evaluated the outcomes in accordance with the usage of fuzzy neural networks, intelligent techniques, and feature selection-based models. They concluded that the presented models were able to extract information from a complex and highly dimensioned dataset. Horst et al. (2019) examined whether XAI techniques can improve the interpretability, explainability, and transparency of the estimations in clinical gait classification. For this purpose, they considered a dataset including information about both healthy people and patients who have gait disorders. They concluded that XAI can be employed for understanding and interpreting the considered machine learning models for gait classification. Besides, they also determined the features that are meaningful and highly correlated with the clinical gait characteristics and considered these features when building machine learning models.

MATERIAL AND METHOD

The main aim of this study is to provide a basic, interpretable, and robust approach to Human Activity Classification (HAC) problems. For this purpose, an approach, called explainable human activity classification (XHAC), is proposed. XHAC provides additional information to help individuals to understand model predictions. In other words, it presents the decision results with an explanation to the users in a humanly understandable and comprehensive manner. XHAC provides a new way to open an ML black-box model and gives an interpretable and transparent decision to users. In this way, XHAC provides a decision-making mechanism that can be understandable by individuals that are not necessarily experts for a HAC problem. XHAC gives a clear understanding of how the ML model achieved a certain result or prediction. Furthermore, it clarifies the validity of the ML model and the evidence for the results. In this way, XHAC provides a basis to improve trust in model inferences.

In this study, HAC has been performed by considering four base learners which have high or moderate explainability properties, including Decision Trees (DT), Partial Decision Tree (PART), Naive Bayes (NB), and K-Nearest Neighbors (KNN).

Decision Trees (DT): Decision trees split the data into branches considering a splitting criterion to perform the classification task. C4.5 is one of the popular decision tree algorithms which considers the normalized information entropy concept (called gain ratio) as the splitting criterion (Witten et al., 2017). DT is considered an explainable or interpretable machine learning technique since the decisions (i.e., node splitting and finalizing) made by the model can be easily interpreted by a human. Besides, the model can be simulated by a user without requiring any mathematical background (Barredo-Arrieta et al., 2020).

Partial Decision Tree (PART): It considers both divide-and-conquer and separate-and-conquer strategies. The main advantage of this algorithm is that it does not require conducting a global optimization to evaluate accurate rule sets. Therefore, it constitutes a rule without considering the covering instances and continuously creates other *rules* for the all-other instances recursively (Frank & Witten, 1998). The algorithm can be simulated by even non-expert users since the rules are readable and manageable. On the other hand, the rules may require decomposition since they may be too large. Besides, since rules may grow so much, they may be so complicated that the model examination may require powerful mathematical tools. In that perspective, PART is an explainable algorithm in terms of its structure. However, it requires additional tools and experts to understand the relations between rules and features for the complex dataset which includes too many rules.

Naive Bayes (NB): Based on Bayes conditional probabilities theorem, the Naive Bayes algorithm presents a probabilistic approach for classification. For continuous data, the Gaussian Naive Bayes model can be employed, which uses the mean and variance values of each feature to evaluate the probability of a given input's class. It is an *explainable* and effective method on datasets that includes a low number of features. Bayesian models can be interpretable by humans who are capable to understand the statistical relationships between variables. However, these relations should be decomposed when the number of variables is too much. Besides, the complexity of the predictors makes the model analyzable only by using mathematical tools.

K-Nearest Neighbors (KNN): It uses the nearest neighbors of an instance to predict its class. The nearest neighbors are usually obtained by employing Euclidean, Manhattan, or Minkowski distance functions. The parameter "k" represents the considered number of neighbors. Although the KNN model can be interpretable by humans for simulations, the complexity of the distance functions and/or features adversely affects its transparency. Therefore, it can be concluded that KNN is a restricted explainable machine learning algorithm. This algorithm is more explainable on datasets that include a low number of features.

Table 1 gives the explainability properties of the four transparent machine learning algorithms under study. Some of the key explainability properties of the machine learning models are Decomposition Requirement, Casualty, Effectiveness, Stability, Simplification, Additional Tool Requirement Informativeness, and Accuracy. *Decomposition Requirement* denotes whether the indicators of the considered machine learning model can be decomposed for interpretation. *Causality* measures the capability of the model in terms of clarifying the relationship between the input and output. *Effectiveness* indicates how capable machine learning to support meaningful decision-making to users. *Stability* denotes the consistent behavior of a model to give similar explanations when similar inputs are considered. *Simplification* is the ability to reduce the variable number considering the set of principal ones (Vilone & Longo, 2020). *Additional Tool Requirement* indicates whether the structure and/or the outputs of the machine learning model need a mathematical tool to make interpretations. *Informativeness* measures whether the model can provide practical knowledge to the end-users. Finally, *Accuracy* is a beneficial metric for the degree of correctness of the machine learning model and how it can generally perform.

Table 1. Explainability properties of transparent machine learning algorithms considered under the XHAC approach

	Explainability Level	Decomposition Requirement	Causalty	Effectiveness	Stability	Simplification	Additional Tool Requirement	Informativeness	Accuracy
DT	High	High Volume and Complex Data	Very High	Effective	High	High	High Volume and Complex Data	Informative	Very High
PART	High	High Volume and Complex Data	Very High	Effective	High	High	High Volume and Complex Data	Informative	Very High
NB	Moderate	All Data Types and Sizes	High	Restricted	Low	High	All Data Types and Sizes	Restricted	High
KNN	Moderate	High Volume and Complex Data	High	Restricted	High	High	All Data Types and Sizes	Restricted	Very High

EXPERIMENTAL STUDIES

In this study, the impact of the type and location of the different sensors on the performance of ML algorithms was investigated. Besides, the features that significantly affect the classification performance were explored by evaluating the characteristic of features. Furthermore, the effect of the window size on the classification performance was taken into account. As for performance metrics, accuracy and confusion matrix were considered by using the 10-fold cross-validation technique.

Dataset Description

In this study, we used the MHEALTH dataset (Banos et al., 2015) which comprises human activity data of ten participants and twelve physical activities. These activities are standing (L1), sitting (L2), lying (L3), walking (L4), climbing stairs (L5), waist bends forward (L6), the frontal elevation of arms (L7), knees bending (L8), cycling (L9), jogging (L10), running (L11), and jumping front and back (L12). Each activity was performed by each participant for approximately one minute. The physical activities were measured individually by an accelerometer, gyroscope, and magnetometer, which were located on three different body parts (ankle, arm, and chest). The data were recorded at a sampling rate of 50 Hz. Each sensor includes measurement data in the x-, y-, and z-axis. The dataset includes a total of 1215714 records for ten participants.

Experimental Results

The experiments were conducted by employing Decision Trees (DT), Partial Decision Tree (PART), Naive Bayes (NB), and K-Nearest Neighbors (KNN) algorithms on the MHEALTH dataset. The results were presented considering three sub-categories namely, Data Exploration, Model Structure Explanation, and Prediction Explanation to provide the explainability of the Human Activity Classification in a comprehensive way.

Data Exploration

Data exploration gives the information about the considered dataset to find the meaningful relations or attributes. Besides, it is useful to understand the data. In this study, the data exploration was performed by visualizing the physical activities' signals and presenting feature importance rankings.

Figure 1 shows visuals of the raw signals obtained from the accelerometer, which is located on the ankle of the first participant. It is seen from Figure 1 that standing (L1), sitting and relaxing (L2), and lying down (L3) have similar activity patterns. Likewise, jogging (L10), running (L11), and jump front & back (L12) also show similar physical behavior.

It may not always be possible to recognize the activity by considering the raw sensor signals so that it is required to perform a feature extraction process. Therefore, the feature extraction process was performed to obtain both time-domain and frequency-domain features for each window, including maximum, minimum, mean, standard deviation, median, peak-to-peak value, the number of zero-crossing, kurtosis, root means squared (RMS) value, skewness, crest factor, root mean squared velocity, and signal entropy. In this procedure, low and high-frequency components were extracted from the original time series and derived three PCA components. Afterward, the extracted features were investigated by using the Information Gain (InfoGain) method (Witten et al., 2017) to understand distinguishing and determinant features.

Figure 2 shows the importance of features in increasing order for human activity classification. It is seen from Figure 2 that the maximum values of the first low-frequency principal component (lpc1.max), the root means squared error values of the second low-frequency principal component (lpc2.rms), and the maximum values of the second principal component (lpc2.max) are the first three most important features. Besides, it is concluded that the maximum, minimum, and RMS values are the most notable features for the classification task.

Figure 1. Raw signals of different activities obtained from the accelerometer sensor located on the ankle

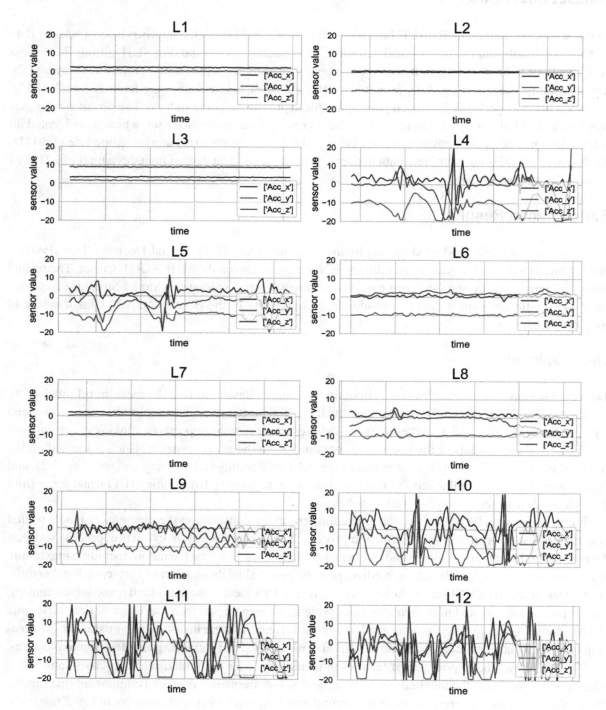

Figure 2. Feature evaluation results obtained by the Information Gain method

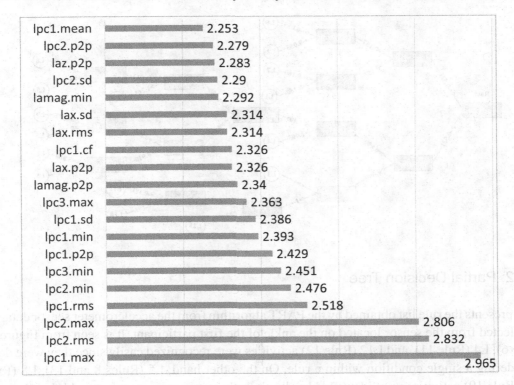

Model Structure Explanation

Model structure explanation aims to explain the learning behavior of the model. By acknowledging the learning behavior, it can be interpreted whether the model can be improved and/or behaved secure and efficiently under unexpected conditions. Besides, by performing model structure explanation, one can understand whether the model is user-friendly in supporting accurate and/or fast user decision-making and presenting meaningful information to the end-users. In this study, the DT, PART, NB, and KNN methods were considered due to their explainability. Therefore, the model structure explanation for these methods was performed under the proposed XHAC approach.

Model-1: Decision Tree

Figure 3 shows the first three and the last three levels of the decision tree structure considering the accelerometer sensor, which is located on the ankle of the first participant.

It is seen from Figure 3 that L1, L2, L3, L4, L6, and L7 activities were recognized at the third level of the decision tree structure. This means that these activities were easily distinguished from each other and remained activities. L11 was detected at the fourth, L10 and L12 were at the fifth, and L5, L8, and L9 were at the sixth level of the tree structure as seen from Figure 3. Among these activities, it is seen that L5, L8, and L9 were the most difficult to detect and distinguish activities since they were detected in multiple levels and different branches.

Figure 3. Decision tree structure

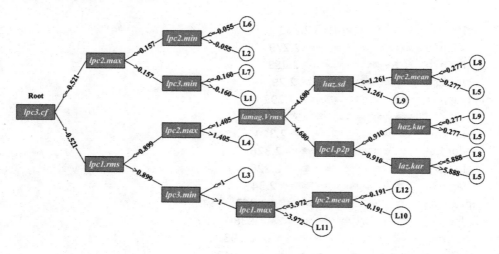

Model-2: Partial Decision Tree

Figure 4 presents the rule list obtained by the PART algorithm from the accelerometer sensor data, which were collected from the sensor located on the ankle of the first participant. It is seen from Figure 4 that L1 (Rule 6), L4 (Rule 11), and L12 (Rule 12) activities were recognized easily since they were detected by considering a single condition within a rule. On the other hand, L5 (Rules 8 and 13), L8 (Rule 9), and L9 (Rule 10) activities were identified hardly since they were recognized in multiple rules or rules in which multiple conditions existed.

Figure 4. Rule list extracted by the partial decision tree (PART) method

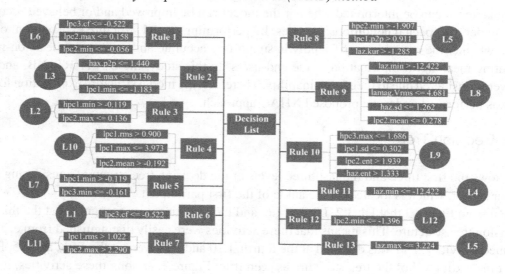

Model-3: Naive Bayes

The Naive Bayes algorithm fits the class data to Gaussian curves for numeric features. Figures 5(a) and 5(b) show the Gaussian curves of the first low-frequency principal component's maximum value (*lpc1. max*) and the peak-to-peak value of the low-frequency component of the y-axis (*lay.p2p*) considering twelve classes. The distribution of mean values of observations belonging to each class is an important criterion for the evaluation of the feature. Therefore, Gaussian curves with different mean values are an important indicator of the classifier's accuracy. However, the mean is not the sole parameter to determine the classifier performance. The standard deviation value increases the width of the curves and decreases their height. Hence, a curve with a high absolute standard deviation may cause a negative effect on the classifier performance since the curves should be distinguished from each other. Thus, it may an adverse effect if the curves overlap each other. It is seen from Figures 5(a) that some of the class-based Gaussian distributions of the feature *lpc1.max* are completely distinguished from those of other classes. Besides, some Gaussian curves have a low absolute standard deviation that causes a partial separation. On the other hand, some class-based Gaussian distributions of the feature *lay.p2p* are not well-separated and have a large absolute standard deviation that causes observing close probabilities in multiple classes for a given input. Estimation is done for each class using their respective Gaussian curves. Hence, the features that are characterized by the well-separated Gaussian curves are more important for the classification task since the probability of observing a given input in a class is independent of another probability of observing the same input in another class.

Model-4: K-Nearest Neighbors

In the KNN algorithm, determining the optimal value of k is critical to obtain accurate and meaningful results. Therefore, in this study, parameter tuning was performed on values $k \in [3, 4, 5, ..., 11]$. As a result, $k=3$ achieved the best result. Figure 6 shows the results obtained by KNN considering the raw signals of the first participant's accelerometer sensor that is located on the ankle. It is seen that the results are not interpretable. Therefore, the feature extraction from the raw data is essential to perform HAR. Figures 7(a) and 7(b) show the KNN results based on two pairs of features. As can be seen, the feature extraction procedure significantly improves the accuracy and the interpretability of the KNN algorithm. On the other hand, the results are more meaningful for the features *lpc1.max* and *lpc2.max* when compared with those of *lax.max* and *lax.min*. Where *lax* indicates the low-frequency component of x-axis. Recalling Figure 2 from the Data Exploration section, it can be concluded that the results were improved when highly correlated features were selected. This indicates that the explainability of a model may significantly improve by choosing appropriate features and applying necessary processes to the raw data.

Prediction Explanation

Generally, multiple sensors (i.e., accelerometer, gyroscope, and magnetometer) are combined in the WSHAR studies. However, in this study, the sensor performances were considered separately to improve the explainability. Table 2 gives the average accuracy values (all participants and all activities) of the four machine learning algorithms considering accelerometer (ACC), gyroscope (GYRO), and magnetometer (MAG) sensors, which are located in the ankle (AN), arm, and chest (CH). When comparing sensor

Figure 5. Class-based Gaussian distributions of the features (a) lpc1.max and (b) lay.p2p

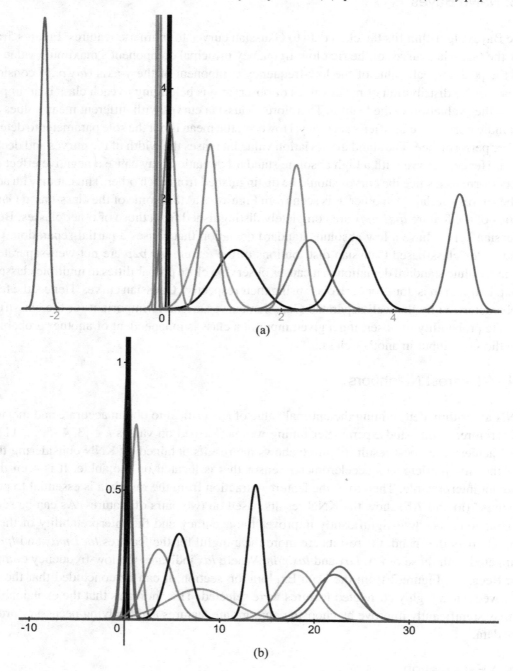

(a)

(b)

locations, it is seen from Table 2 that the highest average accuracy value was obtained for the ankle no matter which sensor was considered. On the other hand, when comparing sensor types, the highest accuracy value (95.79%) was achieved by the accelerometer regardless of the sensor location. When considering all sensor locations and sensor types, the DT method outperformed all the other methods in the study with an accuracy value of 93.79% on average. The best accuracy value (97.36%) was observed with the combination of DT, ankle, and gyroscope.

Figure 6. Visualization of KNN algorithm on the raw accelerometer signals

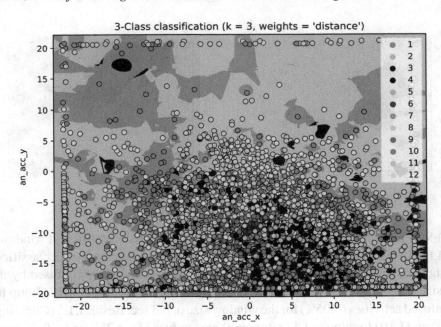

Table 3 gives the standard deviation (STDEV) and the range (*max_value – min_value*) of the accuracy values of all participants when considering sensor location and sensor type combinations.

It is seen from Table 3 that the most stable accuracy values were obtained for the ankle-gyroscope and ankle-accelerometer combinations. On the other hand, the most variation in the accuracy values was observed with the arm-magnetometer and arm-gyroscope combinations. When considering sensor locations and sensor types individually, it can be concluded that the most stable accuracy values were achieved by the accelerometer sensor and the ankle as the sensor location.

In addition to the sensor locations and sensor types, the effect of the window size on the classification performance was investigated in this study. For this purpose, the accuracy values of the DT algorithm considering the accelerometer sensor that is located on the ankle of the first participant were considered. Figure 8 shows the average accuracy values of four machine learning methods when considering different window sizes. According to the results, using the window size of 1.5 sec. produced the best accuracy value for all algorithms. The best accuracy values were achieved by DT for all different window sizes. However, the optimal window size is directly related to sampling time. Increasing window size for a short sampling time reduces the number of instances. Therefore, this may decrease the model performance and causes overfitting. In this study, the window size of 1 sec. was considered for entire analyses since increasing the window size decreases the number of instances, which may cause overfitting. The window sizes of 0.3 sec. and 0.5 sec. decreased the accuracy. Decreasing the window size to such values can adversely affect the machine learning performance since the features may not provide a meaningful data to the model.

Figure 7. Visualization of the KNN algorithm considering (a) lax.max – lay.max and (b) lpc1.max – lpc2. max features

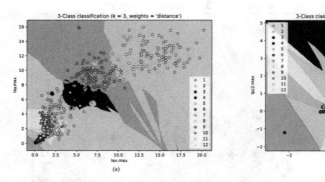

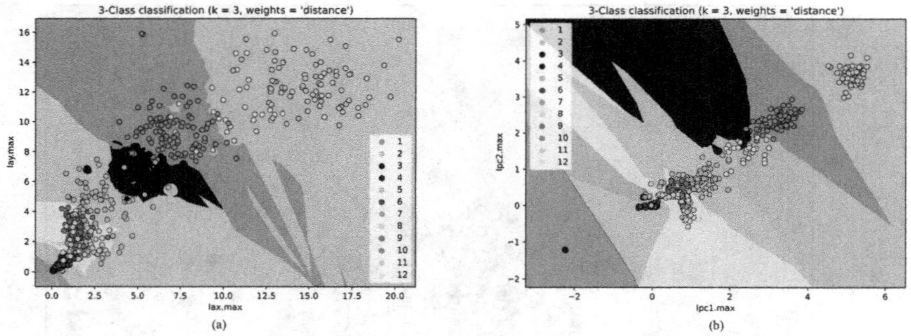

Figures 9(a)-9(d) present the confusion matrices to show the effects of different window sizes on the performance of the decision tree method. It is clearly seen that each activity was classified and distinguished with high accuracy. However, some human activities were slightly confused by the algorithm during the classification task. As can be seen from the figure, L10 (Jogging) – L12 (Jump front & back) are the most confused activities (6.05%) for the window size of 0.3 sec. Besides, L5 (Climbing stairs) – L8 (Knees bending) and L10 (Jogging) – L11 (Running) are confused by 4.75% and 4.05% respectively. On the other hand, as the window size was increased, confusions were decreased in terms of both percentage and the number of confused activities. For example, when the window size of 1 sec. was considered, L5 (Climbing stairs) – L8 (Knees bending) and L5 (Climbing stairs) – L9 (Cycling) were confused by 3.6% and 3.75% respectively. For the window size of 1.5 sec., only L5 (Climbing stairs) – L8 (Knees bending) activities were confused (3.55%).

Table 2. Accuracy values of machine learning algorithms according to location - sensor type pairs

Sensor Location	Sensor Type	KNN	DT	PART	NB	AVERAGE
AN	ACC	95.01	**97.18**	97.11	92.85	95.54
AN	GYRO	95.53	**97.36**	97.12	93.14	**95.79**
AN	MAG	87.22	**91.10**	87.22	87.22	88.19
ARM	ACC	**96.53**	95.44	95.62	86.71	93.57
ARM	GYRO	**95.86**	94.49	94.51	86.95	92.96
ARM	MAG	84.45	84.71	**85.18**	67.85	80.55
CH	ACC	**96.34**	96.22	96.27	88.85	94.42
AVERAGE		92.99	**93.79**	93.29	86.22	
AVERAGE AN		92.59	**95.21**	93.82	91.07	
AVERAGE ARM		**92.28**	91.55	91.77	80.50	

Table 3. Standard deviation and range of accuracy values for all participants

Sensor Location and Sensor Type	STDEV	RANGE
AN-ACC	1.4%	4.5%
AN-GYRO	1.3%	3.5%
AN-MAG	2.7%	7.9%
ARM-ACC	2.8%	7.9%
ARM-GYRO	4.1%	11.6%
ARM-MAG	4.2%	13.4%
CH-ACC	2.1%	7.1%

Figure 8. Average accuracy values of four machine learning algorithms considering four window sizes

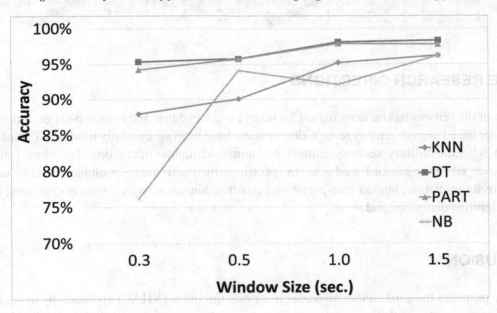

Figure 9. Confusion matrices obtained by DT considering (a) the window size of 0.3 sec., (b) the window size of 0.5 sec., (c) the window size of 1.0 sec., and (d) window size of 1.5 sec.

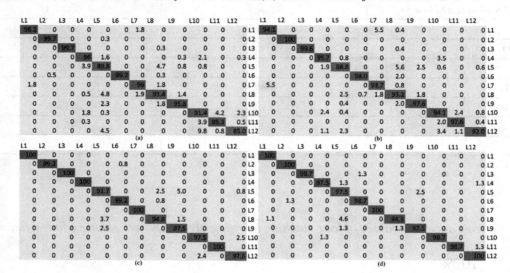

FUTURE RESEARCH DIRECTIONS

The usage of the sensors has been increased for many purposes due to the common usage of the IoT systems. Sensor based human activity recognition systems have been successfully used in IoT implemented areas such as health, military, security, gaming, and human-computer interaction. Therefore, future studies may cover vision or sensor-based domain specific human activities, simultaneous multi-activities, human activity transition, human transportation activities, human activity anomaly detection, physical activity cognitive disorders, and so on.

CONCLUSION

This study proposes the *explainable human activity classification* (XHAC) approach by using multiple wearable sensors within an IoT environment. The proposed approach considers the explainability of the DT, PART, NB, and KNN methods by performing Data Exploration, Model Structure Explanation, and Prediction Explanation. According to the results, the following questions were answered.

Q1: Do raw signals give sufficient information about the performed human activity?
A1: The stationary actions such as lying down, standing, or sitting may be recognized on the raw signals by the machine learning algorithms under study. However, those signals do not give sufficient information for non-stationary actions. Therefore, raw signals should be split into sequential time-series segments (called windows) and statistical features should be extracted from each segment.
Q2: What is the importance of feature extraction in human activity classification? Which features are the most meaningful in human activity classification processes?

A2: Feature extraction provides meaningful data in the time and frequency domain which helps to recognize an activity. It is essential to perform the feature extraction process since using raw signals without processing mostly does not provide enough information for the human activity recognition process. According to the Information Gain evaluation results, the most important features are the maximum, minimum, and root means squared error values of the low-frequency components in the time series.

Q3: What is the role of the window size on the human activity recognition performance?

A3: The smaller window size values (e.g., 0.3, 0.5 sec.) are useful for stationary activities such as sitting or standing. However, it may not be sufficient for non-stationary and complex actions. On the other hand, increasing window size decreases the number of instances, which adversely affects the performance of human activity classification. Therefore, a window size of 1 sec. could be sufficient for distinguishing human activities.

Q4: Which activities were easily and hardly classified?

A4: According to the decision tree structure, standing, sitting, lying down, walking, waist bends forward, and frontal elevation of arms activities were easily recognized since they were classified at the third level of the tree structure. On the other hand, climbing stairs, knees bending, and cycling activities were the hardest to recognize activities since they were classified at the sixth level of the tree structure.

Q5: How well the transparent machine learning models performed in the explainable human activity classification? Does the sensor location affect the algorithm performance?

A5: The average performances obtained by the machine learning methods under study are from best to worst as follows: DT (93.79%), PART (93.29%), KNN (92.99%), and NB (86.22%). On the other hand, the algorithm performances can vary for each sensor location. For example, DT achieved the highest average accuracy (95.21%) with the ankle sensor, while KNN obtained the best average accuracy value (92.28%) with the arm sensor.

Q6: What is the effect of sensor type on the human activity classification performance?

A6: Among the accelerometer, gyroscope, and magnetometer sensors, the best performance was obtained with the accelerometer sensor (94.51%) no matter where the sensors were located. On the other hand, the worst performance was observed with the magnetometer sensor (84.37%) on average.

Q7: Which sensor location gives the most accurate result regardless of the sensor type and machine learning algorithm?

A7: According to results, the most effective sensor location is the ankle since it achieved the highest accuracy results for each sensor and algorithm when compared to the other locations.

Q8: Does the stability of the algorithm performance vary for each participant considering the sensor location and type?

A8: According to the results, considering all participants, the most stable sensor location was the ankle followed by chest, and arm respectively. On the other hand, the most stable sensor type was the accelerometer followed by gyroscope and magnetometer, respectively.

REFERENCES

Anguita-Ruiz, A., Segura-Delgado, A., Alcalá, R., Aguilera, C. M., & Alcalá-Fdez, J. (2020). Explainable Artificial Intelligence (XAI) for the identification of biologically relevant gene expression patterns in longitudinal human studies, insights from obesity research. *PLoS Computational Biology*, *16*(4), 1–34. doi:10.1371/journal.pcbi.1007792 PMID:32275707

Banos, O., Villalonga, C., Garcia, R., Saez, A., Damas, M., Holgado-Terriza, J. A., Lee, S., Pomares, H., & Rojas, I. (2015). Design, implementation and validation of a novel open framework for agile development of mobile health applications. *Biomedical Engineering Online*, *14*(S6), 1–20. doi:10.1186/1475-925X-14-S2-S6 PMID:26329639

Barredo-Arrieta, A., Díaz-Rodríguez, N., Del Ser, J., Bennetot, A., Tabik, S., Barbado, A., Garcia, S., Gil-Lopez, S., Molina, D., Benjamins, R., Chatila, R., & Herrera, F. (2020). Explainable Artificial Intelligence (XAI): Concepts, taxonomies, opportunities and challenges toward responsible AI. *Information Fusion*, *58*, 82–115. doi:10.1016/j.inffus.2019.12.012

Chen, H.-Y., & Lee, C.-H. (2020). Vibration Signals Analysis by Explainable Artificial Intelligence (XAI) Approach: Application on Bearing Faults Diagnosis. *IEEE Access: Practical Innovations, Open Solutions*, *8*, 134246–134256. doi:10.1109/ACCESS.2020.3006491

Daglarli, E. (2021). Explainable Artificial Intelligence (xAI) Approaches and Deep Meta-Learning Models for Cyber-Physical Systems. *Advances in Systems Analysis, Software Engineering, and High Performance Computing*, 42–67. doi:10.4018/978-1-7998-5101-1.ch003

Dosilovic, F. K., Brcic, M., & Hlupic, N. (2018). Explainable artificial intelligence: A survey. In *41st International Convention on Information and Communication Technology, Electronics and Microelectronics (MIPRO)*. (pp. 210-215). IEEE. 10.23919/MIPRO.2018.8400040

Dziubany, M., Garling, M., Schmeink, A., Burger, G., Dartmann, G., Naumann, S., & Gollmer, K.-U. (2019). Machine learning-based artificial nose on a low-cost IoT-hardware. *Big Data Analytics for Cyber-Physical Systems*, 239-257. doi:10.1016/B978-0-12-816637-6.00011-7

Farrugia, D., Zerafa, C., Cini, T., Kuasney, B., & Livori, K. (2021). A Real-Time Prescriptive Solution for Explainable Cyber-Fraud Detection Within the iGaming Industry. *SN Computer Science*, *2*(3), 1–9. doi:10.100742979-021-00623-7 PMID:33880451

Fellous, J.-M., Sapiro, G., Rossi, A., Mayberg, H., & Ferrante, M. (2019). Explainable Artificial Intelligence for Neuroscience: Behavioral Neurostimulation. *Frontiers in Neuroscience*, *13*, 1–14. doi:10.3389/fnins.2019.01346 PMID:31920509

Frank, E., & Witten, I.-E. (1998). Generating Accurate Rule Sets Without Global Optimization. In *Proceedings of the Fifteenth International Conference on Machine Learning*. (pp. 144-151). Academic Press.

Horst, F., Slijepcevic, D., Lapuschkin, S., Raberger, A.-M., Zeppelzauer, M., Samek, W., Breiteneder, C., Schöllhorn, W. I., & Horsak, B. (2019, December 16). On the Understanding and Interpretation of Machine Learning Predictions in Clinical Gait Analysis Using Explainable Artificial Intelligence. *Arxiv*. https://arxiv.org/abs/1912.07737v1

Hossain, M. S., Muhammad, G., & Guizani, N. (2020). Explainable AI and Mass Surveillance System-Based Healthcare Framework to Combat COVID-I9 Like Pandemics. *IEEE Network*, *34*(4), 126–132. doi:10.1109/MNET.011.2000458

Khodabandehloo, E., Riboni, D., & Alimohammadi, A. (2021). HealthXAI: Collaborative and explainable AI for supporting early diagnosis of cognitive decline. *Future Generation Computer Systems*, *116*, 168–189. doi:10.1016/j.future.2020.10.030

Li, H., Ota, K., & Dong, M. (2018). Learning IoT in Edge: Deep Learning for the Internet of Things with Edge Computing. *IEEE Network*, *32*(1), 96–101. doi:10.1109/MNET.2018.1700202

Meske, C., & Bunde, E. (2020). Transparency and Trust in Human-AI-Interaction: The Role of Model-Agnostic Explanations in Computer Vision-Based Decision Support. In H. Degen & L. Reinerman-Jones (Eds.), *Artificial Intelligence in HCI* (pp. 54–69). Springer. doi:10.1007/978-3-030-50334-5_4

Rudin, C. (2019). Stop explaining black box machine learning models for high stakes decisions and use interpretable models instead. *Nature Machine Intelligence*, *1*(5), 206–215. doi:10.103842256-019-0048-x

Shafique, M., Theocharides, T., Bouganis, C.-S., Hanif, M. A., Khalid, F., Hafiz, R., & Rehman, S. (2018). An overview of next-generation architectures for machine learning: Roadmap, opportunities and challenges in the IoT era. In Design, Automation & Test in Europe Conference & Exhibition (DATE) (pp. 827-832). IEEE. doi:10.23919/DATE.2018.8342120

Shanthamallu, U. S., Spanias, A., Tepedelenlioglu, C., & Stanley, M. (2017). A brief survey of machine learning methods and their sensor and IoT applications. In *8th International Conference on Information, Intelligence, Systems & Applications (IISA)* (pp. 1-8), IEEE. 10.1109/IISA.2017.8316459

Slijepcevic, D., Horst, F., Lapuschkin, S., Raberger, A.-M., Zeppelzauer, M., Samek, W., Breiteneder, C., Schöllhorn, W. I., & Horsak, B. (2020, August 19). On the Explanation of Machine Learning Predictions in Clinical Gait Analysis. *Arxiv*. https://arxiv.org/abs/1912.07737

Souza, P. V., Guimaraes, A. J., Araujo, V. S., Batista, L. O., & Rezende, T. S. (2020). An Interpretable Machine Learning Model for Human Fall Detection Systems Using Hybrid Intelligent Models. In H. Ponce, L. Martínez-Villaseñor, J. Brieva, & E. Moya-Albor (Eds.), *Challenges and Trends in Multimodal Fall Detection for Healthcare* (pp. 181–205). Springer. doi:10.1007/978-3-030-38748-8_8

Vilone, G., & Longo, L. (2020, October 12). Explainable Artificial Intelligence: a Systematic Review. *Arxiv*. https://arxiv.org/abs/2006.00093

Walter, K.-D. (2019*)*. AI-based sensor platforms for the IoT in smart cities. *Big Data Analytics for Cyber-Physical Systems*, 145-166. doi:10.1016/B978-0-12-816637-6.00007-5

Wang, Y., Cang, S., & Yu, H. (2019). A survey on wearable sensor modality centred human activity recognition in health care. *Expert Systems with Applications*, *137*, 167–190. doi:10.1016/j.eswa.2019.04.057

Witten, I. H., Frank, E., Hall, M. A., & Pal, C. J. (2017). *Data mining practical machine learning tools and techniques*. Morgan Kaufmann.

Zantalis, F., Koulouras, G., Karabetsos, S., & Kandris, D. (2019). A Review of Machine Learning and IoT in Smart Transportation. *Future Internet*, *11*(4), 1–23. doi:10.3390/fi11040094

ADDITIONAL READING

Hassan, M. M., Uddin, M. Z., Mohamed, A., & Almogren, A. (2018). A robust human activity recognition system using smartphone sensors and deep learning. *Future Generation Computer Systems*, *81*, 307–313. doi:10.1016/j.future.2017.11.029

Janidarmian, M., Roshan Fekr, A., Radecka, K., & Zilic, Z. (2017). A comprehensive analysis on wearable acceleration sensors in human activity recognition. *Sensors (Basel)*, *17*(3), 529. doi:10.339017030529 PMID:28272362

Keshavarzian, A., Sharifian, S., & Seyedin, S. (2019). Modified deep residual network architecture deployed on serverless framework of iot platform based on human activity recognition application. *Future Generation Computer Systems*, *101*, 14–28. doi:10.1016/j.future.2019.06.009

Köping, L., Shirahama, K., & Grzegorzek, M. (2018). A general framework for sensor-based human activity recognition. *Computers in Biology and Medicine*, *95*, 248–260. doi:10.1016/j.compbiomed.2017.12.025 PMID:29361267

Minh Dang, L., Min, K., Wang, H., Jalil Piran, M., Hee Lee, C., & Moon, H. (2020). Sensor-based and vision-based human activity recognition: A comprehensive survey. *Pattern Recognition*, *108*, 107561. doi:10.1016/j.patcog.2020.107561

Yadav, S. K., Tiwari, K., Pandey, H. M., & Akbar, S. A. (2021). A review of multimodal human activity recognition with special emphasis on classification, applications, challenges and future directions. *Knowledge-Based Systems*, *223*, 106970. doi:10.1016/j.knosys.2021.106970

KEY TERMS AND DEFINITIONS

Activity Recognition: Input data labeling by using the corresponding action labels.

Classification: Categorization of the data considering its characteristics.

Feature Extraction: A procedure to obtain specific features from the data by employing appropriate techniques.

Human Activity Recognition: Identification of a physical human activity by examining sensor or visual data.

Internet of Things: A communication network in which physical devices are connected to each other or to bigger systems via the internet.

Machine Learning: The utilization of algorithms to develop meaningful models by training the computers.

Wearable Sensors: Sensor devices, which can be mounted on objects that are worn by humans.

Chapter 9
Animal Activity Recognition From Sensor Data Using Ensemble Learning

Derya Birant

iD https://orcid.org/0000-0003-3138-0432

Dokuz Eylul University, Turkey

Kadircan Yalniz

Dokuz Eylul University, Turkey

ABSTRACT

Animal activity recognition is an important task to monitor the behavior of animals to know their health condition and psychological state. To provide a solution for this need, this study is aimed to build an internet of things (IoT) system that predicts the activities of animals based on sensor data obtained from embedded devices attached to animals. This chapter especially considers the problem of prediction of goat activity using three types of sensors: accelerometer, gyroscope, and magnetometer. Five possible goat activities are of interest, including stationary, grazing, walking, trotting, and running. The utility of five ensemble learning methods was investigated, including random forest, extremely randomized trees, bagging trees, gradient boosting, and extreme gradient boosting. The results showed that all these methods achieved good performance (>94%) on the datasets. Therefore, this study can be successfully used by professionals such as farmers, vets, and animal behaviorists where animal tracking may be crucial.

INTRODUCTION

Activity recognition is a research subject that aims to understand what activities an agent does with the information obtained from an Internet of Things (IoT) environment and the agent. The research subject has been taken into consideration because of playing a significant role in producing personalized applications. There are two main types of activity recognition tasks related to living organisms: human activity recognition and animal activity recognition. This study focuses on animal activity recognition.

DOI: 10.4018/978-1-7998-4186-9.ch009

Animal activity recognition (AAR) is the process of identifying the activity of an animal by analyzing video or sensor data. AAR is in the interest of pet owners, veterinarians, and the agricultural community since it acts as a useful indicator of animal health and welfare. According to researches, when they are not under human supervision, knowing what animals do gives us a lot of information about their health and psychology.

The aim of this study is to make predictions of goats' movements with machine learning algorithms. We consider the problem of prediction of goat activity from sensor data. We developed a pipeline of data pre-processing, segmentation, feature extraction, model construction, and activity classification especially designed for performing decision-making on IoT systems.

The main contributions of this chapter can be summarized as follows. It investigates the utility of ensemble learning algorithms to classify major movement modes of goats from sensor data. Our specific objective is to classify goat behavior into five major activity modes: stationary, grazing, walking, trotting, and running. Our study is also original in that it considers multiple sensor data: accelerometer, gyroscope, and magnetometer. A combination of this variety of IoT sensors gives us a robust insight into goat movements. This study also compares different ensemble learning algorithms to determine the best one for goat activity recognition, including Random Forest (RF), Extremely Randomized Trees (Extra Trees), Bagging Trees (BT), Gradient Boosting (GBoost), and Extreme Gradient Boosting (XGBoost). The experimental results showed that all these ensemble learning methods showed good performance (>94%) on the datasets.

BACKGROUND

In recent years, animal activity recognition has become more popular because of its usability in numerous fields such as health, security, and remote monitoring. Besides, an increased number of IoT-based systems is providing more people to contribute to this field. In the past years, many scientific publications (Arablouei et al., 2021; Alvarenga et al., 2016) suggest that when we get some insight into animal activity patterns, we are in a stronger position to understand an animal's health and wellbeing. Besides, it is desirable to take advantage of tracking the animal's daily routine as a sign of changes in internal or external factors. One approach to monitoring animals is building an IoT system that can gather data and extract information to track animal activities. If the outputs of such an IoT system are localized in areas such as vets and farming, it is quite possible to construct a hypothesis from the daily routine of animals. These hypotheses can be relevant in which environments animals are less stressed, future health problems, and so on. The previous studies on animal activity recognition are given in Table 1.

Generally, animal activity recognition techniques can be categorized under two main groups: sensor-based and vision-based. The *sensor-based technique* (Rahman et al., 2018; den Uijl et al., 2017) uses data gathered by a single or set of IoT sensors placed on an animal body. It has been a fast-growing field because of the benefits of inertial measurement units (IMUs): low-cost, small-size (few mm), light-weight (few grams), ease of programming, and providing reliable information about the body such as force and angular. The *computer vision-based techniques* (Guan et al., 2020; Dandil and Polattimur, 2020; George et al., 2018) use data gathered by a camera placed near the animal. However, there are many problems related to this approach: highly dependent on the light, requiring resolution, limiting the area, high cost, and breaching personal privacy potentially. For this reason, in this study, we carried out the experiments by using a sensor-based approach.

Table 1. Summary of some animal activity recognition systems

Ref	Year	Animal	Method	Class	Sensor			Video
					Acc	Gyr	Magn	
Arablouei et al.	2021	Cattle	SVM, NN, DT, LR, QDA, NB	4	Ö			X
Conners et al.	2021	Bird	HMM	3	Ö		Ö	X
Arabacı et al.	2021	Dog	SVM, MKBoost, SimpleMKL	10	Ö	Ö	Ö	Ö
Guan et al.	2020	Cattle	CNN	2				Ö
Casella et al.	2020	Horse	DT, NB, KNN	3	Ö			X
Dandil and Polattimur	2020	Dog	CNN	6				Ö
Le Roux et al.	2019	Sheep, Rhinoceros	LDA, QDA, DT, RF, SVM, KNN, LR, NB	5	Ö			Ö
Sturm et al.	2019	Calf	Modified OneR	6	Ö			X
Aich et al.	2019	Dog	NN, SVM, KNN, RF, NB	7	Ö	Ö		Ö
Chakravarty et al.	2019	Meerkat	SVM, NB, LDA, LR, RF, KNN	4	Ö			Ö
Decandia et al.	2018	Sheep	DA	3	Ö			Ö
George et al.	2018	Various	SVM, KNN	4				Ö
Mansbridge et al.	2018	Sheep	SVM, RF, KNN, AdaBoost	3	Ö	Ö		Ö
Barwick et al.	2018	Sheep	QDA	4	Ö			Ö
Rahman et al.	2018	Cattle	RF	3	Ö			Ö
Walton et al.	2018	Sheep	RF	3	Ö	Ö		Ö
Fehlmann et al.	2017	Baboon	RF	8	Ö			Ö
den Uijl et al.	2017	Dog	A classification algorithm	8	Ö			Ö
Giovanetti et al.	2017	Sheep	DA	3	Ö			Ö
Le Roux et al.	2017	Rhinoceros, Sheep	LDA	5	Ö			Ö
Hammond et al.	2016	Chipmunk	SVM, HMM	5	Ö			Ö
Painter et al.	2016	Red Fox	KNN, RF	3	Ö		Ö	Ö
Alvarenga et al.	2016	Sheep	DT	5	Ö			Ö
Brugarolas et al.	2016	Dog	A classification algorithm	2	Ö			X
Diosdado et al.	2015	Cow	DT, K-Means, HMM, SVM	3	Ö			X
McClune et al.	2014	Badger	KNN, DT	4	Ö			Ö
Gao et al.	2013	Dog	SVM	5	Ö			X
Escalante et al.	2013	Sow	NN, SVM, NB, RF, Zarbi, LogitBoost	5	Ö			Ö
Gerencser et al.	2013	Dog	SVM	7	Ö	Ö		Ö
Shamoun-Baranes et al.	2012	Oystercatcher	DT	8	Ö			Ö
Nadimi et al.	2012	Sheep	NN	5	Ö			X
Soltis et al.	2012	Elephant	DT	4	Ö			Ö
Grunewalder et al.	2012	Cheetah	SVM, HMM	3	Ö			X
Nathan et al, 2012	2012	Vulture	SVM, CART, RF, NN, LDA	5	Ö			X

Continued on following page

Table 1. Continued

Ref	Year	Animal	Method	Class	Sensor			Video
					Acc	Gyr	Magn	
Proposed Approach		Goat	RF, Extra Trees, BT, GBoost, XGBoost	5	Ö	Ö	Ö	X

Over the past years, embedded devices with inertial measurement units (IMUs) have become much more popular, because of the relatively good performance in tracking movements and accessibility for engineers to build up IoT systems. The most widely-used sensor types are accelerometer (Sturm et al., 2019; Decandia et al., 2018), gyroscope (Aich et al., 2019; Mansbridge et al., 2018; Walton et al., 2018), and magnetometer (Conners et al., 2021; Painter et al., 2016). These types of sensors are attached to animals in various ways for capturing observations at a specific point in time and measuring animal action in all spatial dimensions. Some studies (Arabacı et al., 2021; Gerencser et al., 2013) show that a combination of several different IoT sensors is also possible to build successful predictive models.

Previous studies (Le Roux et al., 2019; Escalante et al., 2013) have proven that applying machine learning algorithms to sensor data provides accurate predictions on identifying numerous animal activities such as walking, running, lying down, and feeding. The characteristics differences among animals make the sensor data unique for each species since some animals have nature move dynamically compared to other ones. Until now, the activity recognition techniques have been applied to a wide variety of animal kinds, including dog (Brugarolas et al., 2015; Gao et al., 2013), horse (Casella et al., 2020), cow (Diasdado et al., 2015), sheep (Giovanetti et al., 2017; Nadimi et al., 2012), elephant (Soltis et al., 2012), rhinoceros (Rous et al., 2017), baboon (Fehlmann et al., 2017), meerkat (Chakravarty et al., 2018), red fox (Painter et al., 2016), badger (McClune et al., 2014), chipmunk (Hammond et al., 2016), cheetah (Grunewalder et al., 2012), and vulture (Nathan et al., 2012). In this study, we consider the classification problem of goat behavior from sensor data.

Related to animal activity recognition systems, Gao et al. (Gao et al., 2013) pointed out that the volume and complexity of the data streams are a big problem in the interpretation and labeling of the data. For this reason, some researchers captured and combined both video recordings and sensor data from different animals to construct a recognition system. Through a visualization tool, experts could interactively use their domain expert knowledge on animal movements.

In the literature, a variety of ML algorithms have been used for animal activity recognition such as Support Vector Machine (SVM) (Gao et al., 2013; Gerencser et al., 2013), Decision Tree (DT) (Shamoun-Baranes et al., 2012), Logistic Regression (LR) (Arablouei et al., 2021), Discriminant Analysis (DA) (Giovanneti et al., 2017), Linear Discriminant Analysis (LDA) (Le Roux et al., 2017), Quadratic Discriminant Analysis (QDA) (Barwick et al., 2018), Random Forest (RF) (Rahman et al., 2018), Naive Bayes (NB) (Casella et al., 2020), Hidden Markov Models (HMM) (Conners et al., 2021), Neural Network (NN) (Aich et al., 2019), Multiple Kernel Boosting (MKBoost) (Arabacı et al., 2021), Simple Multi-Kernel Learning (SimpleMKL) (Arabacı et al., 2021), K-Nearest Neighbors (KNN) (Hammond et al., 2016), and Convolutional Neural Network (CNN) (Dandil and Polattimur, 2020).

Our study differs from the aforementioned studies in several respects. First, our specific objective is to classify goat behavior into five major activity modes: stationary, grazing, walking, trotting, and running. Second, we evaluate the utility of ensemble learning algorithms to classify major movement modes of animals from sensor data. Unlike the previous studies, we used different algorithms such as Extreme Gradient Boosting, Bagging Trees, and Extremely Randomized Trees. Third, we used a dataset that involves multiple sensor data: accelerometer, gyroscope, and magnetometer. A combination of this variety of IoT sensors gives us a robust insight into animal movements.

MATERIALS AND METHODS

Proposed Approach

An intelligent system that can recognize animal movements should have three main focuses. One is the placement of data sources to acquire robust data, the second one is the construction of reliable data streaming to reduce the loss of information, and the last one is the processing steps of the data to establish a correlation between model and activities. For most of the systems, placement has a crucial role in working other steps properly. In particular, cameras and off-body devices must place in the whole environment for tracking animals all day. This approach can be led the projects to create a highly controlled environment, which is caused to restrict animals in a specific location. Our study utilizes the advantage of wearable sensor devices and machine learning algorithms to create a portable system at a low implementation cost.

Figure 1 shows the general overview of the proposed approach which consists of multiple steps. First, raw data are gathered from the IoT sensors which are placed on an animal. Second, the collected data is stored in a database on a private cloud-based platform. After that, in the data preprocessing step, the signal is filtered by a low-pass filter method, and then, segmented into smaller blocks by using a sliding window technique. Third, features are extracted from sensor data streams such as min, max, median, standard deviation, kurtosis, skewness, energy, and entropy. Here, a suitable algorithm can be applied to select a subset of relevant features for use in model construction. In the next step, machine learning algorithms are fed with these features, and a prediction model is built. Finally, the constructed model is used to recognize animal activities such as walking, trotting, running, stationary, and grazing.

Figure 1. The general overview of the proposed approach

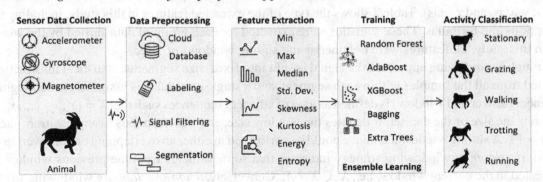

The *data labeling* process is generally made by an annotator with both the video and sensor data. The clock timestamps from the sensors and video are used to provide synchronization. The animals are videotaped from various angles throughout the time performing activities. Sensor data is visualized by a graph and video is viewed at the same time using an application. An annotator labeled the data by clicking on the graph at the point where there is a change in behavior. The annotator markers the start and stop times for one activity by utilizing the video. Transitions between activities are excluded from the data to accurately label the activity associated with the sensor data. All efforts are made carefully to ensure the high quality of the labeling process.

In this work, we aim to give robust and reliable information to animal owners and experts. Informing the experts about animal activity during the day is very important to keep tracking the animal's health status. For example, the activities of an animal, whose health condition is likely to deteriorate, reveal the times of the day when the animal is stressed. In this approach, an animal owner or expert can be informed about dangerous external factors.

Feature Extraction

One of the important steps in working with sensor data is to prepare the data so that it can be used to infer a useful pattern or rule. Sensor data is one of the data that does not provide enough information in its own format. For this reason, we should obtain different information about the data by making statistical inferences and manipulating the features of the data. Making statistical inferences is one of the healthiest methods for sensor data.

Since raw sensor data contains specific values obtained at a particular time instant from observation, it does not carry in-depth and sufficient information itself to describe an animal activity. For this reason, we used a feature extraction technique to transform the original sensor data into more informative features. Through feature extraction, we captured the more useful and exhaustive representation of the sensor data to be able to correctly distinguish different animal activities, such as minimum, maximum, standard deviation, skewness, and kurtosis. The selection of these features is a critical issue to be able to generate a good-performing animal activity classifier.

Features are extracted from each signal segment, called a window, for each one axis of each sensor, such as the minimum value of the x-axis of the accelerometer sensor. In other words, features were individually extracted from three sensor data (accelerometer, gyroscope, and magnetometer) for each axis (x-axis, y-axis, and z-axis). Table 2 shows the type of the extracted features in this study, including their descriptions and formulas. These statistics were extracted for each group of data shifted by the window size. In this study, all features were obtained using sliding windows of 1 sec.

Through a windowing approach, the signal is split into fixed-size segments, statistical information is extracted from all the samples within each segment, and a single class label is assigned to each segment. A segment (also called window) is defined as a set of adjacent sequences such that $X = \{x_r, x_{r+1}, ..., x_{r+w-1}\}$, where n is the size of the dataset, w denotes the window size, and r corresponds to any position, such as $1 \pounds r \pounds n-w+1$. A sliding window technique could be performed in either an overlapping or non-overlapping way. An *overlapping* windowing strategy indicates that some samples from the previous window will be repeated in the current window, i.e., $X_1 \varsigma X_2 \,^1 \, \cancel{E}$. Conversely, a *non-overlapping* windowing strategy refers that the samples in one window do not intersect with the samples of another window, i.e., $X_1 \varsigma X_2 = \cancel{E}$. In this study, fixed sliding windows with overlapping of 50% were used.

Table 2. Extracted features from sensor data

Feature	Description	Formula
Min	Minimum value of a window.	$MIN = \min(X)$
Max	Maximum value of a window.	$MAX = \max(X)$
Mean	Average signal value of a window.	$\bar{x} = \dfrac{1}{n}\sum_{i=1}^{n}x_i$
Interquartile Range	The difference between the 75th percentile and the 25th percentile value of a window.	$IQR = Q3 - Q1$
Standard Deviation	Standard deviation of signal values within a window.	$STD = \sqrt{\dfrac{1}{n-1}\sum_{i=1}^{n}\left(x_i - \bar{x}\right)^2}$
Number of Zero Crossings	The total number of times the signal changes from negative to positive or vice versa.	$ZC = \sum_{i=2}^{n}\left| sign(x_i) - sign(x_{i-1})\right|$
Peak-to-Peak Value	The difference between the maximum value and the minimum value of a window.	$PP = \max(X) - \min(X)$
Root Mean Squared (RMS)	Quadratic mean of a window.	$RMS = \sqrt{\dfrac{1}{n}\sum_{i=1}^{n}x_i^2}$
Kurtosis	The degree of sharpness of the signal distribution within a window.	$KV = \dfrac{1}{n}\sum_{i=1}^{n}\left(\dfrac{x_i - \bar{x}}{\sigma}\right)^4$
Skewness	The degree of asymmetry of the signal distribution within a window.	$SV = \dfrac{1}{n}\sum_{i=1}^{n}\left(\dfrac{x_i - \bar{x}}{\sigma}\right)^3$
Crest Factor	Measure of extreme peaks in a window.	$CF = \dfrac{\max(X)}{RMS}$
Sample Entropy	Measure of the distribution of signal values.	$SaE = -\log_2\dfrac{A}{B}$
Spectral Entropy	Measure of the distribution of Fast Fourier Transformation (FFT) components.	$SpE = -\sum_{i=1}^{n}PSD(f_i)\,log_2\left(PSD(f_i)\right)$ $PSD(f) = \dfrac{\left|X(f)^2\right|}{\sum_{j=1}^{n}X(f_j)}$
Mean Absolute Change	Mean of the consecutive differences of a window.	$\overline{xc} = \dfrac{1}{n}\sum_{i=1}^{n}\left|diff(xi)\right|$
Energy	The sum of the squared signal values of a window.	$E = 1/n\sum_{i=1}^{n}\left(x_i\right)^2$

Continued on following page

Table 2. Continued

Feature	Description	Formula
Frequency Energy	The sum of FFT magnitudes of a window.	$FE = \sum_{i=1}^{n}\left(\left|f_i\right|^2\right)$
Frequency Magnitudes	The first five magnitudes of the FFT analysis.	$F_1 = \|f_1\|^2$ $F_2 = \|f_2\|^2$ $F_3 = \|f_3\|^2$ $F_4 = \|f_4\|^2$ $F_5 = \|f_5\|^2$

In the proposed approach, an embedded device with sensor units is used to acquire a vast amount of data from an animal. Having a huge amount of data provides us to find out the most promising features to train a model. We use these features with multiple classification algorithms to acquire the best fit for our model based on metrics such as accuracy and confusion matrix.

Ensemble Learning Algorithms

This section describes the ensemble learning algorithms used in this study for animal activity recognition, including Random Forest, Extremely Randomized Trees, Bagging Trees, Gradient Boosting, and Extreme Gradient Boosting. We selected these algorithms since they are among the top-10 ensemble learning methods. While the first three ones are *bagging-based* methods, the others are *boosting-based* methods.

Random Forest (RF): The Random Forest algorithm creates multiple diverse models by randomly selecting a set of features out of the total features. This random variation makes it possible to generate decision trees in a forest different from each other. Furthermore, the random forest models are usually good at dealing with unbalanced and missing data.

Extremely Randomized Trees (Extra Trees): The Extremely Randomized Tree algorithm is another ensemble learning algorithm that utilizes the bagging approach. Unlike Random Forest, this method randomly selects samples without replacement from the whole training set. So, the model is built on data that does not contain repetition of observations. In addition, the split process is done on features that are chosen completely randomly, instead of finding the best split on an optimal feature and splitting value like RF. Therefore, Extra Trees maintains its performance even in the presence of noise features.

Bagging Trees (BT): The Bagging Tree method creates multiple decision trees using all the features in the training set. During the prediction step, it uses all the trees together to get accurate output. Each tree votes a prediction and then an estimated probability vector is extracted using the average of the votes given by all trees. This process reduces the problem of overfitting decision trees and provides better results than a single tree.

Gradient Boosting (GBoost): The Gradient Boosting method is an ensemble learning method that uses gradient descent and boosting procedures. In this method, weak learners are defined by gradients. The method boosts by minimizing the defined loss function. Therefore, each model is created to have a lower loss than the previous model.

Extreme Gradient Boosting (XGBoost): The Extreme Gradient Boosting algorithm is a high-performance boosting algorithm. It creates models sequentially like other boosting algorithms. It performs modeling quickly as a result of algorithmic enhancements. In addition, it is good at dealing with missing data.

EXPERIMENTAL STUDIES

We implemented the proposed system with Python which is currently one of the most widely-used programming languages for constructing a machine learning model. We used the *Pandas* and *NumPy* libraries in data manipulation and calculation procedures, especially in the data preprocessing step. The features were extracted from raw data to exhibit all of the characteristics. The extracted features provide us a statistical approach related to the signal and help to estimate the pattern in the signals. In addition, *Tsfresh* was used to eliminate weakly relevant features in the early stage of the machine learning pipeline and to increase the performance of the machine learning model. Finally, we used the *Scikit-learn* machine learning library to build predictive models.

In this study, classification accuracies were obtained by using the k-fold cross-validation technique, in which the dataset is randomly split into k groups, called folds, then one of the groups is taken for test and the remaining groups for the training. This process is repeated k times until each fold is used as a test set. In this study, the value of k is set to five ($k=10$). The performances of the models were evaluated with the accuracy metric.

Dataset Description

The experiments were conducted on a real-world dataset (Kamminga et al., 2017). It is publicly available at the website https://www.utwente.nl/en/eemcs/ps/research/dataset/. The dataset contains labeled multiple sensor data from three goats. These animals were selected from different ages, sizes, and weights to create a variety. Sensors placed on the animals' collars recorded the animals making nine different movements. In this study, four activities were not considered as they occur very rarely, i.e., being insufficient data. The activities to be included in our study are stationary, walking, trotting, grazing, and running activities, which are distributed in the datasets as shown in Table 3. In addition, since one of the main aims of our study was working on different sensor types (3D accelerometer, magnetometer, and gyroscope), we excluded the animals without gyroscope measurement. While accelerometer and gyroscope sensors were collected at 200 Hz, magnetometer was obtained at 100 Hz.

Table 3. Summary of datasets

Dataset	Number of Instances	Number of Features	Number of Classes	Class Distribution
G1	19658	186	5	10043, 3772, 3669, 1789, 389
G2	19266	186	5	11914, 3416, 2676, 824, 437
G3	22311	186	5	16888, 2777, 2325, 295, 5
All	61235	186	5	38845, 9965, 8670, 2908, 831

Experimental Results

In the first experiment, we determined the best ensemble learning method by comparing alternative ones in terms of accuracy. We tested five methods: Random Forest (RF), Extremely Randomized Trees (Extra Trees), Bagging Trees (BT), Gradient Boosting (GBoost), and Extreme Gradient Boosting (XGBoost). The following parameter values were set for the algorithms:

- RF randomly selects some features to perform the best splitting operation. In this experiment, this parameter value was chosen to be the square of the total features. In addition, the Gini impurity function was used to measure the quality of a split. Firstly, the minimal cost-complexity value was varied between 5×10^{-2} and 1×10^{-1}. Secondly, the parameter for the number of trees was varied between 100 and 300.
- Extra Trees was also tried with the same parameters as RF.
- GBoost performs the boosting procedure through loss functions. In the experiments, exponential and deviance functions were tried to be able to determine the optimum one. In addition, the contribution ratio of each tree in the model was tried from 5×10^{-3} to 1×10^{-1}. All other tree-based parameter values were set as the same with RF.
- XGBoost model's learning rate was varied between 0.05 and 0.2. All parameter values related to boosting were set the same with GBoost.

Table 4 shows the accuracy values obtained by each algorithm on each animal dataset. All accuracy results range between 94% and 97.7%, so it can be concluded that ensemble learning methods have the ability to reach high accuracy in animal activity recognition. The best results for all animals were obtained by XGBoost. It is clearly seen that XGBoost outperformed the rest on average with an accuracy of 96.7%. This is probably because of the fact that it involves some algorithmic enhancements that provide solving many data science problems in a fast and accurate way, i.e., considering feature importance, iteratively updating the previous model based on misclassifications, and adding regularizations to the loss function. XGBoost achieved the best accuracy (97.7%) on the third goat data. It is followed by the Extra Tees and RF with the accuracy values of 95.7% and 95.6% on average, respectively.

Table 4. Comparison of ensemble learning methods in terms of accuracy (%)

Dataset	Random Forest	Extra Trees	Bagging Trees	Gradient Boosting	Extreme Gradient Boosting
G1	95.1	95.0	94.3	95.2	**96.3**
G2	95.2	95.3	94.0	95.1	**96.5**
G3	96.7	97.0	95.9	97.0	**97.7**
All	95.4	95.5	94.4	94.7	**96.3**
Average	95.6	95.7	94.7	95.5	**96.7**

Figure 2 shows the confusion matrix of the XGBoost model to present the prediction performance of the method on each animal activity separately. As can be seen, the predictive model usually had no difficulty in identifying animal activities. For instance, 1897 out of 1972 "walking" activities were correctly predicted; nevertheless, only 75 of them were misclassified by the model. Although animal activities were distinguished well with high accuracy, "grazing" and "trotting" activities were slightly confused by the method during prediction. It can be also noted from the confusion matrix that the best performance was achieved on the "stationary" activity.

Figure 2. The confusion matrix of the best model

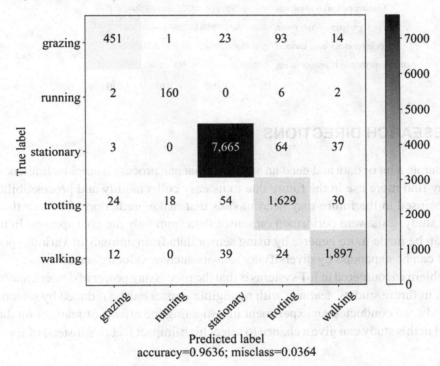

accuracy=0.9636; misclass=0.0364

In the second experiment, we identified the most important features that affect animal activity recognition. Our purpose is not only to construct a good-performing animal activity classifier but also to describe the prediction by means of feature importance. We used the embedding feature importance method in the XGBoost algorithm to evaluate the features. This method forecasts how each feature is correlated with the class attribute (activity) through a pair-wise comparison. Figure 3 shows the top-10 most important features for animal activity prediction in decreasing order. As shown in the figure, feature ranks range between 0.015 and 0.021. According to the results, the most important features for activity prediction are accelerometer z-axis kurtosis and gyroscope z-axis kurtosis. The gyroscope z-axis first magnitude feature (F_1) follows them as one of the important features.

Figure 3. The top-10 important features

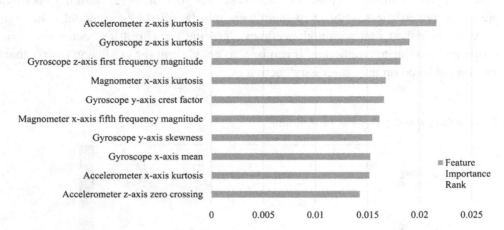

FUTURE RESEARCH DIRECTIONS

IoT devices generate a lot of data and need an approach that can process it quickly. Inferences made from sensor data may find more use in the future due to its easy collectability and processability. Moreover, the system to be used in the future may need models that make predictions for more than one animal species. In this study, tests were performed on sensor data from only the goat species. In future studies, the approach can be made more generic by using sensor data from animals of various species. In addition, the model can be expanded by diversifying sensors such as velocity sensors.

Another problem encountered in IoT systems is that the processing power of devices may not very high. For this reason, in future studies, features with negligible impact can be reduced by selecting important ones. In this study, we conducted an experiment investigating the effects of features on the model. The results obtained in this study can give a chance to select high-impact features instead of less-impact ones.

CONCLUSION

Animal activity is a useful indicator that can be potently utilized to monitor the health and well-being of animals. This study is concerned with the prediction of animal activities based on sensor data obtained from IoT devices placed on animals. The experimental studies are especially focused on the problem of discriminating between the five goat activities (stationary, grazing, walking, trotting, and running) using three different types of sensors (accelerometer, gyroscope, and magnetometer). Five ensemble learning algorithms were compared to determine the best one in classifying goat activities, including Random Forest, Extremely Randomized Trees, Bagging Trees, Gradient Boosting, and Extreme Gradient Boosting.

In this study, two experiments were carried out. The first experiment showed that ensemble learning models achieved very good results in predicting goat activities from sensor data. Especially, the boosting algorithms achieved high accuracy values (~96%) among alternative ensemble learning methods since they progress by correcting previous mistakes. In the second experiment, we observed that the gyroscope sensor data is as important as the accelerometer in animal activity recognition.

REFERENCES

Aich, S., Chakraborty, S., Sim, J. S., Jang, D. J., & Kim, H. C. (2019). The design of an automated system for the analysis of the activity and emotional patterns of dogs with wearable sensors using machine learning. *Applied Sciences (Basel, Switzerland)*, *9*(22), 1–12. doi:10.3390/app9224938

Alvarenga, F. A. P., Borges, I., Palkovič, L., Rodina, J., Oddy, V. H., & Dobos, R. C. (2016). Using a three-axis accelerometer to identify and classify sheep behaviour at pasture. *Applied Animal Behaviour Science*, *181*, 91–99. doi:10.1016/j.applanim.2016.05.026

Arabacı, M. A., Özkan, F., Surer, E., Jančovič, P., & Temizel, A. (2021). Multi-modal egocentric activity recognition using multi-kernel learning. *Multimedia Tools and Applications*, *80*(11), 16299–16328. doi:10.100711042-020-08789-7

Arablouei, R., Currie, L., Kusy, B., Ingham, A., Greenwood, P. L., & Bishop-Hurley, G. (2021). In-situ classification of cattle behavior using accelerometry data. *Computers and Electronics in Agriculture*, *183*, 1–12. doi:10.1016/j.compag.2021.106045

Barwick, J., Lamb, D. W., Dobos, R., Welch, M., & Trotter, M. (2018). Categorising sheep activity using a tri-axial accelerometer. *Computers and Electronics in Agriculture*, *145*, 289–297. doi:10.1016/j.compag.2018.01.007

Brugarolas, R., Latif, T., Dieffenderfer, J., Walker, K., Yuschak, S., Sherman, B. L., Roberts, D. L., & Bozkurt, A. (2015). Wearable heart rate sensor systems for wireless canine health monitoring. *IEEE Sensors Journal*, *16*(10), 3454–3464. doi:10.1109/JSEN.2015.2485210

Casella, E., Khamesi, A. R., & Silvestri, S. (2020). A framework for the recognition of horse gaits through wearable devices. *Pervasive and Mobile Computing*, *67*, 1–19. doi:10.1016/j.pmcj.2020.101213

Chakravarty, P., Cozzi, G., Ozgul, A., & Aminian, K. (2019). A novel biomechanical approach for animal behaviour recognition using accelerometers. *Methods in Ecology and Evolution*, *10*(6), 802–814. doi:10.1111/2041-210X.13172

Conners, M. G., Michelot, T., Heywood, E. I., Orben, R. A., Phillips, R. A., Vyssotski, A. L., Shaffer, S. A., & Thorne, L. H. (2021). Hidden Markov models identify major movement modes in accelerometer and magnetometer data from four albatross species. *Movement Ecology*, *9*(7), 1–16. doi:10.118640462-021-00243-z PMID:33618773

Dandil, E., & Polattimur, R. (2020). Dog behavior recognition and tracking based on faster R-CNN. *Journal of the Faculty of Engineering and Architecture of Gazi University*, *35*(2), 819–834.

Decandia, M., Giovanetti, V., Molle, G., Acciaro, M., Mameli, M., Cabiddu, A., Cossu, R., Serra, M., Manca, C., Rassu, S., & Dimauro, C. (2018). The effect of different time epoch settings on the classification of sheep behaviour using tri-axial accelerometry. *Computers and Electronics in Agriculture*, *154*, 112–119. doi:10.1016/j.compag.2018.09.002

den Uijl, I., Gómez Álvarez, C. B., Bartram, D., Dror, Y., Holland, R., & Cook, A. (2017). External validation of a collar-mounted triaxial accelerometer for second-by-second monitoring of eight behavioural states in dogs. *PLoS One*, *12*(11), 1–13. doi:10.1371/journal.pone.0188481 PMID:29186154

Diosdado, J. A. V., Barker, Z. E., Hodges, H. R., Amory, J. R., Croft, D. P., Bell, N. J., & Codling, E. A. (2015). Classification of behaviour in housed dairy cows using an accelerometer-based activity monitoring system. *Animal Biotelemetry*, *3*(1), 1–14. doi:10.118640317-015-0045-8

Escalante, H. J., Rodriguez, S. V., Cordero, J., Kristensen, A. R., & Cornou, C. (2013). Sow-activity classification from acceleration patterns: A machine learning approach. *Computers and Electronics in Agriculture*, *93*, 17–26. doi:10.1016/j.compag.2013.01.003

Fehlmann, G., O'Riain, M. J., Hopkins, P. W., O'Sullivan, J., Holton, M. D., Shepard, E. L., & King, A. J. (2017). Identification of behaviours from accelerometer data in a wild social primate. *Animal Biotelemetry*, *5*(1), 1–11. doi:10.118640317-017-0121-3

Gao, L., Campbell, H. A., Bidder, O. R., & Hunter, J. (2013). A Web-based semantic tagging and activity recognition system for species' accelerometry data. *Ecological Informatics*, *13*, 47–56. doi:10.1016/j.ecoinf.2012.09.003

George, G., Namdev, A., & Sarma, S. (2018). Animal action recognition: Analysis of various approaches. *International Journal of Engineering Sciences & Research Technology*, *7*(4), 548–554.

Gerencser, L., Vasarhelyi, G., Nagy, M., Vicsek, T., & Miklosi, A. (2013). Identification of behaviour in freely moving dogs (Canis familiaris) using inertial sensors. *PLoS One*, *8*(10), 1–14. doi:10.1371/journal.pone.0077814 PMID:24250745

Giovanetti, V., Decandia, M., Molle, G., Acciaro, M., Mameli, M., Cabiddu, A., Cossu, R., Serra, M., Manca, C., Rassu, S., & Dimauro, C. (2017). Automatic classification system for grazing, ruminating and resting behaviour of dairy sheep using a tri-axial accelerometer. *Livestock Science*, *196*, 42–48. doi:10.1016/j.livsci.2016.12.011

Grunewalder, S., Broekhuis, F., Macdonald, D. W., Wilson, A. M., McNutt, J. W., Shawe-Taylor, J., & Hailes, S. (2012). Movement activity based classification of animal behaviour with an application to data from cheetah (Acinonyx jubatus). *PLoS One*, *7*(11), 1–11. doi:10.1371/journal.pone.0049120 PMID:23185301

Guan, H., Motohashi, N., Maki, T., & Yamaai, T. (2020). Cattle identification and activity recognition by surveillance camera. *Electronic Imaging*, *2020*(12), 174–1. doi:10.2352/ISSN.2470-1173.2020.12.FAIS-174

Hammond, T. T., Springthorpe, D., Walsh, R. E., & Berg-Kirkpatrick, T. (2016). Using accelerometers to remotely and automatically characterize behavior in small animals. *The Journal of Experimental Biology*, *219*(11), 1618–1624. doi:10.1242/jeb.136135 PMID:26994177

Kamminga, J. W., Bisby, H. C., Le, D. V., Meratnia, N., & Havinga, P. J. (2017, September). Generic online animal activity recognition on collar tags. In *Proceedings of the 2017 ACM International Joint Conference on Pervasive and Ubiquitous Computing and Proceedings of the 2017 ACM International Symposium on Wearable Computers* (pp. 597-606). 10.1145/3123024.3124407

Le Roux, S. P., Marias, J., Wolhuter, R., & Niesler, T. (2017). Animal-borne behaviour classification for sheep (Dohne Merino) and Rhinoceros (Ceratotherium simum and Diceros bicornis). *Animal Biotelemetry*, *5*(25), 1–13. doi:10.118640317-017-0140-0

Le Roux, S. P., Wolhuter, R., & Niesler, T. (2019). Energy-aware feature and model selection for onboard behavior classification in low-power animal borne sensor applications. *IEEE Sensors Journal*, *19*(7), 2722–2734. doi:10.1109/JSEN.2018.2886890

Mansbridge, N., Mitsch, J., Bollard, N., Ellis, K., Miguel-Pacheco, G. G., Dottorini, T., & Kaler, J. (2018). Feature selection and comparison of machine learning algorithms in classification of grazing and rumination behaviour in sheep. *Sensors (Basel)*, *18*(10), 1–16. doi:10.339018103532 PMID:30347653

McClune, D. W., Marks, N. J., Wilson, R. P., Houghton, J. D., Montgomery, I. W., McGowan, N. E., Gormley, E., & Scantlebury, M. (2014). Tri-axial accelerometers quantify behaviour in the Eurasian badger (Meles meles): Towards an automated interpretation of field data. *Animal Biotelemetry*, *2*(5), 1–6. doi:10.1186/2050-3385-2-5

Nadimi, E. S., Jørgensen, R. N., Blanes-Vidal, V., & Christensen, S. (2012). Monitoring and classifying animal behavior using ZigBee-based mobile ad hoc wireless sensor networks and artificial neural networks. *Computers and Electronics in Agriculture*, *82*, 44–54. doi:10.1016/j.compag.2011.12.008

Nathan, R., Spiegel, O., Fortmann-Roe, S., Harel, R., Wikelski, M., & Getz, W. M. (2012). Using tri-axial acceleration data to identify behavioral modes of free-ranging animals: General concepts and tools illustrated for griffon vultures. *The Journal of Experimental Biology*, *215*(6), 986–996. doi:10.1242/jeb.058602 PMID:22357592

Painter, M. S., Blanco, J. A., Malkemper, E. P., Anderson, C., Sweeney, D. C., Hewgley, C. W., Červený, J., Hart, V., Topinka, V., Belotti, E., Burda, H., & Phillips, J. B. (2016). Use of bio-loggers to characterize red fox behavior with implications for studies of magnetic alignment responses in free-roaming animals. *Animal Biotelemetry*, *4*(1), 1–20. doi:10.118640317-016-0113-8

Rahman, A., Smith, D. V., Little, B., Ingham, A. B., Greenwood, P. L., & Bishop-Hurley, G. J. (2018). Cattle behaviour classification from collar, halter, and ear tag sensors. *Information Processing in Agriculture*, *5*(1), 124–133. doi:10.1016/j.inpa.2017.10.001

Shamoun-Baranes, J., Bom, R., van Loon, E. E., Ens, B. J., Oosterbeek, K., & Bouten, W. (2012). From sensor data to animal behaviour: An oystercatcher example. *PLoS One*, *7*(5), 1–13. doi:10.1371/journal.pone.0037997 PMID:22693586

Soltis, J., Wilson, R., Douglas-Hamilton, I., Vollrath, F., King, L., & Savage, A. (2012). Accelerometers in collars identify behavioral states in captive African elephants Loxodonta africana. *Endangered Species Research*, *18*(3), 255–263. doi:10.3354/esr00452

Sturm, V., Efrosinin, D., Efrosinina, N., Roland, L., Iwersen, M., Drillich, M., & Auer, W. (2019). A chaos theoretic approach to animal activity recognition. *Journal of Mathematical Sciences*, *237*(5), 730–743. doi:10.100710958-019-04199-9

Walton, E., Casey, C., Mitsch, J., Vázquez-Diosdado, J. A., Yan, J., Dottorini, T., Ellis, K. A., Winterlich, A., & Kaler, J. (2018). Evaluation of sampling frequency, window size and sensor position for classification of sheep behaviour. *Royal Society Open Science*, *5*(2), 1–14. doi:10.1098/rsos.171442 PMID:29515862

ADDITIONAL READING

Dominguez-Morales, J. P., Duran-Lopez, L., Gutierrez-Galan, D., Rios-Navarro, A., Linares-Barranco, A., & Jimenez-Fernandez, A. (2021). Wildlife Monitoring on the Edge: A Performance Evaluation of Embedded Neural Networks on Microcontrollers for Animal Behavior Classification. *Sensors (Basel)*, *21*(9), 2975. doi:10.339021092975 PMID:33922753

Dominguez-Morales, J. P., Rios-Navarro, A., Dominguez-Morales, M., Tapiador-Morales, R., Gutierrez-Galan, D., Cascado-Caballero, D., Jimenez-Fernandez, A., & Linares-Barranco, A. (2016). Wireless sensor network for wildlife tracking and behavior classification of animals in Doñana. *IEEE Communications Letters*, *20*(12), 2534–2537. doi:10.1109/LCOMM.2016.2612652

Glass, T. W., Breed, G. A., Robards, M. D., Williams, C. T., & Kielland, K. (2020). Accounting for unknown behaviors of free-living animals in accelerometer-based classification models: Demonstration on a wide-ranging mesopredator. *Ecological Informatics*, *60*, 101152. doi:10.1016/j.ecoinf.2020.101152

Gutierrez-Galan, D., Dominguez-Morales, J. P., Cerezuela-Escudero, E., Rios-Navarro, A., Tapiador-Morales, R., Rivas-Perez, M., Dominguez-Morales, M., Jimenez-Fernandez, A., & Linares-Barranco, A. (2018). Embedded neural network for real-time animal behavior classification. *Neurocomputing*, *272*, 17–26. doi:10.1016/j.neucom.2017.03.090

Le Roux, S. P., Wolhuter, R., Stevens, N., & Niesler, T. (2018). Reduced energy and memory requirements by on-board behavior classification for animal-borne sensor applications. *IEEE Sensors Journal*, *18*(10), 4261–4268. doi:10.1109/JSEN.2018.2816965

Torres, L. G., Orben, R. A., Tolkova, I., & Thompson, D. R. (2017). Classification of animal movement behavior through residence in space and time. *PLoS One*, *12*(1), 1–18. doi:10.1371/journal.pone.0168513 PMID:28045906

KEY TERMS AND DEFINITIONS

Activity Recognition: The process of labeling input data with action labels.

Animal Activity Recognition: The process of identifying the activity of an animal by analyzing video or sensor data.

Classification: The process of categorizing data based on certain characteristics.

Feature Extraction: The task of generating new features by using some methods from existing information in the data.

Internet of Things: The network of physical devices which are connected via the Internet.

Machine Learning: The application of intelligent algorithms that teach computers to create analytical models.

Sensor Data: Data that are collected from various heterogeneous internet of things (IoT) devices.

Chapter 10
Essentials, Challenges, and Future Directions of Agricultural IoT:
A Case Study in the Indian Perspective

M. Manikandakumar

ⓘ https://orcid.org/0000-0003-2648-7139

Thiagarajar College of Engineering, India

P. Karthikeyan

ⓘ https://orcid.org/0000-0003-2703-4051

Thiagarajar College of Engineering, India

ABSTRACT

Agriculture plays a major role in the socio-economic structure of India. A recent report claimed that population of India is increasing faster than its capability to produce rice, wheat, and vegetables. The challenges in the area of agriculture are farming, watering, weather forecasting, marketing, and transportation. These challenges are to be addressed towards proper solution. If the infrastructure and productivity of the food increases, then India can easily feed its population as well as improve the exports of wheat and rice around the world. Internet of things (IoT) is an emerging technical area of agriculture domain. The advantage of IoT is to implement a smart agriculture management system with the help of analyzing the weather conditions of the field in order to optimize the usage of water, energy, fertilizers so as to maximize the crop yield. The objective of this study is to explore the possible contributions of IoT in Indian agriculture towards the improvements in irrigation infrastructure, agricultural productivity, food security, and rural job opportunities.

DOI: 10.4018/978-1-7998-4186-9.ch010

INTRODUCTION

Agriculture is one of the most important areas of human activity worldwide. India is one of the agriculture background developing nation with more than 70% of its inhabitants depend on agriculture. The escalation in agriculture productivity directly increases the economy of India. As of 2015-16, India has wide-ranging agricultural sector makes about 17% of GDP income. India's 159.7 million hectares (394.6 million acres) of arable land is the second largest in the globe, after the United States. Gross irrigated crop region of 82.6 million hectares is the biggest in the world. India stands in the top three global manufacturers of many crops, such as wheat, rice, cotton, peanuts, vegetables and fruits. India also had the biggest herds of livestock; hence it is the large maker of milk and also has one of the largest poultry industries. As the inhabitants of India increases there is a need to raise the agriculture productivity. But nowadays the Indian farmer's life style and farm practices are swiftly untrustworthy due to the raise in non-agricultural openings. The scientific improvements in farming are not getting closer to the cultivator, because of their illiteracy or due to lack of knowledge. Hence, a greater number of the farmers are failing to gain the expected production profit and business rate. Still the Indian agriculture face the challenges like traditional farming practices, disjointed land farming, dependence on monsoon, poor infrastructure in countryside and less usage of technology applications.

Indian financial system is organized into three sectors: Agriculture sector, Industry sector and Service sector. The Agriculture sector consists of Agriculture, Livestock, Forestry & Logging, Fishing and allied activities. Combination of Agriculture & allied, Industry, and Services sector was 51.45%, 16.69%, and 29.63%, correspondingly at current prices in 1951-52. But now the contribution of Agriculture & allied sector has declined to 17.40% in 2015-16. Meanwhile share of service sector has improved to 56.60% share of industry sector also has raised to 26.00% as shown in fig.1 (Planning Commission department, Government of India). Rural areas in India still faces a greater number of challenges in the agriculture sector, water resources management, environment management, infrastructure administration, cleanliness, access to markets, roads and transport connectivity. The technical contribution and its usability still have to be developed for agriculture sector.

Figure 1. Sector wise contribution of GDP of India (1951 - 2019)

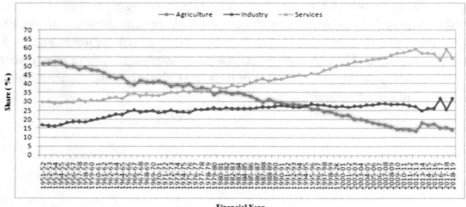

In this Internet era information plays a vital task, agriculture is becoming a very data concentrated area where farm workers need to gather and analyze large amount of data from a diverse number of field devices such as meteorological sensor, fertilizer sensors, farm equipments etc., to turn into more resourceful in production and transporting suitable information. The remaining of the paper is followed as: Section two presents the related literature. Section three shows open challenges and issues on IoT and in the next section the authors discussed the IoT recommendations for agriculture, the fifth section presents the technologies, platforms and standards for agricultural IoT, sixth section lists the possible applications, at the last the work is concluded and throws more ideas on feasible future works.

BACKGROUND

The idea of smart farming, based on IoT technique, is becoming a smart way for organizing natural sources and realizing modernized sustainable agriculture development. It is transporting agriculture into the modern and new information age. Even though some initiatives have already been executed by the government of India for providing web and mobile based online information services to farmers related to agriculture queries, wholesaler detail to farmers, they only provide the static information related to soil quality at each district and state. To counter the requirements of rural farmers and other agriculture allied communities, minimize their poverty and digitalize the agriculture sector, this study focuses the use of information and communication technologies (ICTs), specifically Internet of Things, to serve the rural communities in India. The purpose and aim of this work is to identify the requirements and suggest IoT in response to these requirements with the intention of reducing the impact of scarcity in the countryside areas with prominence on the agricultural sector.

For agricultural practices and in an environment where the initiation of climate change results in unpredictable rainfalls, automatic drip irrigation can be adopted. Robles et al. developed smart water managing system based on IoT technology by implementing business processes management and decision support systems (Robles et al., 2014). The practice of drip irrigation supplies water only to the soil closest to the plant's root. Gathering and connecting data such as humidity, temperature, radiation, and soil water content from various sensors, control the supply of water in required level and appropriate location. In view of the fact that the farm lands in the rural side are capable by means of renewable sources and there is a limited or no facility to get connected with electricity network, these renewable forces such as solar and airstream can provide energy into water pumps which in turn pump water from ground to tanks.

Weather data collection over long periods and analysis can be very much useful for forecast the weather to lessen the risks associated with the agriculture. Big data analytics technology can be the better solution provider for this analysis. The effectiveness of insect can also be monitored and controlled along with the environment data, which allows agriculture experts to predict pest occurrences more clearly for the reason that the pest maturation depends on environmental circumstances. Similarly farm management systems should take the advantages of new characters that the upcoming internet offers. More software modules could be used to develop farm related special digital components. Alexandros Kaloxylos et al., (2014) developed a cloud-based Farm Management System in which a user has the ability to retrieve weather information for any place simply by typing the location name into the input box.

Drought has been a problem disturbing our food security. A challenge of drought research is to implement suitable techniques for forecasting the beginning and termination points of droughts. A synthetic system that integrates drought monitoring and forecasting and irrigation amount forecasting into an IoT platform using hybrid programming and parallel computing has designed by Quingzu Laun et al., (2015). The design of drought impact assessment also can better serve for the disaster prevention and reduction. Processing and analyzing methods have to be improved for multi sourced data, further optimization of the algorithms will gives better efficiency. The advancement in this technology will help farmers increase the crop gain. Architecture has developed and incorporated to a middleware which handles the collection and pre-processing of sensor data, with the support to actuation on the environment. Expand the use of the architecture in other equipments and consequently integrating other types of sensors and actuators might be an intelligent method (Cardozo et al., 2016).

Distributed heterogeneous WSN for facility agriculture environment monitoring and warning system in the early hours based on IoT using ZigBee also has been implemented. In which the perception layer collects the physical information from RFID tags, sensors and cameras, the access layer transfers the data from acquisition layer to network layer. The network level layer performs the functionalities related to transporting data streams from source to target. The application level layer performs the practical application processes for the end consumer. Parameters other than the temperature and humidity also have to be considered for the complete framework development. The distributed information service method of agriculture IoT was proposed by Li Minbo et al., (2013) based on the data service, object identity service, discovery service to provide public information service that includes capturing, processing, managing and querying of enormous business data of agriculture production. This information service can be further enhanced to maintain more types of agricultural products.

The proposed work on implementing precision agriculture using wireless sensor network application by Mohd Kassim et al., (2014) shows WSN as the good method to solve the issues associated to farming resources optimization, making decision support systems and land monitoring. But large data sets need to be collected and tested. IoT gateway for agricultural greenhouse has been implemented and was compatible with multiple access methods such as LAN, Wifi, GPRS, EDGE and 3G. Extendibility issues with new technologies have to be addressed to make it comfortable remote monitoring. A dispersed automated crop disease consultative service to mitigate crop diseases and an innovative tailored agriculture advisory system that bridges information gaps exist between farmers and agricultural scientists. Rising IoT technologies, such as sensor networks, networked weather locations, digital cameras, and smart mobile phones would be used to gather enormous volume of ecological and crop growth status data, ranging time series data from sensors, spatial data from digital cameras, human interpretation composed and recorded through smart mobile phone applications. These data can then be processed to sort out worthless data and calculate personalized crop productivity recommendations for any specific farm land (Jayaraman et al.,). However, still integrating the technologies such as sensor, GPS, bar codes, QR code and streaming image data into a single system and processing multivariate data is an immense problem to researchers.

OPEN CHALLENGES AND ISSUES

Data Storage

Large volume of data stream in agriculture comes from variety of sensors, M2M data systems, satellites, GPS, yield software, and seed planting hardware. The challenge is to store these multiple, heterogeneous data types and formats in order to solve the problems and making decision support system to the farmers and appropriate stakeholders.

Data Analysis

To predict what type of seed to use, the best time to plant, where to plant in order to get better yields and decrease environmental impact from the research data specific to agriculture data analysis plays a vital role. It is difficult to process using usual data processing applications or database management system tools. The challenges also include on historical data comparisons, stream data processing and data transfer, visualization and information retrieval.

Big data analytics mechanisms are necessary to identify significant results from huge amount of different kind of sensor data (Wolfert et al., 2017). These techniques are needed to find preferences of farmers and other stakeholders by exploring the unseen correlations, hidden patterns, detecting disasters and business strategies. Few challenges to the agricultural domain includes,

- Policy development based on data analytics practices for government and industrial regulations.
- Simple farming machinery control mechanisms for larger size farm fields.
- Developing crop growth monitoring structure, disease supervision models based on the collected field data.
- Design of web-based data analytics application to the farmers in order to provide digitalized recommendations on agriculture.
- Decision support system to improve crop productivity and business profit.

Security & Privacy

Farmers are concerned about what could happen if their data falls into the wrong peoples. According to a recent survey summarized at https://www.hpe.com accessed (15 Sep. 2019), 61% of farmers said they were worried that vendors will use their data to influence market decisions, and 77% of farmers want entire control over their data and more transparency from the vendors who collect it. Most vendors collect and store data from sensors and software, and enforce privacy terms stating that the data belongs to the vendor. The battle over who gets to own, use, and profit from the data will likely continue, challenges such as insufficient authentication, Lack of transport encryption, insecure web or mobile interface, poor session management, weak default credentials, lack of secure code practices and cross-site scripting vulnerabilities while data security will also remain a concern. Open nature of wireless communication medium, frequent changing topology with dynamism and inadequate capability of sensors in terms of operational power, energy, storage, bandwidth and integration with an internet also leads to security issues (Manikandakumar et al., 2019). Proper access control schemes for sensor networks in the context of IoT, big data and allied policies have to be designed and practiced for security and privacy needs (Manikandakumar & Ramanujam, 2018; Manikandakumar & Karthikeyan, 2019; Manikandakumar et al., 2019).

Interoperability

A major challenge is the lack of wireless infrastructure in rural areas. Even though the growth of IoT, service providers still establish the connectivity based on the number of people connected, leaving less population area for connectivity. Extendibility issues with new technologies have to be addressed to make it comfortable remote monitoring. Ensuring the interoperability of a vast heterogeneity of IoT devices with open IoT standards, architectures and platforms including the arrangement of horizontal technical IoT standards and specific standards in the agriculture domain is also a challenge to the researchers. Semantic Web ontology has to be designed to increase the interoperability between heterogeneous data sets and heterogeneous big data environments.

Optimization

Lack of optimization algorithms, intelligent methodologies and tools are other challenging factors that has to be solved to attain best results in terms of quality, quantity, sustainability, cost effectiveness and financial return from agricultural production and reduce wastages. The Internet of Things will play a key position to defeat such short comings and gives a new way in the domains of agriculture and irrigation.

IOT RECOMMENDATIONS FOR AGRICULTURE

The development of agricultural IoT and implementations will give excellent opportunities for modernizing conventional farming methods, as well as for spreading advanced awareness to farmers. There is a prediction that by the year 2050, the agriculture IoT will increase the food production by 70% and will be feeds up to 9.6 billion numbers of people. By taking into account the development of IoT till 2000, the usage of sensors in agriculture gives a major shift in agro products. About 525 million farms on global record were connected to the Internet of Things in the year 2000. In the year 2025 about 600 million sensor deployments at connected farms which leads to the foremost transfer towards technical advancements been applied in agriculture sector to carry the Agricultural Internet of Things. In 2035, with 525 million farm fields world-wide, there would be more than threefold enlargement in sensor utilization compared to the year 2020. By 2050, there will be a possibility of two billion sensors deployed in 525 million agriculture farm. It brings the agriculture into the digital era and maximizes the return on investment.

The Sensor technology can be used effectively in organic greenhouses to observe and manage temperature, humidity data, soil aeration status, soil moisture, fertility levels and sun radiance. Integrating all such parameters through a framework to organize them can direct towards smart system that helps former to utilize their resources and diversification. IoT technologies could also support precision agriculture to maximize productivity. It can give alert notifications to keep a crop in a good manner by communicating data wirelessly to water store points on when to supply water. Additionally, farm workers can implement automatic drip irrigation in the areas of water scarce. It could be attained by involving sensor data from a range of resources that manages not only where water is released but also how much is actually needed.

IoT based smart decision support systems running on smart mobiles support farmers preparation for the appropriate farming seasons. These applications also help farmers to track and monitor farm animals, detecting potential signs of diseases, prevent the spread of plant eating pests and plant diseases. With the growing face of IoT technology, the increasing number of agriculture farms can be equipped with smart cameras monitoring the farm situation and status of the crop growth. In-field monitoring is recommended to lessen the crop harm by plant eating pests and animals. Smart mobile phone might be used to take photographs and transmit the images of infected crops or livestock to scientist's lab for prescribe remedies to the identified problems.

Fig 1 describes the proposed framework of agricultural IoT. The entire framework is carefully designed to satisfy the needs of farmers, consumers, storage and analytical engineers. With the help of this framework farmers can increase their productivity and yields due to the advanced technology, analyst and agriculture experts can forecast the future climates and can provide their predicted suggestions, Consumers can utilize the quality products.

Figure 2. Agricultural IoT reference model

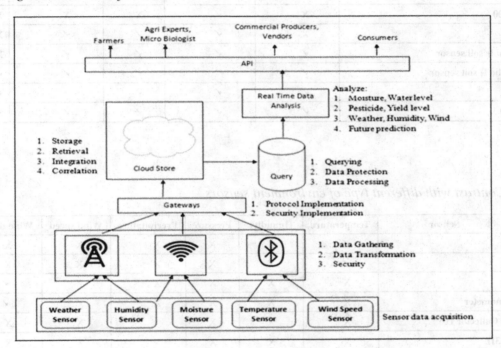

TECHNOLOGIES, PLATFORMS AND STANDARDS FOR AGRICULTURAL IOT

The agricultural IoT reference model is divided into several layers.

Sensor Data Acquisition Layer

Data acquisition level layer consists of various agriculture specific sensors to collect the field data such as weather, humidity, moisture and temperature etc., the authors compared the sensors in this layer into two major categories as soil sensors and environment sensors. Table 1. lists the different type of soil oriented sensors which are deployed for capturing the field data like soil moisture, soil temperature, salinity, conductivity and water content level in the soil.

Environment specific agriculture sensors are compared and listed in Table 2., this type of sensors are deployed to focus on the parameters such as temperature, pressure, humidity, wind speed, wind direction and precipitation. By deploying these soil and environment sensors will ensures the better decision making process, limited usage of pesticides, fertilizers and improved quality monitoring.

Table 1. Contrast with different type of soil sensors

Sensor	Soil Moisture	Soil Temperature	Salinity	Conductivity	Water level
ECH₂O EC-5	✓	X	X	X	X
5TE	✓	✓	✓	✓	✓
GS3	✓	✓	✓	✓	✓
VH-400	✓	X	X	X	✓
THERM200	X	✓	X	X	X
WET-2	X	✓	✓	✓	X
Pogo portable soil sensor	✓	✓	✓	✓	X
Hydra probe II soil sensor	✓	✓	✓	✓	✓
EC-250	✓	✓	✓	✓	✓
SMEC 300	✓	✓	✓	✓	X

Table 2. Contrast with different type of environment sensors

Sensor	Temperature	Humidity	Pressure	Precipitation	Wind speed	Wind direction
HMP60	✓	✓	X	X	X	X
PT1000	✓	X	X	X	X	X
RM Young	X	X	X	X	✓	✓
Davis Anemometer	X	X	X	X	✓	✓
Davis Rain Collector II	X	X	X	✓	X	X
RG13/RG13H	X	X	X	✓	X	X
Met One Series 380 rain gauge	X	X	X	✓	X	X
MSO weather station	✓	✓	✓	X	✓	✓
CM-100 compact weather station	✓	✓	✓	X	✓	✓
WXT530 compact weather station	✓	✓	✓	✓	✓	✓
AIO Weather Sensor	✓	✓	✓	X	✓	✓

Communication Layer

Communication layer establishes the data communication between the data acquisition layer and to higher layers. Data gathering from sensors and secured way of transmitting the data to big data store through the appropriate gateways are the important roles of this layer. This part lists the particulars of various wireless medium standards and their applications in agriculture domain.

WiMAX

WiMAX is a wireless network standard which implements interoperable development of IEEE 802.16 group. It is stands for Worldwide Interoperability for Microwave Access. WiMAX is one of the best suited communication standard for agricultural IoT applications and implementations due to its support over for long range of area coverage along with high speed data communication. IEEE 802.16e standard is referred as Mobile WiMAX (Louta et al., 2014) provides the minimum data rate of 50 MbPs and extends to the maximum of 100 Mbps and shows the energy efficiency than 4G LTE (Long Term Evolution).

ZigBee

ZigBee, a low cost, low power, radio enabled and reliable wireless medium communication scheme based on the standard IEEE 802.15.4, which is best suitable for energy efficient small range (10-20 meter) agricultural farm lands. ZigBee works at the maximum data rate as 250 kbps at 868/915 MHz and 2.4 GHz frequencies of ISM band (Lin, 2011).

Bluetooth

Bluetooth is another low cost, low power wireless communication medium standard based on IEEE 802.15.1 to establish the data communication over short range (upto 10 meter). The data rate of this technology ranges from 1-24 Mbps. This device defines the Personal Area Network (PAN) medium using 2.4 GhZ of ISM band. Due to the AdHoc nature of the Bluetooth, it can be best applicable to the multi layer agricultural applications that include environmental monitoring, precision agriculture, facility automation and tractability systems with RFID.

WiFi

WiFi is a wireless local area network (WLAN) standard based on IEEE 802.11. It works on the data transmission rate of 2 – 54 Mbps at 2.4 GHz ISM band upto 100 meter area range. WiFi can be used in agriculture field to establish the connection between different kind of network devices and sensors in AdHoc fashion.

GPRS

General Packet Radio Service (GPRS) is an ETSI-3GPP standard which uses 900 – 1800 MHz frequency band at the maximum data rate of 115.2 Kb/s over the long distances ranges from 0.5km to 35km. It is a packet based data transmission service for GSM based cells (Zong et al., 2013). The throughput of GPRS depends on the number of user utilizing the same resource. GPRS can be effectively used in large scale agriculture fields for monitoring, tracking and periodically updating the agriculture instruments. GSM and UMTS has the similar features, those can also be used in larger size agriculture farm lands as a part of IoT setup for better cultivation and irrigation process. Table 3 presents the comparison of different communication standards.

Table 3. Contrast with various communication standard

Parameter types	Communication Standards						
	WiMAX	ZigBee	Bluetooth	WiFi	GSM	GPRS	UMTS
Standard	IEEE - 802.16 a /e	IEEE - 802.15.4	IEEE - 802.15.1	IEEE - 802.11 a/b/g	GSM 1900	ETSI – 3GPP Standard	3GPP Standard
Frequency band	2–66 GHz	868/915 MHz, 2.4 GHz	2.4 GHz 2.4 GHz	2.4 GHz 2.4 GHz	900- 1800MHz 1 Mb/s	900-	1.92- 1.98GHz 2.11- 2.17GHz 54 Mb/s
Maximum Data rate	50 Mb/s	250 Kb/s	1 Mb/s 8–10 m	54 Mb/s 20 – 100	14.4 Kb/s	115.2 Kb/s	2 Mb/s
Transmission range	<=50 km	10–20 m	8–10 m	m	0.5 – 35 Km	0.5 – 35 Km	0.1 – 10 Km
Channel Bandwidth	1.25 - 20 MHz	0.3 / 0.6 MHz - 2 MHz	1 MHz 1 MHz	22 MHz 22 MHz	200 KHz	200 KHz	5 MHz
Node Acquisition Time	100ms	30ms	3s 3s	2s 2s	Based on Grade of Service	Based on Grade of Service	Based on Grade of Service
Access Technique	Scheduling Scheme	CSMA - CA	TDMA TDMA	CSMA / CA	TDMA	TDMA	CDMA

The following table summarizes the available technologies, architectures, platforms and standards for Agriculture IoT.

Table 4. Technologies, Architectures, Platforms and Standards for Agricultural IoT

Technology Types	On hand Technologies, Architectures, Platforms and Standards for Agriculture IoT
Hardware	**Sensor types:**
	weather, water, humidity, Moisture, soil respiration wind speed, gas analyzers, chemical, biological, Leaf Area index (LAI) sensors, mechanical, acoustic, ultrasonic, electric, optical cameras, range finders, Radio Frequency Identifiers.
	Sensor device standards:
	SensorML, IEEE 1451, ISO 29182.
	Actuator types:
	Mechanical, Electrical, Thermal, Hydraulic.
	Hardware interfaces:
	RS-232, RS-485.,
	Processors:
	MIPS, ARM, x86, Multi-core processors.
Software	**IoT/Embedded OS:**
	Windows 10, Embedded Linux, RTOS, Tiny OS.
	Smartphone OS:
	Android OS, iOS, Windows mobile OS, Blackberry OS.
	High-level protocols and languages:
	HTTP, Websockets, CoAP, Web REST services, MQTT, WFS, WMS.
Networking Technologies	**Wired medium:**
	IEEE 802.3, IPv6, CAN J1939 bus, ISO11783.
	Wireless medium:
	IEEE802.15.1, IEEE802.15.4, RFID, NFC, ISO11785, ISO14223, ZigBee, WiMAX, Wi-Fi (IEEE802.11), UWB, GSM, GPRS, UMTS, LTE.
Platforms	**Platforms:**
	UBIDOTS, Xively, Thing Speak, Open.Sen.se,SensorCloud, Amazon IoT and IBM IoT platforms. FIWARE, SOFIA2, Carriots, Farmsight, Thingworx, ODBC.
	Architectures:
	IoT-A, IoT World Forum, IIoT Architecture, IEEE, ITU-T.
Services	**Cloud Services:**
	SaaS, IaaS, PaaS, SOA.
	Data analytics services:
	Anomaly detection, trend detection, time series, Hadoop, Spark.
	Weather information systems.

Data Storage and Big Data Analytics Layer

Data resources needed to store in a cloud store kind of shared databases, Storing huge volumes of data on the hybrid storage system is the best approach and commonly accepted solution worldwide for agriculture related purposes in order to trade off the cost and performance (Zong et al., 2013). This layer includes the processes like data storage, data retrieval, data integration and correlation of data. Big Data analytics is the process of collecting, organizing, cleaning, inspecting, analyzing, transforming and modeling the large sets of data to discover new patterns and other useful information. It helps the farmers and agriculture scientists to identify the data pattern that is most recommended to the agriculture business development and for future decisions (Wolfert et al.,). E-Agriculture services are possible using the technologies like Hadoop, HDFS and MapReduce with the aid of IoT and Big data that can change the way of agriculture world to meet the global food needs. Real time data analysis involves to analyze the parameters such as moisture, water level, pesticide level and yield prediction etc.,

Application Programming Interface Layer

The Application Programming Interface (API) Layer will facilitate different kind of persons to be connected with Agricultural IoT framework. Farmers can get the seasonal updates, advises from the agri experts and micro biologists. Agri experts and engineers can do research by using this framework for the betterment of cultivation and irrigation process. Commercial Producers and vendors can improve their business by getting the best practices and features from the system. This framework also has direct beneficial impacts with the consumers.

APPLICATIONS OF AGRICULTURAL IOT

Here the authors list the application possibilities of agriculture which can be implemented in Internet of Things.

Farm Management and Monitoring

To improve the economy and to ensure the food availability, agriculture needs modern farm management systems to optimize the energy, water and other resource usage in farming. Scarcity in the level of ground water, electricity and other resources needs to be carefully managed by developing modern farm management system. In this context, IoT based agriculture development and micro-irrigation systems will be the appropriate techniques for cost - effective, resource - efficient productivity which can be achieved by analyzing the environment and soil related information from the field (Adamala et al., 2014; Lichtenberg et sl., 2015; & Gutierrez et al., 2014).

IoT sensor devices can potentially monitor the field and can be configured to interact each other on the network. Nowadays advanced devices and systems are used in large scale agriculture, such devices can be remotely monitored and managed to do the right operation by using the IoT. These devices can be integrated with the satellite inputs, weather monitoring systems, crop health monitoring systems and yield prediction systems (Kim et al., 2014).

Water Supply Management

The crops may get damaged either by excess water supply or water shortage. An intelligent water supply management system integrated with agricultural IoT sensors and analytical systems provides best suggestions to manage the water requirements and water supply for the crop irrigation. It can smartly analyze the adequate amount of water requirements according to the resources available in order to avoid the water waste. Agricultural IoT would be an ultimate technology in the drought and dry areas as it can decide the optimized water supply by intelligent analytics.

Pesticide and Fertilizer Management

To prevent the losses due to pests, usage of pesticides and other controlling mechanisms helps to improve the quality of the crop. IoT systems can be used in controlling the pesticide in the field by monitoring the occurrence of the pest and other worms in the plant (Bhave et al., 2014). Proper supply of fertilizers exactly at the crop places will also increases the crop quality and growth. It is possible to IoT devises which can monitor the level of Nitrogen-Phosphorous-Potassium (NPK) and suggest the farmer to spray the required combination of nutrition. It leads to the cost effective process, optimized use of resources like pesticides and fertilizers and ensures the healthy cultivation lands (Gonçalves et al., 2015; Karthikeyan et al., 2020).

Livestock Monitoring

Livestock farming and agriculture are closely related to each other. IoT systems can be a better replacement for the traditional livestock farming and monitoring process. It can be implemented to remotely monitor the animal movements outside of the restricted boundary and also monitoring the movements towards the vegetation area. Tags places on the herds can transmit data on everything from livestock's health to their mating patterns. Animal identification and tracking in larger livestock farms using RFID tags, animal health monitoring, precision livestock farming and availability of graze in the field for feeding the cattle can be monitored and managed in an effective manner using the IoT technology (Voulodimos et al.,2010).

Ground Water Monitoring

The augmented amount of fertilizer, pesticide and other chemical composition usage in the farm land leads to lessen the worth of ground water. Deploying the appropriate IoT connected sensors will help in monitoring and alarming the water quality. The effective ground water level monitoring and management will ensure the quantity of ground water to satisfy the agricultural needs.

Asset Tracing and Remote Diagnosis

IoT smart devices and sensors attached to the on-hand machinery and other resources such as tractors, shipping machines, containers, pumps, lights heaters, valves and other farming equipments can be tracked and automated in the best way. The entire irrigation system can be tracked from the farmer's home itself and further it can be diagnosed in case of any malfunctioning such as water leakage and in pesticide sprayers. The advent of IoT along with the application of predictive analytics can help agriculture in cost reduction and improve on asset efficiency and availability (Misra & Singh, 2012).

Greenhouse Gases Analysis

IoT can be extended with Big data analytics to analyze the greenhouse gas emission received from different kind of agriculture resources. Such sort of analytics is highly recommended for agriculture as the impact of greenhouse gases are the most influencing factors in ever-increasing the atmosphere temperature (Malaver et al.,).

CONCLUSION

In this study, a novel idea in the field of Internet of Things in farmer's perspective is explored and opens a new aspect of research. Few applications of agriculture IoT have been identified for the farm development. The work is intended to the deployment of IoT in agriculture development. The authors also listed much business profit that would be achieved from various domains of agriculture by implementing IoT in farm fields. It opens a great way to improve the automation and intelligence of agriculture production by applying the Internet of Things technologies. Further development using IoT helps farmer in all aspects, that is, in water management, weather prediction, crop analysis, transport and storage of agricultural products, plant disease management and also for the developers to build other country-specific challenges which leads to poverty mitigation and enriching the standards of the people.

REFERENCES

Adamala, S., Raghuwanshi, N. S., & Mishra, A. (2014). Development of Surface Irrigation Systems Design and Evaluation Software (SIDES). *Computers and Electronics in Agriculture*, *100*, 100–109. doi:10.1016/j.compag.2013.11.004

Bhave, A. G., Mishra, A., & Raghuwanshi, N. S. (2014). A combined bottom-up and top-down approach for assessment of climate change adaptation options. *Journal of Hydrology (Amsterdam)*, *518*, 150–161. doi:10.1016/j.jhydrol.2013.08.039

Cardozo, A., Yamin, A., Xavier, L., Souza, R., Lopes, J., & Geyer, C. (2016). An architecture proposal to distributed sensing in Internet of Things. *2016 1st International Symposium on Instrumentation Systems, Circuits and Transducers (INSCIT)*. doi:10.1109/inscit.2016.7598208

Gonçalves, L. B. L., Costa, F. G., Neves, L. A., Ueyama, J., Zafalon, G. F. D., Montez, C., & Pinto, A. S. R. (2015). Influence of Mobility Models in Precision Spray Aided by Wireless Sensor Networks. *Journal of Physics: Conference Series*, *574*, 012153. doi:10.1088/1742-6596/574/1/012153

Gutierrez, J., Villa-Medina, J. F., Nieto-Garibay, A., & Porta-Gandara, M. A. (2014). Automated Irrigation System Using a Wireless Sensor Network and GPRS Module. *IEEE Transactions on Instrumentation and Measurement*, *63*(1), 166–176. doi:10.1109/tim.2013.2276487

Jayaraman, P., Yavari, A., Georgakopoulos, D., Morshed, A., & Zaslavsky, A. (2016). Internet of Things Platform for Smart Farming: Experiences and Lessons Learnt. *Sensors (Basel)*, *16*(11), 1884. doi:10.339016111884

Kaloxylos, A., Groumas, A., Sarris, V., Katsikas, L., Magdalinos, P., Antoniou, E., ... Maestre Terol, C. (2014). A cloud-based Farm Management System: Architecture and implementation. *Computers and Electronics in Agriculture*, *100*, 168–179. doi:10.1016/j.compag.2013.11.014

Karthikeyan, P., Manikandakumar, M., Sri Subarnaa, D. K., & Priyadharshini, P. (2020). Weed Identification in Agriculture Field Through IoT. *Advances in Smart System Technologies*, 495–505. doi:10.1007/978-981-15-5029-4_41

Kim, Y.-D., Yang, Y.-M., Kang, W.-S., & Kim, D.-K. (2014). On the design of beacon based wireless sensor network for agricultural emergency monitoring systems. *Computer Standards & Interfaces*, *36*(2), 288–299. doi:10.1016/j.csi.2011.05.004

Lichtenberg, E., Majsztrik, J., & Saavoss, M. (2015). Grower demand for sensor-controlled irrigation. *Water Resources Research*, *51*(1), 341–358. doi:10.1002/2014wr015807

Lin, Y. G. (2011). An Intelligent Monitoring System for Agriculture Based on Zigbee Wireless Sensor Networks. *Advanced Materials Research*, *383-390*, 4358–4364. doi:10.4028/www.scientific.net/amr.383-390.4358

Louta, M., Sarigiannidis, P., Misra, S., Nicopolitidis, P., & Papadimitriou, G. (2014). RLAM: A Dynamic and Efficient Reinforcement Learning-Based Adaptive Mapping Scheme in Mobile WiMAX Networks. *Mobile Information Systems*, *10*(2), 173–196. doi:10.1155/2014/213056

Luan, Q., Fang, X., Ye, C., & Liu, Y. (2015). An integrated service system for agricultural drought monitoring and forecasting and irrigation amount forecasting. *2015 23rd International Conference on Geoinformatics*. doi:10.1109/geoinformatics.2015.7378617

Malaver, A., Motta, N., Corke, P., & Gonzalez, F. (2015). Development and Integration of a Solar Powered Unmanned Aerial Vehicle and a Wireless Sensor Network to Monitor Greenhouse Gases. *Sensors (Basel)*, *15*(2), 4072–4096. doi:10.3390150204072

Manikandakumar, M., & Ramanujam, E. (2018). Security and Privacy Challenges in Big Data Environment. *Advances in Information Security, Privacy, and Ethics*, 315–325. doi:10.4018/978-1-5225-4100-4.ch017

Manikandakumar, M., Sri Subarnaa D. K., & Monica Grace R. (2019). A Detailed Study on Security Concerns of VANET and Cognitive Radio VANETs. *Cognitive Social Mining Applications in Data Analytics and Forensics*, 252–264. doi:10.4018/978-1-5225-7522-1.ch013

Minbo, L., Zhu, Z., & Guangyu, C. (2013). Information Service System Of Agriculture IoT. *Automatika (Zagreb)*, *54*(4), 415–426. doi:10.7305/automatika.54-4.413

Misra, S., & Singh, S. (2012). Localized policy-based target tracking using wireless sensor networks. *ACM Transactions on Sensor Networks*, *8*(3), 1–30. doi:10.1145/2240092.2240101

Mohd Kassim, M. R., Mat, I., & Harun, A. N. (2014). Wireless Sensor Network in precision agriculture application. *2014 International Conference on Computer, Information and Telecommunication Systems (CITS)*. doi:10.1109/cits.2014.6878963

Muthusamy, M., & Periasamy, K. (n.d.). A Comprehensive Study on Internet of Things Security. *Advancing Consumer-Centric Fog Computing Architectures*, 72–86. doi:10.4018/978-1-5225-7149-0.ch004

Robles, T., Alcarria, R., Martin, D., Morales, A., Navarro, M., Calero, R., … Lopez, M. (2014). An Internet of Things-Based Model for Smart Water Management. *2014 28th International Conference on Advanced Information Networking and Applications Workshops*. doi:10.1109/waina.2014.129

Voulodimos, A. S., Patrikakis, C. Z., Sideridis, A. B., Ntafis, V. A., & Xylouri, E. M. (2010). A complete farm management system based on animal identification using RFID technology. *Computers and Electronics in Agriculture*, *70*(2), 380–388. doi:10.1016/j.compag.2009.07.009

Wolfert, S., Ge, L., Verdouw, C., & Bogaardt, M.-J. (2017). Big Data in Smart Farming – A review. *Agricultural Systems*, *153*, 69–80. doi:10.1016/j.agsy.2017.01.023

Zong, Z., Fares, R., Romoser, B., & Wood, J. (2013). FastStor: Improving the performance of a large scale hybrid storage system via caching and prefetching. *Cluster Computing*, *17*(2), 593–604. doi:10.100710586-013-0304-5

Chapter 11
Optimization of Consensus Mechanism for IoT Blockchain:
A Survey

Shailesh Pancham Khapre
Amity University, Noida, India

Shraddha P. Satpathy
Amity University, Noida, India

Chandramohan D.
Madanapalle Institute of Technology and Science, India

ABSTRACT

The essence of blockchain is a decentralized distributed ledger system; the IoT is formed by accessing and interconnecting a large number of heterogeneous terminals and has a natural distributed feature. Therefore, the combination of the two IoT blockchains is widely optimistic. At the same time, due to the heterogeneity of IoT sensing terminals, limited computing storage, and data transmission capabilities, the IoT blockchain is facing greater challenges, among which cryptographic consensus technology has become a key issue. In this chapter, based on the summary of the current blockchain consensus algorithm, applicability to the IoT-blockchain has been analyzed, the application status of several major IoT-blockchain platforms and consensus mechanisms have been introduced, and also the IoT-blockchain research progress on optimization of consensus mechanism has been expounded. Looking forward to the optimization techniques of the IoT blockchain, potential research directions have been summarized.

INTRODUCTION

With the advent of IoT (Khodadadi *et.al*, 2017), information sensing equipment is widely used in smart communities, smart agriculture, smart transportation, shared economy, and other fields to promote

DOI: 10.4018/978-1-7998-4186-9.ch011

comprehensive interconnection and integration of man-machine-things. IoT research institutions predict that by the end of 2020 (Ashton, 2009), the number of IoT terminal devices will increase to 26 billion.

The main access control methods in the Internet of Things environment are: role-based access control RBAC, attribute-based access control ABAC, access control based on usage control model UCON, and capability-based access control CapABC. The aforementioned RBAC, ABAC and UCON IoT solutions rely on a centralized server-client architecture to connect to cloud servers via the Internet. In order to meet the growth, the decentralized architecture CapABC was proposed to create a large-scale P2P wireless sensor network. CapABC achieves lightweight distributed control, dynamics, and scalability, but CapABC cannot guarantee security or user privacy. Compared with the traditional Internet, IoT architecture expands network connections to a richer physical space. In view of its massive heterogeneous and resource-constrained IoT terminal, data sharing, privacy protection, intrusion detection, access control, and cross-domain authentication and other problems (Wang *et.al*, 2019, Kouicem *et.al*, 2018), traditional security technologies with large computing requirements and high deployment costs cannot be directly applicable to the IoT platform, we need to find new security solutions.

As shown in Figure 1, from the past closed centralized framework to the open cloud centralized architecture, and the next step is to distribute cloud functions to multiple nodes, blockchain technology can play a big role in the next trend effect.

Figure 1. The IoT architecture of the past, present and future

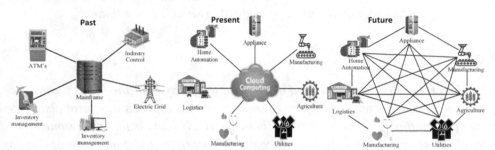

Blockchain is a decentralized distributed technology, a peer-to-peer distributed ledger based on cryptographic algorithms. The blockchain technology extracted from the underlying architecture of Bitcoin can be applied to the transfer of value between any media that does not require mutual trust, thereby spawning a general blockchain application platform such as Ethereum and hyperledger (Qi-feng *et.al*, 2017). Blockchain has the basic characteristics of decentralization, tamper-proof information, open and transparent data, and three guarantee mechanisms: consensus mechanism, smart contract, and asymmetric encryption. Blockchain technology can solve the following challenges in large-scale IoT systems: Most IOT solutions are still expensive because of the high cost of deploying and maintaining central clouds and servers. When the supplier does not provide the above facilities, these costs are transferred to the middleman. Maintenance is also a big issue, when software needs to be regularly updated for millions of smart devices. After the Snowden leak, it is difficult for IOT adopters to trust other technology partners, give them access and control, and allow them to collect and analyze user data. Therefore, privacy and anonymity should be the core of the future development of IOT. The closed source code also leads to a lack of trust. To increase trust and security, transparency is important, so open source solutions should be taken into consideration when developing next-generation IOT solutions.

As shown in Figure 2, the blockchain can generally be divided into six parts: data layer, network layer, consensus layer, incentive layer, contract layer, and application layer (Sun *et.al*, 2018).

Figure 2. The typical layered structure of Blockchain

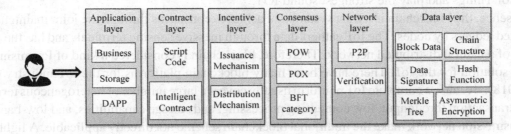

What Blockchain can Accomplish for IOT?

1. Reduce Operating Costs

Blockchain technology focuses on the point-to-point direct connection of data to be transmitted, rather than through the central processing unit. This distributed computing method can handle hundreds of millions of exchanges. At the same time, it can also make full use of nodes distributed in different locations around the world to develop hundreds of millions of idle computing power, storage capacity and network resources, which are used for transaction processing on the Internet of Things, which is costly for calculation and storage. The amplitude is reduced.

2. Reduce Security Risks

The core problem of IoT security is the lack of original mutual trust mechanism between devices. In the early stage of the development of the Internet of Things, all devices need to be verified with the data of the Internet of Things center. Once the central database collapses, it will cause great damage to the entire Internet of Things.

What is gratifying is that in a distributed blockchain network, a new mechanism can be provided to ensure that consensus can be maintained between devices without the need to go to the data center for verification. In this way, even if one or more nodes on the Internet of Things are compromised, the data on the overall network is still reliable and safe.

3. Efficient and Intelligent Network Operation Mechanism

Since the blockchain has a decentralization and consensus mechanism, on the Internet of Things, cross-system data transmission will be transferred from the upper layer to the underlying blockchain. In this way, the complexity of IoT applications can be greatly reduced. The Internet of Things will also evolve into the era of "Internet of Things" and build a new world on the chain.

The combination of blockchain technology and the Internet of Things can eliminate the verification and certification links between nodes, directly build a communication bridge for multiple contacts, and improve network operation efficiency. At the same time, the decentralized consensus mechanism based on the blockchain can also ensure the security and privacy of the Internet of Things and facilitate the transmission of real information. In view of this, the blockchain will definitely come together with the Internet of Things and play the strongest sound IOT.

In essence, the blockchain is a trust system that achieves consensus through the joint maintenance of distributed ledgers by nodes. The IoT gathers data through massive sensing terminals and has the characteristics of a natural distributed network. Therefore, blockchain is considered a kind of Promising basic security solution for the IoT. There have been many blockchain platforms for the IoT industry (Pan & Yang, 2018). Because a complete IoT platform usually covers a large number of heterogeneous terminals, its high transaction throughput, low computing processing, and storage capabilities, and low-bandwidth data transmission network make the traditional blockchain scheme not directly applicable. A lightweight optimized blockchain system must be studied. Among them, the direct factor affecting the throughput of the blockchain is the cryptographic consensus mechanism. In fact, the consensus mechanism usually consists of two parts, one part is the cryptographic algorithm required to reach consensus, namely the consensus algorithm; the other part is the rules for reaching consensus, the consensus rules. The consensus algorithm belongs to the basic application research of cryptography, and its innovative breakthrough faces great challenges. Therefore, how to improve the blockchain data layer, network layer, application layer, and optimize the traditional consensus rules, and how to make the consensus mechanism more applicable to the IoT application environment has become the focus of current research and development.

This chapter outlines the research on IOT Blockchain Consensus algorithms, how Blockchain and IOT can help each other to outcome the shortcoming's in smart applications, author describes the basic working of Blockchain Consensus Mechanism followed by the development status of IOT-Blockchain Consensus Mechanism, author then describes and analyze the hybrid IOT-Blockchain architecture. At the end author outline the research prospects of optimization of consensus mechanism in IOT Blockchain.

Basics of Blockchain Consensus Algorithm

With the popularity and the development of blockchain technology, more and more consensus algorithms have been proposed. In order to enable readers to have a deeper understanding of different consensus algorithms, this section gives a mainstream of the blockchain consensus process Model. It should be noted that this model is not a general model and may not cover all types of consensus processes, but it can reflect the core ideas of most mainstream consensus algorithms.

The blockchain system is built on the P-2-P network. P denotes the collection of all nodes, which is generally split up into ordinary nodes that produce data or transactions, which are accountable for verifying, packaging, and updating the data or transactions generated by ordinary nodes(). The set of "miner" nodes for mining operations (denoted as M), the two types of nodes may have an intersection; usually, miner nodes will all participate in the consensus competition process, and specific representative nodes will be elected in specific algorithms to replace them Participate in the consensus process and compete for accounting rights. The collection of these representative nodes is recorded as D; the accounting node selected through the consensus process is recorded as A. The consensus process is repeated in rounds, and each round of the consensus process generally re-selects the accounting node of the round.

The core of the consensus process is the "master election" and "accounting" two parts. In the specific operation process, each round can be divided into leader election, block generation, data validation and chaining. (Chain Updation, that is, accounting) 4 stages. As shown in Figure 3, the input of the consensus process is the transaction or data generated and verified by the data node, and the output is the encapsulated data block and the updated blockchain .The 4 stages are executed cyclically, and each round of execution will generate a new block.

Figure 3. A basic model of blockchain consensus processes

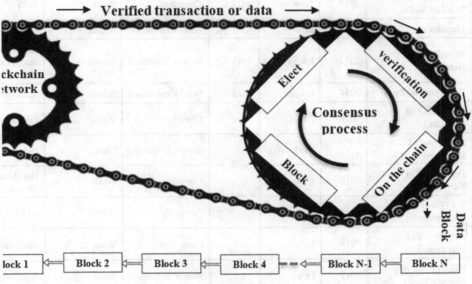

Phase 1: Master election. Master election is the core of the consensus process, that is, the process of selecting accounting node A from the set of all miner nodes M: We can use the formula f(M) → A to represent the master election process, where the function f represents the specific implementation of the consensus algorithm. Generally speaking, |A| = 1, that is, the only miner node is finally selected for accounting.

Phase 2: Block building. The accounting node selected in the first phase packages the transactions or data generated by all nodes P in the current time period into a block according to a specific strategy, and broadcasts the generated new block to all miners Node M or its representative node D. These transactions or data are usually sorted according to various factors such as block capacity, transaction fees, transaction waiting time, etc., and then packaged into new blocks in order. Block-building strategy is the key to the performance of the blockchain system Factors are also a concentrated manifestation of the strategic behavior of miners such as greedy transaction packaging and selfish mining.

Phase 3: Verification. After the miner node M or representative node D receives the broadcasted new block, they will each verify the correctness and rationality of the transaction or data encapsulated in the block. If the new block obtains the majority of verification/representative nodes If approved, the block will be updated to the blockchain as the next block.

Table 1. Comparison of blockchain consensus algorithms

Classification	Consensus algorithm	Proposed time	Calculation overhead	Tolerance of malicious nodes	Degree of decentralization	Manageability	Application
Proof of consensus	POW(Proof of Work)	1999	Large	<1/2	Complete	Weak	Bitcoin, Permacoin
	POS(Proof of Stake)	2011	Moderate	<1/2	Complete	Weak	Peercoin
	DPos (Delegated Proof of Stake)	2013	Low	<1/2	Complete	Weak	EOS
	Ouroboros	2017	Low	<1/2	Semi-Centralised	Strong	Cardno
	POA(Proof of Activity)	2014	Large	<1/2	Semi-Centralised	Strong	Ethereum private chain, Oracles Network
	PoB(Proof of Burn)	2014	Large	<1/2	Semi-Centralised	Strong	Slimcoin
	POC(Proof of Capacity)	2016	Large	—	Complete	Weak	File Sharing
	PoD(Proof of Devotion)	—	Medium	—	Semi-Centralised	Strong	Nebula Chain
	PoE((Proof of Existence)	2016	Unknown	—	Complete	Weak	HeroNode, DragonChain
	PoI (Proof of Importance)	2015	Low	—	Complete	Weak	NEM
	PoR (Proof of Retrievability)	2014	Low	<1/4	Complete	Weak	File Sharing
	PoET (Proof of Elapsed Time)	2017	Low	<1/2	Semi-Centralised	Strong	Sawtooth Lake
	PoP (Proof of Publication)	2012	Large	<1/4	Complete	Weak	BitCoin
Byzantine consensus	PBFT	1999	low	<1/3	Semi-Centralised	Strong	Super Ledger
	Raft	2013		—	Semi-Centralised	Strong	etcd
Directed Acyclic Graph	DAG	—	low	—	Complete	Weak	IoTA

Phase 4: On-chain. The accounting node adds the new block to the main chain to form a complete and longer chain from the genesis block to the latest block. If there are multiple fork chains in the main chain, you need to According to the main chain discrimination criteria stipulated by the consensus algorithm, one of the appropriate branches is selected as the main chain.

As the core of the blockchain, the consensus algorithm mainly has two characteristics: Firstly, consistency, removing the k end blocks of the blockchain to make the block prefixes saved by trusted nodes the same; secondly, effectiveness, transaction information published by trusted nodes will be recorded in the blockchain by other trusted nodes. Table 1 compares the commonly used traditional blockchain consensus from the aspects of classification, proposed time, computational consumption, tolerance of malicious nodes, degree of decentralization, manageability, and application. For example, in the proof consensus, the PoW mechanism applied by Bitcoin obtains the authority of accounting by calculating the accurate Nonce value, which consumes a lot of computing power, and Permacoin uses PoW to provide data preservation services (Miller *et.al*, 2014); In the Byzantine consensus, PBFT (Castro *et.al*, 2002 & Androulak *et.al*, 2018) is applied to the super ledger and can tolerate 1/3 of the wrong nodes. The Byzantine-based consensus also includes Quorum / Update (Abd-El-Malek *et.al*, 2005), Hybrid Quorum (Cowling *et.al*, 2006), FaB (Martin *et.al*, 2005), Spinning (Martin *et.al*, 2005), Robust BFT SMR (Veronese *et.al*, 2009) and Aliph (Clement et.al, 2009), etc.; Others are different from the traditional chain structure, with transaction as the granularity of block-free consensus DAG (directed acyclic graph) (Popov, 2018), this new type of blockchain topology provides new thinking for consensus research.

The consensus mechanism currently used in the cloud blockchain still cannot achieve a perfect balance in terms of computing power consumption, supervisability, decentralization, and security. However, in the field of IoT, massive heterogeneous terminal devices have limited computing and storage capabilities, relatively complex network architecture, and strong expansion requirements. As a result, the current consensus is not fully applicable to the IoT.

IOT-BLOCKCHAIN CONSENSUS MECHANISM APPLICATION STATUS

Examples of deep integration of blockchain and IoT are still in continuous innovation and practice phase. The IoT realizes communication calculation and data transmission and interaction in a peer-to-peer open network environment through sensor nodes, protocols, and other related technologies. Each terminal device can serve as a node of the district chain and participate in the consensus maintenance of the blockchain network. The following will explain the status of projects based on the IoT blockchain from two aspects: the project overview of the IoT blockchain consensus mechanism and the analysis of consensus advantages and disadvantages.

Project Overview of Consensus Mechanism

The IoT blockchain project optimizes and improves the existing consensus algorithm, and uses the main sub-chain and computing power chips to help strengthen the consensus rules, thus reducing the contradictions in the application of the IoT in the blockchain. The existing IoT blockchain systems mainly include IoTA, IoTEX, μNEST, and EOSIoT.

IoTA

IoTA (Popov, 2018) is a new type of transaction settlement blockchain system designed for the IoT. Different from the traditional chain-type blockchain, IoTA adopts a Tangle (DAG) architecture inside. No transfer fees are required for transfers, which is extremely scalable. As the number of nodes increases, the stability of the system increases. In the DAG system, new transactions need to be verified through two historical transaction pointers. The elimination of miner settings in this mechanism can prevent the blockchain from being threatened by computing power and double attacks. At the same time, changes in the consensus mechanism effectively improve transaction efficiency and throughput, and most double-spend attacks will be caught by the system and immediately stopped. DAG's network topology also gives users a clearer and more concise model architecture. Although PoW still consumes computing power as part of DAG, the advantages of a new blockchain based on DAG data structure are emerging, and the IoTA project has also been recognized and developed rapidly.

However, high TPS (transactions per second, the number of transactions per second) will bring the following problems: In Tangle, the time from a transaction to the confirmation is unknown. In addition, high performance will bring low security, and attackers can attack the network through lower computing costs (Lathif *et.al*, 2018).

IoTEX

The IoTEX project has good scalability, privacy, and isolation. As shown in figure 4, in terms of architecture, the project adopts a chain-in-chain form that includes a root chain and a sub-chain, and the chain structure of ledgers is still used internally. In terms of function, the root chain is a public chain, which

Figure 4. IoTEX root chain sub-chain structure diagram

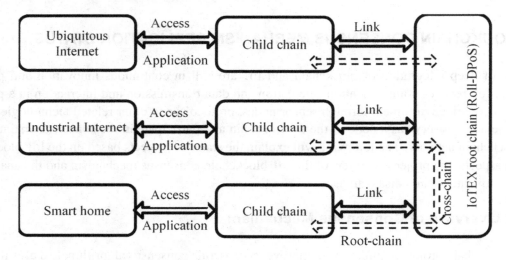

plays a management role on the child chain; in terms of scalability, the sub-chain can design different extensions according to needs to adapt to the diversity of IoT functions; in terms of security, the attack of the sub-chain does not affect the operation of the root chain; in terms of value, data between sub-chains can also be transferred through the root chain.

In the IoTEX project, the consensus mechanism is a random consensus mechanism that can be verified based on random functions (Roll-DPoS) (Fan & Chai, 2018). IoTEX is based on the Byzantine Fault Tolerance Algorithm (PBFT), which votes for nodes, settles quickly, and builds an efficient and scalable blockchain. In terms of node selection, in order to improve efficiency, the system randomly selects group nodes according to the RDPoS algorithm. Compared to DPOS, Roll-DPoS draws on the Algorand algorithm (Gilad *et.al*, 2017) for random node selection, so that each node has the opportunity to participate in consensus building and avoid node isolation.

Application of IoTEX to the IoT, the changes in the architecture can adapt to the distributed environment of the IoT, it also enhances the randomness of consensus, but it has not responded to the disadvantages of low power consumption, poor storage capacity, and small communication bandwidth of IoT devices.

μNEST

The μNEST project is quite different from the above two. The project uses the DPoS consensus mechanism. Although DPoS has improved PoS and optimized the verification efficiency and block production speed, it is still helpless against the current situation of low energy consumption and high concurrency in the IoT, and the internal token mechanism is not applicable in the field of IoT. The μNEST team through the research on cryptography and the application of high-performance hardware reduced the consumption of computing power in the consensus mechanism, improve the computing power of IoT devices so that blockchain programs can run stably on IoT devices. Currently, the project is still under development.

EOSIoT

EOSIoT is an extension of the IoT of the EOS project. Through the RFID system, RFID electronic tags can be sent to the EOS chain, which is used in new supply chains, manufacturing, tracking, and access control. The project is different from the above using physical devices as nodes, retaining the existing architecture of blockchain and IoT, and providing EOS-based blockchain services for IoT systems through smart contracts. EOS adopts DPoS consensus mechanism.

Advantages and Disadvantages of the Consensus Mechanism

Table 2 combines the above projects on the consensus mechanism to summarize and compare the applicability of existing IoT blockchain technologies. The application of consensus mainly depends on the performance, scalability, and security of IoT devices. μNEST and EOSIoT use DPoS consensus, and the existing token mechanism has little effect in the field of IoT, so the scalability is poor. Among them, in the μNEST project, the hardware is used to enhance device performance and optimize the efficiency of the consensus algorithm. The IoTEX project adopts the main sub-chain form, which has strong scalability and is suitable for various IoT fields. However, the inherent weakness of IoT devices has not been greatly improved. The storage method of the chain ledger still limits the low power consumption and weak storage. The IoTA project adopts a novel DAG consensus. Although the performance has been improved and it is easy to expand, when the number of nodes is too small, the degree of decentralization is much lower than the chain structure blockchain, resulting in low security, risks such as untimely transaction verification.

For other consensus that is not used by the project, PoW has high security in an open network, but the huge computing resource requirements are not realistic to implement in IoT devices, so PoW consensus is not adopted in the project. Compared with PoW consensus, PoS consensus can significantly reduce energy consumption, but it still needs to consume a certain amount of computing resources for mining, and it still has certain operating pressure for low-power IoT devices. While increasing the number of nodes, PBFT will reduce the performance of the entire network and cannot improve reliability. Therefore, most of the consensus algorithms and rules currently used still have room for improvement in the field of IoT.

Table 2. Advantages and disadvantages of the project and its consensus

Project Name	Consensus algorithm	App types	Disadvantages	Advantage	Scalability	Security	Performance
µNEST EOSIoT	DPoS	Public chain	The degree of decentralization is low, and internal consensus relies on tokens. Representation is not strong when there are few nodes.	The efficiency is better than PoW and PoS. The block generation speed is faster	Weak	Strong	Higher
IoTEX	Roll-DPoS	Public chain	Depending on the token, the method of selecting representative nodes may not be suitable for completely decentralized scenarios	By randomly selecting nodes, each node has the opportunity to participate in the accounting process	Stronger	Strong	Higher
IoTA	DAG	Public chain	No global ordering, does not support strong oneness, efficient implementation is more complicated	High throughput, no central control for asynchronous communication	Strong	Weak	High

RESEARCH ON OPTIMIZATION OF IOT BLOCKCHAIN CONSENSUS MECHANISM

Through the above analysis and comparison, the application of the consensus mechanism in the IoT is still insufficient. Combining the characteristics of the IoT environment, academia has put forward many optimization solutions. As shown in Table 3, through consensus algorithm improvement, data layer optimization, and architecture service optimization, the consensus rules are strengthened to help the IoT- blockchain.

Improvements in Consensus Algorithms

The consensus algorithm needs to rely on the computing power of the nodes, and the new blocks generated at the same time are synchronized to all nodes through the consensus rules for backup. In the field of the IoT, there are far more mass heterogeneous devices than the Internet environment, and the computing power and throughput are limited by itself and the operating environment. In addition, there are problems such as easy intrusion, easy to simulate, and easy tampering, which increase the hidden dangers of traditional consensus in the field of IoT. The method of using hardware to increase computing power in µNEST is not suitable for all devices. Therefore, how to optimize the consensus mechanism is crucial in node selection, reducing complexity, and improving security and throughput. The Enhanced intelligent consensus model is shown in Figure 5 and selects normal nodes to construct consensus by detecting node data to improve security.

Table 3. Current status and characteristics of research on consensus mechanism optimization of IoT-blockchain

Application direction	Related work	Overview	Performance advantages
Consensus algorithm improvement	Improved Algorithm based on trust PoW (Huang *et.al*, 2019)	Evaluate the trustworthiness of nodes and adjust the mining difficulty of each node through the coefficient	Increase the computing power consumption of malicious nodes, so that they do not get the right to keep accounts, and at the same time reduce the probability of selecting malicious nodes, increasing fault tolerance
	Fault-tolerant optimization based on PBFT (Salimitari *et.al*, 2019)	Use outlier detection algorithms to divide malicious nodes through data.	The consensus algorithm is layered, the first layer uses anomaly node detection algorithm to detect and distinguish malicious nodes, the second layer carries out PBFT consensus. Enhanced fault tolerance.
	DRL boosts consensus mechanism (Liu et.al, 2019)	Use deep reinforcement learning for block generation and other adjustments.	Apply DRL technology to block generation and adjustment, and dynamically adjust the system to achieve balance and efficiency
	DAG main chain sub-chain combination (Jiang et.al. 2018)	DAG-based main chain sub-chain form distinguishes domain and block	The main subchain form of DAG effectively increases the throughput of the blockchain, while reducing the storage of block data.
Data layer optimization	Blockchain system based on data compression (Kim *et.al*, 2019)	Compress the data blocks in the blockchain to reduce storage space and ease the storage pressure of the device.	Greatly enhance the storage capacity of the device and reduce the performance problems caused by the small storage space of the device.
	High-performance data read-write architecture based on FPGA memory module (Sakakibara *et.al*, 2017)	Make an external storage module, and request a high-performance storage module instead of a server during the communication process.	The high-performance storage module effectively improves the reading and writing of data, reduces the performance consumption of data during transmission, and improves the efficiency of consensus.
	Data optimization through edge computing (Casado-Vara *et.al*, 2018)	Verify data quality through a combination of edge computing and distributed computing.	In the blockchain architecture, the edge computing layer is proposed to improve data quality and error data detection, and enhance the consensus fault tolerance rate.
Architecture Service Optimization	IoT+Blockchain Architecture and Services (Sagirlar *et.al*, 2018 & Dorri - *et.al*, 2017)	Combine different layers in the blockchain with different layers in the IoT to build a new architecture	The integration of the architecture circumvents the shortcomings of the IoT, and combines the two to form a stable new structure, so that the blockchain can be applied to the IoT.

Malicious Detection Boosts Consensus Mechanism

The trust-based PoW mechanism (Huang *et.al*, 2019) can effectively enhance the security of the block-chain network. In this mechanism, whether a node is malicious is measured by two parts, the positive part, and the negative part. These two parts can be adjusted by configuring weights. The positive part is obtained by calculating the number of effective transactions and the number of transaction verifications; the negative part is determined by the joint effect of the time for the node to perform malicious actions and the penalty coefficient, there are two types of penalty coefficients, one is to identify the node as a lazy node, that is, to contribute less in the consensus process, the other is to identify the node as a double-spend node, that is, to send malicious transactions such as repeated transactions. These two penalty coefficients will be dynamically adjusted according to the actual situation. The verification of the mechanism by the Raspberry Pi proves that the node judged as malicious will set a higher penalty coefficient, resulting in a larger difficulty value, and the time for the node to run the PoW consensus algorithm will be much longer than that of the normal node. At the same time, when simulating a malicious attack on a node, the coefficient of the passive response part will immediately increase. In this way, the 51% fault tolerance rate of the traditional PoW is enhanced, and the malicious node will never get the authority to keep accounts. (Huang *et.al*, 2019). Node selection through this method can effectively reduce the performance consumption of non-malicious nodes, and at the same time, increase the computational complexity of malicious nodes' PoW algorithm, which is conducive to the stability and robustness of the consensus algorithm under the IoT blockchain system.

Figure 5. Enhanced Intelligent Consensus Model

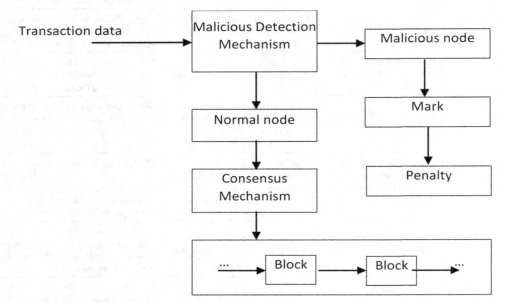

Based on hyperledger fabric and consensus protocol PBFT, (Salimitari *et.al*, 2019) proposed a malicious detection mechanism to improve the fault tolerance of IoT blockchain. Through data collection of IoT devices, a data matrix D is formed, and two probability values are obtained through outlier detection algorithm and low-rank subspace recovery model training data matrix D: Detection probability Pd and false alarm probability Pfa to determine abnormal nodes. In this consensus mechanism, the anomaly node detection algorithm runs as the first-level consensus in each node in the form of a script to verify the compatibility of new data and discard suspicious data. The algorithm will no longer select the node with malicious data as the accounting node to generate the blockchain, enhancing the fault tolerance of the second layer of consensus PBFT. In the experiment, it was found that only when the outlier detection setting is very unreasonable and there is a false alarm probability and a low detection probability, a fault tolerance rate of less than 33.3% will occur. After a lot of experiments, it is proved that while improving network performance, according to different model parameters, a fault tolerance rate of more than 33.3% can be obtained, and even more than 50%. In the experimental environment, the detection probability Pd = 46% and the false alarm probability Pfa = 5%, the available fault tolerance rate is 57.82% (Salimitari *et.al*, 2019). The results show that outlier detection can greatly enhance the fault tolerance rate of the consensus algorithm and increase the stability and security of the IoT blockchain network.

Consensus Building on Dynamic Regulation of Deep Reinforcement Learning

The traditional blockchain has a ternary paradox that can only satisfy two of the three attributes: decentralization, scalability, and security. The traditional blockchain has a ternary paradox that can only satisfy two of the three attributes: decentralization, scalability, and security. Liu et.al, 2019 proposed a dynamic adjustment architecture for IoT blockchain based on deep reinforcement learning (DRL) technology. DRL technology is used to select and adjust the block generator, consistency algorithm, block size and block generation interval, internally combined with PBFT, Zyzzyva (Kotla *et.al*, 2007) and Quorum (Aublin *et.al*, 2015) proposed a new fault-tolerant consensus to achieve a dynamic balance of scalability, decentralization, security, and throughput.

The scheme uses Gini coefficient, block delay, and error tolerance rate to represent decentralization, throughput, and security, and uses deep reinforcement learning (mainly Q-Network) for training to obtain appropriate parameters to select the appropriate block generation node, consensus algorithm, block size, and block generation interval.

After `a lot of experiments, by comparing with the existing unmodified system, the proposed scheme has higher performance and throughput (Liu et.al, 2019), which effectively proves that the design improves the performance of the IoT-Blockchain, and the dynamic adaptation to the distributed heterogeneous architecture of the IoT.

DAG Segmentation Technology to Improve the Consensus Rule

As a new blockchain architecture, there are many improvements and optimizations based on DAG. Different from the traditional DAG in Section 3.1.1 and the main chain model based on the traditional chain structure in Section 3.1.2, Jiang *et al.* 2018 complemented the advantages of DAG and the main chain, and proposed a DAG-based cross-chain solution. The scheme is based on the main sub-chain architecture of directed acyclic graphs. Nodes in a domain jointly maintain a ledger to form a sub-chain. At the same time, the sub-chain is connected to the main chain in the form of an alliance chain for management and maintains the main chain ledger. This kind of scheme connects different nodes to the main chain after fragmenting consensus, which solves the situation that consensus is difficult to establish due to a large number of devices in the IoT environment, and reduces the network consumption caused by large-scale ledger synchronization. After a lot of experiments, running in different memory and different processor-server environments, compared with traditional blockchain, the throughput of this architecture has been significantly improved, at the same time, in the storage of block information, the sub-chain only stores block data in specific areas, and the storage capacity is much smaller than the main chain, reducing the storage pressure of the main chain nodes and sub-chain nodes.

Data Layer Optimization

The IoT collects, stores data, and provides centralized services from various types of terminal devices. If the server is attacked, there is a risk of data leakage. In order to solve the problem of centralized data storage, blockchain technology was introduced, but the low storage capacity of lightweight devices has led to the blockchain consensus mechanism not being able to operate for a long time. At the same time, various sensors in the sensing layer of the IoT generate a large amount of real-time data. If the entire chain is stored by the blockchain, it will exert great pressure on the nodes and the network.

Block Compression Mechanism Saves Storage Space

Combining consensus rules, compressing early data to ensure the consistency of the blockchain, and reducing the storage of block data is a way to solve the storage limitations of IoT devices. Kim *et al.* 2019 proposed a block compression storage method to increase the storage space of the device. The uninterrupted operation of IoT devices will generate massive real-time data. Such data has the characteristics of large data volume and a short validity period. The effective compression of the pre-blocks under the premise of ensuring the establishment of the blockchain consensus can ensure the storage capacity of the lightweight IoT devices in the blockchain network. After the IoT device node joins the network, it is required to synchronize the storage capacity of the node to the entire network, improving the PBFT consensus, as shown in Figure 6.

Figure 6. Block compression model (Fan & Chai, 2018)

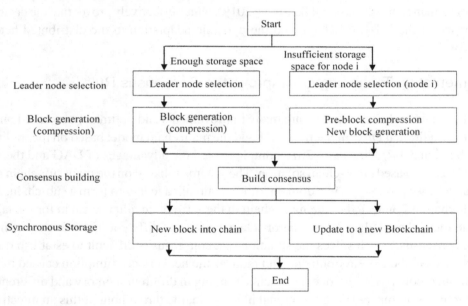

In the process of selecting the Leader node for transaction block, through the evaluation of the storage capacity of its own equipment; if it is less than the set threshold, the consensus mechanism is established normally: if it is greater than the set threshold, the data compression program is started to compress the original block, that is, a new block is generated by Hash operation, the hash value of the parent block of the new block is the compressed block hash value, and the network-wide node synchronization operation is performed on the compressed block and the newly generated block, and the network-wide node is updated to a new blockchain. Based on the comparison between the blockchain model based on block compression and the traditional blockchain model, as the number of nodes increases, the block delay increases by less than 1, and the average storage space of each data block in the blockchain decreases by nearly 63%. After running for a period of time, the compressed model reduces the total storage space by about 63% and tends to be stable (Kim *et.al*, 2019). Although the compression algorithm consumes a certain amount of block time, data compression combined with consensus effectively solves the problem of insufficient data storage space in IoT devices.

High-Performance Cache and Edge Computing Increase Throughput

There is still a contradiction between the heterogeneous data of IoT devices and low communication bandwidth. The transmission delay of a large amount of heterogeneous data in low-bandwidth channels will inevitably greatly affect the operation of the blockchain consensus algorithm and affect the establishment of consensus. Sakakibara *et.al,* 2017, proposed a high-performance cache device to improve the read and write performance. Hardware cache module is added made of an external high-efficiency read-write device to the IoT. Store transaction information in the cache module, reduces the workload of the server, and improve the storage capacity of physical devices in the IoT blockchain. In the network, if there is target data in the cache, it is directly read in the cache module, otherwise, it is obtained from the node. Use cache technology to reduce the resource consumption of data and improves throughput. After extensive experiments, it is seen that IoT blockchain using the cache module shows throughput several times smaller than the one without using it. As the transaction volume increases, throughput shows an inversely proportional curve and gradually converges to stabilize, while the hit rate of the data in the cache shows a proportional trend with the increasing number of transactions, continuously increasing (38). This shows that the application of the cache module can effectively reduce the increase in throughput caused by heterogeneous data transmission in the IoT blockchain, and reduce the load on the device caused by low-bandwidth communications. At the same time, a distributed cooperative algorithm based on game theory can also be used (Huang *et.al,* 2019), which improves the security of incoming data and improves network throughput by improving data quality and performing error data detection in network edge devices.

ARCHITECTURE OPTIMIZATION SERVICES

Blockchain + IoT

General IoT-Blockchain Architecture

The architecture is the combination of a traditional 5 layer Blockchain system with the existing IoT system (Lao et.al, 2020). Figure 7 shows the general 5 layers of IoT Blockchain Architecture. The IoT Blockchain's physical layer has the same functionality as the IoT physical layer. It consists of IoT devices related to application scenarios like home devices, mobile phones, Car sensors, etc. The second layer in IoT Blockchain architecture i.e. the network layer is similar to the traditional blockchain network layer. This layer is responsible for overall communication among the entities involved in the system, i.e. inter-networking, routing, and multicasting. Blockchain functions i.e. data storage, data sharing, and consensus are the part of Blockchain layer. The main purpose of the IoT Blockchain middle layer is to manage blockchain, service integration, and to provide additional security services. The topmost layer i.e. the application layer of IoT Blockchain is similar to the IoT system and Blockchain system application layer, the purpose of the application layer is to provide user interaction, abstraction service, and API services.

Figure 7. General IoT Blockchain Architecture

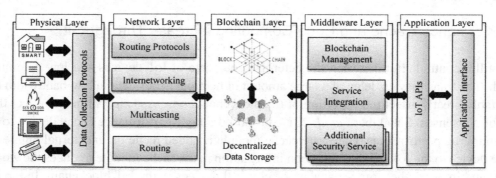

Table 4. Comparison between different IoT-Blockchain applications

IoT-Blockchain	Blockchain	Consensus	Service	IoT devices
Slock.it (sloct.it 2018)	Ethereum	PoW	Commission shop	Electronic lock
ElectriCChain (ectriCChain 2018)	SolarCoin	PoS	Process data of solar panel	Solar panel
LO3 Energy (O3 2018)	Public blockchain solution	PoW	Solar energy marketplace	Grid Edge, Solar plane
LeewayHertz (LewayHertz)	Public blockchain	PoW	IoT-blockchain solutions	Robots, Audio devices
Xage (Xage 2018)	Fabric	Fabric consensus	Security service	Broker, Enforcement Point
Filament (Filament. 2018)	Hardware-based Consortium Blockchain	PoW	Transaction service to embedded IoT	Blocklet USB Enclave, Blocklet Chip
UniquID (UniquID 2018)	Litecoin	PoW	Integrated service to IoT and blockchain	Sensors, Actuators, Appliances
Atonomi (Atonomi 2019)	Atonomi	Atonomi consensus	IoT-blockchain solutions	Smart devices, Smart home
JD.com (JDChain 2019)	BFT blockchain	BFT	Blockchain platform	IoT devices

In this architecture, the IoT device generates data, and Blockchain is responsible for securely storing the data in a secure distributed environment to avoiding malicious modifications. Conversely, all previous data can be easily retrieved with any loss of information. Still, IoT Blockchain is in an early stage of development. Before starting with the architecture optimization let us summarize the current status of IoT-Blockchain Applications and their Architectures. Table 4 differentiates different IOT-Blockchain applications with Blockchain technology, Consensus, services, and IoT devices. All these applications follow the same architecture as described in figure 5. These applications are further divided into two types as per their field application.

1. **Specific Application:** Standalone applications that use IoT and Blockchain in their operations. The application layer and the physical layer perform as core layers. The middle layers act as a supporting layer that is responsible for storage and communication. IoT Device and the application protocol defines the nature and function of IoT Blockchain application.

2. **Application Platform as a Service:** it is the support software that integrates everything in IoT Blockchain System. Developers are provided with direct access to the management platform, which provides developers to manage connected devices, configure communication protocols, and also control data flow. The middleware layer acts as a core layer defining the nature and functionality of the application service. The application layer and physical layer components are not specified in this kind of service.

Hybrid Blockchain+IoT

Figure 8. The architecture of Hybrid blockchain+IoT

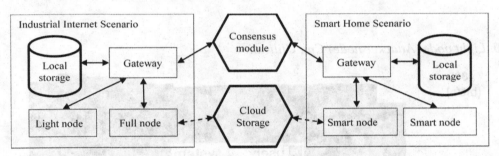

Combining different layers of the blockchain and the IoT a new architecture (Sagirlar *et.al*, 2018 & Dorri *et.al*, 2017) is formed, it is different from the way in which the blockchain is used as a cloud service to provide services to edge devices through smart contracts in Section 3.1.4. As shown in Figure 8, the IoT device nodes in the network are interconnected through network devices such as gateways and routers, at the same time, data storage warehouses are built locally and in the cloud to solve data storage issues for IoT devices.

In a node network, nodes with high-performance computing capabilities and high-availability storage capacity are set as full nodes, and nodes with low power consumption and weak storage capacity are set as light nodes. Full nodes have the ability to participate in maintaining the ledger, establish consensus with other full nodes, and synchronize the ledger; light nodes do not participate in the maintenance of the ledger, and only synchronize the header information of the block (for example, when a new block appears in the blockchain network, the light node download only the block header and send a Merkel certificate request in a specific state). Under such an architecture, blockchain and the IoT are organically combined, and devices exist as light nodes of the blockchain to jointly maintain a network.

Figure 9. Full node (Victim node) Cpu Utilization

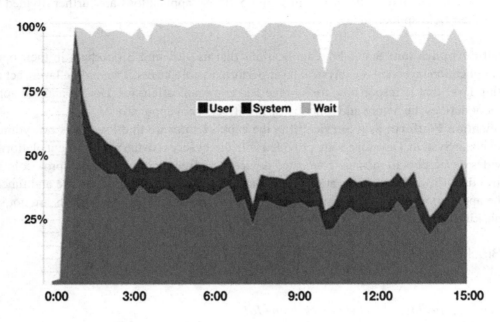

Figure 10. Light node (Attacker node) Cpu Utilization

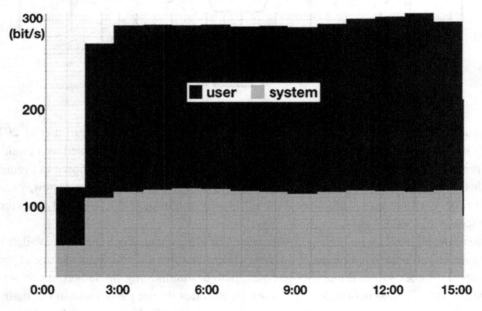

The DDoS attack for stress simulation was carried out in which a set of light nodes repeatedly transmitted data to full nodes. Figure 9 shows the CPU usage of the victim node, it was observed that even though the victim's CPU was almost exhausted, it successfully managed to perform blockchain task without halting or crashing even under heavy load from the attacker. Figure 10 shows the CPU usage of the attacker node, it was observed that nearly 100% of the CPU was exhausted, even though the Attacker node was able to generate transaction load without crashing. The second test was carried out with the varying number of sub-blockchains, it was observed that sub-blockchain having more full nodes the resources usage is averaged with longer consensus rotations. Table 5 shows the performance of the sub-blockchain with varying numbers of full nodes. After the simulation, the architecture can effectively solve the problem of the IoT devices that were not able to meet the blockchain computing power requirements and account storage, and also provide new ideas for the combination of blockchain and IoT.

Table 5. Performance of sub-blockchain with varying number of full nodes

Resource Utilized	20 nodes	40 nodes	100 nodes	200 nodes
Avg. CPU	6.5%	5.1%	2.7%	1.9%
Avg. Memory	110 Mb	106 Mb	105 Mb	104 Mb
Avg. Network	8.2 Kb/s	6.5 Kb/s	4.1 Kb/s	2.1 Kb/s
Avg. Packets	10.1 /s	9.3/s	6.8/s	4.2/s

Blockchain+ IoT+AI

Figure 11. Blockchain+AI+IoT Architecture

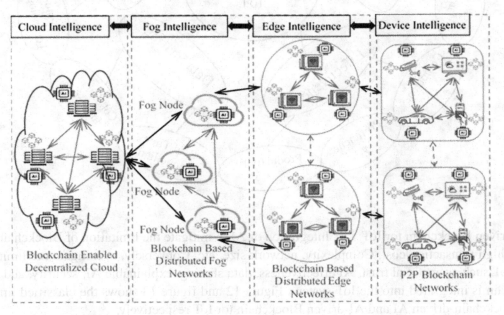

Blockchain + AI+IOT provides a decentralized AI method to share information in cryptographically secured, trusted, and signed manner, it also provides decision-making capabilities for IoT devices in IoT applications. A hierarchically layered structured architecture is proposed consisting of 4 layers of intelligence (S.K. Singh *et.al*, 2019). Figure 11 shows the new Blockchain +IoT+AI. As shown in the figure each layer is enabled with AI, AI at each level is responsible to sense devices, analyzes and processes data, and sends a response to upper or lower layers. At the cloud intelligence layer, AI is associated with data centers that are connected to Blockchain which provide decentralized and secure data for IoT applications. Different consensus protocols can be used in different layers for convergence of Blockchain+AI+IoT for scalability and security. S.K. Singh *et.al*, 2019 further evaluated the architecture in 2 ways, "blockchain-driven AI for IoT" and "AI-driven Blockchain for IoT" depending on the IoT services.

Figure 12. Limitations of Blockchain-driven AI for IoT

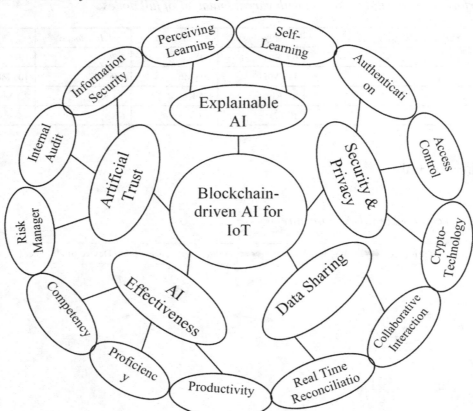

AI-driven Blockchain for IoT, i.e., Integration of AI to mitigate the limitation of Blockchain for IoT such as high transaction cost, Complexity, network size, etc. Conversely, to mitigate the limitation of AI for IoT such as artificial trust, AI effectiveness, data sharing, explainable AI, security, and privacy, Blockchain is integrated into the IoT system. Figure 12 and figure 13 shows the classified limitations from Blockchain-driven AI and AI-driven Blockchain for IoT respectively.

S.K. Singh et.al, 2019 carried out analysis using the proposed Blockchain+AI+IoT Architecture (Table 6) on IoT devices, Edge Layer, Fog Layer, and Cloud Layer with parameters considering security and privacy, accuracy, and latency. By finding the similarity index security & privacy was measured and it was found that at the IoT device layer the similarity index varies from 1.0-0.01, at the edge layer

Figure 13. Limitations of Blockchain-driven AI for IoT

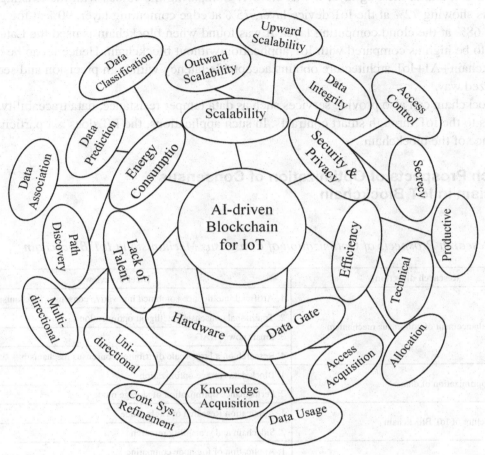

Table 6. Performance of sub-blockchain with varying number of full nodes

Layers	Parameters				
	Security & Privacy(SI)		Accuracy (%)	Latency(ms)	
	Min.	Max.		Min.	Max.
Device Layer	0.01	1.0	72	56	57
Edge Layer	0.4	0.6	75	56	58
Fog Layer	0.1	0.9	90	0	11
Cloud Layer	-	-	68	-	-

it was 0.62-0.4, and at the Fog layer it was 0.9-0.1. Comparing the values with the existing research, accuracy is showing 72% at the IoT device layer, 75% at edge computing layer, 90% at fog computing layer, and 68% at the cloud computing layer. It was found when blockchain is used the Latency value came out to be high as compared with IoT application without blockchain. Hence it can be concluded that Blockchain+AI+IoT architecture obtains acceptable latency with high precision and security in a decentralized way.

The blockchain can also provide services such as data tamper resistance, data traceability, and trust credentials to the IoT through smart contracts. In such applications, the IoT does not participate in the maintenance of the blockchain.

Research Prospects of Optimization of Consensus Mechanism in IoT Blockchain

Table 7. Research Prospects of Optimization of Consensus Mechanism in IoT Blockchain

Research direction	Brief overview
Intelligent enhancement of consensus mechanism	1. Artificial intelligence combined innovative consensus mechanism
	2. Traditional consensus intelligent optimization
	3. Smart power DAG
	4. Research on a large-scale distributed consensus mechanism
Reasonable optimization of data	1. Block data storage optimization
	2. Performance optimization of storage mode
New Architecture of IoT Blockchain	1. Application Research of Light Node
	2. Sidechain and scalability research
Improved transaction performance	1. Application of fog node computing
	2. Development of computing chips for Blockchain
	3. Research and Application of Lightweight cryptography
	4. Segmentation technology for IoT-Blockchain

From the above description table 7, we can see that the combination of IoT and blockchain is mainly limited by the computing power, storage capacity, and throughput of the device. In view of the current blockchain consensus scalability is poor, huge computing power consumption, transaction confirmation efficiency is low, node fault tolerance and performance is difficult to balance, etc., when the IoT and the blockchain are combined, how to choose a consensus algorithm that conforms to the IoT scenario, how to specify a consensus rule that conforms to the IoT business scenario, how to ensure the security, stability, and scalability of the network still need to be done perfectly. Combined with the current research, Table 5 looks at the four aspects of intelligent enhancement of the consensus mechanism, reasonable optimization of data, new architecture of the IoT-blockchain, and transaction performance.

Intelligent Enhancement of Consensus Mechanism

Artificial intelligence is a manual method that simulates, extends, and expands human intelligence. Through data mining, analysis, and training, it realizes the scientific technology of machine intelligence. The combination of blockchain and artificial intelligence provides directions for the internal enhancement of the blockchain and the intelligentization of external governance. The combination of artificial intelligence and the IoT blockchain consensus mechanism is mainly expanded in the following aspects.

Artificial Intelligence Combined Innovative Consensus Mechanism (Salah et.al, 2019).

The current consensus is mainly selected from the proof consensus and the Byzantine consensus, and cannot be fully applied to the special environment of the Internet of Things, combining the characteristics of high real-time data requirements and a large amount of data in the Internet of Things, a new AI-based consensus mechanism is created based on the quality of the learning model, the effective optimization of search strategies, and data quality.

Traditional Consensus Intelligent Optimization

Using deep reinforcement learning's perception and decision-making ability, intelligently improve the computing power consumption and Leader node selection of traditional consensus, in order to achieve the purpose of reasonably distributing the computing power of the IoT-Blockchain, enhancing network fault tolerance, and strengthening the decentralized features.

Smart Power DAG (Pervez et.al, 2018)

The new consensus mechanism model of a directed acyclic graph is still in the development stage, using AI technology to strengthen DAG's shortcomings in transaction confirmation and security is also a direction that requires in-depth research.

Research on a Large-scale Distributed Consensus Mechanism.

The IoT is essentially a large distributed system, the network topology caused by massive nodes is intricate. a multi-layer consensus mechanism can be established through research on the distributed consensus mechanism, so that different regions can establish consensus and then move up to consensus until the entire network reaches consensus, in order to achieve the purpose of reducing throughput and alleviating the limitation of computing power consumption.

Reasonable Optimization of Data

Due to the limitation of throughput, the blockchain cannot adapt to the real-time big data environment of the IoT. Therefore, the following research can be performed on the data.

Block Data Storage Optimization (Taylor et.al, 2019)

IoT device data has real-time characteristics, some of the early data entered into the chain are useless except for the establishment of a consensus mechanism. Therefore, how to reasonably delete the ledger data stored in the blockchain without affecting the establishment of the consensus mechanism, so that the block ledger data can continuously store data that can be deeply studied.

Performance Optimization of Storage Mode

Due to the low storage capacity of IoT devices, it is possible to study in-depth how to improve the existing storage mode, use the caching mechanism or improve block storage middleware, enhance the read and write capabilities of block data, and adapt to the low bandwidth data transmission network of the IoT.

New Architecture of IoT Blockchain

The disadvantages of low computing power and small storage space of the IoT limit the blockchain technology to be fully applied to the IoT environment, but the layered combination of the two can still provide strong assistance for the IoT. Mainly from the following aspects.

Application Research of Light Node (Reilly et.al, 2019)

The characteristic of light nodes is that only the data of the block header is synchronized, and the blockchain architecture based on light nodes and full nodes can be built on IoT devices with different storage performance, and the establishment of a consensus mechanism and the synchronous storage of blocks can be reasonably performed.

Sidechain and Scalability Research (Zhou et.al, 2020)

Through the side chain technology, the field of IoT blockchain application is effectively expanded to achieve more flexible user customization. How to design side chains, how to strengthen extended attributes, and how to realize data interaction between sidechains are the future research directions.

Improved Transaction Performance

Transaction performance is one of the constraints that the blockchain cannot be effectively used in the field of IoT. In the face of the massive data environment of the IoT, the throughput of the blockchain cannot be completely satisfied. Therefore, to improve the throughput of the blockchain, the following directions can be studied.

Application of Fog Node Computing (Xiong et.al, 2020)

Fog computing is a new computing paradigm, sink storage and calculations to a location close to data generation, establishing a local small cloud at the end of the IoT to achieve localized computing or storage, reduce the bandwidth consumption of messages, reduce the computing pressure of the central node, and speed up the establishment of a consensus mechanism.

Development of Computing Chips for Blockchain

The low computing performance of the device is mainly limited by the performance of the processor, and a computing chip for the blockchain can be developed to increase the compatibility of the IoT and the blockchain.

Research and Application of Lightweight Cryptography (Sfar et.al, 2017)

Blockchain is the application of cryptography, it is one of the research focuses to use safe and lightweight passwords to replace the original high-consumption passwords and to improve operational efficiency.

Segmentation Technology for IoT Blockchain (Tong et.al, 2019)

The principle of sharding is to split a large database into small pieces of data and store the pieces on different servers. Combining the consensus mechanism with sharding technology can effectively improve the consistency of the blockchain consensus-building speed.

CONCLUSION

As one of the key areas for future development, the IoT is combined with the blockchain that has the characteristics of decentralization, data tampering, and collective maintenance, or it will have a disruptive impact on the trusted and secure access of massive heterogeneous terminal devices and data security management, becoming one of the indispensable technologies for changing the future. As can be seen from the new research, in the direction of enhancement of consensus mechanism, reasonable optimization of data, a new architecture of IoT blockchain, and improvement of transaction performance, there are still urgent problems to be solved in the combination of IoT and blockchain. It is worth further research.

REFERENCES

O3. (2018). *LO3 Energy The Future of Energy*. Retrieved from https://lo3energy.com/

Abd-El-Malek, M., Ganger, G. R., Goodson, G. R., Reiter, M. K., & Wylie, J. J. (2005). Fault-scalable Byzantine fault-tolerant services. *Operating Systems Review*, *39*(5), 59–74.

Androulaki, E., Barger, A., Bortnikov, V., Cachin, C., Christidis, K., Caro, A. D., Enyeart, D., Ferris, C., Laventman, G., Manevich, Y., Muralidharan, S., Murthy, C., Nguyen, B., Sethi, M., Singh, G., & Smith, K., SornIoTti, A., Stathakopoulou, C., Vukolic, M., Cocco, S.W., & Yellick, J. (2018). Hyperledger fabric: a distributed operating system for permissioned blockchains. In *The Thirteenth EuroSys Conference*. New York: ACM Press.

Ashton, K. (2009). *That "Internet of Things" Thing: In the Real World Things Matter More than Ideas*. RFID Journal.

Atonomi. (2019). *Atonomi—Bringing Trust and Security to IoT*. Retrieved from https://atonomi.io/

Aublin, P., Guerraoui, R., Knezevic, N., Quéma, V., & Vukolic, M. (2015). The Next 700 BFT Protocols. *ACM Trans. Comput. Syst., 32*, 12:1-12:45.

Back, A., Corallo, M., Dashjr, L., Friedenbach, M., Maxwell, G., Miller, A., Poelstra, A., Timón, J., & Wuille, P. (2014). *Enabling Blockchain Innovations with Pegged Sidechains*. Academic Press.

Bentov, I., Lee, C., Mizrahi, A., & Rosenfeld, M. (2014). Proof of Activity: Extending Bitcoin's Proof of Work via Proof of Stake (Extended Abstract). *SIGMETRICS Perform. Evaluation Rev., 42*, 34–37.

Casado-Vara, R., Prieta, F.D., Prieto, J., & Corchado, J.M. (2018). Blockchain framework for IoT data quality via edge computing. *BlockSys'18*.

Castro, M., & Liskov, B. (2002). Practical byzantine fault tolerance and proactive recovery. *ACM Transactions on Computer Systems, 20*, 398–461.

Chen, L., Xu, L., Shah, N., Gao, Z., Lu, Y., & Shi, W. (2017). *On Security Analysis of Proof-of-Elapsed-Time (PoET)*. SSS.

Clark, J., & Essex, A. (2011). CommitCoin: Carbon Dating Commitments with Bitcoin. *IACR Cryptol. ePrint Arch., 2011*, 677.

Clement, A., Wong, E. L., Alvisi, L., Dahlin, M., & Marchetti, M. (2009). *Making Byzantine Fault Tolerant Systems Tolerate Byzantine Faults*. NSDI.

Courtois, N. (2014). *On The Longest Chain Rule and Programmed Self-Destruction of Crypto Currencies*. ArXiv, abs/1405.0534.

Cowling, J.A., Myers, D.S., Liskov, B., Rodrigues, R., & Shrira, L. (2006). HQ replication: A hybrid quorum protocol for byzantine fault tolerance. *OSDI '06*.

Dorri, A., Kanhere, S.S., Jurdak, R., & Gauravaram, P. (2017). *LSB: A Lightweight Scalable BlockChain for IoT Security and Privacy*. ArXiv, abs/1712.02969.

ectriCChain. (2018). *ElectriCChain The Solar Energy Blockchain Project for Climate Change and Beyond*. Retrieved from https://www.electricchain.org/

Eyal, I., Gencer, A. E., Sirer, E. G., & Renesse, R. V. (2016). *Bitcoin-NG: A Scalable Blockchain Protocol*. NSDI.

Fan, X., & Chai, Q. (2018). Roll-DPoS: A Randomized Delegated Proof of Stake Scheme for Scalable Blockchain-Based Internet of Things Systems. In *Proceedings of the 15th EAI International Conference on Mobile and Ubiquitous Systems: Computing, Networking and Services*. ACM Press.

Filament. (2018). *Filament's Industrial Internet of Things Blockchain Solution Wins 2018 IoT Innovator Award*. Retrieved from https://globenewswire.com/news-release/2018/09/26/1576581/0/en/Filament-s-Industrial-Internet-of-Things-Blockchain-Solution-Wins-2018-IoT-Innovator-Award.html

Gilad, Y., Hemo, R., Micali, S., Vlachos, G., & Zeldovich, N. (2017). Algorand: Scaling Byzantine Agreements for Cryptocurrencies. In *Proceedings of the 26th Symposium on Operating Systems Principles*. ACM Press.

Huang, J., Kong, L., Chen, G., Wu, M., Liu, X., & Zeng, P. (2019). Towards Secure Industrial IoT: Blockchain System With Credit-Based Consensus Mechanism. *IEEE Transactions on Industrial Informatics*, *15*, 3680–3689.

JDChain. (2019). *JD Enterprise Blockchain Service*. Retrieved from http://blockchain.jd.com/blockchain_store/pc/index.html#/BlockChainTrace

Jiang, Y., Wang, C., Huang, Y., Long, S., & Huo, Y. (2018). A Cross-Chain Solution to Integration of IoT Tangle for Data Access Management. *2018 IEEE International Conference on Internet of Things (iThings) and IEEE Green Computing and Communications (GreenCom) and IEEE Cyber, Physical and Social Computing (CPSCom) and IEEE Smart Data (SmartData)*, 1035-1041.

Khodadadi, F., Dastjerdi, A. V., & Buyya, R. (2017). Internet of Things: An Overview. ArXiv, abs/1703.06409.

Kiayias, A., Russell, A., David, B.M., & Oliynykov, R. (2016). Ouroboros: A Provably Secure Proof-of-Stake Blockchain Protocol. *IACR Cryptol. ePrint Arch., 2016*, 889.

Kim, T., Noh, J., & Cho, S. (2019). SCC: Storage Compression Consensus for Blockchain in Lightweight IoT Network. *2019 IEEE International Conference on Consumer Electronics (ICCE)*, 1-4.

Kotla, R., Alvisi, L., Dahlin, M., Clement, A., & Wong, E. L. (2007). *Zyzzyva: Speculative byzantine fault tolerance*. TOCS.

Kouicem, D. E., Bouabdallah, A., & Lakhlef, H. (2018). Internet of things security: A top-down survey. *Computer Networks*, *141*, 199–221. doi:10.1016/j.comnet.2018.03.012

Lao, L., Li, Z., Hou, S., Xiao, B., Guo, S., & Yang, Y. (2020). A Survey of IoT Applications in Blockchain Systems: Architecture, Consensus, and Traffic Modeling. *ACM Computing Surveys*, *53*, 1–32.

Lathif, M. R., Nasirifard, P., & Jacobsen, H. (2018). CIDDS: A Configurable and Distributed DAG-based Distributed Ledger Simulation Framework. In *The 19th International Middleware Conference (Posters)*. New Yew: ACM Press.

LewayHertz. (2019). *Blockchain Development for Startups and Enterprises | USA | UAE*. Retrieved from https://www.leewayhertz.com/

Liu, M., Yu, F. R., Teng, Y., Leung, V. C., & Song, M. (2019). Performance Optimization for Blockchain-Enabled Industrial Internet of Things (IIoT) Systems: A Deep Reinforcement Learning Approach. *IEEE Transactions on Industrial Informatics*, *15*, 3559–3570.

Martin, J., & Alvisi, L. (2005). Fast Byzantine Consensus. *IEEE Transactions on Dependable and Secure Computing*, *3*, 202–215.

Miller, A., Juels, A., Shi, E., Parno, B., & Katz, J. (2014). Permacoin: Repurposing Bitcoin Work for Data Preservation. *2014 IEEE Symposium on Security and Privacy*, 475-490.

Miller, A., Juels, A., Shi, E., Parno, B., & Katz, J. (2014). Permacoin: Repurposing Bitcoin Work for Data Preservation. *2014 IEEE Symposium on Security and Privacy*, 475-490.

Nakamoto, S. (2009). *Bitcoin: A Peer-to-Peer Electronic Cash System*. Academic Press.

NOMURA. (2016). *Survey on Blockchain Technologies and Related Services*. FY2015 Report.

Pan, J., & Yang, Z. (2018). Cybersecurity Challenges and Opportunities in the New "Edge Computing + IoT" World. *SDN-NFV Sec'18*.

Pervez, H., Muneeb, M., Irfan, M., & Haq, I. U. (2018). A Comparative Analysis of DAG-Based Blockchain Architectures. *2018 12th International Conference on Open Source Systems and Technologies (ICOSST)*, 27-34.

Popov, S. (2018). *The Tangle*. https://assets.ctfassets.net/r1dr6vzfxhev/2t4uxvsIqk0EUau6g2sw0g/45e ae33637ca92f85dd9f4a3a218e1ec/IoTa1_4_3.pdf

Qi-feng, S., Cheqing, J., Zhao, Z., Weining, Q., & Ao-ying, Z. (2017). *Blockchain: Architecture and Research Progress*. Academic Press.

Reilly, E., Maloney, M., Siegel, M., & Falco, G. (2019). An IoT Integrity-First Communication Protocol via an Ethereum Blockchain Light Client. *2019 IEEE/ACM 1st International Workshop on Software Engineering Research & Practices for the Internet of Things (SERP4IoT)*, 53-56.

Sagirlar, G., Carminati, B., Ferrari, E., Sheehan, J. D., & Ragnoli, E. (2018). Hybrid-IoT: Hybrid Blockchain Architecture for Internet of Things - PoW Sub-Blockchains. *2018 IEEE International Conference on Internet of Things (iThings) and IEEE Green Computing and Communications (GreenCom) and IEEE Cyber, Physical and Social Computing (CPSCom) and IEEE Smart Data (SmartData)*, 1007-1016.

Sakakibara, Y., Nakamura, K., & Matsutani, H. (2017). An FPGA NIC Based Hardware Caching for Blockchain. *HEART2017*.

Salah, K., Rehman, M. H., Nizamuddin, N., & Al-Fuqaha, A. (2019). Blockchain for AI: Review and Open Research Challenges. *IEEE Access: Practical Innovations, Open Solutions*, 7, 10127–10149.

Salimitari, M., Joneidi, M., & Chatterjee, M. (2019). *An Outlier-aware Consensus Protocol for Blockchain-based IoT Networks Using Hyperledger Fabric*. ArXiv, abs/1906.08177.

Sfar, A. R., Natalizio, E., Challal, Y., & Chtourou, Z. (2017). A roadmap for security challenges in the Internet of Things. *Digital Communications and Networks*, 4, 118–137.

Singh, S. K., Rathore, S., & Park, J. H. (2019). BlockIoTIntelligence: A Blockchain-enabled Intelligent IoT Architecture with Artificial Intelligence. *Future Generation Computer Systems*.

sloct.it. (2018). *slock.it A Blockchain Company*. Retrieved from https://slock.it/

Sun, Y. Z., Fan, L., & Hong, X. (2018). Technology Development and Application of Blockchain: Current Status and Challenges. *Chinese Journal of Engineering Science*, 20(2), 27–32. doi:10.15302/J-SSCAE-2018.02.005

Taylor, P. J., Dargahi, T., Dehghantanha, A., Parizi, R. M., & Choo, K. R. (2019). *A systematic literature review of blockchain cyber security*. Digital Communications and Networks.

Tong, W., Dong, X., Shen, Y., & Jiang, X. (2019). A Hierarchical Sharding Protocol for Multi-Domain IoT Blockchains. *ICC 2019 - 2019 IEEE International Conference on Communications (ICC)*, 1-6.

Underwood, S. (2016). Blockchain beyond bitcoin. *Communications of the ACM*, *59*, 15–17.

UniquID. (2018). *UniquID Incorporation Blockchain Identity Access Management*. Retrieved from https://uniquid.com/

Veronese, G. S., Correia, M., Bessani, A. N., & Lung, L. C. (2009). Spin One's Wheels? Byzantine Fault Tolerance with a Spinning Primary. *2009 28th IEEE International Symposium on Reliable Distributed Systems*, 135-144.

Wang, X., Zha, X., Ni, W., Liu, R. P., Guo, Y. J., Niu, X., & Zheng, K. (2019). Survey on blockchain for Internet of Things. *Computer Communications*, *136*, 10–29. doi:10.1016/j.comcom.2019.01.006

Xage. (2018). *Home Page of Xage Security*. Retrieved March 20, 2019 from https://xage.com/

Xiong, Z., Feng, S., Wang, W., Niyato, D., Wang, P., & Han, Z. (2019). Cloud/Fog Computing Resource Management and Pricing for Blockchain Networks. *IEEE Internet of Things Journal*, *6*, 4585–4600.

Yang, F., Zhou, W., Wu, Q., Long, R., Xiong, N. N., & Zhou, M. (2019). Delegated Proof of Stake With Downgrade: A Secure and Efficient Blockchain Consensus Algorithm With Downgrade Mechanism. *IEEE Access: Practical Innovations, Open Solutions*, *7*, 118541–118555.

Zheng, Z., Xie, S., Dai, H., Chen, X., & Wang, H. (2017). An Overview of Blockchain Technology: Architecture, Consensus, and Future Trends. *2017 IEEE International Congress on Big Data (BigData Congress)*, 557-564.

Zhou, Q., Huang, H., Zheng, Z., & Bian, J. (2020). Solutions to Scalability of Blockchain: A Survey. *IEEE Access: Practical Innovations, Open Solutions*, *8*, 16440–16455.

Chapter 12
Critical Nodes Detection in IoT–Based Cyber–Physical Systems:
Applications, Methods, and Challenges

Onur Ugurlu
Izmir Bakircay University, Turkey

Nusin Akram
Ege University, Turkey

Vahid Khalilpour Akram
Ege University, Turkey

ABSTRACT

The new generation of fast, small, and energy-efficient devices that can connect to the internet are already used for different purposes in healthcare, smart homes, smart cities, industrial automation, and entertainment. One of the main requirements in all kinds of cyber-physical systems is a reliable communication platform. In a wired or wireless network, losing some special nodes may disconnect the communication paths between other nodes. Generally, these nodes, which are called critical nodes, have many undesired effects on the network. The authors focus on three different problems. The first problem is finding the nodes whose removal minimizes the pairwise connectivity in the residual network. The second problem is finding the nodes whose removal maximizes the number of connected components. Finally, the third problem is finding the nodes whose removal minimizes the size of the largest connected component. All three problems are NP-Complete, and the authors provide a brief survey about the existing approximated algorithms for these problems.

INTRODUCTION

Internet of Things (IoT) is one the fastest growing and most promising technologies that already have influenced the daily life of most people in different areas. Especially with the emerging of smartphones,

DOI: 10.4018/978-1-7998-4186-9.ch012

people can easily connect to remote devices and control them using their phones. Intelligent homes that automatically control temperature, lights, doors, security, and entertainment facilities is an example of IoT based systems (Zielonka, 2020). The number and diversity of furniture that connects to the internet are growing day by day. Most of the recently produced refrigerators, washing machines, coffeemakers, sound systems, televisions, air conditioning systems, and dishwashers allow their users to control them over the Internet or local network. Intelligent greenhouses (Castañeda-Miranda, 2020), autonomous vehicles (Minovski, 2020), smart manufacturing systems (Tran, 2021), intelligent transportation systems (Lin, 2020), and indoor or outdoor tracking systems (Adardour, 2021) are some other applications areas of IoT.

The recent advances in hardware and electronic technologies have led to the production of small, fast, and energy-efficient devices that can store a large amount of data, precisely sense different events, perform heavy computation, and communicate over different channels such as WiFi, Bluetooth, and 5G technologies. Generally, these devices may run embedded programs to complete the given tasks. They support different communication ports so the users can use them inside other smart things or directly connect them over available ports. The available devices for IoT may connect to the Internet over cabled networks, wireless networks, or multi-hop networks. In this way, we may establish IoT networks almost everywhere, even in harsh environments such as forests or mountains.

One of the most essential requirements in IoT-based systems is communication. Generally, IoT-based systems consist of many different nodes for various tasks such as sensing the events or quantities, processing the gathered data, storing the information, and performing some mechanical tasks such as opening a door or rotating a valve. Most of these tasks are completed by remote nodes which are controlled over the Internet or a communication platform. Based on the application type and available infrastructure, different platforms can be used for establishing the connection between the nodes or end-users. For example, in intelligent home controlling systems, the IoT nodes can connect to the Internet over a local area network or WiFi platform. In a public transportation system or in an outdoor tracking system (for example, tracking cargo packets), the nodes may use 4G or 5G cellular network to communicate with the controlling center. In this way, the users may track the real-time location of the next bus or their cargo. As another example, in a forest fire controlling system, the nodes may use multi-hop ad-hoc connections to cover a wide area and send their gathered data to the controlling center. In this system, each node should send its collected data to the next node until they reach the base station which is connected to the Internet.

Regardless of the type of communication platform, generally, most IoT-based applications need continuous, secure, and fault tolerance communication channels to send their data or receive new commands from the remote nodes. While losing the connection to some nodes for a limited time can be tolerated in some applications (for example, in a forest fire control system), a strict and real-time connection is required in many other applications (for example, in military operations). However, almost all communication platforms may fail due to different hardware problems, software errors, or environmental conditions. The WiFi network may go off because of temporal electric failures. A 5G base station may stop working because of environmental conditions such as a storm. In a multi-hop wireless sensor network, some nodes may stop working because of battery drain. Hence, most IoT-based systems must increase the robustness of the connections as much as possible and should have accurate plans for failure scenarios to improve the reliability of the systems.

Finding the weak points or critical parts of a system is the first step for increasing the system's reliability. In a communication network, failure of a critical node (for example, a router or a node that forwards most of the traffic) or weak communication links (for example, a link with a high error ratio) may disconnect the communication path between the base station and remote nodes. This is an undesirable scenario in most cyber-physical systems because we may lose access to the large collection of active nodes, which may waste many recourses and energy in the system. Finding critical nodes and critical links of a communication platform may provide useful information for increasing the fault tolerance and reliability of systems. After detecting the critical or weak points, we may add redundant nodes or create alternate communication paths to keep the network connectivity after failure in that nodes or links.

In graph theory, a critical node of a graph is a node whose removal disconnects the graph to not connected components. Similarly, a critical edge between two nodes is an edge whose failure divides the graph into disconnected parts. We can model a communication network as a graph where the nodes are the vertices, and the links are the edges between the vertices. Finding the critical nodes of such a graph may reveal the critical parts of the network that their failure imposes a high cost to the system. Critical Nodes Detection Problem (CNDP) is a well-known problem with different variants, most of which are NP-Complete problems. For example, finding the critical nodes that maximize the number of connected components or finding the critical nodes that minimize the largest connected component are NP-Complete problems. In this chapter, we focus on the applications and challenges of finding different kinds of critical nodes in IoT-based cyber-physical systems. In Section 2, we provide the formal definition of critical nodes in a network. In Section 3, we discuss about the application of critical nodes detection in cyber-physical systems. Section 4 covers the main challenges in finding the critical nodes in different kinds of networks. In Section 5, we present the existing central and distributed algorithms for finding the critical nodes. Finally, Section 6 draws the conclusion.

CRITICAL NODES

One of the crucial issues of IoT networks is the reliability of the network. The main factor of reliability is to ensure a sustainable connection between active nodes. Having a large number of alternative connections between nodes can increase connection reliability in the network. In other words, in a reliable network, the failure of one node should not lead to a disconnection between other nodes.

Many problems encountered in daily life can be seen as optimization problems on graphs. In graph theory, connectivity is a fundamental measure that gives information about the reliability and robustness of networks. The connectivity value indicates how well a network is connected or how much effort (by deleting nodes or links) is required to disconnect the network, and pairwise connectivity is the number of connected node pairs. In network analysis, the problem of identifying subsets of nodes that are important for the connectivity of a network has become a popular problem that has been frequently studied by researchers in recent years. Finding important nodes for network connectivity plays a significant role in examining many basic structural features of the network, such as reliability, robustness, and attack tolerance. These important elements are known as "Critical Nodes" in the literature. The primary purpose of detecting critical nodes is to identify the groups that will negatively impact the network in their absence and ensure that this group is protected or strengthened.

In literature, researchers have introduced different definitions for critical nodes. For example, some researchers (Imran, 2013) (Jorgic, 2004) (Alnuem, 2014) (Sheng, 2006) considered the nodes that make the k-neighborhood subgraph disconnect as critical nodes. Ozkaya et al. (Ozkaya, 2018) proposed a new centrality metric to determine critical nodes in distributed networks. Wehmuth and Ziviani (Wehmuth, 2011) defined the nodes closely related to the robustness of a distributed system as critical nodes. Liu et al. (Liu, 2015) consider the nodes that slowed down the average consensus algorithm in their absence as critical nodes. Lastly, Dagdeviren et al. (Dagdeviren, 2019) described the nodes that disrupt the graph's connectivity as critical nodes.

In recent years, a new problem family, namely critical node detection problem, has emerged following the detailed study of Arulselvan et al. (Arulselvan, 2009) on pairwise connectivity. The CNDP is an optimization problem that aims to identify the subsets of the nodes whose deletion minimizes or maximizes a predefined connectivity metric in the residual network (Lalou, 2018). Different definitions of critical nodes can be stated according to different connectivity metrics.

Considering the sample network in Figure 1, if we aim to find the most critical node whose removal minimizes the pairwise connectivity, we need to select node *b* to get the optimal solution which is 90. While if we want to maximizes the number of connected components in the residual network, the most critical node is node *c*, whose removal generates 6 connected components.

Figure 1. A Sample Network

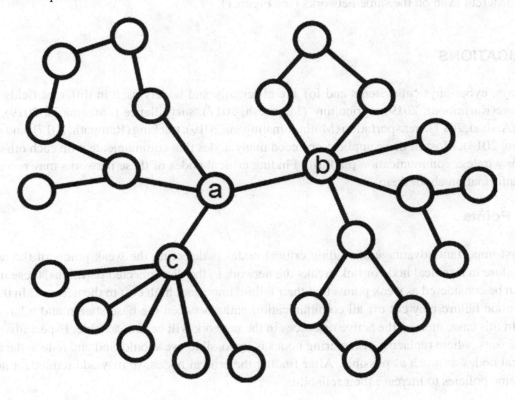

Lastly, if we ask for the most critical node that minimizes the largest connected component's size once deleted, node *a* must be selected to get the optimal solution that constrains each connected component's size to 12 nodes. In all cases, we delete nodes from the given network but according to different connectivity metrics. Although these metrics seem similar, different optimal solutions can be obtained for the same network. These three connectivity metrics form the most important variants of the CNDP, which belong to the NP-complete problem class (Arulselvan, 2009) (Shen, 2012b).

- **Critical Node Problem** (CNP) was introduced by Arulselvan et al. (Arulselvan, 2009). The problem aims to minimize the pairwise connectivity in the residual network by deleting a number of nodes equal to or less than a predefined integer k.
- **Maximize the Number of Connected Components** (MaxNum) problem was introduced by Shen and Smith (Shen, 2012a). The objective of the problem is to maximize the number of connected components in the residual network by removing a number of nodes equal to or less than a predefined integer k.
- **Minimize the Largest Connected Component Size** (MinMaxC) problem was introduced by Shen and Smith (Shen, 2012a). The problem seeks to minimize the size of the largest connected component in the residual network by deleting a number of nodes equal to or less than a predefined integer k.

Although the variants of the CNDP are similar to each other, the optimal solutions of the variants can be different even on the same networks (see Figure1).

APPLICATIONS

Nowadays, cyber-physical systems and IoT are efficiently and widely used in different fields such as healthcare(Karimpour, 2019), agriculture (Jaiganesh, 2017), surveillance (Santamaria, 2019), energy saving (Arshad, 2017), transportation (Muthuramalingam, 2019), tracking (Ramnath, 2017), and military (Johnsen, 2018). Most of these applications need many nodes that communicate with each other over a wired or wireless communication platform. Finding critical nodes of these networks may reveal much useful information about them.

Weak Points

The most important advantage of finding critical nodes is detecting the weak points of the network. Since failure in a critical node or link breaks the network to the disconnected partitions, these nodes or links can be considered as weak points that their failure imposes a high cost to the network. In the worst case, a node failure may cut off all communication paths between the base station and a large set of nodes. In this case, most of the active resources in the network will be unreachable. Especially in harsh environments, where replacing or repairing nodes is impossible, we should find and reduce the number of critical nodes as much as possible. After finding the critical nodes we may add redundant nodes or apply some policies to increase their reliability.

Bottlenecks

The critical nodes usually appear as bottlenecks in the networks that have high traffic flow. Since these nodes connect some partitions with a large set of nodes usually act as a bridge between these nodes. Bottlenecks have many drawbacks in most networks. In battery-powered networks, the nodes which appear as bottleneck consume more energy than other nodes and drain their battery faster than other nodes. This increases the risk of partitioning and reduces the overall network lifetime. In the networks with limited bandwidth on links, the bottlenecks slow down the traffic flow and increase the congestion of packets. Hence, we are usually interested in finding and resolving the bottleneck nodes in any network. Finding the critical nodes may provide very useful information about the possible bottlenecks. After finding the critical nodes, we may add more resources to their location, add new nodes to create alternate paths between other nodes, or move some other nodes to resolve the bottlenecks.

Clustering

Clustering is a well-known problem in almost all kinds of networks that has a wide range of applications. Finding the critical nodes may help to find the clusters or partitions of nodes that have minimal communication paths. Finding these clusters may help to distribute various resources such as base stations, cluster heads, security points, and relay nodes in the networks. For example, in a wireless sensor network, the nodes usually send their collected data to their cluster head. The cluster head gathers data from their cluster combines the collected data and sends them to a base station using secure channels. In this way, we may create a backbone for routing the data packets between the nodes and reduce the overall energy consumption in the network. Generally, appropriate clustering can considerably reduce the data propagation in the network and facilitate network management. Also, the clustering of nodes provides important information for Medium Access Control (MAC) protocols. A MAC protocol allows the nodes to share the communication channel and reduce the packet collision or provide some strategies to handle the packets collisions.

After finding and removing the critical nodes, we will have some disconnected components which show the candidate clusters in the network. The robustness of connections between these partitioned groups is lower than other nodes that remain connected. The critical nodes can be considered as the boundary nodes of the clusters. Therefore, to design an efficient clustering algorithm the first step can be finding the critical nodes or critical edges of the network.

Reliability and Fault Tolerance

The reliability of a network depends on various parameters such as secure communication, reliable hardware, and strong connectivity. The networks that have zero or a limited number of critical nodes may be considered more reliable than the networks that have many critical nodes from the connectivity perspective. The networks that have a limited number of nodes have more than one disjoint path between most of the nodes. Such a network can tolerate many nodes failure without losing its connectivity. In contrast, the networks that have many critical nodes may lose their connectivity after a few nodes failure. Therefore, the number of critical nodes in a network can be used as a benchmark to measure its reliability from the connectivity perspective. Also, by finding and resolving the critical nodes, we may increase the reliability of networks.

Routing

Most of the routing protocols in computer networks try to find the alternate paths between the nodes and avoid using bottlenecks or overused paths. If a network has zero critical nodes, then there are at least 2 disjoint paths between any pair of nodes. Generally, the minimum number of disjoint paths between any pair of nodes in a network equals the number of nodes in its minimum cut. A minimum cut is the minimum number of nodes whose removal destroys the connectivity of the network. Using the available disjoint paths, the sender may push more packets to the network and reduce the overall transmission time. Providing the number of alternate paths between the nodes or providing the bottlenecks information for the routing protocols can considerably increase their performance and improve the packet's delivery time. Based on the available disjoint paths between a sender and receiver, the sender may adjust its packet sending ratio to achieve the best performance and minimize packet loss or congestion.

CHALLENGES

This section presents some major challenges of finding critical nodes in the networks.

Np-Completeness

Most of the provided critical nodes problems in Section 2 are NP-Complete problems that have no well-known approximation solutions. Therefore, not only finding an optimum solution for these problems in a reasonable time is impossible, but also designing an algorithm with a bounded approximation ratio for these problems is a challenging task. Different greedy, random, and heuristic-based algorithms can be used to find an approximated solution; however, their high error ratio may provide inaccurate solutions.

Mobility

Some networks may have mobile nodes that may periodically change their location, which affects the general network topology. For example, in a drone network, the drones usually fly in the network area to collect data or provide some services for the users. As another example, in a vehicular ad hoc network, the vehicles may change their position and in different directions and at different speeds. Moving a node in the network may change the status of many other nodes from critical to noncritical or noncritical to critical. Hence, in a mobile network detecting the critical nodes is a hard and challenging task.

To find the critical nodes in mobile networks, we may follow two general approaches which are proactive and reactive methods. In proactive methods, the critical node detection algorithm runs periodically on the updated network topology to find the latest critical nodes. In the reactive methods, the critical node detection algorithm starts after a dramatic change in the network topology. Both methods have some advantages and disadvantages. The proactive methods may find the new critical nodes faster if they keep the detection interval small. However, these methods may impose message passing and energy consumption overhead for collecting the topology information and running the detection algorithms.

Distributed Environment

In some applications, such as wireless sensor networks, the entire network topology is not available in a specific central node. In these networks, the nodes usually have local neighborhood information of some limited knowledge about the general network such as a number of nodes or their connection. In the distributed systems, finding the critical nodes is much harder than the central systems because any remote connection between the nodes on another side of the network may affect the critical status of any node. Distributed algorithms usually use different message passing-based methods to solve a problem without general knowledge about the network topology. However, they may impose a high amount of message passing, they may need strict synchronization between the nodes, or the message may be lost or corrupted during the transmission. Generally, designing and implementing a distributed algorithm for a problem is more complicated than a central algorithm.

Uncertainty

The communication links in some applications may be unreliable. For example, in a wireless network, if two nodes are at the edges of the communication range of each other, some of their sent messages may receive by the other side and some of them may be lost. This behavior of the communication links leads to uncertainty in the network topology. In such a network, we may have a communication link between two specific nodes for a while and then lose the connection for a random period. Also, the links may be unidirectional in which a node may receive the sent messages by its neighbor but its sent messages may not be delivered to the same neighbor. Also, the links may deliver corrupted data which may affect the algorithm's correctness. Under this uncertainty, finding the critical nodes will be harder than a deterministic platform.

METHODS

This section presents the existing central and distributed algorithms for finding the critical nodes.

Central Methods

The central solution methods for CNDP can be review under two main groups: Exact Solution Methods and Approximate Solution methods. One of the effective ways for finding optimal solutions to optimization problems is integer programming. The first mathematical formulation for the CNP was developed by Arulselvan et al. (Arulselvan, 2009) using integer linear programming. Di Summa et al. (Di Summa, 2012) worked on the first proposed formulation and made several improvements. However, since these two models use a large number of constraints, they can only work on small-sized graphs (up to 150 nodes). Another improved mathematical formulation was proposed by Veremyev et al. (Veremyev, 2014). For the MaxNum and the MinMaxC problems, the most comprehensive study was carried out by Shen et al. (Shen, 2012b). In this study, the researchers developed mathematical formulations for MaxNum and MinMaxC. The effectiveness of the proposed formulations was tested on small-sized graphs (up to 50 nodes). Furthermore, Shen and Smith (Shen, 2012a) proposed dynamic programming approaches for the MaxNum and the MinMaxC problems on special graph types.

Since the variant of the CNDP are NP-Complete problems, it is nearly impossible to find optimal solutions for the large-size problem in reasonable times. Thus, researchers try to find approximate solutions for these types of problems. One of the most used methods for this purpose is greedy heuristics. In literature, several greedy heuristics were proposed for the CNDP (Arulselvan, 2009), (Aringhieri, 2015) (Ventresca, 2014b) (Addis, 2016) (Nguyen, 2013). These algorithms can be classified under two main approaches. In the first approach, algorithms start with an unfeasible solution and try to obtain a feasible solution by removing nodes from the solution set. In the second approach, algorithms start with an empty solution and try to construct a solution. The selection of the nodes depends on the connectivity metric of the problem.

Another approximate solution method used in solving optimization problems is metaheuristic algorithms. Several metaheuristic algorithms were proposed for the CNP in the literature. Ventresca (Ventresca, 2012) investigated the performance of Simulated Annealing and Population-Based Incremental Learning methods on CNP on large graphs (graphs with several thousand nodes). Aringhieri et al. (Aringhieri, 2016a) developed two different metaheuristic algorithms with different local search methods. A greedy randomized adaptive search procedure (GRASP) was proposed by Purevsuren et al. (Purevsuren, 2016), and Zhou et al. (Zhou, 2019) used a Memetic Algorithm to solve the CNP. Also, Aringhieri et al. (Aringhieri, 2016b) presented a genetic algorithm for the MaxNum and the MinMaxC problems. Although the proposed metaheuristic algorithms for these problems can find quality solutions, it can be concluded that these algorithms are not effective for solving large-sized problems.

Distributed Methods

Distributed algorithms have not received as much attention as centralized algorithms for detecting critical nodes. However, when the literature is examined, it is seen that researchers have used two basic methods to construct distributed algorithms to identify critical nodes.

k-neighborhood Method: In this method, nodes learn the information of their neighbors, which are at the most k distance from them. Therefore, first, each node sends a Hello message and sends its ID number to other nodes. Thus, each node learns the 1-hop neighbor list. Then, each node sends its 1-hop neighbor list to its neighbors to form 2-hop local graphs. If each node resends its 2-hop neighbor's list, all nodes can learn about their 3-hop neighbors, and if this process is repeated k times, each node can learn its k-hop neighbors and the edges between those neighbors. The higher the k value, the higher the number of messages sent between nodes and the larger the size of those messages. Therefore, in this method, the value of k is kept less than 3 in general. After constructing the k-neighborhood local graph, each node can run central or heuristic algorithms on these graphs. In this approach, efficient algorithmic rules can be defined. For example, if the degree of a node is less than all the other nodes in the k-neighborhood local graph, then that node or its neighbors are likely to be critical. Several distributed algorithms based on the k-neighborhood method were proposed in the literature (Imran, 2013) (Jorgic, 2004) (Alnuem, 2014) (Sheng, 2006).

Infrastructure Method: In this method, a simple spanning tree, cluster, or ring infrastructure is constructed by another algorithm that uses fewer resources before the algorithm runs on the network. Thus, the algorithm can use the advantages of the infrastructure. Furthermore, since the k-neighborhood method can be used after the infrastructure is created, the hierarchical order of the nodes can be used. One of the most suitable structures to use in this method is spanning trees. Dagdeviren et al. (Dagdeviren, 2019) used connected dominating set and depth-first search tree as an infrastructure to develop distributed algorithms to find critical nodes. As another example, the proposed distributed algorithms for bridge or critical edge detection (Akram, 2013) (Dagdeviren, 2013) can be used for estimating the critical nodes. A bridge or critical edge is an edge whose removal partitions the graph into some disconnected components. So, the endpoints of a bridge can be considered as critical nodes because removing one of them is sufficient to eliminate the edge from the graph and generate a disconnected graph. Therefore, the bridge detection algorithms can be used to provide initial information about the possible critical nodes in the network.

CONCLUSION

Internet of Things and Cyber-Physical Systems have a wide range of applications in different areas such as health care, smart cities, and industrial automation. Recent advances in electronic and hardware technology allow producing the small and energy efficient devices that can connect to the internet sent the collected data or perform remote tasks. However, without a reliable and fault tolerance communication platform, we can not use these devices in most applications. One of the metrics that allow measuring the fault tolerance and reliability of a network is the number and status of existing critical nodes in that network. Generally, a critical node is a node whose failure considerably decreases the robustness of the network connectivity. In this chapter, we discussed three different problems related to the critical nodes. The first problem is finding the nodes whose removal minimizes the pairwise connectivity in the residual network. The second problem is finding the nodes whose removal maximizes the number of connected components. Finally, the third problem is finding the nodes whose removal minimizes the size of the largest connected component. All three problems are NP-Complete. We discussed the applications and challenges of finding the critical nodes in IoT-based cyber-physical systems. Finding the critical nodes may help to identify the weak points of the network, may help to find the best possible clusters, may provide information about the number of existing paths between the nodes, and may reveal the existing bottlenecks in the network. We also briefly discussed the existing and possible distributed and central algorithms for finding each type of critical nodes.

Generally, the existing methods for critical nodes detection can be classified into distributed and central categories. The central methods use different techniques such as integer programming, randomization, heuristics, and metaheuristics to find an approximation of critical nodes. The distributed algorithms may use k-neighborhood information or other infrastructure-based methods to approximate the critical nodes set. In the k-neighborhood methods, each node uses local neighborhood information to decide about its or the neighbor's status (critical or non-critical). Hence, for small k values, the total sent and received bytes by the nodes in k-neighborhood methods will be lower than the other methods. In the infrastructure-based methods, the proposed approaches for different related problems such as clustering, bridge detection, spanning trees, partitioning, and connectivity detection are used to provide an infrastructure to find the critical nodes. The main advantage of the infrastructure-based method is the existence of various efficient algorithms for the related problems. For example, an efficient spanning-tree algorithm may be used to establish the spanning tree in the network and then this tree can be used to find the critical nodes.

However, due to different challenges such as NP-Completeness, mobility, uncertainty, and distributed environment designing an accurate algorithm with a bounded approximation ratio for these problems is a complicated task. The problems are still open and more researches are required to design accurate algorithms to find the mentioned critical nodes.

ACKNOWLEDGMENT

This research was supported by the TUBITAK (Scientific and Technical Research Council of Turkey) [Project number 121F092].

REFERENCES

Adardour, H. E., Hadjila, M., Irid, S. M. H., Baouch, T., & Belkhiter, S. E. (2021). Outdoor Alzheimer's patients tracking using an IoT system and a Kalman Filter estimator. *Wireless Personal Communications*, *116*(1), 249–265. doi:10.100711277-020-07713-4

Addis, B., Aringhieri, R., Grosso, A., & Hosteins, P. (2016). Hybrid Constructive Heuristics for the Critical Node Problem. *Annals of Operations Research*, *238*(1–2), 637–649. doi:10.100710479-016-2110-y

Akram, V. K., & Dagdeviren, O. (2013). Breadth-first search-based single-phase algorithms for bridge detection in wireless sensor networks. *Sensors (Basel)*, *13*(7), 8786–8813. doi:10.3390130708786 PMID:23845930

Alnuem, M., Zafar, N. M., Imran, M., Ullah, S., & Fayed, M. (2014). Formal Specification and Validation of a Localized Algorithm for Segregation of Critical/Noncritical Nodes in MAHSNs. *International Journal of Distributed Sensor Networks*, *10*(6), 1–14. doi:10.1155/2014/140973

Aringhieri, R., Grosso, A., Hosteins, P., & Scatamacchia, R. (2015). VNS Solutions for the Critical Node Problem. *Electronic Notes in Discrete Mathematics*, *47*, 37–44. doi:10.1016/j.endm.2014.11.006

Aringhieri, R., Grosso, A., Hosteins, P., & Scatamacchia, R. (2016a). Local Search Metaheuristics for the Critical Node Problem. *Networks*, *67*(3), 209–221. doi:10.1002/net.21671

Aringhieri, R., Grosso, A., Hosteins, P., & Scatamacchia, R. (2016b). A General Evolutionary Framework for Different Classes of Critical Node Problems. *Engineering Applications of Artificial Intelligence*, *55*, 128–145. doi:10.1016/j.engappai.2016.06.010

Arshad, R., Zahoor, S., Shah, M. A., Wahid, A., & Yu, H. (2017). Green IoT: An investigation on energy saving practices for 2020 and beyond. *IEEE Access: Practical Innovations, Open Solutions*, *5*, 15667–15681. doi:10.1109/ACCESS.2017.2686092

Arulselvan, A., Commander, C. W., Elefteriadou, L., & Pardalos, P. M. (2009). Detecting Critical Nodes in Sparse Graphs. *Computers & Operations Research*, *36*(7), 2193–2200. doi:10.1016/j.cor.2008.08.016

Castañeda-Miranda, A., & Castaño-Meneses, V. M. (2020). Internet of things for smart farming and frost intelligent control in greenhouses. *Computers and Electronics in Agriculture*, *176*, 105614. doi:10.1016/j.compag.2020.105614

Dagdeviren, O., & Akram, V. K. (2013). Energy-efficient bridge detection algorithms for wireless sensor networks. *International Journal of Distributed Sensor Networks*, *9*(4), 867903. doi:10.1155/2013/867903

Dagdeviren, O., Akram, V. K., & Tavli, B. (2019). Design And Evaluation of Algorithms for Energy Efficient and Complete Determination of Critical Nodes for Wireless Sensor Network Reliability. *IEEE Transactions on Reliability*, *68*(1), 280–290. doi:10.1109/TR.2018.2873917

Di Summa, M., Grosso, A., & Locatelli, M. (2012). Branch and Cut Algorithms for Detecting Critical Nodes in Undirected Graphs. *Computational Optimization and Applications*, *53*(3), 649–680. doi:10.100710589-012-9458-y

Imran, M., Alnuem, M. A., Fayed, M. S., & Alamri, A. (2013). Localized Algorithm for Segregation of Critical/Non-critical Nodes in Mobile Ad Hoc and Sensor Networks. *Procedia Computer Science*, *19*, 1167–1172. doi:10.1016/j.procs.2013.06.166

Jaiganesh, S., Gunaseelan, K., & Ellappan, V. (2017). IOT agriculture to improve food and farming technology. In *2017 Conference on Emerging Devices and Smart Systems (ICEDSS)* (pp. 260-266). IEEE. 10.1109/ICEDSS.2017.8073690

Johnsen, F. T., Zieliński, Z., Wrona, K., Suri, N., Fuchs, C., Pradhan, M., Furtak, J., Vasilache, B., Pellegrini, V., Dyk, M., & Marks, M. (2018). Application of IoT in military operations in a smart city. In *2018 International Conference on Military Communications and Information Systems (ICMCIS)* (pp. 1-8). IEEE. 10.1109/ICMCIS.2018.8398690

Jorgic, M., Hauspie, M., Simplot-Ryl, D., & Stojmenovic, I. (2004). Localized Algorithms for Detection of Critical Nodes and Links for Connectivity in Adhoc Networks. *Proceedings of the 3rd IFIP MED-HOC-NET Workshop*, 360-371.

Karimpour, N., Karaduman, B., Ural, A., Challenger, M., & Dagdeviren, O. (2019). Iot based hand hygiene compliance monitoring. In *2019 International Symposium on Networks, Computers and Communications (ISNCC)* (pp. 1-6). IEEE.

Lalou, M., Tahraoui, M. A., & Kheddouci, H. (2018). The critical node detection problem in networks: A survey. *Computer Science Review*, *28*, 92–117. doi:10.1016/j.cosrev.2018.02.002

Lin, C., Han, G., Du, J., Xu, T., Shu, L., & Lv, Z. (2020). Spatiotemporal congestion-aware path planning toward intelligent transportation systems in software-defined smart city IoT. *IEEE Internet of Things Journal*, *7*(9), 8012–8024. doi:10.1109/JIOT.2020.2994963

Liu, H., Cao, X., He, J., Cheng, P., Li, C., Chen, J., & Sun, Y. (2015). Distributed Identification of the most Critical Node for Average Consensus. *IEEE Transactions on Signal Processing*, *63*(16), 4315–4328. doi:10.1109/TSP.2015.2441039

Minovski, D., Åhlund, C., & Mitra, K. (2020). Modeling quality of IoT experience in autonomous vehicles. *IEEE Internet of Things Journal*, *7*(5), 3833–3849. doi:10.1109/JIOT.2020.2975418

Muthuramalingam, S., Bharathi, A., Gayathri, N., Sathiyaraj, R., & Balamurugan, B. (2019). IoT based intelligent transportation system (IoT-ITS) for global perspective: A case study. In *Internet of Things and Big Data Analytics for Smart Generation* (pp. 279–300). Springer. doi:10.1007/978-3-030-04203-5_13

Nguyen, D. T., Shen, Y., & Thai, M. T. (2013). Detecting Critical Nodes in Interdependent Power Networks for Vulnerability Assessment. *IEEE Transactions on Smart Grid*, *4*(1), 151–159. doi:10.1109/TSG.2012.2229398

Ozkaya, M. Y., Sarıyuce, A. E., Pınar, A., & Çatalyurek, U. V. (2018). Local Detection of Critical Nodes in Active Graphs. *2018 IEEE/ACM International Conference on Advances in Social Networks Analysis and Mining (ASONAM)*, 107-110. 10.1109/ASONAM.2018.8508323

Purevsuren, D., Cui, G., Win, N. N. H., & Wang, X. (2016). Heuristic Algorithm for Identifying Critical Nodes in Graphs. *International Journal of Advanced Computer Science*, *5*(3), 1–4.

Ramnath, S., Javali, A., Narang, B., Mishra, P., & Routray, S. K. (2017). IoT based localization and tracking. In *2017 International Conference on IoT and Application (ICIOT)* (pp. 1-4). IEEE.

Santamaria, A. F., Raimondo, P., Tropea, M., De Rango, F., & Aiello, C. (2019). An IoT surveillance system based on a decentralised architecture. *Sensors (Basel)*, *19*(6), 1469. doi:10.339019061469 PMID:30917519

Shen, S., & Smith, J. C. (2012a). Polynomial-time Algorithms for Solving a Class of Critical Node Problems on Trees and Series-Parallel Graphs. *Networks*, *60*(2), 103–119. doi:10.1002/net.20464

Shen, S., Smith, J. C., & Goli, R. (2012b). Exact Interdiction Models and Algorithms for Disconnecting Networks via Node Deletions. *Discrete Optimization*, *9*(3), 172–188. doi:10.1016/j.disopt.2012.07.001

Sheng, M., Li, J., & Shi, Y. (2006). Critical Nodes Detection in Mobile Ad Hoc Network. *20th International Conference on Advanced Information Networking and Applications (AINA'06)*, 336-340.

Tran, M. D., Tran, T. H., Vu, D. T., Nguyen, T. C., Nguyen, V. H., & Tran, T. T. (2021). Development of a Stimulated Model of Smart Manufacturing Using the IoT and Industrial Robot Integrated Production Line. In *Research in Intelligent and Computing in Engineering* (pp. 931–940). Springer. doi:10.1007/978-981-15-7527-3_89

Ventresca, M. (2012). Global Search Algorithms using a Combinatorial Unranking based Problem Representation for the Critical Node Detection Problem. *Computers & Operations Research*, *39*(11), 2763–2775. doi:10.1016/j.cor.2012.02.008

Ventresca, M., & Aleman, D. (2014b). A Fast Greedy Algorithm for the Critical Node Detection Problem. *Combinatorial Optimization and Applications*, *8881*, 603–612. doi:10.1007/978-3-319-12691-3_45

Veremyev, A., Boginski, V., & Pasiliao, E. L. (2014). Exact Identification of Critical Nodes in Sparse Networks via New Compact Formulations. *Optimization Letters*, *8*(4), 1245–1259. doi:10.100711590-013-0666-x

Wehmuth, K., & Ziviani, A. (2011). Distributed Location of the Critical Nodes to Network Robustness based on Spectral Analysis. *7th Latin American Network Operations and Management Symposium*, 1-8. 10.1109/LANOMS.2011.6102259

Zhou, Y., Hao, J. K., & Glover, F. (2019). Memetic Search for Identifying Critical Nodes in Sparse Graphs. *IEEE Transactions on Cybernetics*, *49*(10), 3699–3712. doi:10.1109/TCYB.2018.2848116 PMID:29994417

Zielonka, A., Sikora, A., Woźniak, M., Wei, W., Ke, Q., & Bai, Z. (2020). Intelligent Internet of things system for smart home optimal convection. *IEEE Transactions on Industrial Informatics*, *17*(6), 4308–4317. doi:10.1109/TII.2020.3009094

KEY TERMS AND DEFINITIONS

Bottleneck: A subset of nodes or links that slow down the traffic flow in the network.

Connected Component: A set of nodes in a partitioned graph that have at least one path to each other.

Critical Nodes: A node whose failure reduce the fault tolerance or destroys the connectivity of the network.

Distributed System: A set of independent nodes with local memory and processor that can communicate over a communication platform.

Fault Tolerance: Tolerating the failure of nodes or links in a network while keeping the network functionality.

Internet of Things: A set of devices that can communicate over the internet to perform some tasks.

Routing: The process of finding a communication path between two nodes in a network.

Chapter 13

Mesh Network of eHealth Intelligent Agents for Visually Impaired and Blind People:
A Review Study on Arduino and Raspberry Pi Wearable Devices

Dmytro Zubov

University of Central Asia, Kyrgyzstan

ABSTRACT

Smart assistive devices for blind and visually impaired (B&VI) people are of high interest today since wearable IoT hardware became available for a wide range of users. In the first project, the Raspberry Pi 3 B board measures a distance to the nearest obstacle via ultrasonic sensor HC-SR04 and recognizes human faces by Pi camera, OpenCV library, and Adam Geitgey module. Objects are found by Bluetooth devices of classes 1-3 and iBeacons. Intelligent eHealth agents cooperate with one another in a smart city mesh network via MQTT and BLE protocols. In the second project, B&VIs are supported to play golf. Golf flagsticks have sound marking devices with a buzzer, NodeMcu Lua ESP8266 ESP-12 WiFi board, and WiFi remote control. In the third project, an assistive device supports the orientation of B&VIs by measuring the distance to obstacles via Arduino Uno and HC-SR04. The distance is pronounced through headphones. In the fourth project, the soft-/hardware complex uses Raspberry Pi 3 B and Bytereal iBeacon fingerprinting to uniquely identify the B&VI location at industrial facilities.

INTRODUCTION

Over 253 million people across the world today are estimated to be blind or visually impaired (B&VI) (World Health Organization, 2020). Around 30 million B&VI Europeans need assistance for the spatial cognition indoor and outdoor (European Commission, 2020). About 90% of B&VI live at a low income that means these people cannot buy expensive assistive devices for spatial cognition. Approximately 20%

DOI: 10.4018/978-1-7998-4186-9.ch013

of young B&VI in the UK do not leave their home, approximately 30% had traveled locally, and only 40% left their home alone and walked (Bruce, McKennell, & Walker, 1991). Most of the B&VI who explore new routes feel disorientation, fear, stress, and panic associated with being lost (Golledge, 1993). Being mobile is the crucial factor that contributes to the success of the B&VI (Goodwyn, Bell, & Singletary, 2009). The white canes and guide dogs remain the common aid associated with this disability despite over a hundred different assistive electronic devices developed last three decades (Chaudary et al, 2017; Elmannai & Elleithy, 2017). The additional training of B&VI, especially children (Gori et al, 2016), to use the innovative hardware and its integration into existing networks are the main sticking points nowadays. The first problem is solved by short-term courses, where B&VI people learn the assistive devices. The second problem does not have a single solution due to the heterogeneous soft-/hardware, as well as the standard smart city infrastructure, which is a dominant platform for communication of assistive devices, was not developed yet.

Internet of Things (IoT) hardware is produced by many companies such as Raspberry Pi Foundation, Arduino, Bosch, Silicon Labs. IoT software is represented by different operating systems like Raspbian, Android Things, Windows 10 IoT, Ubuntu Core. The assistive devices exchange data in metropolitan area networks (Yaqoob et al, 2017) via IoT data protocols like MQTT and CoAP (Dizdarevic et al, 2020) and different network technologies such as WiFi, Bluetooth, Ethernet (Rackley, 2007). On a short distance of up to 10 m, most IoT hardware, smartphones, and tablets implement the Bluetooth classes 2 or 3 to be connected directly (Woodford, 2020). Standard iBeacons (Trent, Abdelgawad, & Yelamarthi, 2017; Shovic, 2016; Lin & Lin, 2018) have an approximate range of 70 meters for the peer-to-peer Bluetooth low energy (BLE) connection. For larger distances, the client-server and/or wireless mesh network architectures (Zarzycki, 2016) are recommended.

For the spatial cognition, B&VI require specific functionality from the assistive devices:

1.   Geographic Information and Global Positioning Systems (GIS and GPS) for navigation.
2.   Ultrasonic/optical detection of the obstacles and distances to them.
3.   Computer vision detection and recognition of the people and other objects like animals in front of and/or around the B&VI.
4.   Indication of objects and places around B&VI via the BLE techniques, e.g. RSSI, AoA, and ToF, and recently proposed BLE based protocols, e.g. iBeacon, Apple Inc., and Eddystone, Google Inc., (Zafari, Gkelias, & Leung, 2020).
5.   Integration into existing smart city infrastructure via wireless technologies, e.g. Bluetooth and WiFi.
6.   Navigation assistance to solve the last 10 meters problem, e.g. the sound marking of the objects like the entrances and exits.

Nowadays, none of existing B&VI assistive devices implement together above-stated functionality (1)-(6). The most promising approach is the mesh network of eHealth intelligent agents since the number of network-connected devices is estimated to be 6.58 per person around the world in 2020 (Statista, 2020). It is a huge increase compared with 2003 (0.08), 2010 (1.84), and 2015 (3.47) that reflects the global tendency – IoT becomes the Internet of Everything, i.e. almost every new smart device might be connected to the network and humans are associated with these devices sometimes. BLE is preferable technology to connect the nodes directly, i.e. peer-to-peer (Draishpits, 2016), dynamically, and non-hierarchically in the mesh network on the short distances of up to 90 m due to the energy efficiency.

WiFi is commonly used to connect the nodes for larger distances in the smart city networks (Suzuki, 2017; Muhendra et al, 2017). The low-cost iBeacon mesh network might be developed with Raspberry Pi, Bluetooth module HM-10, and Python library Bluepy for interfacing with BLE devices through Bluez, the official Linux Bluetooth protocol stack (Hrisko, 2020). However, the prices of assistive devices for B&VI with advanced features such as the computer vision and iBeacon object identification are still high. For instance, the price of wearable assistive device OrCam MyEye (Holton, 2020) is USD 3,500; it detects what the B&VI is looking at, recognizes the presence of text, and speaks the text aloud.

RELATED WORK

Previous studies on the mesh network of eHealth intelligent agents for B&VI were mostly published in the Artificial Intelligence (AI) and IoT journals and conference proceedings since assistive devices are based on the intelligent algorithms and IoT soft-/hardware. They can be classified by the above-stated functionality (1)-(6).

In (Jacobson & Kitchin, 1997), the GIS acquires information from the obstacle avoidance sensors, positioning devices, and the end-user, and then forwards these to the spatial knowledge base. This spatial information is delivered to the end-user via audio- and/or tactile-based interfaces a few steps forward. In (Ramadhan, 2018), the wearable smart navigation system is presented using GPS and ultrasonic sensor. A solar panel provides additional power to the system. Microsoft Australia has launched the Soundscape app that uses audio beacons and AI technology to provide navigational information for B&VI (Campos, 2020). However, image processing is not implemented in (Jacobson, 1997; Ramadhan, 2018; Campos, 2020). Nowadays, the B&VI have explicit navigation instructions provided by ordinary smartphones with GPS.

In (Zubov, 2017), the spatial cognition of B&VI is based on the measurement of the distance to an obstacle via ultrasonic sensor HC-SR04. The information is pronounced to the B&VI through headphone and MP3 player based on Arduino Uno. Assistive devices were successfully tested at the Instituto para Ciegos y Débiles Visuales "Ezequiel Hernández Romo", San Luis Potosi, Mexico.

There are different types of the computer vision detection and recognition algorithms (Mallick, 2020; Salton, 2020; Takuya, Akinori, & Takio 2008; Viola & Jones, 2004), e.g. Eigenfaces, Fisherfaces, Histogram of Oriented Gradients (HOG), Local Binary Patterns, Scale Invariant Feature Transform, Speed Up Robust Features, Viola-Jones Face Detection. These methods extract the image features and perform the matching with the input image. Some of them like HOG might be used for the detection and recognition of different categories of objects, e.g. humans and animals. The support vector machine classifier with the HOG feature extractor is the most popular solution for object detection and classification (Ilas & Ilas, 2018). In (Marco, Young, & Turner, 1987), a comparison of the sample linear discriminant function (LDF) and Euclidean distance classifier (EDC) shows that the sample EDC outperforms the sample LDF if the number of features is large relative to the training sample size. Nowadays, different computer vision libraries, e.g. OpenCV, Vlfeat, PCL, and SimpleCV (Rosebrock, 2020c; Demaagd et al, 2012), use the above-stated methods to analyze images via local features extraction and matching. In (Zubov, 2018), the modified Viola-Jones fast face detector with the combination of features "eye" and "nose" is proposed to speed up the image processing, but its detection rate is not 100%. In general, the problem specifies the method(s) to detect and recognize object(s).

In (Bai et al, 2017), the depth-based algorithm finds candidate traversable directions using the depth image. The proposed approach assumes that the nearest obstacle is always at the bottom of the depth image, and it selects only a line at the bottom of the image as input. The ultrasonic sensor is applied, but object recognition is not discussed in (Bai et al, 2017). The wearable assistive device is developed with the RGBD camera and FPGA CPU in (Poggi & Mattoccia, 2016). The semantic categorization of detected obstacles is based on the convolutional neural network. The experiments showed good detection performance close to 98%, although the object categorization is less than 72% of correctness. The sensed area for obstacle detection is from 0.5 m to 3 m only (Poggi & Mattoccia, 2016).

In (Trent et al, 2017), iBeacons are proposed for the spatial marking in the low-cost and energy-effective IoT navigation system for the B&VI. The Raspberry Pi board detects the obstacles with the ultrasonic sensor. The information is provided to the end-user via the Bluetooth headphones.

There is no commonly accepted definition for the smart city assistive/inclusive infrastructure (Commission on Science and Technology, 2016; Al-Hader & Rodzi, 2009). A concept of the inclusive smart infrastructure (de Oliveira Neto & Kofuji, 2016), where physical and digital barriers are eliminated, targets the needs of the B&VI. This idea is implemented through mesh networks (Muhendra et al, 2017; Hrisko, 2020) with eHealth intelligent agents (Bergenti & Poggi, 2010; Chan, Ray, & Parameswaran, 2008) that communicate via IoT data protocols such as MQTT, CoAP, XMPP, DDS, AMQP (Dizdarevic, Carpio, Jukan, & Masip-Bruin, 2020; Suzuki, 2017). MQTT IoT software can be executed on thin clients like Arduino Uno since it takes approximately 10 KB of the random-access memory. It was shown that MQTT brokers work reliably with 100,000 publishers and 100 subscribers (ScalAgent Distributed Technologies, 2020) that satisfies the requirements to smart city networks.

In (Zubov, 2017), the assistive device supports the golf game of B&VI with sound marking of flagsticks and Wi-Fi NodeMcu Lua ESP8266 ESP-12 boards with active buzzers that are remotely controlled by a person with good vision via Intranet HTML websites. The same concept go-to-sound G2S is used in the assistive system (Navigation Complex G2S, 2020) developed for the Ukrainian Association of the Blind.

In (Elmannai & Elleithy, 2017), twenty five different assistive devices are compared using the following parameters: real-time / not real-time mode, coverage (indoor, outdoor, both), time (day, night, both), range (less than 1 m, 1 m to 5 m, over 5 m), object type (static, dynamic, both). 72% of the presented products have at least three characteristics that are not fully satisfied, e.g. the device Eye Subs provides only outdoor coverage, the detection ranges up to 5 m due to the ultrasonic limits, and it detects only static objects. The authors pointed out that the ideal device always must recognize the surrounding environment.

The practical use of B&VI assistive devices shows the following:

- GIS and GPS are standard components of smartphone soft-/hardware nowadays.
- The ultrasonic detectors are preferable to the optical one for the wearable hardware because of price and operational distance. For instance, an ultrasonic sensor HC-SR04 (price USD 1.5 approx.) measures a distance of up to 5 m and an infrared proximity sensor GP2Y0A21 (price USD 3.5 approx.) – up to 0.8 m only.
- Developers prefer Bluetooth transmitters/receivers based on standard BLE protocols such as iBeacon. Devices are connected by Bluetooth on a short distance of up to 90 m, by WiFi – larger distances within the local area network of the smart city.
- Smartphones are used for general-purpose tasks such as face detection/recognition during daytime and GPS navigation. IoT electronics like Raspberry Pi 3 B (Patnaik & Dinkar, 2017) and Arduino

Tian (Embedded Computing, 2020) are applied for specific solutions, e.g. night vision and ultrasonic sensing, since additional sensors are utilized.

- Python is the leading programming language to implement intelligent algorithms on the Raspbian platform.
- Standard libraries are common for face recognition, e.g. OpenCV with Python on the palm-sized computer Raspberry Pi 3 B (Rosebrock, 2020a).
- The sound marking is turned on only if the B&VI is next to the target object since the continuous sound bothers the people with normal vision.
- The B&VI need only specific information about surrounding objects because of their diversity and large quantities.

Analysis of the above-stated work shows that today the spatial cognition is based on the GPS navigation via smartphones, the ultrasonic sensing of obstacles, computer vision detection / recognition / categorization of the surrounding objects, and BLE technology for the spatial marking. None of the known assistive devices for the B&VI combine all the above-stated functionality (1)-(6), they are not the standard components of the smart city infrastructure, as well as they do not implement the mesh networking for the communication with other IoT equipment.

Mesh Network of eHealth Intelligent Agents for the B&VI: A Methodology Outline

This section summarizes projects based on the palm-sized computer Raspberry Pi 3 B with Pi camera and ultrasonic sensor HC-SR04, and it features MQTT IoT protocol allowing it to communicate with other intelligent eHealth agents (Zubov et al, 2018).

We use the meet-in-the-middle methodology (Gajski et al, 2009) to design the mesh network of eHealth intelligent agents to support the B&VI. The proposed smart city inclusive component with the mesh network of eHealth intelligent agents for B&VI is presented in Fig. 1. The data-driven assistive approach is the core of this component. Here, MQTT IoT protocol connects the eHealth intelligent agents, as well as other parts of smart city (smart buildings, smart mobility, smart energy, smart water, smart health, smart waste management, smart industry, smart infrastructure development and monitoring, etc.) communicate with one another via IoT protocols (Dizdarevic et al, 2020). The Python programs, addresses of MQTT brokers and Bluetooth devices, MQTT passwords, MQTT topics, recognition rules, MP3 files, and other relevant information might be downloaded from the file server to the eHealth agents by request. If the Internet is not connected, previously downloaded files are loaded from the internal drive, e.g. SD card on Raspberry Pi 3 B. In addition, the eHealth devices might transmit/receive the information by Bluetooth, e.g. classes 1-3, and iBeacons.

Figure 1. A smart city inclusive component with a mesh network of eHealth intelligent agents for B&VI.

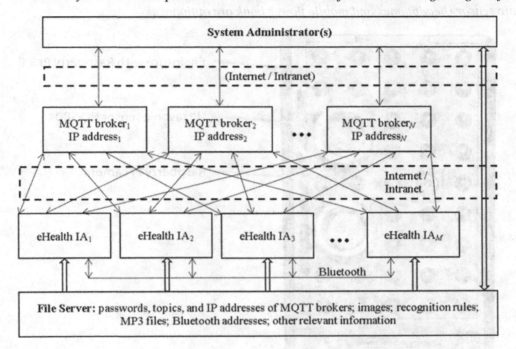

Raspberry Pi 3 B boards can handle all three MQTT roles – broker, publisher, and subscriber (Wireless Communication, 2020). For this purpose, the following software is installed:

- The open-source MQTT message broker Mosquitto to start the MQTT broker, publisher, and subscriber on Raspberry Pi 3 B through the main repository:
  sudo apt-get install -y mosquitto mosquitto-clients
- The Python library paho-mqtt for implementing the publisher and subscriber in the Python 3 program:
  sudo pip3 install paho-mqtt

The Python code (Wireless Communication, 2020) can be replicated with small corrections such as MQTT topic and IP address of MQTT broker.

In the proposed hardware configuration, the Raspberry Pi 3 B is a basic microcomputer. The final product is presented in Fig. 2. Headphones and mobile power banks are optional since the board might be supplied directly from the power grid, as well as headphones might be connected via Bluetooth and cables. The Raspberry Pi 3 B+ board is not considered since it is sensitive to the power supply. In particular, the warning "under-voltage detected" is displayed if Raspberry Pi 3 B+ is supplied by the mobile power banks; two power banks have been applied, and the microcomputer restarted every two minutes. The same external batteries are working well with Raspberry Pi 3 B board. The Arduino boards might be used in a mesh network for simple operations like the data acquisition, e.g. the heart rate measurement via sensor KY-039, Arduino Uno, and Ethernet Shield (Fass, 2020; From KY-039 To Heart Rate, 2020; Doukas, 2012).

Figure 2. The final product of the B&VI assistive device: Raspberry Pi 3 B board with the camera, ultrasonic sensor (headphones and mobile power bank are optional).

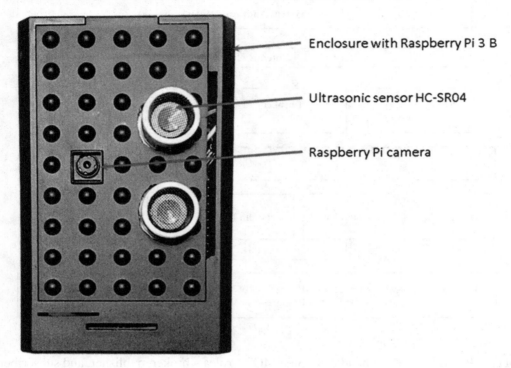

Enclosure with Raspberry Pi 3 B

Ultrasonic sensor HC-SR04

Raspberry Pi camera

The basic options of B&VI assistive device are as follows: ultrasonic measurement of the distance of up to 5 m to the nearest obstacle via the range detector HC-SR04; computer vision detection and recognition of the human faces in front of the B&VI based on the Raspberry Pi camera; indication of the objects and places around B&VI using the Bluetooth devices of classes 1-3 and iBeacons; integration of the assistive device into existing smart city infrastructure through the MQTT IoT data protocol.

Four Python programs were developed to implement the above-stated tasks (1)-(6). They start in parallel using the launch script (Kildall, 2020) when the assistive device is turning on. The launch script is made executable on startup as follows:

1st step. The script file launcher.sh is developed in the text editor as follows:

```
cd /home/pi/Documents/Download
sudo python Download1.py
7z x Files.zip -y
sudo python3 pi_face_recognition.py --cascade haarcascade_frontalface_default.
xml --encodings encodings.pickle & sudo python3 Ultra4.py & sudo python3 Blue-
tooth4.py & sudo python3 MQTT1.py
```

In the first line of file launcher.sh, the current directory is changed to "/home/pi/DIP/Experiment/Download". This directory includes all project files. In the second line of file launcher.sh, the Python program Download1.py is started. This program downloads zip-file Files.zip from the Internet file server.

The URL is unique for every assistive device to satisfy the requirements of the B&VI person. The Python code in Download1.py is as follows:

```
import requests
url = 'http://URL_is_here'
fileName = '/home/pi/Documents/Download/Files.zip'
req = requests.get(url)
file = open(fileName, 'wb')
for chunk in req.iter_content(100000):
    file.write(chunk)
file.close()
```

In the third line of file launcher.sh, zip-file Files.zip is unzipped by program 7z. Command "x" extracts all files from the archive Files.zip to the current directory. Switch "-y" assumes YES on all queries. In the fourth line of file launcher.sh, four Python programs start in parallel: pi_face_recognition.py (detection and recognition of the human face), Ultra4.py (ultrasonic measurement of the distance to nearest obstacle), Bluetooth4.py (an indication of the Bluetooth devices of classes 1-3 and iBeacons), MQTT1.py (communication with other intelligent agents via the MQTT IoT data protocol). These four Python programs are discussed below.

2nd step. Make the script file launcher.sh executable:

```
chmod 755 launcher.sh
```

3rd step. Add the logs directory for records of any errors in crontab, which is a background (daemon) process that executes scripts at specific times (at the start in our case):

```
mkdir logs
```

4th step. Add the script launcher.sh to crontab. The following command is executed in terminal:

```
sudo crontab -e
```

Then, the following code is added at the bottom of the text file:

```
@reboot sh /home/pi/Documents/Download/launcher.sh /home/pi/Documents/Download/logs/cronlog 2>&1
```

The information is pronounced to the B&VI through headphones. All phrases are stored in MP3 files, and hence the language localization might be easily done by simple replacement of the MP3 files on the file server in the end-user specific folder. In the Python program, the command-line MP3 player mpg321 is implemented as follows (MP3 file DeviceIsStarting.mp3 is an example):

```
os.system("mpg321 DeviceIsStarting.mp3")
```

To start MP3 files sequentially, the following Python code is applied (psutil is a cross-platform library for retrieving information on running processes and system utilization):

```
flag=1 # This variable is the semaphore: 1 - another MP3 file is playing
# In the while loop, we wait while another mpg321 player is stopped, i.e.
flag=0
while flag==1:
    flag=0
    try:
      for pid in psutil.pids():
        p = psutil.Process(pid)
        if p.name()=="mpg321":
            flag=1
    except:
     flag=1
     time.sleep(2)
     print("We have an error in PIDs")
```

The presented approach of the microcomputer Raspberry Pi 3 B has the following drawbacks:

- Despite the low cost, USD 70 approx., the price is still high for some B&VI. The solution is to develop the mobile application(s) for Android and iOS mobile platforms using cross-platform technologies such as Apache Cordova and Microsoft Xamarin (Bennett, 2018). In this case, the B&VI will use their smartphones to download and install software at no cost.
- The B&VI listen surrounding environment to identify objects. At the same time, they use a head-phone to acquire audio information from smartphones and other devices. If they have different equipment, the audio mixer is additionally needed to manage audio from each service.

Ultrasonic measurement of the distance to the nearest obstacle up to 5 m is based on the hardware that uses the ultrasonic range sensor HC-SR04 (HC-SR04 Ultrasonic Range Sensor, 2020). Since the device is small-sized, the B&VI can easily rotate it. The Raspberry Pi 3 B GPIO pins are of maximum voltage 3.3 V and the power supply is 5 V. Hence, the voltage divider with resistors 1 kOhm and 2 kOhm is applied to the Echo output of the sensor. The Python code for acquiring the information from the sensor HC-SR04 is presented in (HC-SR04 Ultrasonic Range Sensor, 2020). For the user-friendly representation of distances, the range is split into five intervals – less than 100 m, 200 cm, 300 cm, 400 cm, and 500 cm. This information is repeated every two minutes if it is not changed. The fragment of Python program is as follows:

```
if (distance<=100 and distance>0.5):
os.system("mpg321 LessThanOneMeter.mp3")
else:
   if (distance<=200):
     os.system("mpg321 LessThanTwoMeters.mp3")
   else:
     if (distance<=300):
       os.system("mpg321 LessThanThreeMeters.mp3")
     else:
       if (distance<=400):
         os.system("mpg321 LessThanFourMeters.mp3")
       else:
         if (distance<=500):
           os.system("mpg321 LessThanFiveMeters.mp3")
         else:
           os.system("mpg321 DistanceUnidentified.mp3")
```

The ultrasonic sensor has the following drawbacks (Nguyen, 2014): it cannot detect objects that distract sound due to the complex surface texture or too large angle between sensor and object; the sound could hit another surface before returning to the sensor instead of bouncing back from the target directly (the ghost echo) causing miscalculated timing; the temperature and sound noise interference.

Detection of the obstacle in front of the B&V takes approximately 0.3 sec, which is quite acceptable for the slowly walking B&VI. If the calculated value of the distance is greater than 500 cm or less than 0, the end-user receives a message that distance is unidentified. The most likely future improvement is the use of a range sensor with better measurement accuracy and/or detector based on another principle, e.g. the optical one.

Computer vision detection and recognition of human faces in front of the B&VI is based on the hardware with Raspberry Pi camera (Rosebrock, 2020a) and computer vision library OpenCV (Rosebrock, 2020b) without Python virtual environment. It was found that OpenCV is not working properly from the script file at the Raspberry Pi 3 B startup if it is installed in the Python virtual environment. The face recognition part detects and recognizes the known faces and number of the unknown one; it is developed as follows (Rosebrock, 2020a):

1st step. Install OpenCV 3.2 Python/C++ on Raspberry Pi 3 B.
2nd step. Install Davis King's dlib toolkit software.
3rd step. Install Adam Geitgey's face recognition module.
4th step. Install imutils package of convenient functions.

The project consists of the following files and directories:

- 31 MP3 files with audio information on the device state, spatial cognition, and the number of unknown faces: DeviceIsReady.mp3, InACenter.mp3, OnTheRight.mp3, OnTheLeft. mp3, NoUnidentifiedFaces.mp3, OneUnidentifiedFace.mp3, TwoUnidentifiedFaces.mp3, …, NineteenUnidentifiedFaces.mp3, TwentyUnidentifiedFaces.mp3, OverTwentyUnidentifiedFaces.

mp3. The localization is based on the replacement of these audio files with other files in the specified language, e.g. Chinese, English, Japanese, Macedonian, Ukrainian, Russian, Spanish.

- MP3 files with names of the people, which faces are detected and recognized.
- A directory dataset/ contains sub-directories with .jpg photos for each person that the facial recognition system detects and recognizes.
- A Python file encode_faces.py finds faces in the directory dataset/ and encode them into 128-D vectors (Rosebrock, 2020a; Szeliski, 2011).
- A file encodings.pickle contains the face encodings (128-D vectors, one for each face).
- The OpenCV's pre-trained Haar cascade file haarcascade_frontalface_default.xml is used to detect and localize faces in frames. It is not changed in this project.
- A Python file pi_face_recognition.py is the main execution script.

The Python program pi_face_recognition.py is based on the code presented in (Rosebrock, 2020a). The corrections are as follows: playing MP3 files with audio information on the device state, spatial cognition, and the number of unknown faces; the code for displaying the image on a screen and drawing of predicted face name on the image was deleted to speed up the program.

It was found that the accuracy of face detection and recognition is better if the knowledge base contains more photos of different people (Zubov, 2017). Initially, the directory dataset/ includes two sub-directories with photos of two developers – Dmytro Zubov and Iryna Zubova.

The drawback of the presented approach is an impossibility to estimate the accuracy of face recognition. Hence, the most likely future improvement is the implementation of the new algorithm (Rosebrock, 2020c) for face detection and recognition with the calculation of correct result probability.

1.1 Indication of Objects and Places Around B&VI via the Bluetooth Devices of Classes 1-3 and iBeacons

Indication of objects around B&VI via the Bluetooth devices of classes 1-3, e.g. smartphones and Raspberry Pi boards, and BLE equipment, e.g. iBeacons, is based on the Python library bluetooth is installed using the package libbluetooth-dev:

```
sudo apt-get install python-dev libbluetooth-dev
```

The following Python program shows the Bluetooth devices of classes 1-3 (Raspberry Pi Bluetooth):

```
import bluetooth
nearby_devices = bluetooth.discover_devices(lookup_names = True)
print ("found %d devices" % len(nearby_devices))
for name, addr in nearby_devices:
    print("%s - %s" % (addr, name))
```

To find the iBeacons around the B&VI, the Python code was developed similar to the presented in (Raspberry Pi Bluetooth, 2020). In addition, the bluepy library is installed:

```
sudo pip3 install bluepy
```

The difference of developed Python code with presented in (Hrisko, 2017) and (Raspberry Pi Bluetooth, 2020) is as follows: the audio is produced by the mpg321 player and MP3 files; comparison of the addresses of detected Bluetooth devices with the database of known objects – if coincidence is found, the information is pronounced to the B&VI.

A drawback of the presented approach is the last 10 meters problem – the B&VI cannot identify the direction where the Bluetooth device is. The most likely solution to this problem is the RSSI based localization with iBeacon fingerprinting (Zubov, 2019).

The final recommendations are as follows:

- develop the mobile version of the assistive device;
- improve the connection of power cable;
- replace the headphone to provide the audibility of the surrounding environment and assistive device information both.

Spatial Cognition of Surrounding Objects by the B&VI People Using Sound Patterns and Ultrasonic Sensing

This section summarizes two assistive projects on the spatial cognition by the B&VI using the sound patterns and ultrasonic sensing. The first device supports sports activities of B&VI, the golf game specifically. Every golf flagstick has the sound marking device with the active buzzer and WiFi remote control by the person with a good vision. The NodeMcu Lua ESP8266 ESP-12 WiFi boards in devices are controlled through cross-platform HTML websites, and hence any WiFi smartphone and/or computer can be in use to start the HTML webpage. The second device supports the orientation of B&VI by measuring the distance to the obstacle based on the ultrasonic sensor HC-SR04 and Arduino Uno. The distance is pronounced to the B&VI using headphone and MP3 player with SD card. (Zubov, 2017).

Nowadays, the budget assistance devices for the B&VI can be efficiently developed using Arduino Uno/Mega (Warren, Adams, & Molle, 2011; Norris, 2015) and/or Arduino-compatible hardware like NodeMcu Lua ESP8266 ESP-12 Wi-Fi board (User Manual for ESP-12E DevKit based on ESP8266, 2016) of the price up to USD 10. Here, soft-/hardware is based on the technology Internet of Things (Charalampos, 2012; Norris, 2015; Slama et al, 2015). Polytechnic University of San Luis Potosi and Tecnológico de Monterrey (campus San Luis Potosi) developed two assistive devices – for the golf game (the sound marking of the golf flagsticks) using a mobile app connected to the NodeMcu Lua ESP8266 ESP-12 Wi-Fi boards and for the distance measurement using Arduino Uno together with an ultrasonic sensor. These devices are in use at Instituto para Ciegos y Débiles Visuales "Ezequiel Hernández Romo" nowadays.

Two assistive projects were made by Polytechnic University of San Luis Potosi and Tecnológico de Monterrey for B&VI at Instituto para Ciegos y Débiles Visuales "Ezequiel Hernández Romo":

1. An assistive project for the golf game. In this project, the golf flagsticks have the sound marking devices with the active buzzer and NodeMcu Lua ESP8266 ESP-12 Wi-Fi board, which are remotely controlled by Wi-Fi. Hence, B&VI people play golf almost without help. The person with good vision controls the sound of an appropriate device based on cross-platform HTML website.

2.   An assistive project to support the orientation of B&VI by the measurement of the distance to the obstacle using an ultrasonic sensor and Arduino Uno. Then, the distance info is pronounced to the person using headphone and embedded MP3 player.

The assistive device supports B&VI to play the golf game using an appropriate sound pattern. Every golf flagstick has a sound marking device with Wi-Fi remote control by the person with a good vision. In this case, B&VI person hears the sound (five types of beep signals of different duration) from the appropriate golf stick and then kicks the ball towards it. In other words, B&VI play golf almost without help. The NodeMcu Lua ESP8266 ESP-12 Wi-Fi boards in devices are controlled by the cross-platform HTML websites, and hence any Wi-Fi smartphone and / or computer can be in use to start the HTML web-page. Mini portable 3G/4G Wi-Fi 150Mbps RJ45 USB wireless router with power supply 5 V links all devices in the wireless local area network. Hence, the hardware can work outdoor supplied by 5 V power banks. The manual control is provided by an additional button to the NodeMcu Lua Wi-Fi board if the network is not working; in this case, special beep signal is generated when Wi-Fi board starts. End-users are securely connected to the network using the password to the wireless router. Ten devices were assembled of price USD 7 each, i.e. the total budget is USD 80 including the portable wireless router and power banks. The accumulators for power banks were taken free of charge from the Fujitsu and Samsung old laptop batteries with the capacity approximately 1500 mA each, which provides about 5 hours of the stable working. The software was developed in the Arduino Integrated Development Environment (IDE) under free software license, and hence it does not affect the price.

Figure 3. The electronics hardware part of the assistive device for the golf game.

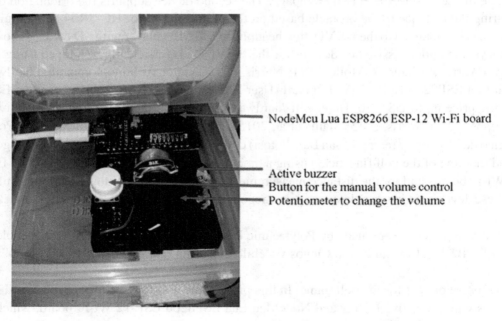

NodeMcu Lua ESP8266 ESP-12 Wi-Fi board

Active buzzer
Button for the manual volume control
Potentiometer to change the volume

Figure 4. The assistive device attached to the top of the golf flagstick using Velcro straps.

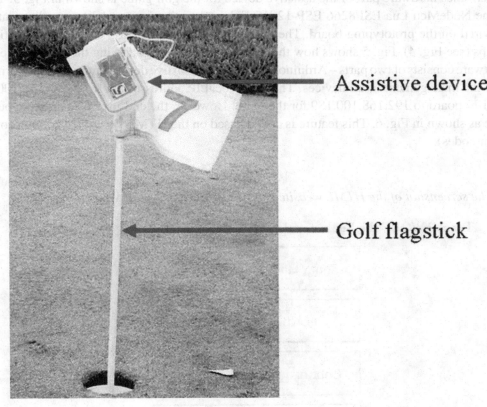

Figure 5. The B&VI person plays golf using an assistive device.

The electronics hardware part of the assistive device for the golf game is shown in Fig. 3. The main parts are the NodeMcu Lua ESP8266 ESP-12 Wi-Fi board, active buzzer, button, and potentiometer. They are wired on the prototyping board. The device is attached to the top of the golf flagstick using Velcro straps (see Fig. 4). Fig. 5 shows how the B&VI person plays golf using the assistive device.

The software consists of two parts – Arduino sketch for the assistive devices and cross-platform HTML website for the management of all devices. The static local IP addresses are from 192.168.100.180 for the first Wi-Fi board to 192.168.100.189 for the tenth. However, the end-user sees only the buttons on the website as shown in Fig. 6. This feature is coded based on the HTML tag *href* as follows (other tags have similar codes):

Figure 6. The screenshot of the HTML website for the management of all Wi-Fi devices.

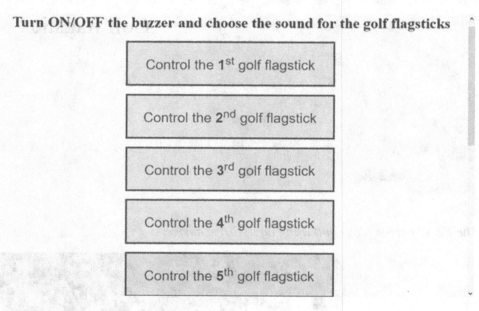

```
<a href="http://192.168.100.180"><button style='color:green; font-size:30px;
width:450px; height:100px; border-style:solid; border-width:4px; border-
color:green;'>Control the <b>1</b><sup>st</sup> golf flagstick</button></a>
```

The configuration of the static local IP address in Arduino sketch for the first Wi-Fi board is as follows (other boards are configured similarly):

```
// The IP address for the Wi-Fi board:
IPAddress ip(192, 168, 100, 180);
// Set gateway to match the network:
IPAddress gateway(192, 168, 100, 1);
// Set subnet mask to match the network:
IPAddress subnet(255, 255, 255, 0);
```

```
// Set the static local IP address:
WiFi.config(ip, gateway, subnet);
```

Figure 7. The screenshot of the HTML website for the management of the ninth Wi-Fi board.

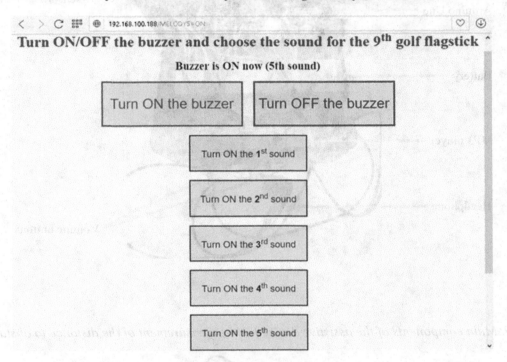

The screenshot of the HTML website hosted on the ninth Wi-Fi board is presented in Fig. 7 (other boards have similar websites).

The assistive device for the golf game was successfully implemented at the Instituto para Ciegos y Débiles Visuales "Ezequiel Hernández Romo", San Luis Potosi, Mexico. Three stages of the project's development are as follows: specification of the device, development of the prototype with intermediate testing, and assembling of ten assistive devices together with Wi-Fi router and power banks.

The assistive wearable device supports the orientation of B&VI by measuring the distance to the obstacle based on the ultrasonic sensor. Then, the distance is pronounced to the person using headphone. The electronics hardware part consists of the ultrasonic sensor HC-SR04, Arduino Uno, MP3 player with SD card, headphone, and two buttons to control the volume (see Fig. 8). The red button decreases the volume, the green one increases it. The device is shown in Fig. 9. The position of the device is not fixed on the clothes, and hence the obstacles can be detected on different levels (ground, knee, body, head, etc.) by the simple changing of the device orientation. The hardware is supplied by 5 V power banks. Several devices were assembled of price USD 8 each including the power banks. The power bank accumulators were taken free of charge from the Fujitsu and Samsung old laptop batteries as well. The

Figure 8. The assistive device hardware for the measurement of the distance to obstacle.

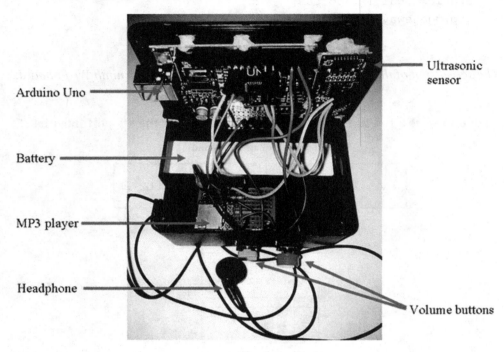

Figure 9. Main components of the assistive device for the measurement of the distance to obstacle.

testing shows that the embedded battery provides a stable power supply for at least an hour. The software was developed in the Arduino IDE under free software license, and hence it does not affect the price.

The ultrasonic sensor HC-SR04 measures the distance up to 4.5 m. Because of practical needs, this length is split into five intervals as follows: less than 1 m, greater than 1 m, 2 m, 3 m, and 4 m. To avoid the chatter mode, the dead bands (Dead Band Plus Hysteresis Estimation with ValveLink Diagnostics, 2020) are used with a length of 10 cm around the setpoints 100 cm, 200 cm, 300 cm, and 400 cm. MP3 files with appropriate info are written on the SD card, and hence the sound patterns can be modified easily by the replacing/adding new files on the SD card. In other words, this device can be adapted for usage in many countries by replacing MP3 files. Here, the main problem is about unidentified distance (usually greater than 5 m). It was found that the ultrasonic sensor HC-SR04 generates the signal about the distance less than 1 m after the unidentified one. Hence, the additional analysis of this ambiguity is implemented in the Arduino sketch.

The assistive device for the measurement of the distance to the obstacle was successfully tested for spatial cognition by about 15 people with good vision and B&VI. By blindfolding the user's eyes, the deficiency of the visual system was simulated. Then, the user was disoriented by several rotations. The testee only uses the device to know at which distance he / she is from the obstacles. Different indoor and outdoor environments were applied. This method is similar to the presented in (Cardin, Thalmann, & Vexo, 2007).

Two stages of the project's development are the specification of a device and the development of the prototype with intermediate testing at the Instituto para Ciegos y Débiles Visuales "Ezequiel Hernández Romo" and Lions Clubs International (Mexico, Distrito B3). Nowadays, Polytechnic University of San Luis Potosi is negotiating with several organizations to produce this device. Other applications were found during the testing as follows:

1. Museums: to tell the info about an exhibit when the visitors are near an interactive area. In this case, the loudspeaker is used instead of headphone.
2. The wall installation: the device says the distance to the person. In this case, the passive infrared sensor (Fernandez-Luque, Zapata, & Ruiz, 2013) is used to identify the biological objects.

Remote Localization and Assistance of Visually Impaired Employees using Bytereal iBeacon Fingerprinting

This section summarizes the project based on the soft-/hardware complex that uses wearable Raspberry Pi 3 B microcomputer and the Bytereal iBeacon fingerprinting (Peng et al, 2018) to uniquely identify the B&VI location at the three-workroom industrial facilities of 40 m². (Qasim, Abdulrahman, & Zubov, 2019; Zubov, Siniak, & Grenčíková, 2018).

Industry 4.0 is commonly called as a fourth industrial revolution today (Hopali & Vayvay, 2018; Hozdić, 2015; Eurostat, 2020). Cyber-physical systems, IoT, cloud and cognitive computing are the main constituents of this concept (Hozdić, 2015; Strobel et al, 2004). These technologies significantly affect almost every aspect of smart enterprises including the employment of people with disabilities and eye problems (blind and visually impaired, B&VI) in particular (Strobel et al, 2004; Gilchrist, 2016; French, 2017). Nowadays, the B&VI employment rate is about 30% worldwide (French, 2017). The solution to this problem brings many benefits to both sides – enterprises have qualified employees and show social responsibility, B&VI have money, companionship, and a positive and valued self-identity (French, 2017).

The B&VI employees design mental maps of the premises based on the infrastructure elements such as tables and walls. This activity takes a few hours or days – the duration depends on the dimensions and

B&VI experience. Main difficulties of B&VI are about the detection of unexpected obstacles such as trolleys and boxes. The main drawback of blind companions is about remote localization of the B&VI. In this work, a case study on the B&VI spatial cognition within three-workroom industrial facilities is discussed using the assistive device with the following features:

- detection of unexpected obstacles in front of the B&VI on the distances of up to 1 m with ultrasonic range sensor HC-SR04 (MODMYPI, 2020) installed on the Raspberry Pi 3 B board (Shovic, 2016);
- Raspberry Pi 3 B based indoor localization (Zafari et al, 2020; Zubov, 2018) of the B&VI using the RSSI from the Bytereal iBeacon Bluetooth low energy (BLE) 4.0 near field orientation modules with a cover range of 50 m (Shovic, 2016; Zafari et al, 2020; Zubov, 2018; Paek, Ko, & Shin; 2016; Gast, 2015), MQTT IoT protocol (Raspberry Pi Tutorials, 2020), and HTML dynamic website.

Then, this information is said to the B&VI and/or transmitted to the blind companion. This specific configuration satisfies the basic requirements for assistive devices at the industrial facilities. This functionality was designed via interviewing of B&VI at the Instituto para Ciegos y Débiles Visuales "Ezequiel Hernández Romo" (San Luis Potosi, Mexico) and the analysis of literature, e.g. (Zafari et al, 2020; Nicolau, Guerreiro, & Jorge, 2009; Hudec & Smutny, 2017; Duarte et al, 2008; Al-Khalifa, 2008; Joseph, 2014), and Internet, e.g. (RNIB, 2020; ORCAM, 2020), resources.

Most of the literature deals with IT-based technologies for the B&VI spatial cognition within the smart factories. The results were mainly published in the journals and conference proceedings related to the IoT and assistive devices for B&VI since these technologies are based on intelligent algorithms and IoT soft-/hardware.

Nowadays, location systems use two principal techniques for positioning – radio frequency (RF) / acoustic / optical triangulation/trilateration (Röbesaat et al, 2017; Wang et al, 2013) and fingerprinting (Flores, Griffin, & Jadav, 2017; Faragher & Harle, 2015). Triangulation (Wang et al, 2013) and trilateration (Röbesaat et al, 2017) determine absolute or relative locations by the measurement of distances using the geometry of triangles and circles / spheres, respectively. The ranges are identified via RF (e.g. WiFi, Bluetooth, RFID) technologies, acoustic (e.g. HC-SR04) and/or optical (e.g. GP2Y0A21) sensors. The fingerprinting uses machine learning to match the B&VI location based on a predefined set of characteristics of sensor signals at each of the locations.

In (Zafari et al, 2020), different indoor localization techniques (Angle of Arrival (AoA), Time of Flight (ToF), Return Time of Flight (RTOF), RSSI, Channel State Information (CSI), etc.) and technologies (WiFi, Ultra Wideband (UWB), Visible Light, etc.) are described in detail. Three approaches of the object localization are presented: the user device utilizes the reference or anchor nodes to obtain its relative location; a set of the reference or anchor nodes passively obtains the position of the user connected to the reference node; proximity detection of the distance between a user and a point of interest. Existing localization systems are evaluated from the perspective of energy efficiency, availability, cost, reception range, latency, scalability, and tracking accuracy. It is pointed out that the final solution depends on the various factors such as smart factory infrastructure, existing soft-/hardware, localization techniques.

In (Nicolau, et al, 2009), the behavior of B&VI is discussed when they explore unknown places. It helps to build a more appropriate interface and dialogue system. A study on how the B&VI verbalize a route with a set of elements and rules is presented. A concept of the blind companion is shown but the soft-/hardware is not discussed.

In (Hudec & Smutny, 2017), an ambient intelligent system RUDO for B&VI is presented. It consists of several modules: recognition of approaching people, alerting to other household members' movement in the apartment, work on a computer including writing in Braille on a regular keyboard, supervision of sighted children, cooperation of a sighted and B&VI, control of heating and zonal regulation by the B&VI. Here, the home solution is discussed only.

In (Duarte et al, 2008), the information and assisted navigation system for the B&VI performs voice-controlled navigation inside the building. The location system was developed based on Bluetooth technology. The system locates the user and sends the instructions to reach the desired destination if sensors are installed in the building. Here, the obstacle detection relies on the user abilities only.

In (Paek et al, 2016), a measurement study of the Estimote, GELO, and Wizturn Pebble iBeacons and iOS / Android mobile device platforms shows that iBeacon RSSI values vary significantly across iBeacon vendors, mobile device platforms, deployment height of the device, indoor/outdoor environmental factors, and obstacles. Also; it was pointed out that iBeacons can be used indoor and outdoor both, but GPS is unusable inside buildings. Hence, the design of the location estimation model is a complicated problem.

In (Al-Khalifa, 2008; Joseph, 2014), QR code based indoor navigation systems are presented. This approach is feasible if the QR code is in front of the camera. In (Intorobotics. 2020), a camera reads AprilTags and then calculates the location and orientation of the device. However, it is a common situation when QR codes and AprilTags cannot be captured by the camera, and hence the B&VI location is unidentifiable.

In (Flores et al, 2017; Faragher & Harle, 2015), a promising approach of the location fingerprinting with iBeacons is presented. In (Flores et al, 2017), the training data is collected from a Bluetooth-enabled iOS client device, and then is pushed to and stored in the computational cloud for future retrieval and use. In (Faragher & Harle, 2015), a detailed study of the user fingerprinting localization with 19 BLE beacons distributed around 600 m2 testbed is presented. The results show advantages of BLE beacons for positioning compared with WiFi fingerprinting. Machine learning algorithms are not applied in (Flores et al, 2017; Faragher & Harle, 2015).

Nowadays, Industry 4.0 applies several IoT protocols such as MQTT, CoAP, XMPP, DDS, and AMQP (Dizdarevic et al, 2020; Scalagent, 2020). MQTT IoT software can be executed on thin clients like Arduino Uno since it takes approximately 10 KB of random access memory. It was shown that MQTT brokers work reliably with 100,000 publishers and 100 subscribers (Dizdarevic et al, 2020) that satisfies the requirements to the smart enterprise networks.

In (Zubov, Siniak, & Grenčíková, 2018), the Raspberry Pi 3 B microcomputer and ultrasonic range sensor HC-SR04 are the main hardware components in a project on the spatial cognition within industrial facilities. Alao, a small 5 MP Raspberry Pi camera was installed in the enclosure for the future image processing projects. The Arduino Mega board with an Ethernet shield implements the simple web-server to start the HTML dynamic website based on the data acquired from the MQTT broker. The interaction between MQTT clients and broker is as follows: the B&VI with wearable Raspberry Pi microcomputers are the MQTT publishers (Python library paho-mqtt is applied), Arduino Mega board with Ethernet shield (Arduino library PubSubClient is included) is the MQTT subscriber, the blind companion computer (Mosquitto software is installed) with Windows 10 operating system is the MQTT broker. In this project, the Arduino hardware is used since additional sensors can be utilized additionally. This possibility is crucial for the future scaling of the system. The price of one kit for ten B&VI is about USD 700.

Analysis of the above-stated work shows that Industry 4.0 and smart city technologies simplify the B&VI employment and make their work conditions more B&VI friendly via IoT. For the time being, there is no universal soft-/hardware solution for smart factories. Hence, the development of case-oriented projects with four-hospitality criterion is the most effective approach to support the B&VI working activities.

In the experiments, the Bytereal iBeacon (see Fig. 10, A) and the Raspberry Pi 3 B microcomputer (Zubov, 2018) are used. The testbed is a small industrial facility of approximately 40 m² (see Fig. 10, B;

Figure 10. Three Bytereal iBeacons (A) and the map of experimental testbed (B)

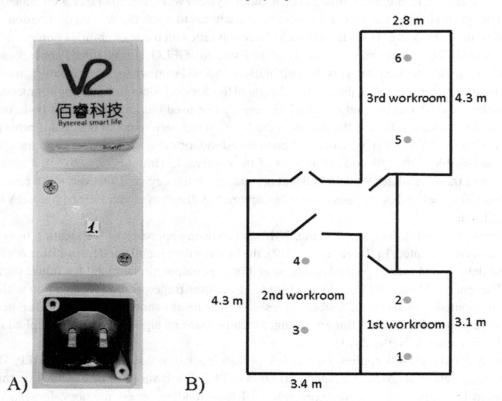

six blue dots represent the iBeacon fingerprinting points) in Vinnitsa city that is common to Ukraine. The area has an existing WiFi network with one access point at the testbed.

There is a major factor, which affects the accuracy of distance measurements: the orientation of the iBeacon antenna. We did two experiments to find the relationship between the RSSI values observed on the assistive device and the following:

- the angle of iBeacon mount orientation – vertical and horizontal;
- the iBeacon installation in workrooms – in a center, in the corners with nearest and farthest distances.

Table 1. RSSIs measured by the assistive device around the iBeacon

Angle, i.e. positions of the clock's hour hand	1	2	3	4	5	6	7	8	9	10	11	12
iBeacon and Raspberry Pi 3 B are both placed horizontally												
RSSI, dBm	-68	-67	-62	-68	-63	-65	-64	-62	-64	-70	-63	-70
iBeacon and Raspberry Pi 3 B are placed horizontally and vertically, respectively												
RSSI, dBm	-64	-66	-65	-70	-67	-70	-69	-70	-66	-67	-66	-70
iBeacon and Raspberry Pi 3 B are placed vertically and horizontally, respectively												
RSSI, dBm	-66	-70	-69	-64	-72	-76	-61	-71	-68	-68	-73	-67

In the first experiment, the RSSIs were measured by the assistive device around the iBeacon on the distances of 1 m in twelve points corresponding to the twelve positions of the clock's hour hand. The results are presented in Table 1.

Analysis of the results presented in Table 1 shows the following:

Figure 11. Installation of the Bytereal iBeacons in workrooms: in the center (A), in the corners with nearest (B) and farthest (C) distances

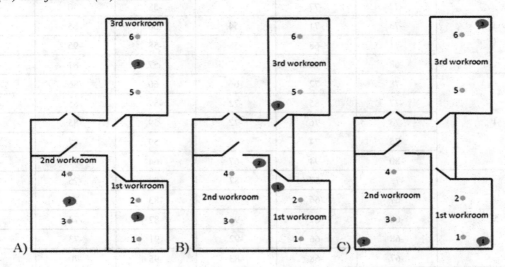

- the mean values are -65.5, -67.5, and -68.75 dBm, respectively;
- the corrected sample standard deviations are 2.97, 2.2, and 3.44 dBm, respectively.

We assume that the mean values and the corrected sample standard deviations are differentiated insignificantly. Hence, we conclude that the positions of iBeacon and Raspberry Pi 3 B boards do not affect the RSSI on the distances of 1 m in twelve points corresponding to the twelve positions of the clock's hour hand.

In the second experiment, the iBeacons are installed in a center (on the ceiling), in the corners (one meter above the floor) with nearest and farthest distances of the workrooms (see Fig. 11; three red dots

Table 2. RSSIs of Bytereal iBeacons, installation in the center

No. of the point	1st workroom iBeacon RSSI, dBm		2nd workroom iBeacon RSSI, dBm		3rd workroom iBeacon RSSI, dBm	
1	-57	-51	-80	-79	-87	-93
	-47	-48	-73	-81	-90	-95
	-50	-61	-82	-76	-88	-86
	-52	-57	-83	-80	-85	-97
	-46	-52	-86	-76	-87	-89
2	-53	-54	-84	-71	-88	-93
	-73	-53	-72	-73	-84	-90
	-71	-71	-76	-75	-82	-86
	-69	-71	-72	-74	-90	-87
	-52	-84	-70	-73	-93	-90
3	-78	-88	-71	-54	-90	-88
	-72	-77	-54	-58	-90	-86
	-73	-71	-54	-56	-85	-88
	-71	-68	-58	-58	-95	-83
	-68	-78	-67	-57	-81	-83
4	-78	-72	-66	-60	-86	-85
	-77	-85	-72	-57	-85	-92
	-73	-76	-72	-59	-85	-94
	-75	-74	-75	-59	-87	-98
	-80	-94	-67	-64	-83	-93
5	-73	-67	-87	-87	-75	-72
	-67	-66	-96	-83	-72	-72
	-68	-67	-96	-82	-74	-73
	-68	-66	-92	-91	-73	-74
	-67	-68	-83	-95	-70	-72
6	-81	-86	-80	-93	-82	-71
	-83	-88	-92	-95	-72	-72
	-83	-89	-91	-94	-73	-71
	-83	-88	-91	-92	-75	-71
	-83	-95	-97	-92	-71	-67

represent the iBeacon points). The Raspberry Pi 3 B board measures the RSSIs of Bytereal iBeacons at six points (blue dots in Fig. 10, B and Fig. 11) using the Python library Bluepy. The 1st workroom iBeacon has a name BR522827 and Bluetooth address 20:18:ff:00:33:5d, 2nd – BR523803 and 20:18:ff:00:33:16, 3rd – BR523809 and 20:18:ff:00:33:19. The results are presented in Tables 2-4.

Analysis of the iBeacon fingerprinting RSSIs presented in Table 2 shows that the B&VI location can be uniquely identified with two following rules:

Table 3. RSSIs of Bytereal iBeacons, installation in the corners with nearest distances

No. of the point	1st workroom iBeacon RSSI, dBm		2nd workroom iBeacon RSSI, dBm		3rd workroom iBeacon RSSI, dBm	
	-87	-66	-83	-86	-81	-83
	-77	-72	-91	-79	-95	-80
1	-73	-75	-76	-79	-81	-86
	-72	-66	-76	-73	-81	-87
	-64	-70	-88	-79	-83	-84
	-77	-69	-80	-75	-87	-77
	-74	-77	-78	-88	-91	-76
2	-80	-72	-81	-77	-82	-77
	-72	-75	-82	-82	-83	-81
	-81	-66	-80	-80	-81	-88
	-79	-72	-79	-76	-81	-81
	-72	-75	-81	-70	-77	-81
3	-70	-69	-79	-76	-77	-78
	-70	-70	-76	-71	-82	-76
	-70	-71	-76	-70	-82	-73
	-72	-67	-70	-66	-76	-77
	-70	-67	-61	-72	-80	-78
4	-69	-67	-62	-70	-77	-79
	-70	-68	-62	-63	-79	-81
	-71	-62	-64	-60	-77	-74
	-85	-82	-85	-83	-90	-76
	-85	-83	-91	-85	-83	-75
5	-77	-80	-84	-86	-85	-76
	-83	-81	-83	-86	-74	-76
	-84	-80	-84	-84	-72	-73
	-97	-89	-90	-97	-88	-83
	-91	-91	-97	-99	-81	-82
6	-84	-87	-95	-95	-92	-83
	-92	-96	-100	-89	-82	-78
	-95	-97	-97	-81	-81	-84

Table 4. RSSIs of Bytereal iBeacons, installation in the corners with farthest distances

No. of the point	1st workroom iBeacon RSSI, dBm		2nd workroom iBeacon RSSI, dBm		3rd workroom iBeacon RSSI, dBm	
1	-72	-72	-83	-78	-88	-85
	-73	-72	-85	-80	-81	-91
	-68	-74	-76	-78	-92	-85
	-68	-70	-78	-77	-83	-87
	-70	-75	-82	-78	-82	-87
2	-74	-75	-72	-75	-94	-85
	-76	-82	-77	-78	-88	-87
	-77	-85	-81	-78	-90	-87
	-77	-78	-77	-80	-85	-97
	-76	-74	-84	-79	-86	-85
3	-76	-81	-72	-67	-95	-94
	-70	-83	-70	-72	-98	-96
	-80	-73	-72	-72	-96	-95
	-74	-77	-71	-79	-99	-96
	-78	-76	-84	-70	-91	-97
4	-80	-77	-74	-77	-99	-99
	-84	-72	-79	-72	-99	-98
	-72	-80	-71	-74	-96	-94
	-77	-77	-77	-77	-92	-91
	-80	-83	-78	-87	-90	-99
5	-83	-91	-89	-97	-85	-80
	-84	-81	-95	-99	-80	-78
	-85	-84	-95	-93	-94	-83
	-80	-91	-92	-92	-80	-90
	-80	-85	-96	-96	-87	-85
6	-95	-88	-98	-95	-71	-82
	-89	-93	-99	-97	-77	-63
	-97	-89	-99	-95	-72	-65
	-99	-93	-99	-98	-83	-72
	-94	-92	-99	-95	-70	-73

- if RSSI of first or second iBeacon is greater than -65 dBm then the B&VI is in the workroom where this iBeacon is installed;
- if RSSI of the third iBeacon is greater than -75 dBm then the B&VI is in the third workroom.

Analysis of the iBeacon fingerprinting RSSIs presented in Tables 2 and 3 shows that it is impossible to apply two above-stated rules. Moreover, it is much more complicated to uniquely identify dependencies between the iBeacon RSSIs and the B&VI location. Hence, the recommendation is to install the iBeacons in the center of workrooms.

CONCLUSION

In this chapter, four assistive projects for B&VI people are discussed. In the first project, the mesh network of eHealth intelligent agents for the B&VI is presented as the smart city inclusive component. The main constituents are as follows:

- Hardware: microcomputer Raspberry Pi 3 B with the ultrasonic range sensor HC-SR04, camera, headphone, mobile power bank.
- MQTT IoT protocol for the connection of eHealth agents and other components of the mesh network. The Python programs, addresses of MQTT brokers and Bluetooth devices, MQTT passwords / topics, recognition rules, MP3 files, and other relevant information are downloaded from the file servers to the eHealth agents by request.
- Ultrasonic measurement of the distance to the nearest obstacle via the range sensor HC-SR04.
- Computer vision detection and recognition of human faces in front of the B&VI using the Raspberry Pi camera, OpenCV library, and face recognition module of Adam Geitgey.
- Indication of objects around the B&VI through the Bluetooth devices of classes 1-3 and iBeacons.

All information is conveyed to the B&VI aurally via the headphone. The presented mesh network of eHealth intelligent agents was successfully tested with a score of 95.5% at the city Vinnitsa, Ukraine.

In the second project, an assistive device supports the visually impaired person to play golf. Every golf flagstick has the sound marking device with active buzzer and Wi-Fi remote control by the person with a good vision. B&VI person hears the sound from the appropriate golf stick and then kicks the ball towards it. The NodeMcu Lua ESP8266 ESP-12 Wi-Fi boards in devices are controlled by the cross-platform HTML websites. Mini portable 3G/4G Wi-Fi 150Mbps RJ45 USB router links all devices in the network. The manual control is provided by an additional button to the NodeMcu Lua Wi-Fi board if the network is not accessible.

In the third project, the assistive wearable supports the orientation of B&VI by measuring the distance to obstacle based on the ultrasonic sensor HC-SR04, Arduino Uno, MP3 player with SD card, headphone, and two buttons to control the volume. The distance is pronounced to the B&VI using headphone.

In the fourth project, the remote localization and assistance of visually impaired employees are based on the Bytereal iBeacon fingerprinting. The experimental testbed is a small industrial facility of 40 m^2 with three workrooms with one Bytereal iBeacon in each. Analysis of the iBeacon RSSI fingerprinting showed that the B&VI location is uniquely identified with two following rules:

- if RSSI of first or second iBeacon is greater than -65 dBm then the B&VI is in the workroom where this iBeacon is installed;
- if RSSI of the third iBeacon is greater than -75 dBm then the B&VI is in the third workroom.

Based on two above-stated rules, the blind companion can identify the location of the visually impaired employee and assist him/her.

REFERENCES

Al-Hader, M., & Rodzi, A. (2009). The Smart City Infrastructure Development & Monitoring. Theoretical and Empirical Researches in Urban Management. Research Centre in Public Administration and Public Services.

Al-Khalifa, H. S. (2008). Utilizing QR Code and Mobile Phones for Blinds and Visually Impaired People. In Computers Helping People with Special Needs. ICCHP 2008. Lecture Notes in Computer Science (vol. 5105, pp. 1065-1069). Berlin: Springer.

Bai, J., Lian, S., Liu, Z., Wang, K., & Liu, D. (2017). Smart Guiding Glasses for Visually Impaired People in Indoor Environment. *IEEE Transactions on Consumer Electronics*, *63*(3), 258–266.

Bennett, J. (2018). *Xamarin in Action: Creating native cross-platform mobile apps*. Manning Publications Co.

Bergenti, F., & Poggi, A. (2010). Multi-Agent Systems for the Application and Employing of E-Health Services. In M. M. Cruz-Cunha, A. J. Tavates, & R. Simoes (Eds.), *Handbook of Research on Developments in E-Health and Telemedicine: Technological and Social Perspectives* (pp. 247–264). IGI Global Publishing.

Bruce, I., McKennell, A., & Walker, E. (1991). *Blind and Partially Sighted Adults in Britain: The RNIB Survey* (Vol. 1). Her Majesty's Stationery Office.

Campos, G. (2020, January 3). *Microsoft's Audio Wayfinding App for the Visually Impaired*. Retrieved from https://www.avinteractive.com/news/ai/microsoft-launches-audio-wayfinding-app-visually-impaired-18-09-2018/

Cardin, S., Thalmann, D., & Vexo, F. (2007). A Wearable System for Mobility Improvement of Visually Impaired People. *The Visual Computer Journal*, *23*(2), 109–118.

Chan, V., Ray, P., & Parameswaran, N. (2008). Mobile e-Health Monitoring: An Agent-Based Approach. *IET Communications*, *2*(2), 223–230.

Charalampos, D. (2012). Building Internet of Things with the Arduino. CreateSpace Independent Publishing Platform, Amazon.com.

Chaudary, B., Paajala, I., Keino, E., & Pulli, P. (2017). Tele-guidance Based Navigation System for the Visually Impaired and Blind Persons. In eHealth 360° (LNICST, vol. 181, pp 9-16). Cham: Springer.

Commission on Science and Technology for Development, Nineteenth session: Smart cities and infrastructure, Report of the Secretary-General. (2016). Geneva: United Nations.

de Oliveira Neto, J. S., & Kofuji, S. T. (2016). Inclusive Smart City: An Exploratory Study. In UAHCI 2016 (LNCS, vol. 9738, 456-465). Cham: Springer.

Dead Band Plus Hysteresis Estimation with ValveLink Diagnostics. (2020, January 10). Product Bulletin, Fisher Controls International. Retrieved from http://www.documentation.emersonprocess.com/groups/public/documents/bulletins/d103549x012.pdf

Demaagd, K., Oliver, A., Oostendorp, N., & Scott, K. (2012). *Practical Computer Vision with SimpleCV*. O'Reilly Media.

Dizdarevic, J., Carpio, F., Jukan, A., & Masip-Bruin, X. (2020, January 10). *Survey of Communication Protocols for Internet-of-Things and Related Challenges of Fog and Cloud Computing Integration*. Retrieved from https://arxiv.org/abs/1804.01747

Doukas, C. (2012). Building Internet of Things with the Arduino. Amazon.com, CreateSpace Independent Publishing Platform.

Draishpits, G. (2016). *Peer-to-Peer Communication in Wireless Networks as an Alternative to Internet Access*. Open University of Israel.

Duarte, K., Cec'ilio, J., S'a Silva, J., & Furtado, P. (2008). Information and Assisted Navigation System for Blind People. *8th International Conference on Sensing Technology*, 470-473.

Elmannai, W., & Elleithy, K. (2017). Sensor-Based Assistive Devices for Visually-Impaired People: Current Status, Challenges, and Future Directions. *Sensors (Basel)*, *17*(3), 565.

Embedded Computing: Arduino Tian. (2020, January 3). Retrieved from https://embeddedcomputing. weebly.com/arduino-tian.html

European Commission announces a €3 million Horizon Prize to develop a tactile display for the visually impaired. (2020, January 2). Retrieved from https://ec.europa.eu/digital-single-market/en/news/european-commission-announces-eu3-million-horizon-prize-develop-tactile-display-visually

Eurostat. (2020, January 10). *Sustainable development in the European Union: Monitoring Report on Progress Towards the SDGS in an EU Context*. Retrieved from http://ec.europa.eu/budget/img/budget-4results/SustainableDevelopmentInTheEU.pdf

Faragher, R., & Harle, R. (2015). Location Fingerprinting With Bluetooth Low Energy Beacons. *IEEE Journal on Selected Areas in Communications*, *33*(11), 2418–2428.

Fass, B. (2020, January 3). *A Heart Rate During a Heart Attack*. Retrieved from https://www.livestrong.com/article/344010-the-normal-heart-rate-during-a-panic-attack/

Fernandez-Luque, F., Zapata, J., & Ruiz, R. (2013). PIR-Based Motion Patterns Classification for AmI Systems. *Proc. of Conference on the Interplay Between Natural and Artificial Computation*, 355-364.

Flores, G. H., Griffin, T. D., & Jadav, D. (2017). An iBeacon Training App for Indoor Fingerprinting. *5th IEEE International Conference on Mobile Cloud Computing, Services, and Engineering*, 173-176.

French, S. (2017). *Visual impairment and work: experiences of visually impaired people*. Routledge.

From KY-039 To Heart Rate. (2020, January 3). Retrieved from https://www.hackster.io/Johan_Ha/from-ky-039-to-heart-rate-0abfca

Gajski, D. D., Abdi, S., Gerstlauer, A., & Schirner, G. (2009). Embedded System Design: Modeling, Synthesis and Verification. Springer-Verlag.

Gast, M. S. (2015). *Building Applications with iBeacon: Proximity and Location Services with Bluetooth Low Energy*. O'Reilly Media.

Gilchrist, A. (2016). *Industry 4.0: The Industrial Internet of Things*. Apress.

Golledge, R. G. (1993). Geography and the Disabled: A Survey with Special Reference to Vision Impaired and Blind Populations. *Transactions of the Institute of British Geographers, 18*, 63–85.

Goodwyn, M., Bell, E. C., & Singletary, C. (2009). *Factors that Contribute to the Success of Blind Adults. Research Report of the Professional Development and Research Institute on Blindness*. Louisiana Tech University.

Gori, M., Cappagli, G., Tonelli, A., Baud-Bovy, G., & Finocchietti, S. (2016). Devices for Visually Impaired People: High Technological Devices with Low User Acceptance and no Adaptability for Children. *Neuroscience and Biobehavioral Reviews, 69*, 79–88.

HC-SR04 Ultrasonic Range Sensor on the Raspberry Pi. (2020, January 3). Retrieved from https://www.modmypi.com/blog/hc-sr04-ultrasonic-range-sensor-on-the-raspberry-pi

Holton, B. (2020, January 13). *MyReader and MyEye from OrCam: Text and Item Recognition at the Touch of a Finger. AccessWorld*. Retrieved from https://www.afb.org/afbpress/pubnew.asp?DocID=aw180205

Hopali, E., & Vayvay, Ö. (2018). Industry 4.0 as the Last Industrial Revolution and its Opportunities for Developing Countries. In R. Brunet-Thornton & F. Martinez (Eds.), *Analyzing the Impacts of Industry 4.0 in Modern Business Environments* (pp. 65–80). IGI Global.

Hozdić, E. (2015). Smart Factory for Industry 4.0: A Review. *International Journal of Modern Manufacturing Technologies, 7*(1), 28–35.

Hrisko, J. (2020, January 3). *Using Raspberry Pi, HM-10, and Bluepy To Develop An iBeacon Mesh Network (Part 1)*. Retrieved from https://engineersportal.com/blog/2017/12/31/using-raspberry-pi-hm-10-and-bluepy-to-develop-an-ibeacon-mesh-network-part-1

Hudec, M., & Smutny, Z. (2017). RUDO: A Home Ambient Intelligence System for Blind People. *Sensors (Basel), 17*(8), 1926.

Ilas, M.-E., & Ilas, C. (2018). A New Method of Histogram Computation for Efficient Implementation of the HOG Algorithm. *Computers, 7*(1), 18.

Intorobotics. (2020, January 10). *5 Cheap Methods For Indoor Robot Localization: BLE Beacon, AprilTags, WiFi SubPos, NFC and RFID*. Retrieved from https://www.intorobotics.com/5-cheap-methods-for-indoor-robot-localization-ble-beacon-apriltags-wifi-subpos-nfc-and-rfid/

Jacobson, R. D., & Kitchin, R. M. (1997). GIS and People with Visual Impairments or Blindness: Exploring the Potential for Education, Orientation, and Navigation. *Transactions in GIS, 2*(4), 315–332.

Joseph, J. (2014). QR Code Based Indoor Navigation with Voice Response. *International Journal of Scientific Research, 3*(11), 923–926.

Kildall, S. (2020, January 3). *Raspberry Pi: Launch Python Script on Startup*. https://www.instructables.com/id/Raspberry-Pi-Launch-Python-script-on-startup/

Lin, Y. W., & Lin, C. Y. (2018). An Interactive Real-Time Locating System Based on Bluetooth Low-Energy Beacon Network. *Sensors (Basel)*, *18*(5), 1637.

Mallick, S. (2020, January 3). *Histogram of Oriented Gradients*. Retrieved from https://www.learnopencv.com/histogram-of-oriented-gradients/

Marco, V.R., Young, D.M., & Turner, D.W. (1987). The Euclidean Distance Classifier: An Alternative to the Linear Discriminant Function. *Communications in Statistics – Computation and Simulation, 16*, 485-505.

MODMYPI. (2020, January 10). *HC-SR04 Ultrasonic Range Sensor on the Raspberry Pi*. Retrieved from https://www.modmypi.com/blog/hc-sr04-ultrasonic-range-sensor-on-the-raspberry-pi

Muhendra, R., Rinaldi, A., Budimana, M., & Khairurrijal, K. (2017). Development of WiFi Mesh Infrastructure for Internet of Things Applications. *Procedia Engineering, 170*, 332–337.

Navigation Complex G2S. (2020, January 3). Retrieved from http://cputos.org.ua/technologies/navi-hatsijnyj-kompleks-g2s-go-to-the-sound-idy-na-zvuk/

Nguyen, C. (2014). *Haptic Obstacle Detector for the Blind*. KTH Royal Institute of Technology.

Nicolau, H., Guerreiro, T., & Jorge, J. (2009). Designing Guides for Blind People. In *27th International Conference Extended Abstracts on Human Factors in Computing Systems* (pp. 3601-3606). ACM.

Norris, D. (2015). *The Internet of Things: Do-It-Yourself at Home Projects for Arduino, Raspberry Pi, and BeagleBone Black*. McGraw-Hill Education.

ORCAM. (2020, January 10). *Employment for the Blind and Visually Impaired*. Retrieved from https://www.orcam.com/en/blog/employment-for-the-blind-and-visually-impaired/

Paek, J., Ko, J., & Shin, H. (2016). A Measurement Study of BLE iBeacon and Geometric Adjustment Scheme for Indoor Location-Based Mobile Applications. *Mobile Information Systems*.

Patnaik, P., & Dinkar, R. (2017). A Comparative Study of Arduino, Raspberry Pi and ESP8266 as IoT Development Board. *International Journal of Advanced Research in Computer Science*, 8(5), 2350–2352.

Peng, Y., Niu, X., Tang, J., Mao, D., & Qian, C. (2018). Fast Signals of Opportunity Fingerprint Database Maintenance with Autonomous Unmanned Ground Vehicle for Indoor Positioning. *Sensors (Basel)*, *18*(10), 3419.

Poggi, M., & Mattoccia, S. (2016). A Wearable Mobility Aid for the Visually Impaired based on Embedded 3D Vision and Deep Learning. In *2016 IEEE Symposium on Computers and Communication Proceedings* (pp. 208-213). University of Messina.

Qasim, M. A., Abdulrahman, S. S., & Zubov, D. (2019). Remote Localization and Assistance of Visually Impaired Employees: A Case Study on Bytereal iBeacon Fingerprinting. *Proc. Conf. Computer Intelligent Systems and Networks*, 160-172.

Rackley, S. (2007). *Wireless Networking Technology: From Principles to Successful Implementation*. Newnes.

Ramadhan, A. J. (2018). Wearable Smart System for Visually Impaired People. *Sensors (Basel)*, *18*(3), 843.

Raspberry Pi Bluetooth In/Out Board Or "Who's Home". (2020, January 3). Retrieved from https://www.instructables.com/id/Raspberry-Pi-Bluetooth-InOut-Board-or-Whos-Hom/

Raspberry Pi Tutorials. (2020, January 10). *Wireless communication between Raspberry Pi's via MQTT broker/client*. Retrieved from https://tutorials-raspberrypi.com/raspberry-pi-mqtt-broker-client-wireless-communication/

RNIB. (2020, January 10). *Smart Glasses*. Retrieved from https://www.rnib.org.uk/smart-glasses

Röbesaat, J., Zhang, P., Abdelaal, M., & Theel, O. (2017). An Improved BLE Indoor Localization with Kalman-Based Fusion: An Experimental Study. *Sensors (Basel)*, *17*(5), 951.

Rosebrock, A. (2020a, January 2). *Raspberry Pi Face Recognition*. Retrieved from https://www.pyimagesearch.com/2018/06/25/raspberry-pi-face-recognition/

Rosebrock, A. (2020b, January 3). *Raspbian Stretch: Install OpenCV 3 + Python on your Raspberry Pi*. Retrieved from https://www.pyimagesearch.com/2017/09/04/raspbian-stretch-install-opencv-3-python-on-your-raspberry-pi/

Rosebrock, A. (2020c, January 11). *OpenCV Face Recognition*. Retrieved from https://www.pyimagesearch.com/2018/09/24/opencv-face-recognition/

Salton, K. (2020, January 3). *Face Recognition: Understanding LBPH Algorithm*. Retrieved from https://towardsdatascience.com/face-recognition-how-lbph-works-90ec258c3d6b

Scalagent. (2020, January 10). *Benchmark of MQTT servers: ActiveMQ 5.10.0, Apollo 1.7, JoramMQ 1.1.3 (based on Joram 5.9.1), Mosquitto 1.3.5, RabbitMQ 3.4.2*. Retrieved from http://www.scalagent.com/IMG/pdf/Benchmark_MQTT_servers-v1-1.pdf

Shovic, J.C. (2016). *Raspberry Pi IoT Projects: Prototyping Experiments for Makers*. Apress.

Slama, D., Puhlmann, F., Morrish, J., & Bhatnagar, R. M. (2016). *Enterprise IoT: Strategies and Best Practices for Connected Products and Services*. O'Reilly Media.

Statista: Forecast on Connected Devices per Person Worldwide 2003-2020. (2020, January 3). https://www.statista.com/statistics/678739/forecast-on-connected-devices-per-person/

Strobel, W., Fossa, J., Panchura, C., Beaver, K., & Westbrook, J. (2004). *The Industry Profile on Visual Impairment*. Rehabilitation Engineering Research Center on Technology Transfer.

Suzuki, L. R. (2017). Smart Cities IoT: Enablers and Technology Road Map. In S. T. Rassia & P. M. Pardalos (Eds.), *Smart City Networks: Through the Internet of Things, Springer Optimization and Its Applications* (Vol. 125, pp. 167–190). Springer.

Szeliski, R. (2011). *Computer Vision: Algorithms and Applications* (1st ed.). Springer-Verlag.

Takuya, K., Akinori, H., & Takio, K. (2008). Selection of Histogram of Oriented Gradients Features for Pedestrian Detection. In ICONIP 2007 (LNCS, vol. 4985, pp. 598-607). Springer.

Trent, M., Abdelgawad, A., & Yelamarthi, K. (2017). A Smart Wearable Navigation System for Visually Impaired. In GOODTECHS 2016 (LNICST, vol. 195, pp. 333-341). Cham: Springer.

User Manual for ESP-12E DevKit based on ESP8266. (2020, January 10). Retrieved from https://smart-arduino.gitbooks.io/user-manual-for-esp-12e-devkit/content/index.html

Viola, P., & Jones, M. J. (2004). Robust Real-Time Face Detection. *International Journal of Computer Vision, 57*(2), 137–154.

Wang, Y., Yang, X., Zhao, Y., Liu, Y., & Cuthbert, L. (2013). Bluetooth positioning using RSSI and triangulation methods. In *IEEE 10th Consumer Communications and Networking Conference*. Las Vegas, NV: IEEE.

Warren, J.-D., Adams, J., & Molle, H. (2011). *Arduino Robotics*. Apress Media LLC.

Wireless Communication between Raspberry Pi's via MQTT Broker/Client. (2020, January 3). Retrieved from https://tutorials-raspberrypi.com/raspberry-pi-mqtt-broker-client-wireless-communication/

WoodfordC. (2020, January 2). *Bluetooth*. Retrieved from https://www.explainthatstuff.com/howbluetoothworks.html

World Health Organization: Blindness and Visual Impairment. (2020, January 2). Retrieved from, http://www.who.int/news-room/fact-sheets/detail/blindness-and-visual-impairment

Yaqoob, I., Hashem, I., Mehmood, Y., Gani, A., Mokhtar, S., & Guizani, S. (2017). Enabling Communication Technologies for Smart Cities. *IEEE Communications Magazine, 55*(1), 112–120.

Zafari, F., Gkelias, A., & Leung, K. K. (2020, January 10). *A Survey of Indoor Localization Systems and Technologies*. Retrieved from https://arxiv.org/abs/1709.01015

Zarzycki, A. (2016). Adaptive Designs with Distributed Intelligent Systems – Building Design Applications. In *34th eCAADe Conference Proceedings* (*vol. 1*, pp. 681-690). University of Oulu.

Zubov, D. (2017). A Case Study on the Spatial Cognition of Surrounding Objects by the B&VI People Using Sound Patterns and Ultrasonic Sensing. In P. Kocovic, R. Behringer, M. Ramachandran, & R. Mihajlovic (Eds.), *Emerging Trends and Applications of the Internet of Things* (pp. 105–116). IGI Global.

Zubov, D. (2018). A Smart City Assistive Infrastructure for the Blind and Visually Impaired People: A Thin Client Concept. *BRAIN – Broad Research in Artificial Intelligence and Neurosciences J., 9*(4), 25-37.

Zubov, D., Kose, U., Ramadhan, A. J., & Kupin, A. (2018). Mesh Network of eHealth Intelligent Agents in Smart City: A Case Study on Assistive Devices for B&VI. *Proc. Workshop "1st International Workshop on Informatics & Data-Driven Medicine"*, 65-81.

Zubov, D., Siniak, N., & Grenčíková, A. (2018). Impact of Industry 4.0 Technologies on the Employment of the People with Eye Problems: A Case Study on the Spatial Cognition within Industrial Facilities. *Proc. Conf. "The Impact of Industry 4.0 on Job Creation"*, 254-263.

Chapter 14

Prototype Implementation of Innovative Braille Translator for the Visually Impaired With Hearing Deficiency

Soumen Santra
Techno International NewTown, India

Arpan Deyasi
ⓘ https://orcid.org/0000-0003-3056-896X
RCC Institute of Information Technology, India

ABSTRACT

Text-to-Braille conversion as well as speech-to-Braille conversion are not available in combined form so far for the visually impaired, and there is tremendous need of a device that can look after this special class of people. The present chapter deals with a novel model that is designed to help both types of impaired people, be it visual problem or related with hearing. The proposal is itself unique and is also supported by experimental results available within the laboratory condition. This device will help people to read from text with their Braille language and will also help to convert the same form to audio signal. Since text and audio are the two main interfaces for any person to communicate with the external world apart from functionalities of sensory organs, the work has relevance. With the help of DANET, the same data, in text or speech form, can be accessed in more than one digital device simultaneously.

1. INTRODUCTION

In 1821 a blind Frenchman Louis Braille invented a writing system to help blind people read and write (Choi et al., 2004; Fritz & Barner, 1999; Fukumoto & Tonomura, 1997), later nomenclature of his name. Now engineers invented many modern techniques in different wings of life, but blind peoples are still facing problems related to traditional lifestyle. They still use traditional Braille set-up for the purpose

DOI: 10.4018/978-1-7998-4186-9.ch014

reading and understanding content of materials or books etc. As per Fig 1, (Wikipedia, n.d.a) Braille consists of a cell of six raised dots arranged in two columns of three dots, which the user can read by feeling using a finger (Fritz & Barner, 1999; Fukumoto & Tonomura, 1997), (Ng et al., 1999). The Braille system is used worldwide by blind people and has also been translated in other languages. Braille is a series of raised dots that can be read with the fingers by people who are blind or whose eyesight is not enough for reading printed material. General people who are not visually impaired ordinarily read Braille with their eyes (Choi et al., 2004), (Fukumoto & Tonomura, 1997), (Ng et al., 1999). In Fig 2, (Wikipedia, n.d.b) we have shown the different alphabets overview structure in Braille. The visually impaired people who can touch and feel objects around them to picture their surroundings their finger tactile receptors get exceptionally well developed. This allows them to be able to feel details sighted people barely notice. Braille is not a language, but it is a code by which other languages may be written and read device (Blenkhorn, 1995; Blenkhorn, 1997; Lahiri et al., 2005). The standard cells have one to six dots. The dots are arranged in two parallel columns of three positions each shows the representation of the English alphabet in Braille. This in turn makes the blind people independent and well educated. Blind people play a vital role in the development of the society and without consideration of the blind gross improvement of the community is not possible. There is a clear need for a device which can overcome these obstacles for the blind (Matsuda et al., 2007; Moore & Murray, 2001).

Figure 1. Basic Braille Structure

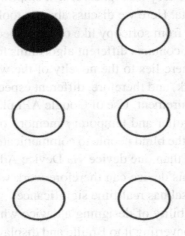

All over the world all the countries have adapted the system 'Braille' as a universal approach to get the information for the visually impaired. A novel prototype is designed for both 'Text to Braille conversion' as well as 'audio signal to Braille conversion' for visually impaired people. The novelty of the design lies in the fact that it will also help to those blind persons who have hearing deficiency. These types of composite devices are not proposed so far as per the best of knowledge of authors, however, it should be acknowledged that individual devices are proposed a few though not practically realized in the commercial stage. All over the world all the countries have adapted the system 'Braille' as a universal approach to get the information for the visually impaired. Henceforth, prolong demand has been raised in all area across the world to help them for adapting with the real world situations, and therefore, electronic devices are proposed for the said purpose. The great problem faced by the blind are how to read digital

Figure 2. Different Alphabets and Numeric Special Character Overview in Braille Structure (Wikipedia, n.d.b)

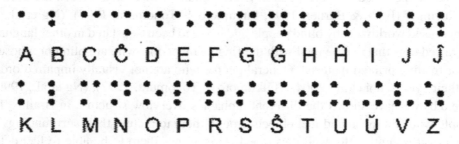

data with their Braille language. With our proposed independent electronic device, visually impaired person will be able to read messages from text and speech. Generally, especially able persons may have the deficiency in either hearing or viewing, and for their purpose, individual or isolated devices are proposed. But if a person has sort of problems, then the volume or degree problem is enlarged and solution becomes more complex, precisely in the realization stages. As in Braille language the manner of six dots arrangement in 3x2 matrix manner and it can only be sense by tactile means. The blind person could not read it without touching to the arrangement of the dots for the text. This technology describes the hardware implementation of a text and speech to Braille translator using Arduino UNO which is an open source microcontroller that occupies very less space. It will empower the blind people to communicate freely through reading of digital data. Here we discuss about a tool based on Internet of Things where visual impairment people can learn from softcopy like ordinary people can learn from mobile devices. The composite device, as proposed, contains different algorithms for '*audio to text*' conversion as well as '*pdf to text*' transcription; and there lies to the novelty of the work that one individual work is not assembled with another type of work, and therefore, different especially able people can work with the device as per his/her individual requirement. Use of Google API plays a vital role in this context where it is connected with the microcontroller and temporary memory of the device is utilized for primary storage of the data. It will empower the blind people to communicate freely. Using this tool blind people can access a single content in more than one device via Device Adhoc Network (DANET) by Internet of Things and wireless network. This device can therefore work wonder when security purpose is associated, and henceforth, the proposal has real-time significance.

This project introduces the feasibility of designing a device which would allow a blind user to access any digital text document by converting it to Braille and displaying it in a manner suitable for them to read. We have used a servo motor and the Braille cell contains only six dots, only six of the Input/output pins of the development board are used (Blenkhorn, 1997), (Blenkhorn, 1995), (Al-Salman & Al-Khalifa, 2003; Slaby, 1990). There are various applications based on Braille already developed but we introduce here IoT applications into Braille.

2. BRIEF DISCUSSION ON IOT

IoT (Internet of Things) is a technology where we can import the essence of internet in the daily activities of human's life. IoT is known as an emerging technological world where anyone or anything can be connected, interacted, communicated with each other anytime and anywhere in a perceptive way through different types of gadgets like smartphones, computers etc. In IOT the physical objects like actuators and sensors which are wirelessly or physically connected to the internet. Enormous amount of data is produced by the network to the analytical devices to scrutinize it (Prakash et al., 2018; Usikalu et al., 2019). IoT is working as a monitor in a smarter way upon the education, home, car etc. appliances. It gives a smart shape to the future by which human can maintain their life very easily and faster way. Using IoT we can easily reach to our data or devices through internet easily without traversing the distance physically. Due to high speed of Cloud service people easily connect with their devices within a span of time and can access their data. Using IoT we can acquire, fetch, manage, collect, process and share the data among more than one device over internet. In Internet of Things multiple physical objects of the real world associated with each other to collect and interchange the data. The application areas of IOT spread out at various segments including healthcare environments.

The objective of IOT is to generate a new technological era to raise the real-world objects or things by enabling communication, storage, application and computing abilities. IOT is recognized as an open network paradigm which made with the ability of smart things or objects of the real world with the capabilities of information sharing, properly organized data, resource and storage handling, automatic organizing facility and reacting in case of environmental changes (Prakash et al., 2018). The environment must be distributed for any type of IOT application areas. Many different origins and devices which are used to gather data from different entities and different vendors are used to collaborate to achieve the desired objective. Devices from other manufacturer are used to sharing data in a way which maintain the interoperability from different protocol and system. Each object should be a part of the network which maintains scalability. IOT has given a wide range of application area in each segment of daily life. IOT application have the advantages which are very much related with internet to share data, proper connectivity etc. Embedded devices are used to collect data and always connected to the global and local networks. IOT provides a huge amount of data which belongs to object, human, space and time always combines with internet to gain the cost-effective communication techniques.

IoT acts as various roles in the platform of programming language. It uses as third party External Interfaces as an intermediate layer in relationship-based system like CRM, ERP etc. through Application Programming Interface, Software Development Kit, gateways etc. It also imports Machine Learning algorithms for analysis purpose. It can help to build up prototyping tool or development module for access management or reporting purpose. Real time data visualization for graphics implementation through sensor data can also be done through Internet of Things. IoT technology provides a lots of application areas which are commonly known as a cyber-physical system including the smart concept in the areas of city, transportation, medical facility, home etc. Each individual thing is identified uniquely with the help emerging embedded system along with incorporating within the existing infrastructure with the help of internet technology (Nellore & Hancke, 2016). Fig. 3 shows the architecture of the Internet of Things. Traffic Control Management is one of the fundamental areas which is rising with the help of IoT. It can process and change its activity management based on changing of incoming data from sensors and devices. As a backend service, IoT manages the devices for its updated version and deploy the software time to time. It ensures the connection with existing library files and normalized data format. IoT gives its services to the user as an agent of data repository which serves the necessary dataset through the connection of internet.

3. LITERATURE SURVEY

As per the digitized world, Braille is one type of coding technique by which we can predict the language tactic or meaningful pronunciation. The latest trend which is based on Automated and Intelligent Education management is controlling the learning system for the blind people through Mobile Devices. In this dynamic and automated network system, the signal is automatically changed depend upon the density of the Devices at the congested network traffic with the help of sensors (Usikalu et al., 2019). In this system the proximity sensors are used to detect the number of Devices present in a congested network

Figure 3. Schematic architecture of Internet of Things

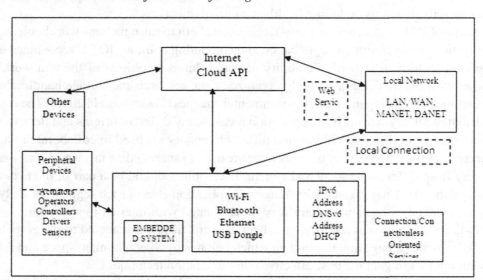

and convey this message to the Arduino microcontroller where the decision is made that extra time duration of the signaling of reading articles is required or not to clear the congestion network (Usikalu et al., 2019).The next trend is reducing the waiting time of the Devices at any tollbooth with the help of mobile technology and sensor technology. The next trend is depending upon the DANET (Device Ad hoc Network) which is a subclass of MANET (Mobile Ad Hoc Network). The DANET scheme combines the automobile infrastructure and wireless technology to develop the congestion less road and to improve the road much safer. DANET consists of Device to infrastructure (D2I) and Device to Device (D2D) wireless communication with the help of different wireless technologies such as IEEE 802.11. In this DANET the nodes are the vehicles who can exchange data within this Devices Ad hoc Network to develop an Intelligent Education System (IES) for blind people. Shivakumar *et. al* (Shivakumar & Thipathi, 2013) described the tool for Braille conversion using Client-Server architecture (Shivakumar & Thipathi, 2013). Blenkhorn *et. al* (Blenkhorn, 1997), (Blenkhorn, 1995) introduced the hardcopy conversion of Braille set through printer and typewriter (Ng et al., 1999) respectively. A group of researchers have shown the way of conversion of Braille display into tactile display (Choi et al., 2004; Fritz & Barner, 1999). People with visual impairment can use Braille using advance technique through wireless approach (Ng et al., 1999). As per Fukumoto *et al* (Fukumoto & Tonomura, 1997), wireless communication also introduces a new way to overcome traffic congestion of DANET when more devices want to access single text content via wireless media.

Several works are published related with Braille translation in the last decade, where a few proposals also claim about novelty from the implementation point of view. Christensen (Christensen, 2006) earlier proposed an automated textual information transformation through email-based RoboBraille service for the visually impaired people. At the same time, Zhang and his co-workers (Zhang et al., 2006) proposed a hardware implementation of Braille translator using FPGA. The work is primarily based on the translating algorithm of Paul Blenkhorn, and superior throughput is claimed. The same group proposed another improved version (Zhang et al., 2007) in the next year, and claimed equally efficient output as earlier obtained by software based algorithm. Hoffmann (Hersh et al., 2008) proposes possibility of speech conversion through its spectral analysis, and therefore claims about bi-directional conversion of both speech-to-text and text-to-speech. Dharme *et. al.* (Dharme & Karmore, 2015) made a detailed survey earlier related with all English language to Braille conversions, and focussed on conversion of printed data. Gadag (Gadag & Udayashankara, 2016) showed that proper character recognition may be possible if 5VM classifier is used along with proper pre-processing techniques. This method may also eliminate noise and improves contrast through image acquisition. FSM has been developed for automatic conversion (Moise et al., 2017) very recently using microcontroller, where experimental results for initial phase are reported. 3D visual representation for children is proposed, followed by 3D printed material through Braille conversion (Arbes et al., 2019), and therefore, a repository can be developed. For multimedia contents and also for conversion of massive texts, Kim and co-workers (Kim et al., 2019) proposed eBook reader application for DAISY and EPUB formats.

4. RELATIONSHIP BETWEEN IOT AND CLOUD COMPUTING

Internet of Thing (IoT) is a collection of interlinked of more than one device or system based on network which fully controlled by Cloud Computing (CC). IoT is a system which mainly works on data and it changes its flow of mechanism based on variation of data. Without intervention of Human interaction with system, it gives output and the structure format of output changes properly when the input data varies time to time. It means the communication of data with system and its process structure is independent in nature. IoT serves as a digital computing device which mainly acts as machine for solving human problems without interaction of Human Being without directly access of devices. The knowledge-based communication between Human and device are taken place through remote places. We know CC working as Software-as-a-Service, Platform-as-a-Service, Infrastructure-as-a-Service, Human-as-a-Service, Data-as-a-Service, Development-as-a-Service, Education-as-a-Service, Health-as-a-Service etc. Apart from this when Cloud architecture connects with IoT it works as Device-as-a-Service. Using IoT through wireless communication we can access the device through any terminal like Smartphone, Notebook, Desktop-PC etc. CC is used as not only data communicator with device, but it also acts as storage of data, recovery of data, testing of data, analysis of data and more important prediction of data. As in CC we know data communicate with high scalable server, large storage structure, so different types of efficient analysis-based algorithm may apply for the generation better data. When data can communicate with a device from a different storage structure, there may be possibilities of loss of data. In CC all terminal devices as client computers relate to Data centre via distributed servers through internet. When

IoT enabled devices communicate with client devices over Cloud network then all the security issues controlled by this network which is known as federated network, whereas non-federated network is one kind of public one where unauthenticated issue is still alive. In CC (Avastystem, n.d.; Elprocus, n.d.) the components are Client, Data-centre, Distributed Servers, Cloud Provisioner, Cloud Storage, Cloud Application, Cloud Services, Cloud Platform, and Cloud Infrastructure. When IoT device connects with CC network, the nit would be act as Device-as-a-service where the Client connects with Cloud storage or Data-centre through this device. Since all components i.e. computing elements of CC relate to each other or interlinked with each other so the remote device i.e. interface of Cloud Client like smart phones is controlling all the components. It is not only connected with target device also it connects with Cloud Storage or Data-centre through Cloud Platform or Distributed Server as guest or Cloud Client for accessing Cloud Application. Through this Smart interface the Client access the target device or IoT enable device and after authentication the target device connect to Cloud platform and all System commands are controlling the one using Cloud APIs. So, due to the development of internet (high bandwidth up to 3 to 300 GHz with 1 Gbps speed) enable to 5G this IoT technology gives a new wing to Cloud architecture which supports to enhance business growth of Cloud platform. In Fig. 4 we have shown how IoT device get connected through Cloud network and access all functionalities of CC technologies for e.g. Transportation, Health-care services, Educational managements, Signal Transformation, Home-Automation etc. Data scalability, Data mobilization, Time-to-reach, Data Security, Cost effective these are the key factors for Cloud based IoT devices (Avastystem, n.d.; Elprocus, n.d.; Instructible Circuits, n.d.).

As per subscription, the Client's details store in Cloud database which given by Cloud Client through Client's device such as smart interface for authentication. After successful verification the Cloud Client can access the target device through the Federated Cloud Network. To reduce the hardware complexity and software computation all necessity support given to IoT devices through Cloud APIs' from Cloud set-up through that mentioned network which is classified as private, public or hybrid as per one or more than one user (Santra et al., 2014; Santra & Mali, 2015).

Figure 4. IoT Device with Cloud Computing Platform

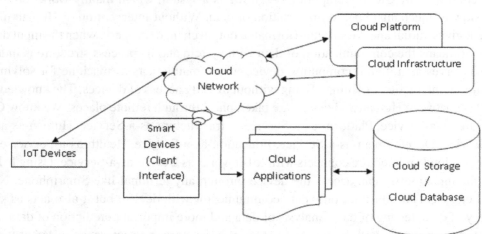

Figure 5. Relationship between More IoT devices with Cloud Network (Google, n.d.)

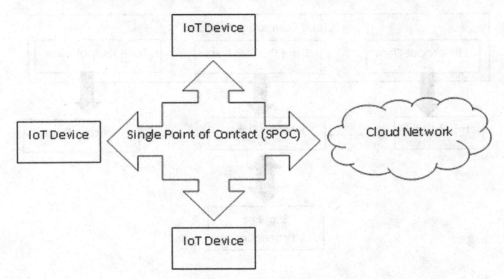

Basically, in IoT device the software coding technique are written in a memory and that memory import into port which is access by IoT enable devices. There is a concept of virtual machine (VM) which gives the essence of presence of a server nearest to the Client. All services are coming from Datacentre regarding various activities of Cloud user.

The IoT device's information stores in a Cloud Information Service Register (CIS Registry) which maintains the device IP addresses to identify them. This CIS Registry stores all information regarding the device which can track its location through this IP address. The Data-centre Broker gives the access permission to the IoT device after verification by CIS Registry and then the resource of Data-centre is distributed to IoT devices and Client Interface. The availability of Data-centre depends upon accessibility of Cloud network only. Because of the authorization procedures are the only gateway point as the key operators of the performance of operations of Cloud based IoT Device. In Fig. 5 we have shown how more than one IoT devices are connected with Cloud Platform through Single Point of Contact (SPOC) or gateway (Google, n.d.). Here gateway means Cloud Client Interfaces or Smart devices like Mobile or Notebook or Desktop PC etc.

5. INPUT METHODOLOGY OF CLOUD BASED IOT DEVICE

Input operations of IoT device where it is acting as DaaS based on Sensors, Connectivity, Tuning operations, Smart Client Interface. The sensors those are taking input from environment are known as actuator and transfer the input data to the Cloud service, upon which Cloud APIs' computed and perform tuning operations. After tuning operation by Cloud platform, the tuned data passes to IoT device as input data. This type of tuning operations would be happening for processing and output data. In Fig. 5 we have shown the activities regarding data input, process and output of IoT device interrelated with CC Platform.

This IoT device can take input either in 0/1 format as digital or within a range of 0 to 1024 as analog. In both the case we need sensors which work as resistor (potentiometer) (Instructible Circuits, n.d.).

Figure 6. Data input, process and output of IoT device interrelated with CC Platform

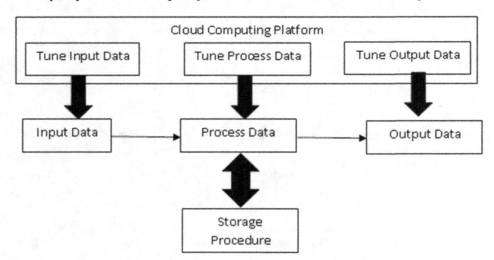

Here we need library files which get support by Cloud APIs' (as e.g. Google APIs'). The software code which is written in memory card of Arduino and ports into its memory slot to connect the software code to Cloud APIs' to download libraries and install the drives into IoT device as SaaS which initiates PaaS, IaaS and all necessary services through Cloud Network. After setting and making this IoT device we connect it with the Smart interface of Cloud Client.

Sometimes IoT device uses Telemetry with sensors where the input data is collected through channelling method (Google, n.d.). All input data store in Cloud due to the delay of processing and might passes one after another to the IoT device. When the input data store for processing, it is identified with a unique field which is device id. The data row also mentioned with another important attribute which the location of the device is to represents the state of the actuators. The actuator or sensor we use which capture the input the data is specially based on the purpose of the device. This kind of actuators or sensors can trace any kind of motions or sense any specified smell to find out any sensitivity or complexity about the data which are coming from environment randomly (Google, n.d.). These data are coming to serial interfaces through the sensors or actuators. These data are converted, collected, validated, arranged, enhanced, reduced and at last combined with state of the values (Google, n.d.). IoT device takes input data from external source like temperature, humidity etc. and passes them to sensors or different control unit for analysis purpose. Here we can also use transducer for conversion of energies. The input-output port connects with a central processing unit (CPU) or a microcontroller which connect with memory (primary and secondary both). These input-output ports can handle either in analog or digital and use an analog digital converter and vice-versa for the changing of format of raw input and output data.

6. FLOW DIAGRAM

Here we discuss the flow process or flow diagram of this methodology, shown in Fig 7. First, we scan the serial port whether to read the pdf files from internet or database as text or capture sound as audio files from internet resources. If read the pdf files, then extract each character from text and send it to

Arduino. In case for audio we send the content of recording which is capture through device microphone from internet resources to the temporary memory and then forward to the Google API. After conversion from audio to text by Google, it is sent to microcontroller and whatever received by it, converted to binary form. From This binary form if it is 1 then raise the Braille dot otherwise not for 0. Using format of Braille cell set blind people can get the idea about the content of pdf or audio.

Figure 7. Flow Diagram of Mechanism.

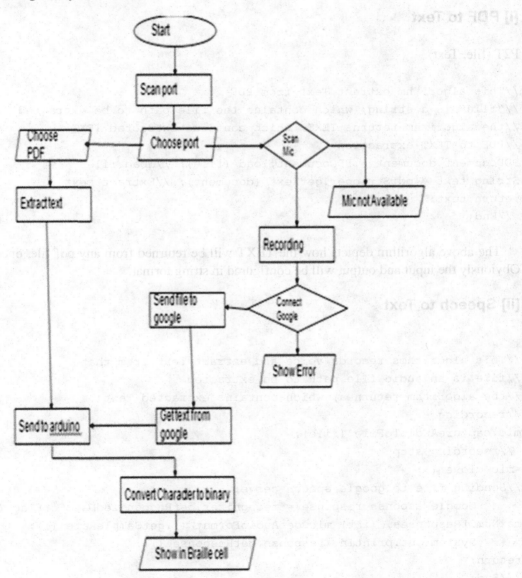

7. ALGORITHM

In this section, we are giving the algorithm for

[i]   pdf to text conversion
[ii]   speech to text conversion
[iii] data sent to Arduino

[i] PDF to Text

P2T (file, Text)

```
//This algorithm extract Text from PDF
//"file" is a string, which contains the file path to be extracted
//the algorithm returns TEXT, which contains extracted TEXT
//PDF to TEXT extraction
PDDocument document = PDDocument.load (file); //load file
String text = pdfStripper.getText (document); //Extract text
return text;
 //End
```

The above algorithm depicts how the TEXT will be returned from any pdf file, once it is loaded. Obviously the input and output will be configured in string format.

[ii] Speech to Text

```
//This algorithms records voice and extract Text from that
//file is an audio file path to be extracted
//the algorithm return a, which contains extracted Text
//recording
mic.captureAudioToFile (file);
 //recording stop
 mic.close ();
//Sending file to google speech server
     GoogleResponse response = recognizer.getRecognizedDataForFlac (file,
maxNumOfResponses, (int) mic.getAudioFormat ().getSampleRate ());
     System.out.println (response.getResponse ());
return;
 //End
```

This algorithm shows that after capturing an audio file, it is sent to google server. Once the data is recognized, then corresponding string is extracted. However, complexity of the algorithm obviously lies on the clarity of the speech. Error will occur during the conversion process if the audio is comprises of complex signals.

[iii] Send To Arduino

```
SerialPort [] portNames= SerialPort.getCommPorts ();
 //Scan for ports chosenPort.setComPortTimeouts (SerialPort.TIMEOUT_SCANNER,
0, 0);
//Connect
output.print (b);
output.flush ();
//Send
```

After extracting the TEXT (either from pdf or from Audio), the file is sent to Arduino. The transfer is occurred through dedicated serial ports.

8. CODE DEVELOPMENT

Corresponding code development part is given in this section

[i] PDF to Text Extraction

```
File file = new File (path);
PDDocument document = PDDocument.load (file);
PDFTextStripper pdfStripper = new PDFTextStripper ();
String text = pdfStripper.getText (document);
System.out.println (text);
document. close ();
return text;
```

[ii] Speech to Text Extraction

```
try
{
     int maxNumOfResponses = 1;
GoogleResponse response = recognizer.getRecognizedDataForFlac (file, maxNumO-
fResponses, (int) mic.getAudioFormat ().getSampleRate ());
 System.out.println (response.getResponse ());
     a=response.getResponse ();
   }
```

```
    catch (Exception ex) {
System.out.println ("ERROR: Google cannot be contacted");
    ex.printStackTrace ();
    }
    file.deleteOnExit ();
    return a
```

[iii] Serial Connection to Arduino

```
SerialPort [] portNames = SerialPort.getCommPorts ();
chosenPort = SerialPort.getCommPort (jComboBox1.getSelectedItem ().toString
());
chosenPort.setComPortTimeouts (SerialPort.TIMEOUT_SCANNER, 0, 0);
PrintWriter output = new PrintWriter (chosenPort.getOutputStream ());
while (true) {
output.print (b);
output.flush ();
}
```

9. RESULT

Schematic circuit diagram and corresponding graphical result are displayed in Fig 8 to Fig 10. Fig 8 shows the Arduino sketch diagram, where all the virtual connections are displayed for implementation of the algorithms. Corresponding incoming sinusoidal waves at different time-instants are represented in Fig 9, which is naturally phase shifted of 90°, and therefore, all the waves will be either sine or cosine. A particular time slot is given in Fig 9, which is real-time generated. Fig 10 displays it visually, and therefore, Fig 9 is validated. X-axis of Fig 10 shows real-time data, and therefore it justifies the variation and working of the experiment at any time-instant.

A summarized analysis or the critical evaluation of the chapter is represented here. Since we have already obtained the variation n of audio signal (which is graphically symbolized), and the algorithm is working fine for text interaction, henceforth, at least under laboratory condition, the model is working fine. Algorithms are already provided in the result section, which should be critically re-examined and modified as per the requirement for further implementation under real-time situation. This algorithm is so far good for English language, and to make it marketable, complex words or various types of speeches have to check so that it can work suitable for different people irrespective of its geographical territories and difference in pronunciation. The initial step runs successfully, however, more modifications and corresponding hardware set-up is required for further development.

Figure 8. Schematic Sketch Diagram of Arduino Code

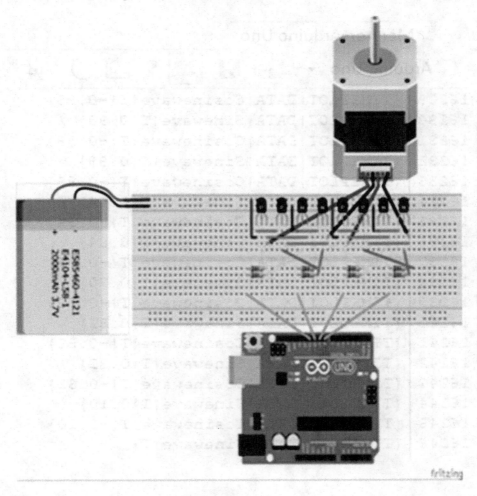

Figure 9. Time plot of Arduino Code with incoming Data

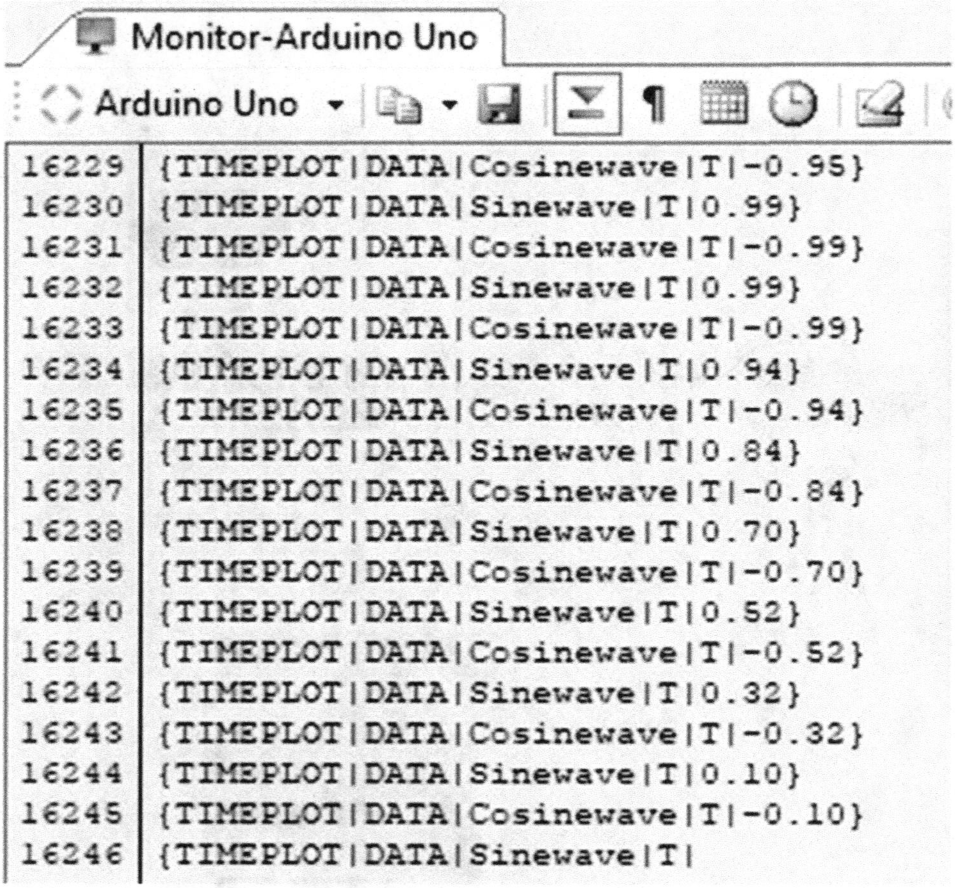

Monitor-Arduino Uno
Arduino Uno
16229 {TIMEPLOT|DATA|Cosinewave|T|-0.95}
16230 {TIMEPLOT|DATA|Sinewave|T|0.99}
16231 {TIMEPLOT|DATA|Cosinewave|T|-0.99}
16232 {TIMEPLOT|DATA|Sinewave|T|0.99}
16233 {TIMEPLOT|DATA|Cosinewave|T|-0.99}
16234 {TIMEPLOT|DATA|Sinewave|T|0.94}
16235 {TIMEPLOT|DATA|Cosinewave|T|-0.94}
16236 {TIMEPLOT|DATA|Sinewave|T|0.84}
16237 {TIMEPLOT|DATA|Cosinewave|T|-0.84}
16238 {TIMEPLOT|DATA|Sinewave|T|0.70}
16239 {TIMEPLOT|DATA|Cosinewave|T|-0.70}
16240 {TIMEPLOT|DATA|Sinewave|T|0.52}
16241 {TIMEPLOT|DATA|Cosinewave|T|-0.52}
16242 {TIMEPLOT|DATA|Sinewave|T|0.32}
16243 {TIMEPLOT|DATA|Cosinewave|T|-0.32}
16244 {TIMEPLOT|DATA|Sinewave|T|0.10}
16245 {TIMEPLOT|DATA|Cosinewave|T|-0.10}
16246 {TIMEPLOT|DATA|Sinewave|T|

Figure 10. Mapping Plot of sinusoidal waveforms of Arduino Code

*Mapping
*Time Plot-Arduino Uno
Arduino Uno
All (auto)
Sine and Cosine Function Waveforms
1.5
1.0
0.5
0.0
-0.5
-1.0
-1.5
05:10
05:15
05:20
Time

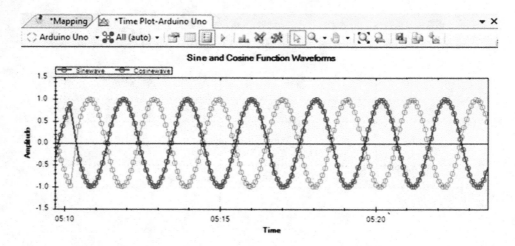

10. CONCLUSION

In Education management system for a smart city we always try to reduce the eccentricity of unnecessary wastage of tree leaves to prepare Braille as well as the methodologies must reduce time and cost consumption. So, we use IoT where we can monitor the Education system through hand-held devices automatically and all the necessary actions taken through network against certain serious situation automatically. For reading situation we can control devices through reading content with their learning speed, order of understanding, time modulation with knowledge accommodation, emergency support system etc. Here we connect all IoT devices through MANET, DANET etc. those are working as Adhoc network topology and maintaining databases which is based on real time data. The proposed work can be developed such a way so that network congestion will be sorted out very quickly using the DANET application. In this proposed system we have successfully created a Low-Cost Text to Braille Converter using IoT. We've also added an added functionality of Audio to text to help people having visually as well as hearing impaired in reading books like ordinary people use Mobile devices. The content of article or book stores in cloud as pdf or soft-connect with Braille devices via DANET can easily access by blind person through feel of Braille or audio using this tool by IoT. Some of the essential information such as cab or train or flight or hospitals booking will also be possible as future prospect, which will be very easily, fulfill all kind of basic needs and requirements of visual impairment people in different situations. This proposed system also will involve exchanging of data between more than one device based on broadcast or multicast network technique which will help to improve the safety and security system of blind persons.

11. FUTURE SCOPE

We are trying to develop it using our own system driver to minimize the cost most. Here we can add some more entertaining features for blind people for listening songs, booking cabs, hotels, flights, Train ticket, restaurant's seat, finding articles or books through internet. They can also use smart hospital management system, Automated Home control systems and appliances etc.

ACKNOWLEDGMENT

We are thankful to research and development cell of Techno International New Town (Formerly known as Techno India College of Technology) and RCC Institute of Information Technology for necessary support for this experimental work.

REFERENCES

Al-Salman, A. M. S., & Al-Khalifa, H. S. (2003). Towards a computerized Arabic Braille environment. *Journal of Software: Practice and Experience*, *33*(6), 497–508.

Arbes, L. A. D., Baybay, J. M. J., Turingan, J. E. E., & Samonte, M. J. C. (2019). Tagalog text-to-braille translator tactile story board with 3D printing. *IOP Conference Series. Materials Science and Engineering*, *482*, 012023. doi:10.1088/1757-899X/482/1/012023

Avastystem. (n.d.). *Benefits of a cloud platform in the IoT*. Retrieved from: https://www.avsystem.com/blog/iot-cloud-platform/

Blenkhorn, P. (1995). A System for Converting Braille to Print. *IEEE Transactions on Rehabilitation Engineering*, *3*(2), 215–221. doi:10.1109/86.392366 PMID:9184898

Blenkhorn, P. (1997). A system for converting print into Braille. *IEEE Transactions on Rehabilitation Engineering*, *5*(3), 121–129. doi:10.1109/86.593266 PMID:9184898

Choi, H. R., Lee, S. W., Jung, K. M., Koo, J. C., Lee, S. I., Choi, H. G., Jeon, J. W., & Nam, J. D. (2004). Tactile Display as Braille Display for the Visually Disabled. *Proceedings of the IEEE/RSJ International Conference on Intelligent Robots and Systems*, *2*, 1985–1990. doi:10.1109/IROS.2004.1389689

Christensen, L. B. (2006). RoboBraille – Automated Braille Translation by Means of an E-Mail Robot. *International Conference on Computers for Handicapped Persons - Computers Helping People with Special Needs*, *4061*, 1102-1109. 10.1007/11788713_160

Dharme, V. S., & Karmore, S. P. (2015). Designing of English text to braille conversion system: A survey. *International Conference on Innovations in Information, Embedded and Communication Systems*. 10.1109/ICIIECS.2015.7193267

Elprocus. (n.d.). *What is Cloud Computing and How it Works?* Retrieved from: https://www.elprocus.com/cloud-computing-technology

Fritz, J. P., & Barner, K. E. (1999). Design of a haptic data visualization system for people with visual impairments. *IEEE Transactions on Rehabilitation Engineering*, *7*(3), 372–384. doi:10.1109/86.788473 PMID:10498382

Fukumoto, M., & Tonomura, Y. (1997). Body coupled Finger Ring: wireless wearable keyboard. *CHI '97: Proceedings of the ACM SIGCHI Conference on Human factors in computing systems*, 147-154 10.1145/258549.258636

Gadag, M., & Udayashankara, V. (2016). Efficient Approach for English Braille to Text Conversion. *International Journal of Advanced Research in Electrical, Electronics and Instrumentation Engineering*, *5*(4), 3343–3348.

Google. (n.d.). *Technical overview of Internet of Things*. Retrieved from: https://cloud.google.com/solutions/iot-overview

Hoffmann, R. (2008). Speech, Text and Braille Conversion Technology. In M. Hersh & M. Johnson (Eds.), *Assistive Technology for Visually Impaired and Blind People* (pp. 497–554). Springer. doi:10.1007/978-1-84628-867-8_14

Instructible Circuits. (n.d.). *IoT Analog Input - Getting Started With IoT*. Retrieved from: https://www.instructables.com/id/IoT-Analog-Input-Getting-Started-With-IoT/

Kim, S., Park, E. S., & Ryu, E. S. (2019). Multimedia Vision for the Visually Impaired through 2D Multiarray Braille Display. *Applied Sciences (Basel, Switzerland)*, *9*(5), 878. doi:10.3390/app9050878

Lahiri, A., Chattopadhyay, S. J., & Basu, A. (2005). Sparsha: A comprehensive Indian language toolset for the blind. *Proceedings of the 7th International ACM SIGACCESS conference on Computers and accessibility*, 114-120 10.1145/1090785.1090807

Matsuda, Y., Isomura, T., Sakuma, I., Kobayashi, E., Jimbo, Y., & Arafune, T. (2007). Finger Braille Teaching System for People who Communicate with Deafblind People. *IEEE International Conference on Mechatronics and Automation*. 10.1109/ICMA.2007.4304074

Moise, A., Bucur, G., & Popescu, C. (2017). Automatic system for text to Braille conversion. *9th International Conference on Electronics, Computers and Artificial Intelligence*. 10.1109/ECAI.2017.8166391

Moore, C., & Murray, I. (2001). An electronic design of a low cost Braille typewriter. *IEEE 7th Australian and New Zealand Intelligent Information Systems Conference*.

Nellore, K., & Hancke, G. P. (2016). Traffic Management for Emergency Vehicle Priority Based on Visual Sensing. *Sensors (Basel)*, *16*(11), 1892. doi:10.339016111892 PMID:27834924

Ng, C. M., Ng, V., & Lau, Y. (1999). Regular feature extraction for recognition of Braille. *Proceedings of IEEE 3rd International Conference on Computational Intelligence and Multimedia Applications*, 302-306. 10.1109/ICCIMA.1999.798547

Prakash, U. E., Vishnupriya, K. T., Thankappan, A., & Balakrishnan, A. A. (2018). Density Based Traffic Control System using Image Processing. *IEEE International Conference on Emerging Trends and Innovations In Engineering and Technological Research*. 10.1109/ICETIETR.2018.8529111

Santra, S., Dey, H., Majumdar, S., & Jha, G. S. (2014). New Simulation Toolkit for Comparison of Scheduling algorithm on Cloud Computing. *IEEE International Conference on Control, Instrumentation, Communication and Computational Technologies*. 10.1109/ICCICCT.2014.6993007

Santra, S., & Mali, K. (2015). A new approach to survey on load balancing in VM in cloud computing: Using CloudSim. *IEEE International Conference on Computer, Communication and Control*. 10.1109/IC4.2015.7375671

Shivakumar, B. L., & Thipathi, M. R. (2013). English to Braille Conversion Tool using Client Server Architecture Mode. *International Journal of Advanced Research in Computer Science and Software Engineering*, *3*(8), 300–303.

Slaby, W. A. (1990). Computerized braille translation. *Journal of Microcomputer Applications*, *13*(2), 107–113. doi:10.1016/0745-7138(90)90013-W

Usikalu, M. R., Okere, A., Ayanbisi, O., Adagunodo, T. A., & Babarimisa, I. O. (2019). Design and Construction of Density Based Traffic Control System. *IOP Conference Series. Earth and Environmental Science*, *331*, 012047. doi:10.1088/1755-1315/331/1/012047

Wikipedia. (n.d.a). *Braille Ï.svg*. Retrieved from: https://commons.wikimedia.org/wiki/File:Braille_%C3%8F.svg

Wikipedia. (n.d.b). *Brajla alfabeto.gif*. Retrieved from: https://commons.wikimedia.org/wiki/File:Brajla_alfabeto.gif

Zhang, X., Ortega-Sanchez, C., & Murray, I. (2006). Text-to-Braille Translator in a Chip. *International Conference on Electrical and Computer Engineering*.

Zhang, X., Ortega-Sanchez, C., & Murray, I. (2007). A System for Fast Text-to-Braille Translation Based on FPGAs. *3rd Southern Conference on Programmable Logic*. 10.1109/SPL.2007.371735

Compilation of References

Matsuda, Y., Isomura, T., Sakuma, I., Kobayashi, E., Jimbo, Y., & Arafune, T. (2007). Finger Braille Teaching System for People who Communicate with Deafblind People. *IEEE International Conference on Mechatronics and Automation.* 10.1109/ICMA.2007.4304074

Moore, C., & Murray, I. (2001). An electronic design of a low cost Braille typewriter. *IEEE 7th Australian and New Zealand Intelligent Information Systems Conference.*

Slaby, W. A. (1990). Computerized braille translation. *Journal of Microcomputer Applications, 13*(2), 107–113. doi:10.1016/0745-7138(90)90013-W

Al-Salman, A. M. S., & Al-Khalifa, H. S. (2003). Towards a computerized Arabic Braille environment. *Journal of Software: Practice and Experience, 33*(6), 497–508.

Prakash, U. E., Vishnupriya, K. T., Thankappan, A., & Balakrishnan, A. A. (2018). Density Based Traffic Control System using Image Processing. *IEEE International Conference on Emerging Trends and Innovations In Engineering and Technological Research.* 10.1109/ICETIETR.2018.8529111

Usikalu, M. R., Okere, A., Ayanbisi, O., Adagunodo, T. A., & Babarimisa, I. O. (2019). Design and Construction of Density Based Traffic Control System. *IOP Conference Series. Earth and Environmental Science, 331,* 012047. doi:10.1088/1755-1315/331/1/012047

Nellore, K., & Hancke, G. P. (2016). Traffic Management for Emergency Vehicle Priority Based on Visual Sensing. *Sensors (Basel), 16*(11), 1892. doi:10.339016111892 PMID:27834924

Shivakumar, B. L., & Thipathi, M. R. (2013). English to Braille Conversion Tool using Client Server Architecture Mode. *International Journal of Advanced Research in Computer Science and Software Engineering, 3*(8), 300–303.

Christensen, L. B. (2006). RoboBraille – Automated Braille Translation by Means of an E-Mail Robot. *International Conference on Computers for Handicapped Persons - Computers Helping People with Special Needs, 4061,* 1102-1109. 10.1007/11788713_160

Zhang, X., Ortega-Sanchez, C., & Murray, I. (2006). Text-to-Braille Translator in a Chip. *International Conference on Electrical and Computer Engineering.*

Choi, H. R., Lee, S. W., Jung, K. M., Koo, J. C., Lee, S. I., Choi, H. G., Jeon, J. W., & Nam, J. D. (2004). Tactile Display as Braille Display for the Visually Disabled. *Proceedings of the IEEE/RSJ International Conference on Intelligent Robots and Systems, 2,* 1985–1990. doi:10.1109/IROS.2004.1389689

Zhang, X., Ortega-Sanchez, C., & Murray, I. (2007). A System for Fast Text-to-Braille Translation Based on FPGAs. *3rd Southern Conference on Programmable Logic.* 10.1109/SPL.2007.371735

Hoffmann, R. (2008). Speech, Text and Braille Conversion Technology. In M. Hersh & M. Johnson (Eds.), *Assistive Technology for Visually Impaired and Blind People* (pp. 497–554). Springer. doi:10.1007/978-1-84628-867-8_14

Dharme, V. S., & Karmore, S. P. (2015). Designing of English text to braille conversion system: A survey. *International Conference on Innovations in Information, Embedded and Communication Systems*. 10.1109/ICIIECS.2015.7193267

Gadag, M., & Udayashankara, V. (2016). Efficient Approach for English Braille to Text Conversion. *International Journal of Advanced Research in Electrical, Electronics and Instrumentation Engineering, 5*(4), 3343–3348.

Moise, A., Bucur, G., & Popescu, C. (2017). Automatic system for text to Braille conversion. *9th International Conference on Electronics, Computers and Artificial Intelligence*. 10.1109/ECAI.2017.8166391

Arbes, L. A. D., Baybay, J. M. J., Turingan, J. E. E., & Samonte, M. J. C. (2019). Tagalog text-to-braille translator tactile story board with 3D printing. *IOP Conference Series. Materials Science and Engineering, 482*, 012023. doi:10.1088/1757-899X/482/1/012023

Kim, S., Park, E. S., & Ryu, E. S. (2019). Multimedia Vision for the Visually Impaired through 2D Multiarray Braille Display. *Applied Sciences (Basel, Switzerland), 9*(5), 878. doi:10.3390/app9050878

Elprocus. (n.d.). *What is Cloud Computing and How it Works?* Retrieved from: https://www.elprocus.com/cloud-computing-technology

Avastystem. (n.d.). *Benefits of a cloud platform in the IoT*. Retrieved from: https://www.avsystem.com/blog/iot-cloud-platform/

Instructible Circuits. (n.d.). *IoT Analog Input - Getting Started With IoT*. Retrieved from: https://www.instructables.com/id/IoT-Analog-Input-Getting-Started-With-IoT/

Fritz, J. P., & Barner, K. E. (1999). Design of a haptic data visualization system for people with visual impairments. *IEEE Transactions on Rehabilitation Engineering, 7*(3), 372–384. doi:10.1109/86.788473 PMID:10498382

Santra, S., & Mali, K. (2015). A new approach to survey on load balancing in VM in cloud computing: Using CloudSim. *IEEE International Conference on Computer, Communication and Control*. 10.1109/IC4.2015.7375671

Santra, S., Dey, H., Majumdar, S., & Jha, G. S. (2014). New Simulation Toolkit for Comparison of Scheduling algorithm on Cloud Computing. *IEEE International Conference on Control, Instrumentation, Communication and Computational Technologies*. 10.1109/ICCICCT.2014.6993007

Google. (n.d.). *Technical overview of Internet of Things*. Retrieved from: https://cloud.google.com/solutions/iot-overview

Fukumoto, M., & Tonomura, Y. (1997). Body coupled Finger Ring: wireless wearable keyboard. *CHI '97: Proceedings of the ACM SIGCHI Conference on Human factors in computing systems*, 147-154 10.1145/258549.258636

Wikipedia. (n.d.a). *Braille Ï.svg*. Retrieved from: https://commons.wikimedia.org/wiki/File:Braille_%C3%8F.svg

Ng, C. M., Ng, V., & Lau, Y. (1999). Regular feature extraction for recognition of Braille. *Proceedings of IEEE 3rd International Conference on Computational Intelligence and Multimedia Applications*, 302-306. 10.1109/ICCIMA.1999.798547

Wikipedia. (n.d.b). *Brajla alfabeto.gif*. Retrieved from: https://commons.wikimedia.org/wiki/File:Brajla_alfabeto.gif

Blenkhorn, P. (1997). A system for converting print into Braille. *IEEE Transactions on Rehabilitation Engineering, 5*(3), 121–129. doi:10.1109/86.593266 PMID:9184898

Lahiri, A., Chattopadhyay, S. J., & Basu, A. (2005). Sparsha: A comprehensive Indian language toolset for the blind. *Proceedings of the 7th International ACM SIGACCESS conference on Computers and accessibility*, 114-120 10.1145/1090785.1090807

Blenkhorn, P. (1995). A System for Converting Braille to Print. *IEEE Transactions on Rehabilitation Engineering*, *3*(2), 215–221. doi:10.1109/86.392366 PMID:9184898

Abbas, F., Liu, G., Fan, P., & Khan, Z. (2020). An Efficient Cluster Based Resource Management Scheme and its Performance Analysis for V2X Networks. *IEEE Access: Practical Innovations, Open Solutions*, *8*, 87071–87082. doi:10.1109/ACCESS.2020.2992591

Abdelgawad, A., & Yelamarthi, K. (2017). Internet of Things (IoT) Platform for Structure Health Monitoring. *Wireless Communications and Mobile Computing*, *2017*, 1–10. doi:10.1155/2017/6560797

Abd-El-Malek, M., Ganger, G. R., Goodson, G. R., Reiter, M. K., & Wylie, J. J. (2005). Fault-scalable Byzantine fault-tolerant services. *Operating Systems Review*, *39*(5), 59–74.

Adamala, S., Raghuwanshi, N. S., & Mishra, A. (2014). Development of Surface Irrigation Systems Design and Evaluation Software (SIDES). *Computers and Electronics in Agriculture*, *100*, 100–109. doi:10.1016/j.compag.2013.11.004

Adardour, H. E., Hadjila, M., Irid, S. M. H., Baouch, T., & Belkhiter, S. E. (2021). Outdoor Alzheimer's patients tracking using an IoT system and a Kalman Filter estimator. *Wireless Personal Communications*, *116*(1), 249–265. doi:10.100711277-020-07713-4

Addis, B., Aringhieri, R., Grosso, A., & Hosteins, P. (2016). Hybrid Constructive Heuristics for the Critical Node Problem. *Annals of Operations Research*, *238*(1–2), 637–649. doi:10.100710479-016-2110-y

Aditya, S., Molisch, A. F., & Behairy, H. M. (2018). A survey on the impact of multipath on wideband time-of-arrival based localization. *Proceedings of the IEEE*, *106*(7), 1183–1203. doi:10.1109/JPROC.2018.2819638

Ahmad, E., Alaslani, M., Dogar, F. R., & Shihada, B. (2020). Location-Aware, Context-Driven QoS for IoT Applications. *IEEE Systems Journal*, *14*(1), 232–243. doi:10.1109/JSYST.2019.2893913

Aich, S., Chakraborty, S., Sim, J. S., Jang, D. J., & Kim, H. C. (2019). The design of an automated system for the analysis of the activity and emotional patterns of dogs with wearable sensors using machine learning. *Applied Sciences (Basel, Switzerland)*, *9*(22), 1–12. doi:10.3390/app9224938

Ai, Z., Liu, Y., Chang, L., Lin, F., & Song, F. (2020). A Smart Collaborative Authentication Framework for Multi-Dimensional Fine-Grained Control. *IEEE Access: Practical Innovations, Open Solutions*, *8*, 8101–8113. doi:10.1109/ACCESS.2019.2962247

Akram, V. K., Asci, M., & Dagdeviren, O. (2018). Design and Analysis of a Breadth First Search based Connectivity Robustness Estimation Approach in Wireless Sensor Networks. *2018 6th International Conference on Control Engineering & Information Technology (CEIT)*, 1-6. 10.1109/CEIT.2018.8751850

Akram, V. K., Arapoglu, O., & Dagdeviren, O. (2018). A Depth-First Search based Connectivity Estimation Approach for Fault Tolerant Wireless Sensor Networks. *2018 International Conference on Artificial Intelligence and Data Processing (IDAP)*, 1-6. 10.1109/IDAP.2018.8620883

Akram, V. K., & Dagdeviren, O. (2013). Breadth-first search-based single-phase algorithms for bridge detection in wireless sensor networks. *Sensors (Basel)*, *13*(7), 8786–8813. doi:10.3390130708786 PMID:23845930

Akram, V. K., & Dagdeviren, O. (2018). DECK: A distributed, asynchronous and exact k-connectivity detection algorithm for wireless sensor networks. *Computer Communications*, *116*, 9–20. doi:10.1016/j.comcom.2017.11.005

Akram, V. K., & Dagdeviren, O. (2018). k-Connectivity Estimation from Local Neighborhood Information in Wireless Ad Hoc and Sensor Networks. *2018 IEEE International Black Sea Conference on Communications and Networking (BlackSeaCom)*, 1-5. 10.1109/BlackSeaCom.2018.8433701

Akram, V. K., Dagdeviren, O., & Tavli, B. (2021). Distributed k-connectivity restoration for fault tolerant wireless sensor and actuator networks: Algorithm design and experimental evaluations. *IEEE Transactions on Reliability, 70*(3), 1112–1125. doi:10.1109/TR.2020.2970268

Akyildiz, I. F., Su, W., Sankarasubramaniam, Y., & Cayirci, E. (2002). Wireless sensor networks: a survey. *Computer Networks, 38*(4), 393-422.

Akyildiz, I. F., Su, W., Sankarasubramaniam, Y., & Cayirci, E. (2002). Wireless sensor networks: A survey. *Computer Networks, 38*(4), 393–422. doi:10.1016/S1389-1286(01)00302-4

Alam, M. F., Katsikas, S., Beltramello, O., & Hadjiefthymiades, S. (2017) Augmented and virtual reality based monitoring and safety system: A prototype IoT platform. *Journal of Network and Computer Applications, 89*, 109-119. doi:10.1016/j.jnca.2017.03.022

Alameer, A., & Halfond, W. (2016). An Empirical Study of Internationalization Failures in the Web. *Proceedings of the International Conference on Software Maintenance and Evolution (ICSME)*. 10.1109/ICSME.2016.55

Alemdar, H., & Ersoy, C. (2010). Wireless sensor networks for healthcare: A survey. *Computer Networks, 54*(15), 2688-2710.

Al-Fuqaha, A., Guizani, M., Mohammadi, M., Aledhari, M., & Ayyash, M. (2015). Internet of Things: A survey on enabling technologies, protocols, and applications. *IEEE Communications Surveys and Tutorials, 4*(17), 2347–2376. doi:10.1109/COMST.2015.2444095

Al-Hader, M., & Rodzi, A. (2009). The Smart City Infrastructure Development & Monitoring. Theoretical and Empirical Researches in Urban Management. Research Centre in Public Administration and Public Services.

Ali, M. U., Hur, S., & Park, Y. (2019). Wi-Fi-based effortless indoor positioning system using IoT sensors. *Sensors (Basel), 19*(7), 1496. doi:10.339019071496 PMID:30934799

Al-Karaki, J. N., & Gawanmeh, A. (2017). The optimal deployment, coverage and connectivity problems in wireless sensor networks: Revisited. *IEEE Access: Practical Innovations, Open Solutions, 5*, 18051–18065. doi:10.1109/ACCESS.2017.2740382

Al-Kaseem, B. R., Al-Dunainawi, Y., & Al-Raweshidy, H. S. (2019). End-to-End Delay Enhancement in 6LoWPAN Testbed Using Programmable Network Concepts. *IEEE Internet of Things Journal, 6*(2), 3070–3086. doi:10.1109/JIOT.2018.2879111

Al-Khalifa, H. S. (2008). Utilizing QR Code and Mobile Phones for Blinds and Visually Impaired People. In Computers Helping People with Special Needs. ICCHP 2008. Lecture Notes in Computer Science (vol. 5105, pp. 1065-1069). Berlin: Springer.

Al-Masri, E., Kalyanam, K. R., Batts, J., Kim, J., Singh, S., Vo, T., & Yan, C. (2020). Investigating Messaging Protocols for the Internet of Things (IoT). *IEEE Access: Practical Innovations, Open Solutions, 8*, 94880–94911. doi:10.1109/ACCESS.2020.2993363

Alnuem, M., Zafar, N. M., Imran, M., Ullah, S., & Fayed, M. (2014). Formal Specification and Validation of a Localized Algorithm for Segregation of Critical/Noncritical Nodes in MAHSNs. *International Journal of Distributed Sensor Networks, 10*(6), 1–14. doi:10.1155/2014/140973

Alonso, R. S., Sittón-Candanedo, I., García, O., Prieto, J., & Rodríguez-González, S. (2020). An intelligent Edge-IoT platform for monitoring livestock and crops in a dairy farming scenario. *Ad Hoc Networks, 98*.

Al-Sarawi, S., Anbar, M., Alieyan, K., & Alzubaidi, M. (2017). Internet of Things (IoT) communication protocols: Review. *2017 8th International Conference on Information Technology (ICIT), Amman*, 685-690.

Alvarenga, F. A. P., Borges, I., Palkovič, L., Rodina, J., Oddy, V. H., & Dobos, R. C. (2016). Using a three-axis accelerometer to identify and classify sheep behaviour at pasture. *Applied Animal Behaviour Science, 181*, 91–99. doi:10.1016/j.applanim.2016.05.026

Amadeo, R. (2015). *Meet Google's "Eddystone"-a flexible open source iBeacon fighter*. Ars Technica.

Amjad, M., Sharif, M., Afzal, M. K., & Kim, S. W. (2016). TinyOS-New Trends, Comparative Views, and Supported Sensing Applications: A Review. *IEEE Sensors Journal, 16*(9), 2865–2889. doi:10.1109/JSEN.2016.2519924

Andersen, M. P., Fierro, G., & Culler, D. E. (2016). Enabling Synergy in IoT: Platform to Service and Beyond. *2016 IEEE First International Conference on Internet-of-Things Design and Implementation (IoTDI)*, 1-12. 10.1109/IoTDI.2015.45

Androulaki, E., Barger, A., Bortnikov, V., Cachin, C., Christidis, K., Caro, A. D., Enyeart, D., Ferris, C., Laventman, G., Manevich, Y., Muralidharan, S., Murthy, C., Nguyen, B., Sethi, M., Singh, G., & Smith, K., SornIoTti, A., Stathakopoulou, C., Vukolic, M., Cocco, S.W., & Yellick, J. (2018). Hyperledger fabric: a distributed operating system for permissioned blockchains. In *The Thirteenth EuroSys Conference*. New York: ACM Press.

Anguita-Ruiz, A., Segura-Delgado, A., Alcalá, R., Aguilera, C. M., & Alcalá-Fdez, J. (2020). Explainable Artificial Intelligence (XAI) for the identification of biologically relevant gene expression patterns in longitudinal human studies, insights from obesity research. *PLoS Computational Biology, 16*(4), 1–34. doi:10.1371/journal.pcbi.1007792 PMID:32275707

Arabacı, M. A., Özkan, F., Surer, E., Jančovič, P., & Temizel, A. (2021). Multi-modal egocentric activity recognition using multi-kernel learning. *Multimedia Tools and Applications, 80*(11), 16299–16328. doi:10.100711042-020-08789-7

Arablouei, R., Currie, L., Kusy, B., Ingham, A., Greenwood, P. L., & Bishop-Hurley, G. (2021). In-situ classification of cattle behavior using accelerometry data. *Computers and Electronics in Agriculture, 183*, 1–12. doi:10.1016/j.compag.2021.106045

Arampatzis, T., Lygeros, J., & Manesis, S. (2005). A Survey of Applications of Wireless Sensors and Wireless Sensor Networks. *Proceedings of the 2005 IEEE International Symposium on, Mediterrean Conference on Control and Automation Intelligent Control*, 719-724. 10.1109/.2005.1467103

Aringhieri, R., Grosso, A., Hosteins, P., & Scatamacchia, R. (2015). VNS Solutions for the Critical Node Problem. *Electronic Notes in Discrete Mathematics, 47*, 37–44. doi:10.1016/j.endm.2014.11.006

Aringhieri, R., Grosso, A., Hosteins, P., & Scatamacchia, R. (2016a). Local Search Metaheuristics for the Critical Node Problem. *Networks, 67*(3), 209–221. doi:10.1002/net.21671

Aringhieri, R., Grosso, A., Hosteins, P., & Scatamacchia, R. (2016b). A General Evolutionary Framework for Different Classes of Critical Node Problems. *Engineering Applications of Artificial Intelligence, 55*, 128–145. doi:10.1016/j.engappai.2016.06.010

Arshad, R., Zahoor, S., Shah, M. A., Wahid, A., & Yu, H. (2017). Green IoT: An investigation on energy saving practices for 2020 and beyond. *IEEE Access: Practical Innovations, Open Solutions, 5*, 15667–15681. doi:10.1109/ACCESS.2017.2686092

Arslan, S., Challenger, M., & Dagdeviren, O. (2017). Wireless sensor network based fire detection system for libraries. In *2017 International Conference on Computer Science and Engineering (UBMK 2017)*, (pp. 271-276). IEEE 10.1109/UBMK.2017.8093388

Arulselvan, A., Commander, C. W., Elefteriadou, L., & Pardalos, P. M. (2009). Detecting Critical Nodes in Sparse Graphs. *Computers & Operations Research*, *36*(7), 2193–2200. doi:10.1016/j.cor.2008.08.016

Ashton, K. (2009). *That "Internet of Things" Thing: In the Real World Things Matter More than Ideas*. RFID Journal.

Asici, T. Z., Karaduman, B., Eslampanah, R., Challenger, M., Denil, J., & Vangheluwe, H. (2019). Applying model driven engineering techniques to the development of contiki-based IoT systems. In *2019 IEEE/ACM 1st International Workshop on Software Engineering Research & Practices for the Internet of Things (SERP4IoT)* (pp. 25-32). IEEE. 10.1109/SERP4IoT.2019.00012

Atonomi. (2019). *Atonomi—Bringing Trust and Security to IoT*. Retrieved from https://atonomi.io/

Aublin, P., Guerraoui, R., Knezevic, N., Quéma, V., & Vukolic, M. (2015). The Next 700 BFT Protocols. *ACM Trans. Comput. Syst., 32*, 12:1-12:45.

Awwad, A., & Slany, W. (2016). Automated Bidirectional Languages Localization Testing for Android Apps with Rich GUI. *Mobile Information Systems, 2016*.

Awwad, A. (2017). Localization to Bidirectional Languages for a Visual Programming Environment on Smartphones. *International Journal of Computer Science Issues*, *14*, 3.

Awwad, A., & Rez, N. (2018). Automatic Internationalization and Localization Based on Android Location Services. *IJCSI International Journal of Computer Science Issues*, *15*, 5.

Baccelli, E., Hahm, O., Günes, M., Wählisch, M., & Schmidt, T. C. (2013). RIOT OS: Towards an OS for the Internet of Things. In 2013 IEEE conference on computer communications workshops (INFOCOM WKSHPS) (pp. 79-80). IEEE.

Baccelli, E., Gundogan, C., Hahm, O., Kietzmann, P., Lenders, M. S., Petersen, H., Schleiser, K., Schmidt, T. C., & Wahlisch, M. (2018). RIOT: An Open Source Operating System for Low-End Embedded Devices in the IoT. *IEEE Internet of Things Journal*, *5*(6), 4428–4440. doi:10.1109/JIOT.2018.2815038

Back, A., Corallo, M., Dashjr, L., Friedenbach, M., Maxwell, G., Miller, A., Poelstra, A., Timón, J., & Wuille, P. (2014). *Enabling Blockchain Innovations with Pegged Sidechains*. Academic Press.

Badii, C., Bellini, P., Difino, A., & Nesi, P. (2020). Smart City IoT Platform Respecting GDPR Privacy and Security Aspects. *IEEE Access: Practical Innovations, Open Solutions*, *8*, 23601–23623. doi:10.1109/ACCESS.2020.2968741

Bai, S., & Wu, T. (2013). *Analysis of K-Means algorithm on fingerprint based indoor localization system*. Paper presented at the meeting of the 5th IEEE International Symposium on Microwave, Antenna, Propagation and EMC Technologies for Wireless Communications. 10.1109/MAPE.2013.6689952

Bai, J., Lian, S., Liu, Z., Wang, K., & Liu, D. (2017). Smart Guiding Glasses for Visually Impaired People in Indoor Environment. *IEEE Transactions on Consumer Electronics*, *63*(3), 258–266.

Balaji, S., Nathani, K., & Santhakumar, R. (2019). IoT Technology, Applications and Challenges: A Contemporary Survey. *Wireless Personal Communications*, *108*(1), 363–388. doi:10.100711277-019-06407-w

Banos, O., Villalonga, C., Garcia, R., Saez, A., Damas, M., Holgado-Terriza, J. A., Lee, S., Pomares, H., & Rojas, I. (2015). Design, implementation and validation of a novel open framework for agile development of mobile health applications. *Biomedical Engineering Online*, *14*(S6), 1–20. doi:10.1186/1475-925X-14-S2-S6 PMID:26329639

Barredo-Arrieta, A., Díaz-Rodríguez, N., Del Ser, J., Bennetot, A., Tabik, S., Barbado, A., Garcia, S., Gil-Lopez, S., Molina, D., Benjamins, R., Chatila, R., & Herrera, F. (2020). Explainable Artificial Intelligence (XAI): Concepts, taxonomies, opportunities and challenges toward responsible AI. *Information Fusion*, *58*, 82–115. doi:10.1016/j.inffus.2019.12.012

Barwick, J., Lamb, D. W., Dobos, R., Welch, M., & Trotter, M. (2018). Categorising sheep activity using a tri-axial accelerometer. *Computers and Electronics in Agriculture*, *145*, 289–297. doi:10.1016/j.compag.2018.01.007

Battisti, A. L., & Wen, M.-S. (2021). Enabling Internet of Media Things with edge-based virtual multimedia sensors. *IEEE Access: Practical Innovations, Open Solutions*, *9*, 59255–59269. doi:10.1109/ACCESS.2021.3073240

Benammar, M., Abdaoui, A., Ahmad, S. H. M., Touati, F., & Kadri, A. (2018). A Modular IoT Platform for Real-Time Indoor Air Quality Monitoring. *Sensors (Basel)*, *18*(2), 581. doi:10.339018020581 PMID:29443893

Bennett, J. (2018). *Xamarin in Action: Creating native cross-platform mobile apps*. Manning Publications Co.

Bentov, I., Lee, C., Mizrahi, A., & Rosenfeld, M. (2014). Proof of Activity: Extending Bitcoin's Proof of Work via Proof of Stake (Extended Abstract). *SIGMETRICS Perform. Evaluation Rev.*, *42*, 34–37.

Bergenti, F., & Poggi, A. (2010). Multi-Agent Systems for the Application and Employing of E-Health Services. In M. M. Cruz-Cunha, A. J. Tavates, & R. Simoes (Eds.), *Handbook of Research on Developments in E-Health and Telemedicine: Technological and Social Perspectives* (pp. 247–264). IGI Global Publishing.

Berz, E. L., Tesch, D. A., & Hessel, F. P. (2015). *RFID indoor localization based on support vector regression and k-means*. Paper presented at the meeting of the 2015 IEEE 24th International Symposium on Industrial Electronics (ISIE), Rio de Janeiro, Brazil. 10.1109/ISIE.2015.7281681

Bhave, A. G., Mishra, A., & Raghuwanshi, N. S. (2014). A combined bottom-up and top-down approach for assessment of climate change adaptation options. *Journal of Hydrology (Amsterdam)*, *518*, 150–161. doi:10.1016/j.jhydrol.2013.08.039

Bojkovic, Z., Milovanovic, D., & Fowdur, T. P. (Eds.). (2020). *5G Multimedia Communication: Technology, multiservices, and deployment*. CRC Press. doi:10.1201/9781003096450

Bonte, P., Ongenae, F. D., & Backere, F. (2017). The MASSIF platform: A modular and semantic platform for the development of flexible IoT services. *Knowledge and Information Systems*, *51*(1), 89–126. doi:10.100710115-016-0969-1

Botta, A., Donato, W., Persico, V., & Pescape, A. (2016). Integration of cloud computing and Internet of Things: A survey. *Future Generation Computer Systems*, *56*, 684–700. doi:10.1016/j.future.2015.09.021

Bozkurt, S., Elibol, G., Gunal, S., & Yayan, U. (2015, September). *A comparative study on machine learning algorithms for indoor positioning*. Paper presented at the meeting of the 2015 International Symposium on Innovations in Intelligent SysTems and Applications (INISTA), Madrid, Spain. 10.1109/INISTA.2015.7276725

Bracciale, L., Loreti, P., Detti, A., Paolillo, R., & Melazzi, N. B. (2019). Lightweight Named Object: An ICN-Based Abstraction for IoT Device Programming and Management. *IEEE Internet of Things Journal*, *6*(3), 5029–5039. doi:10.1109/JIOT.2019.2894969

Bredin, J. L., Demaine, E. D., Hajiaghayi, M. T., & Rus, D. (2010). Deploying sensor networks with guaranteed fault tolerance. *IEEE/ACM Transactions on Networking*, *18*(1), 216–228. doi:10.1109/TNET.2009.2024941

Bruce, I., McKennell, A., & Walker, E. (1991). *Blind and Partially Sighted Adults in Britain: The RNIB Survey* (Vol. 1). Her Majesty's Stationery Office.

Brugarolas, R., Latif, T., Dieffenderfer, J., Walker, K., Yuschak, S., Sherman, B. L., Roberts, D. L., & Bozkurt, A. (2015). Wearable heart rate sensor systems for wireless canine health monitoring. *IEEE Sensors Journal, 16*(10), 3454–3464. doi:10.1109/JSEN.2015.2485210

Campos, G. (2020, January 3). *Microsoft's Audio Wayfinding App for the Visually Impaired.* Retrieved from https://www.avinteractive.com/news/ai/microsoft-launches-audio-wayfinding-app-visually-impaired-18-09-2018/

Cardeñosa, J., Gallardo, C., & Martín, A. (2006). *Internationalization and Localization after System Development: A Practical Case.* https://www.lionbridge.com/blog/translationlocalization/localizationglobalizationinternationalization-whats-the-difference/

Cardin, S., Thalmann, D., & Vexo, F. (2007). A Wearable System for Mobility Improvement of Visually Impaired People. *The Visual Computer Journal, 23*(2), 109–118.

Cardozo, A., Yamin, A., Xavier, L., Souza, R., Lopes, J., & Geyer, C. (2016). An architecture proposal to distributed sensing in Internet of Things. *2016 1st International Symposium on Instrumentation Systems, Circuits and Transducers (INSCIT).* doi:10.1109/inscit.2016.7598208

Casado-Vara, R., Prieta, F.D., Prieto, J., & Corchado, J.M. (2018). Blockchain framework for IoT data quality via edge computing. *BlockSys'18.*

Casella, E., Khamesi, A. R., & Silvestri, S. (2020). A framework for the recognition of horse gaits through wearable devices. *Pervasive and Mobile Computing, 67*, 1–19. doi:10.1016/j.pmcj.2020.101213

Castañeda-Miranda, A., & Castaño-Meneses, V. M. (2020). Internet of things for smart farming and frost intelligent control in greenhouses. *Computers and Electronics in Agriculture, 176*, 105614. doi:10.1016/j.compag.2020.105614

Castro, M., & Liskov, B. (2002). Practical byzantine fault tolerance and proactive recovery. *ACM Transactions on Computer Systems, 20*, 398–461.

Censor-Hillel, K., Ghaffari, M., & Kuhn, F. (2014). Distributed connectivity decomposition. *Proc. ACM Symp. Principl. Distrib. Comput. (PODC)*, 56–165.

Chakravarty, P., Cozzi, G., Ozgul, A., & Aminian, K. (2019). A novel biomechanical approach for animal behaviour recognition using accelerometers. *Methods in Ecology and Evolution, 10*(6), 802–814. doi:10.1111/2041-210X.13172

Chan, V., Ray, P., & Parameswaran, N. (2008). Mobile e-Health Monitoring: An Agent-Based Approach. *IET Communications, 2*(2), 223–230.

Charalampos, D. (2012). Building Internet of Things with the Arduino. CreateSpace Independent Publishing Platform, Amazon.com.

Chaudary, B., Paajala, I., Keino, E., & Pulli, P. (2017). Tele-guidance Based Navigation System for the Visually Impaired and Blind Persons. In eHealth 360° (LNICST, vol. 181, pp 9-16). Cham: Springer.

Chen, H.-Y., & Lee, C.-H. (2020). Vibration Signals Analysis by Explainable Artificial Intelligence (XAI) Approach: Application on Bearing Faults Diagnosis. *IEEE Access: Practical Innovations, Open Solutions, 8*, 134246–134256. doi:10.1109/ACCESS.2020.3006491

Chen, I., Guo, J., & Bao, F. (2016). Trust Management for SOA-Based IoT and Its Application to Service Composition. *IEEE Transactions on Services Computing, 9*(3), 482–495. doi:10.1109/TSC.2014.2365797

Chen, L., Xu, L., Shah, N., Gao, Z., Lu, Y., & Shi, W. (2017). *On Security Analysis of Proof-of-Elapsed-Time (PoET).* SSS.

Chéour, R., Khriji, S., & Kanoun, O. (2020). Microcontrollers for IoT: Optimizations, Computing Paradigms, and Future Directions. In *2020 IEEE 6th World Forum on Internet of Things (WF-IoT)* (pp. 1-7). IEEE.

Chernyshev, M., Baig, Z., Bello, O., & Zeadally, S. (2018). Internet of Things (IoT): Research, Simulators, and Testbeds. *IEEE Internet of Things Journal, 5*(3), 1637–1647. doi:10.1109/JIOT.2017.2786639

Choudhury, N., Matam, R., Mukherjee, M., & Lloret, J. (2020). A Performance-to-Cost Analysis of IEEE 802.15.4 MAC with 802.15.4e MAC Modes. *IEEE Access: Practical Innovations, Open Solutions, 8*, 41936–41950. doi:10.1109/ACCESS.2020.2976654

Chriki, A., Toutai, H., & Snoussi, H. (2017). *SVM-Based Indoor Localization in Wireless Sensor Networks.* Paper presented at the meeting of the 13th International Wireless Communications and Mobile Computing Conference (IWCMC), Valencia, Spain. 10.1109/IWCMC.2017.7986446

Clark, J., & Essex, A. (2011). CommitCoin: Carbon Dating Commitments with Bitcoin. *IACR Cryptol. ePrint Arch., 2011*, 677.

Clement, A., Wong, E. L., Alvisi, L., Dahlin, M., & Marchetti, M. (2009). *Making Byzantine Fault Tolerant Systems Tolerate Byzantine Faults.* NSDI.

Čolaković, A., & Hadžialić, M. (2018). Internet of Things (IoT): A review of enabling technologies, challenges, and open research issues. *Computer Networks, 144*, 17–39. doi:10.1016/j.comnet.2018.07.017

Commission on Science and Technology for Development, Nineteenth session: Smart cities and infrastructure, Report of the Secretary-General. (2016). Geneva: United Nations.

Conners, M. G., Michelot, T., Heywood, E. I., Orben, R. A., Phillips, R. A., Vyssotski, A. L., Shaffer, S. A., & Thorne, L. H. (2021). Hidden Markov models identify major movement modes in accelerometer and magnetometer data from four albatross species. *Movement Ecology, 9*(7), 1–16. doi:10.118640462-021-00243-z PMID:33618773

Courtois, N. (2014). *On The Longest Chain Rule and Programmed Self-Destruction of Crypto Currencies.* ArXiv, abs/1405.0534.

Cowling, J.A., Myers, D.S., Liskov, B., Rodrigues, R., & Shrira, L. (2006). HQ replication: A hybrid quorum protocol for byzantine fault tolerance. *OSDI '06.*

Cristian, L. (2015). On Internationalization (I18N). Studia Universitatis Petru Maior. *Philologia, 19*, 151–160.

Dagdeviren, O., & Akram, V. K. (2017). PACK: Path coloring based k-connectivity detection algorithm for wireless sensor networks. *Ad Hoc Networks, 64*, 41-52.

Dagdeviren, O., Akram, V. K., & Farzan, A. (2019). A Distributed Evolutionary algorithm for detecting minimum vertex cuts for wireless ad hoc and sensor networks. *Journal of Network and Computer Applications, 127*, 70-81. doi:10.1016/j.jnca.2018.10.009

Dagdeviren, O., & Akram, V. K. (2013). Energy-efficient bridge detection algorithms for wireless sensor networks. *International Journal of Distributed Sensor Networks, 9*(4), 867903. doi:10.1155/2013/867903

Dagdeviren, O., & Akram, V. K. (2014). An energy-efficient distributed cut vertex detection algorithm for wireless sensor networks. *The Computer Journal, 57*(12), 1852–1869. doi:10.1093/comjnl/bxt128

Dagdeviren, O., & Akram, V. K. (2019). KEIP: A distributed k-connectivity estimation algorithm based on independent paths for wireless sensor networks. *Wireless Networks, 25*(8), 4479–4491. doi:10.100711276-018-1739-7

Dagdeviren, O., Akram, V. K., & Tavli, B. (2019). Design And Evaluation of Algorithms for Energy Efficient and Complete Determination of Critical Nodes for Wireless Sensor Network Reliability. *IEEE Transactions on Reliability*, *68*(1), 280–290. doi:10.1109/TR.2018.2873917

Dagdeviren, O., Akram, V. K., Tavli, B., Yildiz, H. U., & Atilgan, C. (2016). Distributed detection of critical nodes in wireless sensor networks using connected dominating set. *IEEE SENSORS*, *1-3*, 2016. doi:10.1109/ICSENS.2016.7808815

Daglarli, E. (2021). Explainable Artificial Intelligence (xAI) Approaches and Deep Meta-Learning Models for Cyber-Physical Systems. *Advances in Systems Analysis, Software Engineering, and High Performance Computing*, 42–67. doi:10.4018/978-1-7998-5101-1.ch003

Dai, F., & Wu, J. (2005) On Constructing k-connected k-dominating Set in Wireless Networks. In *Proc. 19th Int. Parallel and Distributed Processing Symposium (IPDPS)*. IEEE. 10.1109/IPDPS.2005.302

Dai, H., Ying, W., & Xu, J. (2015). Multi-layer neural network for received signal strength-based indoor localisation. *IET Communications*, *10*(6), 717–723. doi:10.1049/iet-com.2015.0469

Dandil, E., & Polattimur, R. (2020). Dog behavior recognition and tracking based on faster R-CNN. *Journal of the Faculty of Engineering and Architecture of Gazi University*, *35*(2), 819–834.

Dawei, X., & Liqiu, J. (2018). Design of Real-Time Communication Social Software Based on XMPP. *2018 IEEE International Conference of Safety Produce Informatization (IICSPI)*, 829-833. 10.1109/IICSPI.2018.8690410

De Donno, M., Tange, K., & Dragoni, N. (2019). Foundations and Evolution of Modern Computing Paradigms: Cloud, IoT, Edge, and Fog. *IEEE Access: Practical Innovations, Open Solutions*, *7*, 150936–150948. doi:10.1109/ACCESS.2019.2947652

de Oliveira Neto, J. S., & Kofuji, S. T. (2016). Inclusive Smart City: An Exploratory Study. In UAHCI 2016 (LNCS, vol. 9738, 456-465). Cham: Springer.

Dead Band Plus Hysteresis Estimation with ValveLink Diagnostics. (2020, January 10). Product Bulletin, Fisher Controls International. Retrieved from http://www.documentation.emersonprocess.com/groups/public/documents/bulletins/d103549x012.pdf

Decandia, M., Giovanetti, V., Molle, G., Acciaro, M., Mameli, M., Cabiddu, A., Cossu, R., Serra, M., Manca, C., Rassu, S., & Dimauro, C. (2018). The effect of different time epoch settings on the classification of sheep behaviour using tri-axial accelerometry. *Computers and Electronics in Agriculture*, *154*, 112–119. doi:10.1016/j.compag.2018.09.002

Demaagd, K., Oliver, A., Oostendorp, N., & Scott, K. (2012). *Practical Computer Vision with SimpleCV*. O'Reilly Media.

den Uijl, I., Gómez Álvarez, C. B., Bartram, D., Dror, Y., Holland, R., & Cook, A. (2017). External validation of a collar-mounted triaxial accelerometer for second-by-second monitoring of eight behavioural states in dogs. *PLoS One*, *12*(11), 1–13. doi:10.1371/journal.pone.0188481 PMID:29186154

Deniz, F., Bagci, H., Korpeoglu, I., & Yazici, A. (2016). An adaptive, energy-aware and distributed fault-tolerant topology-control algorithm for heterogeneous wireless sensor networks. *Ad Hoc Networks*, *44*, 104–117. doi:10.1016/j.adhoc.2016.02.018

Di Summa, M., Grosso, A., & Locatelli, M. (2012). Branch and Cut Algorithms for Detecting Critical Nodes in Undirected Graphs. *Computational Optimization and Applications*, *53*(3), 649–680. doi:10.100710589-012-9458-y

Diosdado, J. A. V., Barker, Z. E., Hodges, H. R., Amory, J. R., Croft, D. P., Bell, N. J., & Codling, E. A. (2015). Classification of behaviour in housed dairy cows using an accelerometer-based activity monitoring system. *Animal Biotelemetry*, *3*(1), 1–14. doi:10.118640317-015-0045-8

Dissanayake, D. M. C., & Jayasena, K. P. N. (2017). A cloud platform for big IoT data analytics by combining batch and stream processing technologies. *2017 National Information Technology Conference (NITC)*, 40-45. 10.1109/NITC.2017.8285647

Dizdarevic, J., Carpio, F., Jukan, A., & Masip-Bruin, X. (2020, January 10). *Survey of Communication Protocols for Internet-of-Things and Related Challenges of Fog and Cloud Computing Integration*. Retrieved from https://arxiv.org/abs/1804.01747

Dobrilovic, D., & Zeljko, S. (2016). Design of open-source platform for introducing Internet of Things in university curricula. *2016 IEEE 11th International Symposium on Applied Computational Intelligence and Informatics (SACI)*, 273-276. 10.1109/SACI.2016.7507384

Dorri, A., Kanhere, S.S., Jurdak, R., & Gauravaram, P. (2017). *LSB: A Lightweight Scalable BlockChain for IoT Security and Privacy*. ArXiv, abs/1712.02969.

Dosilovic, F. K., Brcic, M., & Hlupic, N. (2018). Explainable artificial intelligence: A survey. In *41st International Convention on Information and Communication Technology, Electronics and Microelectronics (MIPRO)*. (pp. 210-215). IEEE. 10.23919/MIPRO.2018.8400040

Doukas, C. (2012). Building Internet of Things with the Arduino. Amazon.com, CreateSpace Independent Publishing Platform.

Draishpits, G. (2016). *Peer-to-Peer Communication in Wireless Networks as an Alternative to Internet Access*. Open University of Israel.

Duarte, K., Cec'ılio, J., S'a Silva, J., & Furtado, P. (2008). Information and Assisted Navigation System for Blind People. *8th International Conference on Sensing Technology*, 470-473.

Dunkels, A. (2003, May). Full TCP/IP for 8-bit architectures. In *Proceedings of the 1st international conference on Mobile systems, applications and services* (pp. 85-98). Academic Press.

Dunkels, A. (2007). Rime-a lightweight layered communication stack for sensor networks. In *Proceedings of the European Conference on Wireless Sensor Networks (EWSN), Poster/Demo session, Delft, The Netherlands* (Vol. 44). Academic Press.

Dunkels, A., Gronvall, B., & Voigt, T. (2004). Contiki-a lightweight and flexible operating system for tiny networked sensors. In *29th annual IEEE international conference on local computer networks* (pp. 455-462). IEEE. 10.1109/LCN.2004.38

Dunkels, A., Schmidt, O., Voigt, T., & Ali, M. (2006). Protothreads: Simplifying event-driven programming of memory-constrained embedded systems. In *Proceedings of the 4th international conference on Embedded networked sensor systems* (pp. 29-42). 10.1145/1182807.1182811

Dupont, C., Vecchio, M., Pham, C., Diop, B., Dupont, C., Koffi, S., & Pathan, K. (2018). An Open IoT Platform to Promote Eco-Sustainable Innovation in Western Africa: Real Urban and Rural Testbeds. *Wireless Communications and Mobile Computing*, *2018*, 1–17. Advance online publication. doi:10.1155/2018/1028578

Dziubany, M., Garling, M., Schmeink, A., Burger, G., Dartmann, G., Naumann, S., & Gollmer, K.-U. (2019). Machine learning-based artificial nose on a low-cost IoT-hardware. *Big Data Analytics for Cyber-Physical Systems*, 239-257. doi:10.1016/B978-0-12-816637-6.00011-7

ectriCChain. (2018). *ElectriCChain The Solar Energy Blockchain Project for Climate Change and Beyond*. Retrieved from https://www.electricchain.org/

Elmannai, W., & Elleithy, K. (2017). Sensor-Based Assistive Devices for Visually-Impaired People: Current Status, Challenges, and Future Directions. *Sensors (Basel)*, *17*(3), 565.

Embedded Computing: Arduino Tian. (2020, January 3). Retrieved from https://embeddedcomputing.weebly.com/arduino-tian.html

Escalante, H. J., Rodriguez, S. V., Cordero, J., Kristensen, A. R., & Cornou, C. (2013). Sow-activity classification from acceleration patterns: A machine learning approach. *Computers and Electronics in Agriculture*, *93*, 17–26. doi:10.1016/j.compag.2013.01.003

European Commission announces a €3 million Horizon Prize to develop a tactile display for the visually impaired. (2020, January 2). Retrieved from https://ec.europa.eu/digital-single-market/en/news/european-commission-announces-eu3-million-horizon-prize-develop-tactile-display-visually

Eurostat. (2020, January 10). *Sustainable development in the European Union: Monitoring Report on Progress Towards the SDGS in an EU Context*. Retrieved from http://ec.europa.eu/budget/img/budget4results/SustainableDevelopmentInTheEU.pdf

Eyal, I., Gencer, A. E., Sirer, E. G., & Renesse, R. V. (2016). *Bitcoin-NG: A Scalable Blockchain Protocol*. NSDI.

Fang, S.-H., & Lin, T.-N. (2008). Indoor Location System Based on Discriminant-Adaptive Neural Network in IEEE 802.11 Environments. *IEEE Transactions on Neural Networks*, *19*(11), 1973–1978. doi:10.1109/TNN.2008.2005494 PMID:19000967

Fan, X., & Chai, Q. (2018). Roll-DPoS: A Randomized Delegated Proof of Stake Scheme for Scalable Blockchain-Based Internet of Things Systems. In *Proceedings of the 15th EAI International Conference on Mobile and Ubiquitous Systems: Computing, Networking and Services*. ACM Press.

Faragher, R., & Harle, R. (2015). Location Fingerprinting With Bluetooth Low Energy Beacons. *IEEE Journal on Selected Areas in Communications*, *33*(11), 2418–2428.

Farjow, W., Chehri, A., Hussein, M., & Fernando, X. (2011). *Support Vector Machines for indoor sensor localization*. Paper presented at the meeting of the 2011 IEEE Wireless Communications and Networking Conference, Cancun, Mexico. 10.1109/WCNC.2011.5779231

Farrugia, D., Zerafa, C., Cini, T., Kuasney, B., & Livori, K. (2021). A Real-Time Prescriptive Solution for Explainable Cyber-Fraud Detection Within the iGaming Industry. *SN Computer Science*, *2*(3), 1–9. doi:10.100742979-021-00623-7 PMID:33880451

Fass, B. (2020, January 3). *A Heart Rate During a Heart Attack*. Retrieved from https://www.livestrong.com/article/344010-the-normal-heart-rate-during-a-panic-attack/

Fehlmann, G., O'Riain, M. J., Hopkins, P. W., O'Sullivan, J., Holton, M. D., Shepard, E. L., & King, A. J. (2017). Identification of behaviours from accelerometer data in a wild social primate. *Animal Biotelemetry*, *5*(1), 1–11. doi:10.118640317-017-0121-3

Fellous, J.-M., Sapiro, G., Rossi, A., Mayberg, H., & Ferrante, M. (2019). Explainable Artificial Intelligence for Neuroscience: Behavioral Neurostimulation. *Frontiers in Neuroscience*, *13*, 1–14. doi:10.3389/fnins.2019.01346 PMID:31920509

Fernandez-Luque, F., Zapata, J., & Ruiz, R. (2013). PIR-Based Motion Patterns Classification for AmI Systems. *Proc. of Conference on the Interplay Between Natural and Artificial Computation*, 355-364.

Ferreira, C., Maia, L. F., Salles, C., Trinta, F., & Viana, W. (2017). A Model-based Approach for Designing Location-based Games. *16th Brazilian Symposium on Computer Games and Digital Entertainment (SBGames)*, 29-38. 10.1109/SBGames.2017.00012

Filament. (2018). *Filament's Industrial Internet of Things Blockchain Solution Wins 2018 IoT Innovator Award*. Retrieved from https://globenewswire.com/news-release/2018/09/26/1576581/0/en/Filament-s-Industrial-Internet-of-Things-Blockchain-Solution-Wins-2018-IoT-Innovator-Award.html

Flores, G. H., Griffin, T. D., & Jadav, D. (2017). An iBeacon Training App for Indoor Fingerprinting. *5th IEEE International Conference on Mobile Cloud Computing, Services, and Engineering*, 173-176.

Floros, G., & Charalampidou, P. (2019). Website localization: Asymmetries and terminological challenges. *The Journal of Internationalization and Localization*, 6(2), 2. doi:10.1075/jial.19004.cha

Foukalas, F. (2020). Cognitive IoT platform for fog computing industrial applications. *Computers & Electrical Engineering, 87*.

Frank, E., & Witten, I.-E. (1998). Generating Accurate Rule Sets Without Global Optimization. In *Proceedings of the Fifteenth International Conference on Machine Learning*. (pp. 144-151). Academic Press.

French, S. (2017). *Visual impairment and work: experiences of visually impaired people*. Routledge.

From KY-039 To Heart Rate. (2020, January 3). Retrieved from https://www.hackster.io/Johan_Ha/from-ky-039-to-heart-rate-0abfca

Gajski, D. D., Abdi, S., Gerstlauer, A., & Schirner, G. (2009). Embedded System Design: Modeling, Synthesis and Verification. Springer-Verlag.

Gama, J. R., & Lopes, F. V. (2017). On compensating synchronization errors in two-terminal based fault location approaches. *Workshop on Communication Networks and Power Systems (WCNPS)*, 1-4. 10.1109/WCNPS.2017.8253082

Gao, L., Campbell, H. A., Bidder, O. R., & Hunter, J. (2013). A Web-based semantic tagging and activity recognition system for species' accelerometry data. *Ecological Informatics*, 13, 47–56. doi:10.1016/j.ecoinf.2012.09.003

Gardašević, G., Veletić, M., Maletić, N., Vasiljević, D., Radusinović, I., Tomović, S., & Radonjić, M. (2016). The IoT Architectural Framework, Design Issues and Application Domains. *Wireless Personal Communications*, 92(1), 127–148. doi:10.100711277-016-3842-3

Gast, M. S. (2015). *Building Applications with iBeacon: Proximity and Location Services with Bluetooth Low Energy*. O'Reilly Media.

Gay, D., Levis, P., Von Behren, R., Welsh, M., Brewer, E., & Culler, D. (2003). The nesC language: A holistic approach to networked embedded systems. *ACM SIGPLAN Notices*, 38(5), 1–11. doi:10.1145/780822.781133

Gazis, V. (2016). A survey of standards for Machine to Machine (M2M) and the Internet of Things. *IEEE Communications Surveys and Tutorials*, 19(1), 482–511. doi:10.1109/COMST.2016.2592948

George, G., Namdev, A., & Sarma, S. (2018). Animal action recognition: Analysis of various approaches. *International Journal of Engineering Sciences & Research Technology*, 7(4), 548–554.

Gerencser, L., Vasarhelyi, G., Nagy, M., Vicsek, T., & Miklosi, A. (2013). Identification of behaviour in freely moving dogs (Canis familiaris) using inertial sensors. *PLoS One*, 8(10), 1–14. doi:10.1371/journal.pone.0077814 PMID:24250745

Gerybadze, A., & Reger, G. (1997). Internationalization of R&D and global management of technological competencies within transnational corporations. Innovation in Technology Management. The Key to Global Leadership. PICMET '97, 979-982. doi:10.1109/PICMET.1997.653755

Gilad, Y., Hemo, R., Micali, S., Vlachos, G., & Zeldovich, N. (2017). Algorand: Scaling Byzantine Agreements for Cryptocurrencies. In *Proceedings of the 26th Symposium on Operating Systems Principles*. ACM Press.

Gilchrist, A. (2016). *Industry 4.0: The Industrial Internet of Things*. Apress.

Giovanetti, V., Decandia, M., Molle, G., Acciaro, M., Mameli, M., Cabiddu, A., Cossu, R., Serra, M., Manca, C., Rassu, S., & Dimauro, C. (2017). Automatic classification system for grazing, ruminating and resting behaviour of dairy sheep using a tri-axial accelerometer. *Livestock Science*, *196*, 42–48. doi:10.1016/j.livsci.2016.12.011

Girau, R., Martis, S., & Atzori, L. (2017, February). Lysis: A Platform for IoT Distributed Applications Over Socially Connected Objects. *IEEE Internet of Things Journal*, *4*(1), 40–51. doi:10.1109/JIOT.2016.2616022

Giri, A., Dutta, S., Neogy, S., Dahal, K., & Pervez, Z. (2017). Internet of things (IoT): a survey on architecture, enabling technologies, applications and challenges. In *Proceedings of the 1st International Conference on Internet of Things and Machine Learning (IML '17)*. Association for Computing Machinery. 10.1145/3109761.3109768

Golledge, R. G. (1993). Geography and the Disabled: A Survey with Special Reference to Vision Impaired and Blind Populations. *Transactions of the Institute of British Geographers*, *18*, 63–85.

Gonçalves, L. B. L., Costa, F. G., Neves, L. A., Ueyama, J., Zafalon, G. F. D., Montez, C., & Pinto, A. S. R. (2015). Influence of Mobility Models in Precision Spray Aided by Wireless Sensor Networks. *Journal of Physics: Conference Series*, *574*, 012153. doi:10.1088/1742-6596/574/1/012153

Goodwyn, M., Bell, E. C., & Singletary, C. (2009). *Factors that Contribute to the Success of Blind Adults. Research Report of the Professional Development and Research Institute on Blindness*. Louisiana Tech University.

Gori, M., Cappagli, G., Tonelli, A., Baud-Bovy, G., & Finocchietti, S. (2016). Devices for Visually Impaired People: High Technological Devices with Low User Acceptance and no Adaptability for Children. *Neuroscience and Biobehavioral Reviews*, *69*, 79–88.

GPS. (2017). GPS: Global Positioning System (or Navstar Global Positioning System). In *Wide Area Augmentation System (WAAS) Performance Standard, Section B.3, Abbreviations and Acronyms*. Wayback Machine.

Grunewalder, S., Broekhuis, F., Macdonald, D. W., Wilson, A. M., McNutt, J. W., Shawe-Taylor, J., & Hailes, S. (2012). Movement activity based classification of animal behaviour with an application to data from cheetah (Acinonyx jubatus). *PLoS One*, *7*(11), 1–11. doi:10.1371/journal.pone.0049120 PMID:23185301

Guan, H., Motohashi, N., Maki, T., & Yamaai, T. (2020). Cattle identification and activity recognition by surveillance camera. *Electronic Imaging*, *2020*(12), 174–1. doi:10.2352/ISSN.2470-1173.2020.12.FAIS-174

Guo, A., Satake, S., & Imai, M. (2008). Home-Explorer: Ontology-based Physical Artifact Search and Hidden Object Detection System. *Mobile Information Systems*, *4*(2), 2. doi:10.1155/2008/463787

Guo, B., Fujimura, R., Zhang, R., & Imai, M. (2011). Design-in-Play: Improving the Variability of Indoor Pervasive Games. *Multimedia Tools and Applications*, *59*(1), 259–277. doi:10.100711042-010-0711-z

Gutierrez, J., Villa-Medina, J. F., Nieto-Garibay, A., & Porta-Gandara, M. A. (2014). Automated Irrigation System Using a Wireless Sensor Network and GPRS Module. *IEEE Transactions on Instrumentation and Measurement*, *63*(1), 166–176. doi:10.1109/tim.2013.2276487

Gutierrez, N., Belmonte, C., Hanvey, J., Espejo, R., & Dong, Z. (2014, April). Indoor localization for mobile devices. In *Proceedings of the 11th IEEE International Conference on Networking, Sensing and Control* (pp. 173-178). IEEE. 10.1109/ICNSC.2014.6819620

Haghi, A., Burney, K., Kidd, F. S., Valiente, L. & Peng, Y. (2017). Fast-paced development of a smart campus IoT platform. *2017 Global Internet of Things Summit (GIoTS),* 1-6. . doi:10.1109/GIOTS.2017.8016214

Hammond, T. T., Springthorpe, D., Walsh, R. E., & Berg-Kirkpatrick, T. (2016). Using accelerometers to remotely and automatically characterize behavior in small animals. *The Journal of Experimental Biology, 219*(11), 1618–1624. doi:10.1242/jeb.136135 PMID:26994177

Haq, M. A. U., Kamboh, H. M. A., Akram, U., Sohail, A., & Hifsa, I. (2017). Indoor Localization Using Improved Multinomial Naïve Bayes Technique. In *Proceedings of the Third International Afro-European Conference for Industrial Advancement — AECIA 2016* (vol. 565, pp. 321-329). Springer.

Hau, E., & Aparício, M. (2008). Software internationalization and localization in web based ERP. *Proceedings of the 26th annual ACM international conference on Design of communication,* 175-180. 10.1145/1456536.1456570

HC-SR04 Ultrasonic Range Sensor on the Raspberry Pi. (2020, January 3). Retrieved from https://www.modmypi.com/blog/hc-sr04-ultrasonic-range-sensor-on-the-raspberry-pi

He, C., Guo, S., Wu, Y., & Yang, Y. (2016). A novel radio map construction method to reduce collection effort for indoor localization. *Measurement, 94,* 423–431. doi:10.1016/j.measurement.2016.08.021

Henzinger, M. R., Rao, S., & Gabow, H. N. (2000). Computing vertex connectivity: New bounds from old techniques. *Journal of Algorithms, 34*(2), 222–250. doi:10.1006/jagm.1999.1055

Holm, S. (2009, April). Hybrid ultrasound-RFID indoor positioning: Combining the best of both worlds. In *2009 IEEE International Conference on RFID* (pp. 155-162). IEEE.

Holt, J., & Perry, S. (2008). *SysML for systems engineering* (Vol. 7). IET. doi:10.1049/PBPC007E

Holton, B. (2020, January 13). *MyReader and MyEye from OrCam: Text and Item Recognition at the Touch of a Finger. AccessWorld.* Retrieved from https://www.afb.org/afbpress/pubnew.asp?DocID=aw180205

Hopali, E., & Vayvay, Ö. (2018). Industry 4.0 as the Last Industrial Revolution and its Opportunities for Developing Countries. In R. Brunet-Thornton & F. Martinez (Eds.), *Analyzing the Impacts of Industry 4.0 in Modern Business Environments* (pp. 65–80). IGI Global.

Horst, F., Slijepcevic, D., Lapuschkin, S., Raberger, A.-M., Zeppelzauer, M., Samek, W., Breiteneder, C., Schöllhorn, W. I., & Horsak, B. (2019, December 16). On the Understanding and Interpretation of Machine Learning Predictions in Clinical Gait Analysis Using Explainable Artificial Intelligence. *Arxiv.* https://arxiv.org/abs/1912.07737v1

Hossain, M. S., Muhammad, G., & Guizani, N. (2020). Explainable AI and Mass Surveillance System-Based Healthcare Framework to Combat COVID-I9 Like Pandemics. *IEEE Network, 34*(4), 126–132. doi:10.1109/MNET.011.2000458

Hozdić, E. (2015). Smart Factory for Industry 4.0: A Review. *International Journal of Modern Manufacturing Technologies, 7*(1), 28–35.

Hrisko, J. (2020, January 3). *Using Raspberry Pi, HM-10, and Bluepy To Develop An iBeacon Mesh Network (Part 1).* Retrieved from https://engineersportal.com/blog/2017/12/31/using-raspberry-pi-hm-10-and-bluepy-to-develop-an-ibeacon-mesh-network-part-1

Huang, J., Kong, L., Chen, G., Wu, M., Liu, X., & Zeng, P. (2019). Towards Secure Industrial IoT: Blockchain System With Credit-Based Consensus Mechanism. *IEEE Transactions on Industrial Informatics*, *15*, 3680–3689.

Huang, X., Chen, H., Wang, L., & Zeng, S. (2019). How Does Leader Narcissism Influence Firm Internationalization? *IEEE Transactions on Engineering Management*, 1–14. doi:10.1109/TEM.2019.2900169

Hudec, M., & Smutny, Z. (2017). RUDO: A Home Ambient Intelligence System for Blind People. *Sensors (Basel)*, *17*(8), 1926.

Hu, H., Wen, Y., Chua, T.-S., & Li, X. (2014). Toward scalable systems for Big Data analytics: A technology tutorial. *IEEE Access: Practical Innovations, Open Solutions*, *2*, 652–687. doi:10.1109/ACCESS.2014.2332453

IEEE Draft Recommended. (2019). *Practice for Common Framework of Location Services (LS) for Healthcare*. IEEE P1847/D1.

Ilas, M.-E., & Ilas, C. (2018). A New Method of Histogram Computation for Efficient Implementation of the HOG Algorithm. *Computers*, *7*(1), 18.

Imran, M., Alnuem, M. A., Fayed, M. S., & Alamri, A. (2013). Localized Algorithm for Segregation of Critical/Non-critical Nodes in Mobile Ad Hoc and Sensor Networks. *Procedia Computer Science*, *19*, 1167–1172. doi:10.1016/j.procs.2013.06.166

Intorobotics. (2020, January 10). *5 Cheap Methods For Indoor Robot Localization: BLE Beacon, AprilTags, WiFi SubPos, NFC and RFID*. Retrieved from https://www.intorobotics.com/5-cheap-methods-for-indoor-robot-localization-ble-beacon-apriltags-wifi-subpos-nfc-and-rfid/

ISO/IEC JTC1/SC42/WG2 IS 20547-3 (2019) *Big data Reference architecture*.

ISO/IEC JTC1/WG10 (2015) *Internet of Things*. Retrieved from http://isotc.iso.org/livelink/livelink/open/jtc1wg10 ISO/IEC JTC1/WG9

ISO/IEC JTC1/WG9 (2014) *Big data Preliminary report*.

ITU-Telecommunication Standardization Sector. (2012). *ITU-T Y.4000/Y.2060 Overview of the Internet of things*. Retrieved from https://www.itu.int/en/ITU-T/gsi/iot/

ITU-Telecommunication Standardization Sector. (2016). *ITU-T Series Y Supplement 40, Big data standardization roadmap*. Retrieved from https://www.itu.int/en/ITU-T/techwatch/Pages/big-data-standards.aspx

Iyer, V., Nandakumar, R., Wang, A., Fuller, S. B., & Gollakota, S. (2019). Living IoT: A Flying Wireless Platform on Live Insects. In *The 25th Annual International Conference on Mobile Computing and Networking (MobiCom '19)*. Association for Computing Machinery. 10.1145/3300061.3300136

Jacobson, R. D., & Kitchin, R. M. (1997). GIS and People with Visual Impairments or Blindness: Exploring the Potential for Education, Orientation, and Navigation. *Transactions in GIS*, *2*(4), 315–332.

Jaiganesh, S., Gunaseelan, K., & Ellappan, V. (2017). IOT agriculture to improve food and farming technology. In *2017 Conference on Emerging Devices and Smart Systems (ICEDSS)* (pp. 260-266). IEEE. 10.1109/ICEDSS.2017.8073690

Jamborsalamati, P., Fernandez, E., Hossain, M. J., & Rafi, F. H. M. (2017). Design and implementation of a cloud-based IoT platform for data acquisition and device supply management in smart buildings. *2017 Australasian Universities Power Engineering Conference (AUPEC)*, 1-6. 10.1109/AUPEC.2017.8282504

Jayaraman, P. P., Palmer, D., Zaslavsky, A., & Georgakopoulos, D. (2015). Do-it-Yourself Digital Agriculture applications with semantically enhanced IoT platform. *2015 IEEE Tenth International Conference on Intelligent Sensors, Sensor Networks and Information Processing (ISSNIP)*, 1-6. 10.1109/ISSNIP.2015.7106951

Jayaraman, P. P., Yavari, A., Georgakopoulos, D., Morshed, A., & Zaslavsky, A. (2016). Internet of Things Platform for Smart Farming: Experiences and Lessons Learnt. *Sensors (Basel)*, 6(11), 1884. doi:10.339016111884 PMID:27834862

JDChain. (2019). *JD Enterprise Blockchain Service*. Retrieved from http://blockchain.jd.com/blockchain_store/pc/index.html#/BlockChainTrace

Jiang, Q., Li, K., Zhou, M., & Tian, Z. (2015). Indoor Location in WLAN Based on Competitive Agglomeration Algorithm. *International Journal of Innovative Science, Engineering & Technology, 2*(1).

Jiang, Y., Wang, C., Huang, Y., Long, S., & Huo, Y. (2018). A Cross-Chain Solution to Integration of IoT Tangle for Data Access Management. *2018 IEEE International Conference on Internet of Things (iThings) and IEEE Green Computing and Communications (GreenCom) and IEEE Cyber, Physical and Social Computing (CPSCom) and IEEE Smart Data (SmartData)*, 1035-1041.

Jino Ramson, S. R., & Moni, D. J. (2017). Applications of wireless sensor networks - A survey. *International Conference on Innovations in Electrical, Electronics, Instrumentation and Media Technology (ICEEIMT)*, 325-329. 10.1109/ICIEEIMT.2017.8116858

Johnsen, F. T., Zieliński, Z., Wrona, K., Suri, N., Fuchs, C., Pradhan, M., Furtak, J., Vasilache, B., Pellegrini, V., Dyk, M., & Marks, M. (2018). Application of IoT in military operations in a smart city. In *2018 International Conference on Military Communications and Information Systems (ICMCIS)* (pp. 1-8). IEEE. 10.1109/ICMCIS.2018.8398690

Jorgic, M., Goel, N., Kalaichevan, K., Nayak, A., & Stojmenovic, I. (2007). Localized detection of k-connectivity in wireless ad hoc, actuator and sensor networks. *Proceedings of 16th International Conference on Computer Communications and Networks, ICCCN 2007*, 33-38. 10.1109/ICCCN.2007.4317793

Jorgic, M., Hauspie, M., Simplot-Ryl, D., & Stojmenovic, I. (2004). Localized Algorithms for Detection of Critical Nodes and Links for Connectivity in Adhoc Networks. *Proceedings of the 3rd IFIP MED-HOC-NET Workshop*, 360-371.

Joseph, J. (2014). QR Code Based Indoor Navigation with Voice Response. *International Journal of Scientific Research*, 3(11), 923–926.

Kafle, V. P., Fukushima, Y., & Hara, H. (2016). Internet of Things Standardization in ITU and prospective networking technologies. *IEEE Communications Magazine*, 54(9), 43–49. doi:10.1109/MCOM.2016.7565271

Kaloxylos, A., Groumas, A., Sarris, V., Katsikas, L., Magdalinos, P., Antoniou, E., ... Maestre Terol, C. (2014). A cloud-based Farm Management System: Architecture and implementation. *Computers and Electronics in Agriculture, 100*, 168–179. doi:10.1016/j.compag.2013.11.014

Kamgueu, P. O., Nataf, E., & Djotio, T. (2017). Architecture for an efficient integration of wireless sensor networks to the Internet through Internet of Things gateways. *International Journal of Distributed Sensor Networks, 13*(11), 1550147717744735. doi:10.1177/1550147717744735

Kamminga, J. W., Bisby, H. C., Le, D. V., Meratnia, N., & Havinga, P. J. (2017, September). Generic online animal activity recognition on collar tags. In *Proceedings of the 2017 ACM International Joint Conference on Pervasive and Ubiquitous Computing and Proceedings of the 2017 ACM International Symposium on Wearable Computers* (pp. 597-606). 10.1145/3123024.3124407

Kanmaz, M., & Aydın, M. A. (2019). Comparison of dv-hop based indoor positioning methods in wireless sensor networks and new approach with k-means++ clustering method. *Journal of the Faculty of Engineering and Architecture of Gazi University, 34*(2), 975–986.

Karaduman, B., Aşıcı, T., Challenger, M., & Eslampanah, R. (2018). A cloud and Contiki based fire detection system using multi-hop wireless sensor networks. In *Proceedings of the Fourth International Conference on Engineering & MIS 2018* (pp. 1-5). 10.1145/3234698.3234764

Karaduman, B., Challenger, M., & Eslampanah, R. (2018). ContikiOS based library fire detection system. In *2018 5th International Conference on Electrical and Electronic Engineering (ICEEE)* (pp. 247-251). IEEE. 10.1109/ICEEE2.2018.8391340

Karaduman, B., Challenger, M., Eslampanah, R., Denil, J., & Vangheluwe, H. (2020). Analyzing WSN-based IoT Systems using MDE Techniques and Petri-net Models. Academic Press.

Karaduman, B., Challenger, M., Eslampanah, R., Denil, J., & Vangheluwe, H. (2020). Platform-specific Modeling for RIOT based IoT Systems. In *Proceedings of the IEEE/ACM 42nd International Conference on Software Engineering Workshops* (pp. 639-646). 10.1145/3387940.3392194

Karimpour, N., Karaduman, B., Ural, A., Challenger, M., & Dagdeviren, O. (2019). Iot based hand hygiene compliance monitoring. In *2019 International Symposium on Networks, Computers and Communications (ISNCC)* (pp. 1-6). IEEE.

Karimpour, N., Karaduman, B., Ural, A., Challenger, M., & Dagdeviren, O. (2019). IoT based Hand Hygiene Compliance Monitoring. In *2019 International Symposium on Networks, Computers and Communications (ISNCC)*, (pp. 1-6). IEEE.

Karthikeyan, P., Manikandakumar, M., Sri Subarnaa, D. K., & Priyadharshini, P. (2020). Weed Identification in Agriculture Field Through IoT. *Advances in Smart System Technologies,* 495–505. doi:10.1007/978-981-15-5029-4_41

Khazaei, H., Bannazadeh, H., & Leon-Garcia, A. (2017). SAVI-IoT: A Self-Managing Containerized IoT Platform. *2017 IEEE 5th International Conference on Future Internet of Things and Cloud (FiCloud)*, 227-234. 10.1109/FiCloud.2017.27

Khelifi, F., Bradai, A., Benslimane, A., Rawat, P., & Atri, M. (2019). A survey of localization systems in internet of things. *Mobile Networks and Applications, 24*(3), 761–785. doi:10.100711036-018-1090-3

Khodabandehloo, E., Riboni, D., & Alimohammadi, A. (2021). HealthXAI: Collaborative and explainable AI for supporting early diagnosis of cognitive decline. *Future Generation Computer Systems, 116*, 168–189. doi:10.1016/j.future.2020.10.030

Khodadadi, F., Dastjerdi, A. V., & Buyya, R. (2017). Internet of Things: An Overview. ArXiv, abs/1703.06409.

Kiayias, A., Russell, A., David, B.M., & Oliynykov, R. (2016). Ouroboros: A Provably Secure Proof-of-Stake Blockchain Protocol. *IACR Cryptol. ePrint Arch., 2016*, 889.

Kildall, S. (2020, January 3). *Raspberry Pi: Launch Python Script on Startup.* https://www.instructables.com/id/Raspberry-Pi-Launch-Python-script-on-startup/

Kim, G., Kang, S., Park, J., & Chung, K. (2019). An MQTT-Based Context-Aware Autonomous System in oneM2M Architecture. *IEEE Internet of Things Journal, 6*(5), 8519–8528. doi:10.1109/JIOT.2019.2919971

Kim, T., Noh, J., & Cho, S. (2019). SCC: Storage Compression Consensus for Blockchain in Lightweight IoT Network. *2019 IEEE International Conference on Consumer Electronics (ICCE)*, 1-4.

Kim, Y.-D., Yang, Y.-M., Kang, W.-S., & Kim, D.-K. (2014). On the design of beacon based wireless sensor network for agricultural emergency monitoring systems. *Computer Standards & Interfaces*, *36*(2), 288–299. doi:10.1016/j.csi.2011.05.004

Klein, S. (2017). *IoT Solutions in Microsoft's Azure IoT Suite*. Apress. doi:10.1007/978-1-4842-2143-3

Korobeinikova, T. I., Volkova, N. P., Kozhushko, S. P., Holub, D. O., Zinukova, N. V., Kozhushkina, T. L., & Vakarchuk, S. B. (2020). Google cloud services as a way to enhance learning and teaching at university. *Proceedings of the 7th Workshop on Cloud Technologies in Education (CTE 2019)*.

Kotla, R., Alvisi, L., Dahlin, M., Clement, A., & Wong, E. L. (2007). *Zyzzyva: Speculative byzantine fault tolerance*. TOCS.

Kouicem, D. E., Bouabdallah, A., & Lakhlef, H. (2018). Internet of things security: A top-down survey. *Computer Networks*, *141*, 199–221. doi:10.1016/j.comnet.2018.03.012

Kraijak, S., & Tuwanut, P. (2015). A survey on IoT architectures, protocols, applications, security, privacy, real-world implementation and future trends. *11th International Conference on Wireless Communications, Networking and Mobile Computing (WiCOM 2015)*, 1-6. 10.1049/cp.2015.0714

Krylovskiy, A., Jahn, M., & Patti, E. (2015). Designing a Smart City Internet of Things Platform with Microservice Architecture. *2015 3rd International Conference on Future Internet of Things and Cloud*, 25-30. 10.1109/FiCloud.2015.55

Kubitza, T., & Schmidt, A. (2016). Rapid interweaving of smart things with the meSchup IoT platform. In *Proceedings of the 2016 ACM International Joint Conference on Pervasive and Ubiquitous Computing: Adjunct (UbiComp '16)*. Association for Computing Machinery.:10.1145/2968219.2971379

Kumar, D., Kumar, P., & Ashok, A. (2020). Introduction to multimedia big data computing for IoT. In S. Tanwar, S. Tyagi, & N. Kumar (Eds.), *Multimedia big data computing for IoT applications* (pp. 3–36). Springer.

Kuo, Y., Li, C., Jhang J. & Lin, S. (2018). Design of a Wireless Sensor Network-Based IoT Platform for Wide Area and Heterogeneous Applications. *IEEE Sensors Journal, 18*(12), 5187-5197. . doi:10.1109/JSEN.2018.2832664

Kurniawan, A. (2018). *Learning AWS IoT: Effectively manage connected devices on the AWS cloud using services such as AWS Greengrass, AWS button, predictive analytics and machine learning*. Packt Publishing Ltd.

Lagkas, T. D. (2018). Network Protocols, Schemes, and Mechanisms for Internet of Things (IoT): Features, Open Challenges, and Trends. *Wireless Communications and Mobile Computing*, *2018*, 1–23.

Lalou, M., Tahraoui, M. A., & Kheddouci, H. (2018). The critical node detection problem in networks: A survey. *Computer Science Review*, *28*, 92–117. doi:10.1016/j.cosrev.2018.02.002

Lao, L., Li, Z., Hou, S., Xiao, B., Guo, S., & Yang, Y. (2020). A Survey of IoT Applications in Blockchain Systems: Architecture, Consensus, and Traffic Modeling. *ACM Computing Surveys*, *53*, 1–32.

Lathif, M. R., Nasirifard, P., & Jacobsen, H. (2018). CIDDS: A Configurable and Distributed DAG-based Distributed Ledger Simulation Framework. In *The 19th International Middleware Conference (Posters)*. New Yew: ACM Press.

Le Roux, S. P., Marias, J., Wolhuter, R., & Niesler, T. (2017). Animal-borne behaviour classification for sheep (Dohne Merino) and Rhinoceros (Ceratotherium simum and Diceros bicornis). *Animal Biotelemetry*, *5*(25), 1–13. doi:10.118640317-017-0140-0

Le Roux, S. P., Wolhuter, R., & Niesler, T. (2019). Energy-aware feature and model selection for onboard behavior classification in low-power animal borne sensor applications. *IEEE Sensors Journal*, *19*(7), 2722–2734. doi:10.1109/JSEN.2018.2886890

Lea, R., & Blackstock, M. (2014). City Hub: A Cloud-Based IoT Platform for Smart Cities. *2014 IEEE 6th International Conference on Cloud Computing Technology and Science*, 799-804. doi:10.1109/CloudCom.2014.65

Lee, C., & Lai, Y. H. (2016). Design and implementation of a universal smart energy management gateway based on the Internet of Things platform. *2016 IEEE International Conference on Consumer Electronics (ICCE)*, 67-68. doi: 10.1109/ICCE.2016.7430524

Lee, D., Moon, H., Oh, S., & Park, D. (2020). mIoT: Metamorphic IoT Platform for On-Demand Hardware Replacement in Large-Scaled IoT Applications. *Sensors (Basel)*, *2020*(20), 3337. doi:10.339020123337 PMID:32545495

Lee, S. K., Bae, M., & Kim, H. (2017). Future of IoT Networks: A Survey. *Applied Sciences (Basel, Switzerland)*, *7*(10), 1072. doi:10.3390/app7101072

Leikanger, T., Schuss, C., & Häkkinen, J. (2017). Near field communication as sensor to cloud service interface. 2017 IEEE Sensors, 1-3.

Levis, P., Madden, S., Polastre, J., Szewczyk, R., Whitehouse, K., Woo, A., & Culler, D. (2005). TinyOS: An operating system for sensor networks. In *Ambient intelligence* (pp. 115–148). Springer. doi:10.1007/3-540-27139-2_7

LewayHertz. (2019). *Blockchain Development for Startups and Enterprises | USA | UAE*. Retrieved from https://www. leewayhertz.com/

Li, X., Teng, L., Tang, H., Chen, J., Wang, H., Liu, Y., Fu, M. & Liang, J. (2021). ViPSN: A Vibration-Powered IoT Platform. *IEEE Internet of Things Journal, 8*(3), 1728-1739. . doi:10.1109/JIOT.2020.3016993

Lichtenberg, E., Majsztrik, J., & Saavoss, M. (2015). Grower demand for sensor-controlled irrigation. *Water Resources Research*, *51*(1), 341–358. doi:10.1002/2014wr015807

Li, H., Ota, K., & Dong, M. (2018). Learning IoT in Edge: Deep Learning for the Internet of Things with Edge Computing. *IEEE Network*, *32*(1), 96–101. doi:10.1109/MNET.2018.1700202

Li, J., Andrew, L. L., Foh, C. H., Zukerman, M., & Chen, H.-H. (2009). Connectivity, coverage and placement in wireless sensor networks. *Sensors (Basel)*, *9*(10), 7664–7693. doi:10.339091007664 PMID:22408474

Li, J., Liu, Y., Xie, J., Li, M., Sun, M., Liu, Z., & Jiang, S. (2019). A Remote Monitoring and Diagnosis Method Based on Four-Layer IoT Frame Perception. *IEEE Access: Practical Innovations, Open Solutions*, *7*, 144324–144338. doi:10.1109/ ACCESS.2019.2945076

Lin, Y. G. (2011). An Intelligent Monitoring System for Agriculture Based on Zigbee Wireless Sensor Networks. *Advanced Materials Research, 383-390*, 4358–4364. doi:10.4028/www.scientific.net/amr.383-390.4358

Lin, C., Han, G., Du, J., Xu, T., Shu, L., & Lv, Z. (2020). Spatiotemporal congestion-aware path planning toward intelligent transportation systems in software-defined smart city IoT. *IEEE Internet of Things Journal, 7*(9), 8012–8024. doi:10.1109/JIOT.2020.2994963

Ling, Q., & Tian, Z. (2007). Minimum node degree and *k*-connectivity of a wireless multihop network in bounded area. *IEEE Global Telecommunications Conference. GLOBECOM'07*, 1296-1301. 10.1109/GLOCOM.2007.249

Lin, Y. W., & Lin, C. Y. (2018). An Interactive Real-Time Locating System Based on Bluetooth Low-Energy Beacon Network. *Sensors (Basel)*, *18*(5), 1637.

Li, P., Yan, Y., Yang, P., Li, X., & Lin, Q. (2019). Coexist WiFi for ZigBee Networks With Fine-Grained Frequency Approach. *IEEE Access: Practical Innovations, Open Solutions*, *7*, 135363–135376. doi:10.1109/ACCESS.2019.2941963

Liu, W., Li, W., Yin, X., Yu, Q., & Jiang, H. (2015*).* Single terminal traveling wave fault location based on fault location algorithm integrating MMG with correlation function. *IEEE 5th International Conference on Electronics Information and Emergency Communication*, 289-292. 10.1109/ICEIEC.2015.7284541

Liu, H., Cao, X., He, J., Cheng, P., Li, C., Chen, J., & Sun, Y. (2015). Distributed Identification of the most Critical Node for Average Consensus. *IEEE Transactions on Signal Processing*, *63*(16), 4315–4328. doi:10.1109/TSP.2015.2441039

Liu, M., Yu, F. R., Teng, Y., Leung, V. C., & Song, M. (2019). Performance Optimization for Blockchain-Enabled Industrial Internet of Things (IIoT) Systems: A Deep Reinforcement Learning Approach. *IEEE Transactions on Industrial Informatics*, *15*, 3559–3570.

Louta, M., Sarigiannidis, P., Misra, S., Nicopolitidis, P., & Papadimitriou, G. (2014). RLAM: A Dynamic and Efficient Reinforcement Learning-Based Adaptive Mapping Scheme in Mobile WiMAX Networks. *Mobile Information Systems*, *10*(2), 173–196. doi:10.1155/2014/213056

Luan, Q., Fang, X., Ye, C., & Liu, Y. (2015). An integrated service system for agricultural drought monitoring and forecasting and irrigation amount forecasting. *2015 23rd International Conference on Geoinformatics.* doi:10.1109/geoinformatics.2015.7378617

Luhana, K. K., Schindler, C., & Slany, W. (2018). Streamlining mobile app deployment with Jenkins and Fastlane in the case of Catrobat's pocket code. *IEEE International Conference on Innovative Research and Development (ICIRD)*, 1-6. 10.1109/ICIRD.2018.8376296

Ma, M. (2018). Enhancing Privacy Using Location Semantics in Location Based Services. *IEEE 3rd International Conference on Big Data Analysis (ICBDA)*, 368-373. 10.1109/ICBDA.2018.8367709

Mahmoud, Q. H. & Qendri, D. (2016). The Sensorian IoT platform. *2016 13th IEEE Annual Consumer Communications & Networking Conference (CCNC)*, 286-287. . doi:10.1109/CCNC.2016.7444783

Mahmud, M. A., Bates, K., Wood, T., Abdelgawad, A., & Yelamarthi, K. (2018). A complete Internet of Things (IoT) platform for Structural Health Monitoring (SHM). *2018 IEEE 4th World Forum on Internet of Things (WF-IoT)*, 275-279. 10.1109/WF-IoT.2018.8355094

Makinen, A., Jimenez, J., & Morabito, R. (2017). ELIoT: Design of an emulated IoT platform. *2017 IEEE 28th Annual International Symposium on Personal, Indoor, and Mobile Radio Communications (PIMRC)*, 1-7. 10.1109/PIMRC.2017.8292769

Malaver, A., Motta, N., Corke, P., & Gonzalez, F. (2015). Development and Integration of a Solar Powered Unmanned Aerial Vehicle and a Wireless Sensor Network to Monitor Greenhouse Gases. *Sensors (Basel)*, *15*(2), 4072–4096. doi:10.3390150204072

Mallick, S. (2020, January 3). *Histogram of Oriented Gradients*. Retrieved from https://www.learnopencv.com/histogram-of-oriented-gradients/

Manikandakumar, M., Sri Subarnaa D. K., & Monica Grace R. (2019). A Detailed Study on Security Concerns of VANET and Cognitive Radio VANETs. *Cognitive Social Mining Applications in Data Analytics and Forensics*, 252–264. doi:10.4018/978-1-5225-7522-1.ch013

Manikandakumar, M., & Ramanujam, E. (2018). Security and Privacy Challenges in Big Data Environment. *Advances in Information Security, Privacy, and Ethics*, 315–325. doi:10.4018/978-1-5225-4100-4.ch017

Mansbridge, N., Mitsch, J., Bollard, N., Ellis, K., Miguel-Pacheco, G. G., Dottorini, T., & Kaler, J. (2018). Feature selection and comparison of machine learning algorithms in classification of grazing and rumination behaviour in sheep. *Sensors (Basel)*, *18*(10), 1–16. doi:10.339018103532 PMID:30347653

Marah, H. M., Challenger, M., & Kardas, G. (2020). RE4TinyOS: A Reverse Engineering Methodology for the MDE of TinyOS Applications. In *2020 15th Conference on Computer Science and Information Systems (FedCSIS)* (pp. 741-750). IEEE. 10.15439/2020F133

Marah, H. M., Eslampanah, R., & Challenger, M. (2018). DSML4TinyOS: Code Generation for Wireless Devices. *2nd International Workshop on Model-Driven Engineering for the Internet-of-Things (MDE4IoT), 21st International Conference on Model Driven Engineering Languages and Systems (MODELS2018)*.

Marco, V.R., Young, D.M., & Turner, D.W. (1987). The Euclidean Distance Classifier: An Alternative to the Linear Discriminant Function. *Communications in Statistics – Computation and Simulation*, *16*, 485-505.

Martin, J., & Alvisi, L. (2005). Fast Byzantine Consensus. *IEEE Transactions on Dependable and Secure Computing*, *3*, 202–215.

Martino, B., Cretella, G., & Esposito, A. (2017). Big Data, IoT and semantics. In Handbook of Big Data technologies. Springer.

Maureira, M. A. G., Oldenhof, D., & Teernstra, L. (2011). ThingSpeak–an API and Web Service for the Internet of Things. *World Wide Web (Bussum)*.

McClelland, K., Flinner, E. H., Abler, E. R., & Edu, G. (2017, September). Time Difference of Arrival Localization Testbed: Development, Calibration, and Automation. In *Proceedings of the GNU Radio Conference* (Vol. 2, No. 1, pp. 8-8). Academic Press.

McClune, D. W., Marks, N. J., Wilson, R. P., Houghton, J. D., Montgomery, I. W., McGowan, N. E., Gormley, E., & Scantlebury, M. (2014). Tri-axial accelerometers quantify behaviour in the Eurasian badger (Meles meles): Towards an automated interpretation of field data. *Animal Biotelemetry*, *2*(5), 1–6. doi:10.1186/2050-3385-2-5

Meddeb, A. (2016). Internet of Things standards: Who stands out from the crowd? *IEEE Communications Magazine - Communications Standards Supplement*, *7*(54), 40–47.

Meske, C., & Bunde, E. (2020). Transparency and Trust in Human-AI-Interaction: The Role of Model-Agnostic Explanations in Computer Vision-Based Decision Support. In H. Degen & L. Reinerman-Jones (Eds.), *Artificial Intelligence in HCI* (pp. 54–69). Springer. doi:10.1007/978-3-030-50334-5_4

Migabo, E. M., Djouani, K. D., & Kurien, A. M. (2020). The Narrowband Internet of Things (NB-IoT) Resources Management Performance State of Art, Challenges, and Opportunities. *IEEE Access: Practical Innovations, Open Solutions*, *8*, 97658–97675. doi:10.1109/ACCESS.2020.2995938

Milic, B., & Malek, M. (2007). Adaptation of the breadth first search algorithm for cut-edge detection in wireless multi-hop networks. *Proceedings of the 10th ACM Symposium on Modeling, Analysis, and Simulation of Wireless and Mobile Systems (MSWiM '07)*, 377–386.

Miller, A., Juels, A., Shi, E., Parno, B., & Katz, J. (2014). Permacoin: Repurposing Bitcoin Work for Data Preservation. *2014 IEEE Symposium on Security and Privacy*, 475-490.

Milovanovic, D., Pantovic, V., & Gardasevic, G. (2017). Converging technologies for the IoT: Standardization activities and frameworks. In P. Kocovic, R. Behringer, M. Ramachandran, & R. Mihajlovic (Eds.), *Emerging trends and applications of the Internet of Things* (pp. 71–103). IGI Global. doi:10.4018/978-1-5225-2437-3.ch003

Minbo, L., Zhu, Z., & Guangyu, C. (2013). Information Service System Of Agriculture IoT. *Automatika (Zagreb)*, *54*(4), 415–426. doi:10.7305/automatika.54-4.413

Minoli, D., Sohraby, K., & Occhiogrosso, B. (2017). IoT Considerations, Requirements, and Architectures for Smart Buildings—Energy Optimization and Next-Generation Building Management Systems. *IEEE Internet of Things Journal*, *4*(1), 269–283. doi:10.1109/JIOT.2017.2647881

Minovski, D., Åhlund, C., & Mitra, K. (2020). Modeling quality of IoT experience in autonomous vehicles. *IEEE Internet of Things Journal*, *7*(5), 3833–3849. doi:10.1109/JIOT.2020.2975418

Miranda, J., Cabral, J., Wagner, S. R., Fischer Pedersen, C., Ravelo, B., Memon, M., & Mathiesen, M. (2016). An Open Platform for Seamless Sensor Support in Healthcare for the Internet of Things. *Sensors (Basel)*, *16*(12), 2089. doi:10.339016122089 PMID:27941656

Misra, S., & Singh, S. (2012). Localized policy-based target tracking using wireless sensor networks. *ACM Transactions on Sensor Networks*, *8*(3), 1–30. doi:10.1145/2240092.2240101

MODMYPI. (2020, January 10). *HC-SR04 Ultrasonic Range Sensor on the Raspberry Pi*. Retrieved from https://www.modmypi.com/blog/hc-sr04-ultrasonic-range-sensor-on-the-raspberry-pi

Mohd Kassim, M. R., Mat, I., & Harun, A. N. (2014). Wireless Sensor Network in precision agriculture application. *2014 International Conference on Computer, Information and Telecommunication Systems (CITS)*. doi:10.1109/cits.2014.6878963

Motlagh, N. H., Bagaa, M., & Taleb, T. (2017, February). UAV-Based IoT Platform: A Crowd Surveillance Use Case. *IEEE Communications Magazine*, *55*(2), 128–134. doi:10.1109/MCOM.2017.1600587CM

MPEG (2016a) N16535 *Call for Proposals on Internet of Media Things and Wearables*

MPEG (2016b) N16533 *Use cases for Internet of Media Things and Wearables*

MPEG (2016c) N16534 *Requirements for Internet of Media Things and Wearables*

MPEG (2016d) N16565 Liaison Statement from SC29/WG11 to JTC1/WG9

MPEG (2016e) W16316 *Strategic Standardization Roadmap*

MPEG (2016f) N16540 *Vision, objectives, and plan for Big Media*

MPEG (2018) N17503 *Call For Proposals on NBMP*

MPEG Exploration. (2016). *Internet of Media Things and Wearables*. Retrieved from https://mpeg.chiariglione.org/standards/exploration/internet-media-things-and-wearables

MPEG Exploration. (2020). *Big Media*. Retrieved from https://mpeg.chiariglione.org/standards/exploration/big-media

Muhendra, R., Rinaldi, A., Budimana, M., & Khairurrijal, K. (2017). Development of WiFi Mesh Infrastructure for Internet of Things Applications. *Procedia Engineering*, *170*, 332–337.

Musaddiq, A., Zikria, Y. B., Hahm, O., Yu, H., Bashir, A. K., & Kim, S. W. (2018). A Survey on Resource Management in IoT Operating Systems. *IEEE Access: Practical Innovations, Open Solutions*, *6*, 8459–8482. doi:10.1109/ACCESS.2018.2808324

Muthuramalingam, S., Bharathi, A., Gayathri, N., Sathiyaraj, R., & Balamurugan, B. (2019). IoT based intelligent transportation system (IoT-ITS) for global perspective: A case study. In *Internet of Things and Big Data Analytics for Smart Generation* (pp. 279–300). Springer. doi:10.1007/978-3-030-04203-5_13

Muthusamy, M., & Periasamy, K. (n.d.). A Comprehensive Study on Internet of Things Security. *Advancing Consumer-Centric Fog Computing Architectures*, 72–86. doi:10.4018/978-1-5225-7149-0.ch004

Mvon, Z. (2004). International R&D by Chinese companies. *IEEE International Engineering Management Conference, 1*, 6-10.

Nadimi, E. S., Jørgensen, R. N., Blanes-Vidal, V., & Christensen, S. (2012). Monitoring and classifying animal behavior using ZigBee-based mobile ad hoc wireless sensor networks and artificial neural networks. *Computers and Electronics in Agriculture, 82*, 44–54. doi:10.1016/j.compag.2011.12.008

Naga, R. A., Elias, R., & Nahas, A. E. (2019). Indoor Localization Using Cluster Analysis. In Artificial Intelligence and Soft Computing. ICAISC 2019. Lecture Notes in Computer Science (vol. 11509, pp. 3-13). Springer.

Nakamoto, S. (2009). *Bitcoin: A Peer-to-Peer Electronic Cash System*. Academic Press.

Nathan, R., Spiegel, O., Fortmann-Roe, S., Harel, R., Wikelski, M., & Getz, W. M. (2012). Using tri-axial acceleration data to identify behavioral modes of free-ranging animals: General concepts and tools illustrated for griffon vultures. *The Journal of Experimental Biology, 215*(6), 986–996. doi:10.1242/jeb.058602 PMID:22357592

Nauman, A., Qadri, Y. A., Amjad, M., Zikria, Z. B., Afzal, M. K., & Kim, S. W. (2020). Multimedia Internet of Things: A comprehensive survey. *IEEE Access: Practical Innovations, Open Solutions, 8*, 8202–8250. doi:10.1109/ACCESS.2020.2964280

Navigation Complex G2S. (2020, January 3). Retrieved from http://cputos.org.ua/technologies/navihatsijnyj-kompleks-g2s-go-to-the-sound-idy-na-zvuk/

Newman, N. (2014). Apple iBeacon technology briefing. *Journal of Direct, Data and Digital Marketing Practice, 15*(3), 222–225. doi:10.1057/dddmp.2014.7

Ngu, A. H., Gutierrez, M., Metsis, V., Nepal, S., & Sheng, Q. Z. (2017). IoT Middleware: A Survey on Issues and Enabling Technologies. *IEEE Internet of Things Journal, 4*(1), 1–20.

Nguyen, C. (2014). *Haptic Obstacle Detector for the Blind*. KTH Royal Institute of Technology.

Nguyen, D. T., Shen, Y., & Thai, M. T. (2013). Detecting Critical Nodes in Interdependent Power Networks for Vulnerability Assessment. *IEEE Transactions on Smart Grid, 4*(1), 151–159. doi:10.1109/TSG.2012.2229398

Nicolau, H., Guerreiro, T., & Jorge, J. (2009). Designing Guides for Blind People. In *27th International Conference Extended Abstracts on Human Factors in Computing Systems* (pp. 3601-3606). ACM.

NIST Big Data Public (2019a) NBD-PWG SP 1500-7 *Big Data interoperability framework: Standards roadmap*

NIST Big Data Public (2019b) NBD-PWG *Big Data analytics and beyond roadmap*

NOMURA. (2016). *Survey on Blockchain Technologies and Related Services*. FY2015 Report.

Nordin, H., & Singh, D. (2016). The Internationalization of E-Learning Websites. *Methodology*.

Norris, D. (2015). *The Internet of Things: Do-It-Yourself at Home Projects for Arduino, Raspberry Pi, and BeagleBone Black*. McGraw-Hill Education.

O'Hagan, M. (2009). The evaluation of pragmatic and functionalist aspects in localization: Towards a holistic approach to Quality Assurance. *The Journal of Internationalisation and Localisation, 1*, 60–93. doi:10.1075/jial.1.03jim

O3. (2018). *LO3 Energy The Future of Energy*. Retrieved from https://lo3energy.com/

Ojo, M. O., Giordano, S., Procissi, G., & Seitanidis, I. N. (2018). A Review of Low-End, Middle-End, and High-End Iot Devices. *IEEE Access: Practical Innovations, Open Solutions*, *6*, 70528–70554. doi:10.1109/ACCESS.2018.2879615

ORCAM. (2020, January 10). *Employment for the Blind and Visually Impaired*. Retrieved from https://www.orcam.com/en/blog/employment-for-the-blind-and-visually-impaired/

Ozkaya, M. Y., Sarıyuce, A. E., Pınar, A., & Çatalyurek, U. V. (2018). Local Detection of Critical Nodes in Active Graphs. *2018 IEEE/ACM International Conference on Advances in Social Networks Analysis and Mining (ASONAM)*, 107-110. 10.1109/ASONAM.2018.8508323

Paek, J., Ko, J., & Shin, H. (2016). A Measurement Study of BLE iBeacon and Geometric Adjustment Scheme for Indoor Location-Based Mobile Applications. *Mobile Information Systems*.

Painter, M. S., Blanco, J. A., Malkemper, E. P., Anderson, C., Sweeney, D. C., Hewgley, C. W., Červený, J., Hart, V., Topinka, V., Belotti, E., Burda, H., & Phillips, J. B. (2016). Use of bio-loggers to characterize red fox behavior with implications for studies of magnetic alignment responses in free-roaming animals. *Animal Biotelemetry*, *4*(1), 1–20. doi:10.118640317-016-0113-8

Pan, J., & Yang, Z. (2018). Cybersecurity Challenges and Opportunities in the New "Edge Computing + IoT" World. *SDN-NFV Sec'18*.

Paradis, L., & Han, Q. (2007). A Survey of Fault Management in Wireless Sensor Networks. *Journal of Network and Systems Management*, *15*(2), 171–190. doi:10.100710922-007-9062-0

Park, D., Bang, H., Pyo, C. S., & Kang, S. (2014). Semantic open IoT service platform technology. *2014 IEEE World Forum on Internet of Things (WF-IoT)*, 85-88. 10.1109/WF-IoT.2014.6803125

Park, C. (2020). Security Architecture for Secure Multicast CoAP Applications. *IEEE Internet of Things Journal*, *7*(4), 3441–3452. doi:10.1109/JIOT.2020.2970175

Park, S., Kim, M., & Lee, S. (2018). Anomaly Detection for HTTP Using Convolutional Autoencoders. *IEEE Access: Practical Innovations, Open Solutions*, *6*, 70884–70901. doi:10.1109/ACCESS.2018.2881003

Patnaik, P., & Dinkar, R. (2017). A Comparative Study of Arduino, Raspberry Pi and ESP8266 as IoT Development Board. *International Journal of Advanced Research in Computer Science*, *8*(5), 2350–2352.

Peng, Y., Fan, W., Dong, X., & Zhang, X. (2016). *An Iterative Weighted KNN (IW-KNN) based Indoor Localization Method in Bluetooth Low Energy (BLE) Environment*. Paper presented at the meeting of the 2016 Intl IEEE Conferences on Ubiquitous Intelligence & Computing, Advanced and Trusted Computing, Scalable Computing and Communications, Cloud and Big Data Computing, Internet of People, and Smart World Congress, Toulouse, France.

Peng, Y., Niu, X., Tang, J., Mao, D., & Qian, C. (2018). Fast Signals of Opportunity Fingerprint Database Maintenance with Autonomous Unmanned Ground Vehicle for Indoor Positioning. *Sensors (Basel)*, *18*(10), 3419.

Pérez, J. L., & Carrera, D. (2015). Performance Characterization of the Servioticy API: An IoT-as-a-Service Data Management Platform. *IEEE First International Conference on Big Data Computing Service and Applications*, 62-71. 10.1109/BigDataService.2015.58

Pérez, S., Hernández-Ramos, J. L., Raza, S., & Skarmeta, A. (2020). Application Layer Key Establishment for End-to-End Security in IoT. *IEEE Internet of Things Journal*, *7*(3), 2117–2128. doi:10.1109/JIOT.2019.2959428

Pervez, H., Muneeb, M., Irfan, M., & Haq, I. U. (2018). A Comparative Analysis of DAG-Based Blockchain Architectures. *2018 12th International Conference on Open Source Systems and Technologies (ICOSST)*, 27-34.

Pierris, G., Kothris, D., Spyrou, E., & Spyropoulos, C. (2015). SYNAISTHISI: an enabling platform for the current internet of things ecosystem. In *Proceedings of the 19th Panhellenic Conference on Informatics (PCI '15)*. Association for Computing Machinery. DOI:10.1145/2801948.2802019

Pizzolli, D. (2016). Cloud4IoT: A Heterogeneous, Distributed and Autonomic Cloud Platform for the IoT. *2016 IEEE International Conference on Cloud Computing Technology and Science (CloudCom)*, 476-479. 10.1109/CloudCom.2016.0082

Poggi, M., & Mattoccia, S. (2016). A Wearable Mobility Aid for the Visually Impaired based on Embedded 3D Vision and Deep Learning. In *2016 IEEE Symposium on Computers and Communication Proceedings* (pp. 208-213). University of Messina.

Popov, S. (2018). *The Tangle.* https://assets.ctfassets.net/r1dr6vzfxhev/2t4uxvsIqk0EUau6g2sw0g/45eae33637ca92f85 dd9f4a3a218e1ec/IoTa1_4_3.pdf

Pouyanfar, S., Yang, Y., Chen, S.-C., Shyu, M.-L., & Iyengar, S. S. (2018). Multimedia Big Data Analytics: A Survey. *ACM Computing Surveys*, *51*(1), 10–34. doi:10.1145/3150226

Pritchard, D. (2006). An optimal distributed bridge-finding algorithm. *Proceedings of the 25th Annual ACM SIGACT-SIGOPS Symposium on Principles of Distributed Computing (PODC '06)*.

Purevsuren, D., Cui, G., Win, N. N. H., & Wang, X. (2016). Heuristic Algorithm for Identifying Critical Nodes in Graphs. *International Journal of Advanced Computer Science*, *5*(3), 1–4.

Qasim, M. A., Abdulrahman, S. S., & Zubov, D. (2019). Remote Localization and Assistance of Visually Impaired Employees: A Case Study on Bytereal iBeacon Fingerprinting. *Proc. Conf. Computer Intelligent Systems and Networks*, 160-172.

Qi-feng, S., Cheqing, J., Zhao, Z., Weining, Q., & Ao-ying, Z. (2017). *Blockchain: Architecture and Research Progress*. Academic Press.

Qu, L., Zhang, R., Shin, H., Kim, J., & Kim, H. (2016). Performance enhancement of ground radiation antenna for Z-wave applications using tunable metal loads. *Electronics Letters*, *52*(22), 1827–1828. doi:10.1049/el.2016.1682

Rackley, S. (2007). *Wireless Networking Technology: From Principles to Successful Implementation*. Newnes.

Raei, H., Tabibzadeh, M., Ahmadipoor, B., & Saei, S. (2009). A Self-Stabilizing Distributed Algorithm for Minimum Connected Dominating Sets in Wireless Sensor Networks with Different Transmission Ranges. *Proc. 11th Int. Conf. on Advanced Communication Technology, ICACT'09*, 1, 526–530.

Rahman, A., Smith, D. V., Little, B., Ingham, A. B., Greenwood, P. L., & Bishop-Hurley, G. J. (2018). Cattle behaviour classification from collar, halter, and ear tag sensors. *Information Processing in Agriculture*, *5*(1), 124–133. doi:10.1016/j.inpa.2017.10.001

Ramadhan, A. J. (2018). Wearable Smart System for Visually Impaired People. *Sensors (Basel)*, *18*(3), 843.

Ramallo-Gonzalez, A. P., Gonzalez-Vidal, A., & Skarmeta, A. F. (2021). CIoTVID: Towards an Open IoT-Platform for Infective Pandemic Diseases such as COVID-19. *Sensors (Basel)*, *21*(2), 484. doi:10.339021020484 PMID:33445499

Ramnath, S., Javali, A., Narang, B., Mishra, P., & Routray, S. K. (2017). IoT based localization and tracking. In *2017 International Conference on IoT and Application (ICIOT)* (pp. 1-4). IEEE.

Raspberry Pi Bluetooth In/Out Board Or "Who's Home". (2020, January 3). Retrieved from https://www.instructables.com/id/Raspberry-Pi-Bluetooth-InOut-Board-or-Whos-Hom/

Raspberry Pi Tutorials. (2020, January 10). *Wireless communication between Raspberry Pi's via MQTT broker/client*. Retrieved from https://tutorials-raspberrypi.com/raspberry-pi-mqtt-broker-client-wireless-communication/

Rawat, P., Singh, K. D., Chaouchi, H., & Bonnin, J. M. (2014). Wireless sensor networks: A survey on recent developments and potential synergies. *The Journal of Supercomputing, 68*(1), 1–48. doi:10.100711227-013-1021-9

Rayes, A., & Samer, S. (2019). Internet of Things From Hype to Reality: The Road to Digitization. Springer Publishing Company.

Razavi, A., Valkama, M., & Lohan, E.-S. (2015). *K-Means Fingerprint Clustering for Low-Complexity Floor Estimation in Indoor Mobile Localization.* Paper presented at the meeting of the 2015 IEEE Globecom Workshops (GC Wkshps), San Diego, CA. 10.1109/GLOCOMW.2015.7414026

Razzaque, M. A., Milojevic-Jevric, M., Palade, A., & Clarke, S. (2016). Middleware for Internet of Things: A Survey. *IEEE Internet of Things Journal, 3*(1), 70–95. doi:10.1109/JIOT.2015.2498900

Rehman, H. U., Asif, M., & Ahmad, M. (2017). Future applications and research challenges of IOT. *2017 International Conference on Information and Communication Technologies (ICICT)*, 68-74. 10.1109/ICICT.2017.8320166

Reilly, E., Maloney, M., Siegel, M., & Falco, G. (2019). An IoT Integrity-First Communication Protocol via an Ethereum Blockchain Light Client. *2019 IEEE/ACM 1st International Workshop on Software Engineering Research & Practices for the Internet of Things (SERP4IoT)*, 53-56.

RNIB. (2020, January 10). *Smart Glasses*. Retrieved from https://www.rnib.org.uk/smart-glasses

Röbesaat, J., Zhang, P., Abdelaal, M., & Theel, O. (2017). An Improved BLE Indoor Localization with Kalman-Based Fusion: An Experimental Study. *Sensors (Basel), 17*(5), 951.

Robles, T., Alcarria, R., Martin, D., Morales, A., Navarro, M., Calero, R., ... Lopez, M. (2014). An Internet of Things-Based Model for Smart Water Management. *2014 28th International Conference on Advanced Information Networking and Applications Workshops*. doi:10.1109/waina.2014.129

Rogojanu, T., Ghita, M., Stanciu, V., Ciobanu, R. I., Marin, R. C., Pop, F., & Dobre, C. (2018). Netiot: A versatile iot platform integrating sensors and applications. *2018 Global Internet of Things Summit (GIoTS)*, 1-6.

Rong, P., & Sichitiu, M. L. (2006, September). Angle of arrival localization for wireless sensor networks. In *2006 3rd annual IEEE communications society on sensor and ad hoc communications and networks* (Vol. 1, pp. 374-382). IEEE.

Rosebrock, A. (2020a, January 2). *Raspberry Pi Face Recognition*. Retrieved from https://www.pyimagesearch.com/2018/06/25/raspberry-pi-face-recognition/

Rosebrock, A. (2020b, January 3). *Raspbian Stretch: Install OpenCV 3 + Python on your Raspberry Pi*. Retrieved from https://www.pyimagesearch.com/2017/09/04/raspbian-stretch-install-opencv-3-python-on-your-raspberry-pi/

Rosebrock, A. (2020c, January 11). *OpenCV Face Recognition*. Retrieved from https://www.pyimagesearch.com/2018/09/24/opencv-face-recognition/

Rudin, C. (2019). Stop explaining black box machine learning models for high stakes decisions and use interpretable models instead. *Nature Machine Intelligence, 1*(5), 206–215. doi:10.103842256-019-0048-x

Saadi, M., Ahmad, T., Zhao, Y., & Wuttisttikulkij, L. (2016). *An LED based Indoor Localization System using k-means Clustering.* Paper presented at the meeting of the 2016 15th IEEE International Conference on Machine Learning and Applications. 10.1109/ICMLA.2016.0048

Sagheer, A., Mohammed, M., Riad, K., & Alhajhoj, M. (2021). A Cloud-Based IoT Platform for Precision Control of Soilless Greenhouse Cultivation. *Sensors (Basel)*, *21*(1), 223. doi:10.339021010223 PMID:33396448

Sagirlar, G., Carminati, B., Ferrari, E., Sheehan, J. D., & Ragnoli, E. (2018). Hybrid-IoT: Hybrid Blockchain Architecture for Internet of Things - PoW Sub-Blockchains. *2018 IEEE International Conference on Internet of Things (iThings) and IEEE Green Computing and Communications (GreenCom) and IEEE Cyber, Physical and Social Computing (CPSCom) and IEEE Smart Data (SmartData)*, 1007-1016.

Sakakibara, Y., Nakamura, K., & Matsutani, H. (2017). An FPGA NIC Based Hardware Caching for Blockchain. *HEART2017*.

Sakthidasan Sankaran, K., Vasudevan, N., & Verghese, A. (2020). ACIAR: Application-centric information-aware routing technique for IOT platform assisted by wireless sensor networks. *Journal of Ambient Intelligence and Humanized Computing*, *11*(11), 4815–4825. doi:10.100712652-020-01748-y

Salah, K., Rehman, M. H., Nizamuddin, N., & Al-Fuqaha, A. (2019). Blockchain for AI: Review and Open Research Challenges. *IEEE Access: Practical Innovations, Open Solutions*, *7*, 10127–10149.

Salimitari, M., Joneidi, M., & Chatterjee, M. (2019). *An Outlier-aware Consensus Protocol for Blockchain-based IoT Networks Using Hyperledger Fabric*. ArXiv, abs/1906.08177.

Salton, K. (2020, January 3). *Face Recognition: Understanding LBPH Algorithm*. Retrieved from https://towardsdatascience.com/face-recognition-how-lbph-works-90ec258c3d6b

Sandrini, P. (2014). *Website Localization and Translation*. Project: Website Translation.

Santamaria, A. F., Raimondo, P., Tropea, M., De Rango, F., & Aiello, C. (2019). An IoT surveillance system based on a decentralised architecture. *Sensors (Basel)*, *19*(6), 1469. doi:10.339019061469 PMID:30917519

Sarmento, R. M., Vasconcelos, F. F. X., Filho, P. P. R., & de Albuquerque, V. H. C. (2020). An IoT platform for the analysis of brain CT images based on Parzen analysis. *Future Generation Computer Systems*, *105*, 135-147. doi:10.1016/j.future.2019.11.033

Scalagent. (2020, January 10). *Benchmark of MQTT servers: ActiveMQ 5.10.0, Apollo 1.7, JoramMQ 1.1.3 (based on Joram 5.9.1), Mosquitto 1.3.5, RabbitMQ 3.4.2*. Retrieved from http://www.scalagent.com/IMG/pdf/Benchmark_MQTT_servers-v1-1.pdf

Schiller, J., & Voisard, A. (2004). Location based services. Elsevier.

Seng, K. P., & Ang, L. M. (2018). A Big data layered architecture and functional units for the Multimedia Internet of Things. *IEEE Transaction on Multi-Scale Computing Systems*, *4*(4), 500–512. doi:10.1109/TMSCS.2018.2886843

Sfar, A. R., Natalizio, E., Challal, Y., & Chtourou, Z. (2017). A roadmap for security challenges in the Internet of Things. *Digital Communications and Networks*, *4*, 118–137.

Shafique, M., Theocharides, T., Bouganis, C.-S., Hanif, M. A., Khalid, F., Hafiz, R., & Rehman, S. (2018). An overview of next-generation architectures for machine learning: Roadmap, opportunities and challenges in the IoT era. In Design, Automation & Test in Europe Conference & Exhibition (DATE) (pp. 827-832). IEEE. doi:10.23919/DATE.2018.8342120

Shahzad, A., Kim, Y., & Elgamoudi, A. (2017). Secure IoT Platform for Industrial Control Systems. *2017 International Conference on Platform Technology and Service (PlatCon)*, 1-6. doi:10.1109/PlatCon.2017.7883726

Shamoun-Baranes, J., Bom, R., van Loon, E. E., Ens, B. J., Oosterbeek, K., & Bouten, W. (2012). From sensor data to animal behaviour: An oystercatcher example. *PLoS One*, *7*(5), 1–13. doi:10.1371/journal.pone.0037997 PMID:22693586

Shanthamallu, U. S., Spanias, A., Tepedelenlioglu, C., & Stanley, M. (2017). A brief survey of machine learning methods and their sensor and IoT applications. In *8th International Conference on Information, Intelligence, Systems & Applications (IISA)* (pp. 1-8), IEEE. 10.1109/IISA.2017.8316459

Sharma, N., Shamkuwar, M., & Singh, I. (2019). The history, present and future with IoT. In *Internet of Things and Big Data Analytics for Smart Generation* (pp. 27–51). Springer. doi:10.1007/978-3-030-04203-5_3

Sharma, R., Agarwal, P., & Mahapatra, R. P. (2020). Evolution in Big Data analytics on Internet of Things: Applications and future plan. In S. Tanwar, S. Tyagi, & N. Kumar (Eds.), *Multimedia Big Data computing for IoT applications* (pp. 453–477). Springer. doi:10.1007/978-981-13-8759-3_18

Shchekotov, M. (2014, October). Indoor localization method based on Wi-Fi trilateration technique. In *Proceeding of the 16th conference of fruct association* (pp. 177-179). Academic Press.

Sheng, M., Li, J., & Shi, Y. (2006). Critical Nodes Detection in Mobile Ad Hoc Network. *20th International Conference on Advanced Information Networking and Applications (AINA'06)*, 336-340.

Shen, S., & Smith, J. C. (2012a). Polynomial-time Algorithms for Solving a Class of Critical Node Problems on Trees and Series-Parallel Graphs. *Networks*, *60*(2), 103–119. doi:10.1002/net.20464

Shen, S., Smith, J. C., & Goli, R. (2012b). Exact Interdiction Models and Algorithms for Disconnecting Networks via Node Deletions. *Discrete Optimization*, *9*(3), 172–188. doi:10.1016/j.disopt.2012.07.001

Shovic, J.C. (2016). *Raspberry Pi IoT Projects: Prototyping Experiments for Makers*. Apress.

Silva, R., Silva, J. S., & Boavida, F. (2015). A symbiotic resources sharing IoT platform in the smart cities context. *2015 IEEE Tenth International Conference on Intelligent Sensors, Sensor Networks and Information Processing (ISSNIP)*, 1-6. doi: 10.1109/ISSNIP.2015.7106922

Sinche, S., Raposo, D., Armando, N., Rodrigues, A., Boavida, F., Pereira, V., & Silva, J. S. (2020). A Survey of IoT Management Protocols and Frameworks. *IEEE Communications Surveys and Tutorials*, *22*(2), 1168–1190. doi:10.1109/COMST.2019.2943087

Singh, S. K., Rathore, S., & Park, J. H. (2019). BlockIoTIntelligence: A Blockchain-enabled Intelligent IoT Architecture with Artificial Intelligence. *Future Generation Computer Systems*.

Slama, D., Puhlmann, F., Morrish, J., & Bhatnagar, R. M. (2016). *Enterprise IoT: Strategies and Best Practices for Connected Products and Services*. O'Reilly Media.

Slijepcevic, D., Horst, F., Lapuschkin, S., Raberger, A.-M., Zeppelzauer, M., Samek, W., Breiteneder, C., Schöllhorn, W. I., & Horsak, B. (2020, August 19). On the Explanation of Machine Learning Predictions in Clinical Gait Analysis. *Arxiv*. https://arxiv.org/abs/1912.07737

sloct.it. (2018). *slock.it A Blockchain Company*. Retrieved from https://slock.it/

Sobin, C. C. (2020). A Survey on Architecture, Protocols and Challenges in IoT. *Wireless Personal Communications*, *116*(3), 1383–1429. doi:10.100711277-020-07108-5

Soltis, J., Wilson, R., Douglas-Hamilton, I., Vollrath, F., King, L., & Savage, A. (2012). Accelerometers in collars identify behavioral states in captive African elephants Loxodonta africana. *Endangered Species Research*, *18*(3), 255–263. doi:10.3354/esr00452

Souza, P. V., Guimaraes, A. J., Araujo, V. S., Batista, L. O., & Rezende, T. S. (2020). An Interpretable Machine Learning Model for Human Fall Detection Systems Using Hybrid Intelligent Models. In H. Ponce, L. Martínez-Villaseñor, J. Brieva, & E. Moya-Albor (Eds.), *Challenges and Trends in Multimodal Fall Detection for Healthcare* (pp. 181–205). Springer. doi:10.1007/978-3-030-38748-8_8

Stankovic, J. A. (2014). Research directions for the Internet of Things. *IEEE Internet of Things Journal*, *1*(1), 3–9. doi:10.1109/JIOT.2014.2312291

Statista: Forecast on Connected Devices per Person Worldwide 2003-2020. (2020, January 3). https://www.statista.com/statistics/678739/forecast-on-connected-devices-per-person/

Stojmenovic, I., Seddigh, M., & Zunic, J. (2002). Dominating sets and neighbor elimination-based broadcasting algorithms in wireless networks. *IEEE Transactions on Parallel and Distributed Systems*, *13*(1), 14–25. doi:10.1109/71.980024

Stoyanova, M., Nikoloudakis, Y., Panagiotakis, S., Pallis, E., & Markakis, E. K. (2020). A Survey on the Internet of Things (IoT) Forensics: Challenges, Approaches, and Open Issues. *IEEE Communications Surveys and Tutorials*, *22*(2), 1191–1221. doi:10.1109/COMST.2019.2962586

Strobel, W., Fossa, J., Panchura, C., Beaver, K., & Westbrook, J. (2004). *The Industry Profile on Visual Impairment*. Rehabilitation Engineering Research Center on Technology Transfer.

Sturm, V., Efrosinin, D., Efrosinina, N., Roland, L., Iwersen, M., Drillich, M., & Auer, W. (2019). A chaos theoretic approach to animal activity recognition. *Journal of Mathematical Sciences*, *237*(5), 730–743. doi:10.100710958-019-04199-9

Sun, Y., Xu, Y., Ma, L., & Deng, Z. (2009, December). KNN-FCM hybrid algorithm for indoor location in WLAN. In *2009 2nd International Conference on Power Electronics and Intelligent Transportation System (PEITS)* (Vol. 2, pp. 251-254). IEEE.

Sun, Y. Z., Fan, L., & Hong, X. (2018). Technology Development and Application of Blockchain: Current Status and Challenges. *Chinese Journal of Engineering Science*, *20*(2), 27–32. doi:10.15302/J-SSCAE-2018.02.005

Suroso, D. J., Cherntanomwong, P., Sooraksa, P., & Takada, J. I. (2011, December). Fingerprint-based technique for indoor localization in wireless sensor networks using Fuzzy C-Means clustering algorithm. In *2011 International Symposium on Intelligent Signal Processing and Communications Systems (ISPACS)* (pp. 1-5). IEEE. 10.1109/ISPACS.2011.6146167

Suroso, D. J., Cherntanomwong, P., Sooraksa, P., & Takada, J. I. (2011, November). Location fingerprint technique using Fuzzy C-Means clustering algorithm for indoor localization. In *TENCON 2011-2011 IEEE Region 10 Conference* (pp. 88–92). IEEE. doi:10.1109/TENCON.2011.6129069

Suzuki, L. R. (2017). Smart Cities IoT: Enablers and Technology Road Map. In S. T. Rassia & P. M. Pardalos (Eds.), *Smart City Networks: Through the Internet of Things, Springer Optimization and Its Applications* (Vol. 125, pp. 167–190). Springer.

Szczytowski, P., Khelil, A., & Suri, N. (2012). DKM: Distributed k-connectivity maintenance in wireless sensor networks. *Proc. Annual Conf. Wireless On-Demand Netw. Syst. Serv. (WONS)*, 83–90.

Szeliski, R. (2011). *Computer Vision: Algorithms and Applications* (1st ed.). Springer-Verlag.

Takahashi, M., Hussain, B., & Tang, B. (2009). Demo abstract: Design and implementation of a web service for liteos-based sensor networks. *2009 International Conference on Information Processing in Sensor Networks*, 407-408.

Takuya, K., Akinori, H., & Takio, K. (2008). Selection of Histogram of Oriented Gradients Features for Pedestrian Detection. In ICONIP 2007 (LNCS, vol. 4985, pp. 598-607). Springer.

Taylor, P. J., Dargahi, T., Dehghantanha, A., Parizi, R. M., & Choo, K. R. (2019). *A systematic literature review of blockchain cyber security*. Digital Communications and Networks.

Teng, J., Zhan, X., Xie, L., Zeng, X., Liu, Y., & Huang, L. (2017). A novel location method for distribution hybrid lines. *IEEE Conference on Energy Internet and Energy System Integration (EI2)*, 1-5. 10.1109/EI2.2017.8245425

Terroso-Saenz, F., González Vidal, A., Ramallo-González, A., & Skarmeta, A. (2017). An open IoT platform for the management and analysis of energy data. *Future Generation Computer Systems*, *92*, 1066–1079. Advance online publication. doi:10.1016/j.future.2017.08.046

Tezel, B. T., Challenger, M., & Kardas, G. (2016). A metamodel for Jason BDI agents. In *5th Symposium on Languages, Applications and Technologies (SLATE'16)*. Schloss Dagstuhl-Leibniz-Zentrum fuer Informatik.

Tong, W., Dong, X., Shen, Y., & Jiang, X. (2019). A Hierarchical Sharding Protocol for Multi-Domain IoT Blockchains. *ICC 2019 - 2019 IEEE International Conference on Communications (ICC)*, 1-6.

Toscano, E., & Bello, L. L. (2012). Comparative assessments of IEEE 802.15. 4/ZigBee and 6LoWPAN for low-power industrial WSNs in realistic scenarios. In *2012 9th IEEE International Workshop on Factory Communication Systems* (pp. 115-124). IEEE.

Tran, M. D., Tran, T. H., Vu, D. T., Nguyen, T. C., Nguyen, V. H., & Tran, T. T. (2021). Development of a Stimulated Model of Smart Manufacturing Using the IoT and Industrial Robot Integrated Production Line. In *Research in Intelligent and Computing in Engineering* (pp. 931–940). Springer. doi:10.1007/978-981-15-7527-3_89

Trent, M., Abdelgawad, A., & Yelamarthi, K. (2017). A Smart Wearable Navigation System for Visually Impaired. In GOODTECHS 2016 (LNICST, vol. 195, pp. 333-341). Cham: Springer.

Trilles, S., González-Pérez, A., & Huerta, J. (2020). An IoT Platform Based on Microservices and Serverless Paradigms for Smart Farming Purposes. *Sensors (Basel)*, *20*(8), 2418. doi:10.339020082418 PMID:32344569

Tsokov, T., & Petrova-Antonova, D. (2017). EcoLogic: IoT Platform for Control of Carbon Emissions. Proc. ff ICSOFT, 178-185.

Ünal, P. (2019). Reference architectures and standards for the Internet of Things and Big Data in Smart Manufacturing. *Proc. International Conference on Future Internet of Things and Cloud*, 243-250. 10.1109/FiCloud.2019.00041

Underwood, S. (2016). Blockchain beyond bitcoin. *Communications of the ACM*, *59*, 15–17.

UniquID. (2018). *UniquID Incorporation Blockchain Identity Access Management*. Retrieved from https://uniquid.com/

User Manual for ESP-12E DevKit based on ESP8266. (2020, January 10). Retrieved from https://smartarduino.gitbooks.io/user-manual-for-esp-12e-devkit/content/index.html

Uy, N. Q., & Nam, V. H. (2019). A comparison of AMQP and MQTT protocols for Internet of Things. *2019 6th NAFOSTED Conference on Information and Computer Science (NICS)*, 292-297.

Ventresca, M. (2012). Global Search Algorithms using a Combinatorial Unranking based Problem Representation for the Critical Node Detection Problem. *Computers & Operations Research*, *39*(11), 2763–2775. doi:10.1016/j.cor.2012.02.008

Ventresca, M., & Aleman, D. (2014b). A Fast Greedy Algorithm for the Critical Node Detection Problem. *Combinatorial Optimization and Applications*, *8881*, 603–612. doi:10.1007/978-3-319-12691-3_45

Veremyev, A., Boginski, V., & Pasiliao, E. L. (2014). Exact Identification of Critical Nodes in Sparse Networks via New Compact Formulations. *Optimization Letters*, *8*(4), 1245–1259. doi:10.100711590-013-0666-x

Vergara, P., Marín, E., Villar, J., González, V., & Sedano, J. (2017). An IoT Platform for Epilepsy Monitoring and Supervising. *Journal of Sensors, 2017*, 1–18. doi:10.1155/2017/6043069

Vermesan, O., Friess, P., Guillemin, P., Giaffreda, R., Grindwoll, H., Eisenhauer, M., Serrano, M., Moessner, K., Spirito, M., Blystad, L.-C., & Tragos, E. Z. (2013). Internet of Things beyond the Hype: Research, innovation and deployment. In O. Vermesan & P. Friess (Eds.), *Internet of Things: Converging technologies for smart environments and integrated ecosystems* (pp. 15–118). River Publishers.

Veronese, G. S., Correia, M., Bessani, A. N., & Lung, L. C. (2009). Spin One's Wheels? Byzantine Fault Tolerance with a Spinning Primary. *2009 28th IEEE International Symposium on Reliable Distributed Systems*, 135-144.

Vilone, G., & Longo, L. (2020, October 12). Explainable Artificial Intelligence: a Systematic Review. *Arxiv*. https://arxiv.org/abs/2006.00093

Viola, P., & Jones, M. J. (2004). Robust Real-Time Face Detection. *International Journal of Computer Vision, 57*(2), 137–154.

Voulodimos, A. S., Patrikakis, C. Z., Sideridis, A. B., Ntafis, V. A., & Xylouri, E. M. (2010). A complete farm management system based on animal identification using RFID technology. *Computers and Electronics in Agriculture, 70*(2), 380–388. doi:10.1016/j.compag.2009.07.009

Vresk, T., & Čavrak, I. (2016). Architecture of an interoperable IoT platform based on microservices. *2016 39th International Convention on Information and Communication Technology, Electronics and Microelectronics (MIPRO)*, 1196-1201. 10.1109/MIPRO.2016.7522321

Walter, K.-D. (2019). AI-based sensor platforms for the IoT in smart cities. *Big Data Analytics for Cyber-Physical Systems*, 145-166. doi:10.1016/B978-0-12-816637-6.00007-5

Walton, E., Casey, C., Mitsch, J., Vázquez-Diosdado, J. A., Yan, J., Dottorini, T., Ellis, K. A., Winterlich, A., & Kaler, J. (2018). Evaluation of sampling frequency, window size and sensor position for classification of sheep behaviour. *Royal Society Open Science, 5*(2), 1–14. doi:10.1098/rsos.171442 PMID:29515862

Wang, X., Zhang, L., Xie, T., Mei, H., & Sun, J. (2013). Locating Need-to-Externalize Constant Strings for Software Internationalization with Generalized String-Taint Analysis. *IEEE Transactions on Software Engineering, 39*(4), 516-536.

Wang, X., Zha, X., Ni, W., Liu, R. P., Guo, Y. J., Niu, X., & Zheng, K. (2019). Survey on blockchain for Internet of Things. *Computer Communications, 136*, 10–29. doi:10.1016/j.comcom.2019.01.006

Wang, Y., Cang, S., & Yu, H. (2019). A survey on wearable sensor modality centred human activity recognition in health care. *Expert Systems with Applications, 137*, 167–190. doi:10.1016/j.eswa.2019.04.057

Wang, Y., Jin, J., Li, Y., & Choi, C. (2020). A Reliable Physical Layer Authentication Algorithm for Massive IoT Systems. *IEEE Access: Practical Innovations, Open Solutions, 8*, 80684–80690. doi:10.1109/ACCESS.2020.2989395

Wang, Y., Yang, X., Zhao, Y., Liu, Y., & Cuthbert, L. (2013). Bluetooth positioning using RSSI and triangulation methods. In *IEEE 10th Consumer Communications and Networking Conference*. Las Vegas, NV: IEEE.

Warren, J.-D., Adams, J., & Molle, H. (2011). *Arduino Robotics*. Apress Media LLC.

Wehmuth, K., & Ziviani, A. (2011). Distributed Location of the Critical Nodes to Network Robustness based on Spectral Analysis. *7th Latin American Network Operations and Management Symposium*, 1-8. 10.1109/LANOMS.2011.6102259

Wireless Communication between Raspberry Pi's via MQTT Broker/Client. (2020, January 3). Retrieved from https://tutorials-raspberrypi.com/raspberry-pi-mqtt-broker-client-wireless-communication/

Witten, I. H., Frank, E., Hall, M. A., & Pal, C. J. (2017). *Data mining practical machine learning tools and techniques*. Morgan Kaufmann.

Wolfert, S., Ge, L., Verdouw, C., & Bogaardt, M.-J. (2017). Big Data in Smart Farming – A review. *Agricultural Systems*, *153*, 69–80. doi:10.1016/j.agsy.2017.01.023

WoodfordC. (2020, January 2). *Bluetooth*. Retrieved from https://www.explainthatstuff.com/howbluetoothworks.html

World Health Organization: Blindness and Visual Impairment. (2020, January 2). Retrieved from, http://www.who.int/news-room/fact-sheets/detail/blindness-and-visual-impairment

Wu, Y., Wu, Y., Guerrero, J. M., Vasquez, J. C., Palacios-Garcia, E. J., & Li, J. (2020). Convergence and interoperability for the Energy Internet: From ubiquitous connection to distributed automation. *IEEE Industrial Electronics Magazine*, *14*(4), 91–105. doi:10.1109/MIE.2020.3020786

Xage. (2018). *Home Page of Xage Security*. Retrieved March 20, 2019 from https://xage.com/

Xia, X., Lo, D., Zhu, F., Wang, X., & Zhou, B. (2013). Software Internationalization and Localization: An Industrial Experience. *18th International Conference on Engineering of Complex Computer Systems*, 222-231. 10.1109/ICECCS.2013.40

Xie, Y., Wang, Y., Arumugam, N., & Lina, W. (2016). An Improved K-Nearest-Neighbor Indoor Localization Method Based on Spearman Distance. *IEEE Signal Processing Letters*, *23*(3), 351–355. doi:10.1109/LSP.2016.2519607

Xiong, Z., Feng, S., Wang, W., Niyato, D., Wang, P., & Han, Z. (2019). Cloud/Fog Computing Resource Management and Pricing for Blockchain Networks. *IEEE Internet of Things Journal*, *6*, 4585–4600.

Xu, G., Li, M., Chen, C.-H., & Wei, Y. (2018). Cloud asset-enabled integrated IoT platform for lean prefabricated construction. *Automation in Construction, 93*, 123-134. doi:10.1016/j.autcon.2018.05.012

Xu, L. D., He, W., & Li, S. (2014). Internet of Things in Industries: A Survey. IEEE Transactions on Industrial Informatics, 10(4), 2233-2243. doi:10.1109/TII.2014.2300753

Xu, C., & Xu, C. (2017). Predicting Personal Transitional Location Based on Modified-SVM. *2017 International Conference on Computational Science and Computational Intelligence (CSCI)*, 340-344. 10.1109/CSCI.2017.57

Yang, S., Xu, K., Cui, L., Ming, Z., Chen, Z. & Ming, Z. (2021). EBI-PAI: Toward an Efficient Edge-Based IoT Platform for Artificial Intelligence. *IEEE Internet of Things Journal, 8*(12), 9580-9593. . doi:10.1109/JIOT.2020.3019008

Yang, F., Zhou, W., Wu, Q., Long, R., Xiong, N. N., & Zhou, M. (2019). Delegated Proof of Stake With Downgrade: A Secure and Efficient Blockchain Consensus Algorithm With Downgrade Mechanism. *IEEE Access: Practical Innovations, Open Solutions, 7*, 118541–118555.

Yang, G., Xie, L., Mantysalo, M., Zhou, X., Pang, Z., Xu, L. D., Kao-Walter, S., Chen, Q., & Zheng, L.-R. (2014). A Health-IoT Platform Based on the Integration of Intelligent Packaging, Unobtrusive Bio-Sensor, and Intelligent Medicine Box. *IEEE Transactions on Industrial Informatics, 10*(4), 2180–2191. doi:10.1109/TII.2014.2307795

Yaqoob, I., Hashem, I., Mehmood, Y., Gani, A., Mokhtar, S., & Guizani, S. (2017). Enabling Communication Technologies for Smart Cities. *IEEE Communications Magazine*, *55*(1), 112–120.

Yildirim, P., & Birant, D. (2014, June). Naive Bayes classifier for continuous variables using novel method (NBC4D) and distributions. In *2014 IEEE International Symposium on Innovations in Intelligent Systems and Applications (INISTA) Proceedings* (pp. 110-115). IEEE.

Yıldırım, P., & Birant, D. (2018). Bulut bilişimde veri madenciliği tekniklerinin uygulanması: Bir literatür taraması. *Pamukkale Üniversitesi Mühendislik Bilimleri Dergisi*, *24*(2), 336–343.

Yildirim, P., Birant, D., & Alpyildiz, T. (2018). Data mining and machine learning in textile industry. *Wiley Interdisciplinary Reviews. Data Mining and Knowledge Discovery*, 8(1), e1228. doi:10.1002/widm.1228

Yim, J. (2008). Introducing a decision tree-based indoor positioning technique. *Expert Systems with Applications*, 34(2), 1296–1302. doi:10.1016/j.eswa.2006.12.028

Yiu, S., Dashti, M., Claussen, H., & Perez-Cruz, F. (2017). Wireless RSSI fingerprinting localization. *Signal Processing*, 131, 235–244. doi:10.1016/j.sigpro.2016.07.005

Yuanyuan, Z., Jia, X., & Yanxiang, H. (2006). Energy Efficient Distributed Connected Dominating Sets Construction in Wireless Sensor Networks. *Proc. 2006 Int. Conf. on Wireless Communications and Mobile Computing, IWCMC'06*, 797–802. 10.1145/1143549.1143709

Yugha, R., & Chithra, S. (2020). A survey on technologies and security protocols: Reference for future generation IoT. *Journal of Network and Computer Applications*, 169.

Yu, J., Bang, H. C., Lee, H., & Lee, Y. S. (2016). Adaptive Internet of Things and Web of Things convergence platform for Internet of reality services. *The Journal of Supercomputing*, 72(1), 84–102. doi:10.100711227-015-1489-6

Zafari, F., Gkelias, A., & Leung, K. K. (2020, January 10). *A Survey of Indoor Localization Systems and Technologies*. Retrieved from https://arxiv.org/abs/1709.01015

Zafari, F., Gkelias, A., & Leung, K. K. (2019). A survey of indoor localization systems and technologies. *IEEE Communications Surveys and Tutorials*, 21(3), 2568–2599. doi:10.1109/COMST.2019.2911558

Zamora-Izquierdo, M. A., Santa, J., Martínez, J. A., Martínez, V., & Skarmeta, A. F. (2019). Smart farming IoT platform based on edge and cloud computing. *Biosystems Engineering, 177*, 4-17. doi:10.1016/j.biosystemseng.2018.10.014

Zantalis, F., Koulouras, G., Karabetsos, S., & Kandris, D. (2019). A Review of Machine Learning and IoT in Smart Transportation. *Future Internet, 11*(4), 1–23. doi:10.3390/fi11040094

Zarzycki, A. (2016). Adaptive Designs with Distributed Intelligent Systems – Building Design Applications. In *34th eCAADe Conference Proceedings* (*vol. 1*, pp. 681-690). University of Oulu.

Zelenika, Z., & Pušnik, T. (2016). Reinventing telecom OSS toolkit as an IoT platform. *2016 International Symposium ELMAR*, 21-26. 10.1109/ELMAR.2016.7731746

Zhang, G., & Herring, C. (2012). Globalization or localization? *Proceedings Cultural Attitudes Towards Technology and Communication*, 430-445.

Zhang, J., & Hu, C. (2014). The research and application on the optimal location model of project. *The 26th Chinese Control and Decision Conference (2014 CCDC)*, 2208-2210. 10.1109/CCDC.2014.6852535

Zhang, W., Wang, L., Zhenquan, Q., Zheng, X., Sun, L., Jin, N., & Lei, S. (2014). *INBS: An Improved Naive Bayes Simple Learning Approach for Accurate Indoor Localization*. Paper presented at the meeting of the 2014 IEEE International Conference on Communications (ICC), Sydney, Australia. 10.1109/ICC.2014.6883310

Zhao, H., Huang, B., & Jia, B. (2016). *Applying Kriging Interpolation for WiFi Fingerprinting based Indoor Positioning Systems*. Paper presented at the meeting of the 2016 IEEE Wireless Communications and Networking Conference, Doha, Qatar. 10.1109/WCNC.2016.7565018

Zheng, Z., Xie, S., Dai, H., Chen, X., & Wang, H. (2017). An Overview of Blockchain Technology: Architecture, Consensus, and Future Trends. *2017 IEEE International Congress on Big Data (BigData Congress)*, 557-564.

Zhou, H., & Van, N. N. (2014, January). Indoor fingerprint localization based on fuzzy c-means clustering. In *2014 Sixth International Conference on Measuring Technology and Mechatronics Automation* (pp. 337-340). IEEE. 10.1109/ICMTMA.2014.83

Zhou, Q., Huang, H., Zheng, Z., & Bian, J. (2020). Solutions to Scalability of Blockchain: A Survey. *IEEE Access: Practical Innovations, Open Solutions, 8*, 16440–16455.

Zhou, Y., Hao, J. K., & Glover, F. (2019). Memetic Search for Identifying Critical Nodes in Sparse Graphs. *IEEE Transactions on Cybernetics, 49*(10), 3699–3712. doi:10.1109/TCYB.2018.2848116 PMID:29994417

Zhu, C., Zheng, C., Shu, L., & Han, G. (2012). A survey on coverage and connectivity issues in wireless sensor networks. *Journal of Network and Computer Applications, 35*(2), 619–632.

Zielonka, A., Sikora, A., Woźniak, M., Wei, W., Ke, Q., & Bai, Z. (2020). Intelligent Internet of things system for smart home optimal convection. *IEEE Transactions on Industrial Informatics, 17*(6), 4308–4317. doi:10.1109/TII.2020.3009094

Zong, Z., Fares, R., Romoser, B., & Wood, J. (2013). FastStor: Improving the performance of a large scale hybrid storage system via caching and prefetching. *Cluster Computing, 17*(2), 593–604. doi:10.100710586-013-0304-5

Zubov, D. (2018). A Smart City Assistive Infrastructure for the Blind and Visually Impaired People: A Thin Client Concept. *BRAIN – Broad Research in Artificial Intelligence and Neurosciences J., 9*(4), 25-37.

Zubov, D., Kose, U., Ramadhan, A. J., & Kupin, A. (2018). Mesh Network of eHealth Intelligent Agents in Smart City: A Case Study on Assistive Devices for B&VI. *Proc. Workshop "1st International Workshop on Informatics & Data-Driven Medicine"*, 65-81.

Zubov, D., Siniak, N., & Grenčíková, A. (2018). Impact of Industry 4.0 Technologies on the Employment of the People with Eye Problems: A Case Study on the Spatial Cognition within Industrial Facilities. *Proc. Conf. "The Impact of Industry 4.0 on Job Creation"*, 254-263.

Zubov, D. (2017). A Case Study on the Spatial Cognition of Surrounding Objects by the B&VI People Using Sound Patterns and Ultrasonic Sensing. In P. Kocovic, R. Behringer, M. Ramachandran, & R. Mihajlovic (Eds.), *Emerging Trends and Applications of the Internet of Things* (pp. 105–116). IGI Global.

About the Contributors

Pelin Yildirim Taser is the Assistant Professor Doctor in Computer Engineering Department of İzmir Bakircay University. She received her B.Sc, M.Sc., and Ph.D. degrees in Computer Engineering from Dokuz Eylül University in 2013, 2015, and 2019 respectively. After her B.Sc. graduation, she worked as a project assistant at the Computer Engineering Department of Dokuz Eylül University for six months. Between 2014 – 2019, she worked as a research assistant at the Software Engineering Department of Manisa Celal Bayar University, Turkey. Her research interests include data mining, machine learning, intelligent systems, and deep learning. She is the author of several book chapters and lots of international publications. She is also the advisory board member of some journals and a reviewer for major scientific journals. She is an editor of IGI Global Reference Book. She also served on the organization committee of some conferences and scientific activities. She referees for the assessment of the industrial R&D project proposals. Dr. Yildirim Taser has graduation awards, including certificates of high achievement from her M.S. and Ph.D. educations and certificate of publication honor from her Ph.D.

* * *

Nusin Akram is a PhD Student at International Computer Institute Ege University.

Vahid Khalilpour Akram received the B.Sc. and the M.Sc. degrees in Computer Engineering from Islamic Azad University. He received Ph.D. degree from Ege University, International Computer Institute. He currently is an assistant professor at Ege University, Department of Computer Engineering. His research interests include wireless sensor networks, parallel and distributed algorithms, and graph theory.

Duygu Bagci Das completed her BS in Electronic and Computer Education Department of Mersin University, Turkey in 2009. She received an MS in the Computer Engineering Department of Yalova University, Turkey in 2016. She is currently a Ph.D. candidate in the Computer Engineering Department of Dokuz Eylul University. She has been a Lecturer at the Computer Technologies Department of Dokuz Eylul University since 2013. Her research areas are intelligent systems, data mining, and machine learning. She has several publications that cover her research areas.

Derya Birant received a BS, MS, and Ph.D. in Computer Engineering from Dokuz Eylul University, Turkey in 2000, 2002, and 2006, respectively. Since 2017, she has been an Associate Professor at the Computer Engineering Department of Dokuz Eylul University. She was a Visiting Lecturer at South East European University in 2006 and Ege University between 2010 and 2012. She has been involved in more than twenty long-term interdisciplinary R&D projects on data science. Dr. Birant has supervised more than thirty PhD and MSc students. Her research interests include data mining and machine learning. She is the author of more than 100 publications.

Moharram Challenger received his PhD in IT from International Computer Institute at Ege University (Turkey) in Feb 2016. From 2005 to 2009, he has been a tenure-track faculty member, as a senior lecturer, at the computer engineering department, IAU-Shabestar University. From 2010 to 2013 he was a researcher and team leader of a bilateral project between Slovenia and Turkey (TUBITAK). From 2012 to 2016, he was the R&D director of UNIT IT Ltd. leading one national project funded by TUBITAK and two international software-intensive projects in Europe called ITEA ModelWriter and ITEA Assume. He was also an external post-doc researcher at the IT group of the Wageningen University of Research from 2016 to 2017. In 2017 and 2018, he has been a member of the faculty as an assistant professor at Ege University. From Jan 2019 to July 2020, he was a post-doc researcher at the University of Antwerp working in a Flanders Make projects called PACo and DTDesign. He is currently a tenure-track assistant professor in the Department of Computer Science, University of Antwerp. His research interests include domain-specific modelling languages, multi-agent systems, Cyber-physical Systems, and the Internet of Things.

Deepika Choudhary is a student at Arya Institute of Engineering Technology and Management, Jaipur.

Joachim Denil is an assistant professor at the university of Antwerp. He obtained a bachelor and master degree in Industrial Sciences: Electronics-ICT and a Bachelor and Ph.D. Degree in computer science. After his Ph.D. he did post-doctoral research at McGill University, Canada and at the university of Antwerp on the topic of multi-paradigm modelling of software-intensive and mechatronic systems. His research interests are located at the intersection of model-based systems engineering, simulation and cyber–physical systems. The goal of his research is to create novel methods, techniques and prototype tooling for the design, verification and evolution of technical systems. Finally, Joachim is also a member of the Flanders Make Research Centre Belgium.

Arpan Deyasi is presently working as Assistant Professor in the Department of Electronics and Communication Engineering in RCC Institute of Information Technology, Kolkata, INDIA. He has 13 years of professional experience in academics and industry. He received B.Sc (Hons), B.Tech, M.Tech Degree from University of Calcutta. His work spans around in the field of semiconductor nanostructure, semiconductor photonics. He has published more than 150 peer-reviewed research papers. His major teaching subjects are Solid State Device, Electromagnetics, Photonics. He is associated with different International and National Conferences in various aspects, and organized several technical events under the banner of IE(I) Kolkata section. He is reviewer of a few journals of repute and some prestigious conferences in INDIA and abroad. He is senior member of IEEE, secretary of IEEE Electron Device Society (Kolkata Chapter), member of IE(I), Optical Society of India, IETE, ISTE etc. He is working as SPOC of RCCIIT Local Chapter (NPTEL course), Nodal Coordinator of Internshala & e-outreach programme, Admin of Coursera campus program and Faculty Adviser of the student chapter of Institution of Engineers (INDIA) in ECE Department at RCCIIT.

Arvind Dhaka received his PhD degree in Computer Science and Engineering from NIT Hamirpur, India (an institute of national importance) in 2018. Since 2018, he is working as Assistant Professor in Department of Computer and Communication Engineering at Manipal University Jaipur. His research interests include Wireless Communication, Wireless Sensor Networks, Ad-Hoc Networks, Medical Image Processing, Machine Leaning and Deep Learning in Image Processing.

Raheleh Eslampanah obtained her PhD from Victoria University, Melbourne, Australia in Microelectronics and Telecommunication in 2016. She received a scholarship from Victoria University for 5 years. Furthermore, part of her work, system level design, was funded by Ericsson (Stockholm, Sweden), while Peregrine Semiconductor (San Diego, USA) supported her research by fabricating her designed chips. Highlights of her research include: System level design of an adaptive duplexer as a low cost replacement for the multiple duplexing filters required for the next generation of mobile handsets, and the design of an adaptive duplexer microelectronic circuit compatible with silicon integration. She was a part-time lecturer in several universities (for about 3 years) and Academic Sessional for 3 years at Victoria University. She was an Assistant Prof. in the Department of Electrical and Electronics Engineering of Izmir University of Economics in Izmir, Turkey from Feb. 2017. She joined the department of Mathematics and Computer Science since Jan. 2020 and currently working as a Postdoctoral researcher at the University of Antwerp on Validity Frames for physical systems models.

Burak Karaduman received his BSc diploma as an Electrical and Electronics Engineer at Yaşar University. He focused on embedded technologies, control and automation. He wrote his BSc thesis on "Wireless Home Automation System". He worked as a researcher in scientific research projects, and he also gave lectures for software engineering students as an instructor. At the same time, he started as a master student at the International Computer Institute, Ege University. He developed a platform-independent modelling language for various IoT and WSN operating systems. During his master education, he focused on the Internet of Things (IoT), Cyber-Physical Systems (CPS), Embedded Technologies and Model-driven Engineering (MDE). He completed his master education based on IoT, MDE, CPS and Petri-nets. He conducted his studies with both academics at both Ege University in Turkey and the University of Antwerp in Belgium. After his master's degree, he was granted as a PhD student in Computer Science, University of Antwerp. He currently focuses on the Agent-oriented paradigm and Cyber-physical systems. In addition, he researches model-based descriptions of engineering processes, Petri nets, and Fuzzy Logic. He actively continues his studies with academics from Ryerson University, University of Montreal, Ege University and Dokuz Eylul University.

Jelena Kocovic is a business consulting in the pharmaceutical company Stada IT Solutions. Her professional expertise including skills with SAP.

Petar Kočović is ICT analyst and consultant of company Digital Dreams and full professor at Union University – "Nikola Tesla". Mr. Kočović has more than 30 years of experience working in the IT industry in management and technical positions for end-user organizations and software companies, as well as software developer. Prior to joining Digital Dreams, Mr Kocovic was employer of Gartner company and co-owner of company Tehnicom for 14 years, where he worked in the field of telecommunications, Internet providing and web development. He has experience in all Internet related technologies (including Internet of Things), as well as mathematical foundation for CAD/CAM. On this project he worked in company Energoprojekt-Energodata. He worked in system management, account management, marketing, consulting and systems support, as well as in developing communication and commercial software. "There is never a dull moment in my professional career! It is a delight to work with customers who are constantly seeking out new ways to adopt technology to maximize their business benefit. I feel privileged to be part of that process." He was invited speaker in few universities. He is full professor at the Union University – "Nikola Tesla" from Belgrade, and University of Belgrade-School of Organizational Science. He has around 100 scientific papers, and published 27 books.

Vladimir Kocovic is a full-stack programmer. His professional expertise including programming languages C, C++, Python, PHP. He working as R&D developer in gaming industry.

Mobasshir Mahbub is currently pursuing MSc Engineering in Electrical and Electronic Engineering under the Department of Electrical and Electronic Engineering at Ahsanullah University of Science and Technology, Dhaka, Bangladesh. He graduated (September, 2018) in Electronic and Telecommunication Engineering under the Department of Electronics and Communications Engineering at East West University, Dhaka, Bangladesh with an outstanding academic performance (Merit Scholarship and Dean's List Award). His fields of interest are Circuit Design & Analysis, Embedded Electronics, IoT, IoT Security, IoT-Enabled Intelligent Gadgets, Robotics, Microcontroller Interfacing, Wireless Communications, Data Communication, UAV-Aided Communication, PCB Designing, etc. He served as a Project Engineer, in Transport Network Rollout Department under the Technology Division of Robi Axiata Ltd., a renowned telecom operator of Bangladesh. He has four book chapter publications (in Springer, IGI Global), fourteen research paper publications in reputed international journals (in Elsevier, Springer, EAI), and seven conference publications in reputed international conferences (IEEE Sponsored). He is a member of IEEE Computer Society, Bangladesh Chapter. He is serving as a voluntary editor for IEEE Communications Society (ComSoc) since 2019. He is also serving as a member of several technical committees of several IEEE communities and societies such as IADF, IEEE Geoscience and Remote Sensing Society; Cloud Computing Community; Internet of Things Community; Software Defined Networks Community; Computer Communications, Cloud Computing, Internet of Everything committees of IEEE Computer Society; Connected Vehicles committee of IEEE Vehicular Technology Society, etc. He served as a member of technical committee and reviewer for 5th IEEE FMEC Conference, Paris, France, 2020. He served as organizer, instructor, and keynote speaker in several workshops, seminars, and webinars on Microcontroller Interfacing, Embedded System, IoT, and Robotics (EWU, ULAB, and AUST). He has been serving as a reviewer for journals of reputed publishers such as Springer, IEEE, Wiley, and Emerald and served as reviewer for several international conferences. He obtained certifications and training in IoT, Computer Networking, Routing & Switching, Software Defined Networking (SDN) and Network Function Virtualization (NFV), Network Security, PCB Designing, Industrial IoT on Google Cloud, Digital Marketing, and Google Analytics related courses from Cisco, Huawei, Intel, Microsoft, Google, UCI, GATech, Coursera, Alison, Cybrary, and Udemy. He is currently engaged in research on 5G transmission and IoT.

M. Manikandakumar was awarded the B.Tech., degree in Information Technology in 2009, and M.E., degree in Computer Science and Engineering in 2013 from Anna University, Chennai, India where he is pursuing a Ph.D. He is currently an Assistant Professor in the Information Technology Department,

Thiagarajar Engineering College, Madurai, India. His research interests include data science, wireless networking and machine learning.

Dragorad A. Milovanovic received the Dipl. Electr. Eng. and Magistar degree from the University of Belgrade, Serbia. From 1987 to 1991, he was a Research Assistant and PhD researcher from 1991 to 2001 at the Department of Electrical Engineering, where his interest includes simulation & analysis of digital communications systems. He has been working as R&D engineer for DSP software development in digital television industry. Also, he is serving as an ICT lecturer and consultant in digital television and medicine/sports informatics for implementation standard-based solutions. He participated in research/innovation projects and published more than 250 papers in international journals and conference proceedings. He also, co-authored text-books/chapters in multimedia communications published by Prentice Hall (2002), Wiley (2005), CRC Press (2009, 2019, 2020, 2022), Springer-Verlag (2016, 2017, 2018, 2019) and IGI Global (2017, 2019, 2021). Present projects include adaptive coding of 3D immersive media, IoMT and Big media integration, 5G/6G wireless technology.

Amita Nandal received her Ph.D. degree in Electronics and Communication Engineering from SRM University, Chennai in 2014. Since 2018, she is working as Associate Professor in Department of Computer and Communication Engineering at Manipal University Jaipur. Her research interests include Digital Signal Processing, Machine Learning and Deep learning for Medical Image Processing, Wireless Communication, Circuits Systems and FPGA implementation.

Karthikeyan P. is currently working as an Associate Professor in Thiagarajar College of Engineering, Madurai. He has completed the Ph.D. programme in Information and Communication Engineering under Anna University, Chennai, Tamilnadu, India in the year 2015. He has 16 years of teaching and 6 years of research experiences. He published many papers in refereed international journals, conferences and book chapters. He also published 4 Indian patents. He is a reviewer in various international journals like IEEE Transactions on Cybernetics, Education, IEEE Access, etc. He served as a guest editor in IJMLO (Inderscience). His research interests include evolutionary algorithms, ad hoc networks, educational technology and machine learning.

Soumen Santra is working in the dept of Computer Science & Application in Techno International NewTown. He has already published more than 50 research papers to his credit. He has 10 years of professional experience in academics. He received B.Sc (Hons), MCA, M.Tech Degree. His work spans around in the field of IoT, Cloud Computing, Machine Learning, AI, OOPs.

Arpit Kumar Sharma is PhD scholar at Mnaipal University Jaipur.

Akshat Sinha is a student at Arya Institute of Engineering Technology and Management, Jaipur.

Onur Ugurlu is an assistant professor of Computer Science at the Department of Fundamental Sciences, Izmir Bakircay University, Izmir, Turkey. He completed his undergraduate studies at Ege University with a major in computer science and a minor in mathematics. He has a MS in Computer Science from Ege University, Izmir, in 2013. He obtained his PhD degree in Computer Science from Ege University University, Izmir, Turkey, in 2018. He was a visiting scholar in the Theoretical Computer Science Group at Northwestern University in the U.S. in 2017. He is mainly interested in design and analysis of algorithms, computational theory and graph theory. In particular, his researches focus on finding efficient algorithms for discrete optimization problems on networks.

Hans Vangheluwe is a professor in the Antwerp Systems and Software Modelling (AnSyMo) group within the Department of Mathematics and Computer Science at the University of Antwerp in Belgium, where he is a founding member of the NEXOR Consortium on Cyber-Physical Systems (CPS). AnSyMo is a Core Research Lab of Flanders Make, the strategic research centre for the Flemish manufacturing industry. He heads the Modelling, Simulation and Design Lab (MSDL), founded when he was a professor at McGill University in Montreal, Canada. In a variety of projects, often with industrial partners, he develops and applies the model-based theory and techniques of Multi-Paradigm Modelling (MPM) in application domains as diverse as bio-actived sludge waste-water treatment plant design and optimization, safe automotive software, and autonomic production plants in the context of Industry 4.0. His fundamental work covers the foundations of modelling and (co-)simulation, of model management, model transformation, and collaborative domain-specific (visual) modelling environments. This work is always accompanied by prototype tools such as PythonPDEVS, the Modelverse, T-Core, AToM3 and AToMPM. In the mid '90s, he was one of the original members of the a-causal modelling language Modelica design team, one of the initiatives of the ESPRIT Basic Research Working Group 8467 on "simulation for the future: new concepts, tools and applications" (SiE) which he co-founded. He has published extensively in simulation and in software modelling. He frequently gives tutorials on topics such as Statecharts, DEVS, co-simulation, modelling language engineering and a-causal modelling. He was the chair of the EU COST Action IC1404 "Multi-Paradigm Modelling for Cyber-Physical Systems" (MPM4CPS).

Kadircan Yalnız graduated from Dokuz Eylul University in 2021 as a Computer Engineer. He has been involved in several short-term R&D projects on computer science. His research interests include machine learning and artificial intelligence.

Dmytro Zubov received Dipl. Engineering at V.Dahl East Ukrainian National University in 1995, PhD in Engineering (lower-level doctorate) at Donetsk National Technical University in 1998, and then PhD in Engineering (higher-level doctorate) at Kryvyi Rih Technical University in 2006. He worked as a software engineer at company "Lutri" (1996-1998), as a TA (1996-2000), and then as an assistant/associate professor (2000-2011) at V.Dahl East Ukrainian National University, where he was responsible for several national projects. From Sept 2011 to Jul 2015, he was an assistant professor in Computer Science at the University of Information Science and Technology "St. Paul the Apostle", Macedonia. He was visiting professor in Computer Science at Tecnológico de Monterrey from Aug 2015 to Jul 2016, Universidad Politécnica de San Luis Potosí from Aug 2016 to Jan 2017, Soochow University from Feb to Jul 2017. As of Feb 2020, he was teaching Computer Science subjects at Technical University of Ostrava, Erbil campus, Kurdistan. He is (co)author of over 120 publications including four books. Dr. Zubov got Microsoft (.NET Framework, Web Applications; Server Virtualization with Windows Server Hyper-V and System Center) and IBM (UDB DB2 Programming) certificates, Microsoft Azure Research Award. He supervised Microsoft Azure and AWS grants. He is an IEEE member. Currently, he is working on the project "Spatial Cognition of Surrounding Objects by the B&VI People Using Image Processing and Ultrasonic Sensing".

Index

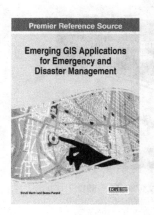

IGI Global Author Services

Providing a high-quality, affordable, and expeditious service, IGI Global's Author Services enable authors to streamline their publishing process, increase chance of acceptance, and adhere to IGI Global's publication standards.

Benefits of Author Services:

Professional Service: All our editors, designers, and translators are experts in their field with years of experience and professional certifications.

Quality Guarantee & Certificate: Each order is returned with a quality guarantee and certificate of professional completion.

Timeliness: All editorial orders have a guaranteed return timeframe of 3-5 business days and translation orders are guaranteed in 7-10 business days.

Affordable Pricing: IGI Global Author Services are competitively priced compared to other industry service providers.

APC Reimbursement: IGI Global authors publishing Open Access (OA) will be able to deduct the cost of editing and other IGI Global author services from their OA APC publishing fee.

Author Services Offered:

English Language Copy Editing
Professional, native English language copy editors improve your manuscript's grammar, spelling, punctuation, terminology, semantics, consistency, flow, formatting, and more.

Scientific & Scholarly Editing
A Ph.D. level review for qualities such as originality and significance, interest to researchers, level of methodology and analysis, coverage of literature, organization, quality of writing, and strengths and weaknesses.

Figure, Table, Chart & Equation Conversions
Work with IGI Global's graphic designers before submission to enhance and design all figures and charts to IGI Global's specific standards for clarity.

Translation
Providing 70 language options, including Simplified and Traditional Chinese, Spanish, Arabic, German, French, and more.

Hear What the Experts Are Saying About IGI Global's Author Services

"Publishing with IGI Global has been *an amazing experience* for me for sharing my research. The *strong academic production* support ensures quality and timely completion." **– Prof. Margaret Niess, Oregon State University, USA**

"The service was *very fast, very thorough, and very helpful* in ensuring our chapter meets the criteria and requirements of the book's editors. I was *quite impressed and happy* with your service." **– Prof. Tom Brinthaupt, Middle Tennessee State University, USA**

Learn More or Get Started Here:

For Questions, Contact IGI Global's Customer Service Team at cust@igi-global.com or 717-533-8845

IGI Global
PUBLISHER of TIMELY KNOWLEDGE
www.igi-global.com

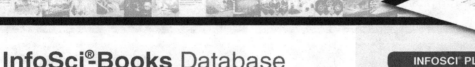

www.igi-global.com

Publisher of Peer-Reviewed, Timely, and
Innovative Academic Research Since 1988

IGI Global's Transformative Open Access (OA) Model:
How to Turn Your University Library's Database Acquisitions Into a Source of OA Funding

Well in advance of Plan S, IGI Global unveiled their OA Fee Waiver (Read & Publish) Initiative. Under this initiative, librarians who invest in IGI Global's InfoSci-Books and/or InfoSci-Journals databases will be able to subsidize their patrons' OA article processing charges (APCs) when their work is submitted and accepted (after the peer review process) into an IGI Global journal.

How Does it Work?

Step 1: **Library Invests in the InfoSci-Databases:** A library perpetually purchases or subscribes to the InfoSci-Books, InfoSci-Journals, or discipline/subject databases.

Step 2: **IGI Global Matches the Library Investment with OA Subsidies Fund:** IGI Global provides a fund to go towards subsidizing the OA APCs for the library's patrons.

Step 3: **Patron of the Library is Accepted into IGI Global Journal (After Peer Review):** When a patron's paper is accepted into an IGI Global journal, they option to have their paper published under a traditional publishing model or as OA.

Step 4: **IGI Global Will Deduct APC Cost from OA Subsidies Fund:** If the author decides to publish under OA, the OA APC fee will be deducted from the OA subsidies fund.

Step 5: **Author's Work Becomes Freely Available:** The patron's work will be freely available under CC BY copyright license, enabling them to share it freely with the academic community.

Note: This fund will be offered on an annual basis and will renew as the subscription is renewed for each year thereafter. IGI Global will manage the fund and award the APC waivers unless the librarian has a preference as to how the funds should be managed.

Hear From the Experts on This Initiative:

"I'm very happy to have been able to make one of my recent research contributions *freely available* along with having access to the *valuable resources* found within IGI Global's InfoSci-Journals database."

— **Prof. Stuart Palmer,**
Deakin University, Australia

"Receiving the support from IGI Global's OA Fee Waiver Initiative *encourages me to continue my research work without any hesitation.*"

— **Prof. Wenlong Liu,** College of Economics and Management at Nanjing University of Aeronautics & Astronautics, China

Printed in the United States
by Baker & Taylor Publisher Services